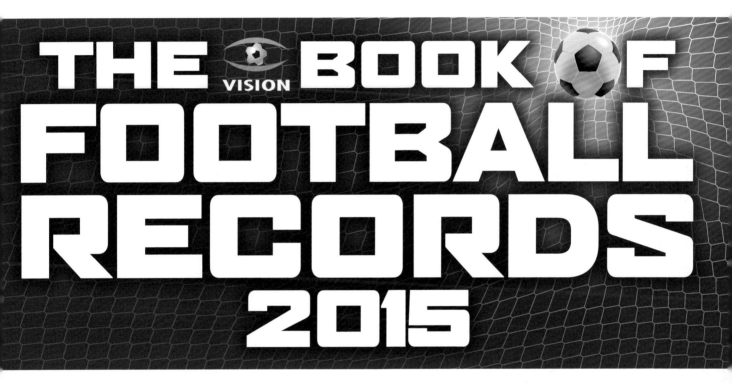

THE VISION BOOK OF FOOTBALL RECORDS 2015

BY CLIVE BATTY

VSP

Published by Vision Sports Publishing in 2014
Vision Sports Publishing
19-23 High Street
Kingston upon Thames
Surrey
KT1 1LL

www.visionsp.co.uk

ISBN: 978-1909534-29-2

Editor: Paul Baillie-Lane
Design: Neal Cobourne
Kit images: David Moor, www.historicalkits.co.uk
All pictures: Getty Images

gettyimages®

Printed and bound in Slovakia by Neografia
A CIP catalogue record for this book is available from the British Library

FSC
www.fsc.org
MIX
Paper from
responsible sources
FSC® C020353

All statistics in the *Vision Book of Football Records 2015*
are correct up until the start of the 2014/15 season

INTRODUCTION

Welcome to the 2015 edition of the *Vision Book of Football Records*. In the 12 months since the previous edition of this tome appeared the established football order has been turned upside down, both here in Britain and on the international stage. Is it only a year ago, for instance, that Spain were still being hailed as possibly the greatest side in history following their impressive triumph at Euro 2012 and smooth qualification for the 2014 World Cup in Brazil, a tournament the Spanish entered as holders and, in the eyes of many, as strong favourites. Well, those who backed the Spanish were made to look pretty foolish as the reigning world and European champions were ejected at the group stage, their much-vaunted 'tiki-taka' passing machine breaking down rather like a rusty old banger with too many miles on the clock. Then there was the weird sight of the hosts, another highly fancied outfit, not just capitulating in the semi-final to eventual winners Germany, but leaving the stage in tears like a bunch of tuneless X-Factor contestants who had just received the thumbs-down from Simon Cowell.

Turning the spotlight on the domestic game, the dramatic decline of reigning champions Manchester United during the 2013/14 season was equally unexpected.

Everything seemed fine and dandy in the Old Trafford camp when long-serving boss Sir Alex Ferguson passed on the baton to fellow Scot David Moyes, but the Red Devils endured a miserable campaign, slumping to their lowest ever Premier League finish and failing to qualify for Europe for the first time in 25 years.

Yet, the nature of football is such that, while some big names see their fortunes wane, other clubs, players and managers are on the rise, forcing their way into contention for major honours and, even more crucially, into the pages of this book! So, you will find new entries for the likes of current Spanish champions Atletico Madrid and League Two newboys Cambridge United and Luton Town; promising England youngsters Ross Barkley, Luke Shaw and Raheem Sterling; recent high-profile additions to the Premier League such as Diego Costa, Radamel Falcao and Alexis Sanchez; and Louis van Gaal and Mauricio Pochettino, the new men in the dug-out at Manchester United and Tottenham Hotspur respectively.

Meanwhile, all the other facts, figures, stats and records have been updated and revised to reflect the many changes that have taken place in the sport over the past year. As in previous editions, you will find

mini-profiles of the top Premier League stars as well as key stats and facts about all 92 English league clubs, the leading Scottish clubs and the top teams in continental Europe. Then there are entries for the biggest international superstars such as Lionel Messi, Cristiano Ronaldo and Arjen Robben, as well as many of the great names from football's past, including the likes of Cantona, Charlton and Cruyff.

Other categories covered, meanwhile, include the main domestic and international competitions, the most important and successful football nations, and the most coveted individual awards. In addition, there are also a host of 'wild card' entries on subjects as diverse as 'Animals' (pitch-invading dogs, squirrels and grasshoppers and the like), 'Sackings' (did you know a record 10 Premier League managers got the boot last season? It's no wonder most bosses have got grey hair and bags under their eyes!) and 'Twitter' (can you guess which player has the most 'followers' on the social media site?).

So, all in all, there's more than enough to keep you occupied here during those rare moments when there's no footy on the telly. Or to put it another way, there's so much to get your teeth into within these pages that even Luis Suarez would be kept busy for weeks on end!

CLIVE BATTY

ABANDONED MATCHES

A record three Football League fixtures were abandoned on 2nd November 2010. The League Two match between Cheltenham and Southend was called off after 66 minutes due to floodlight failure, while waterlogged pitches led to the abandonment of the Hartlepool-Notts County and Rochdale-Oldham League One fixtures after less than 10 minutes total playing time.

• **The shortest ever English game took place in 1894, when a raging blizzard caused the match between Stoke and Wolves at the Victoria Ground to be called off after just three minutes. Only 400 hardy fans had braved the elements, and even they must have been secretly relieved when the referee, Mr Helme, called the game off.**

• Two European finals have been abandoned and they both involved English clubs. The first leg of the 1971 Fairs Cup final between Leeds and Juventus was called off due to a waterlogged pitch, and similar circumstances resulted in a premature halt of the 1973 UEFA Cup final first leg between Liverpool and Borussia Monchengladbach.

• **Bulgarian sides Balkan Belogradchik and Gigant Belene played the shortest match ever on 28th March 2010. Gigant started four players short, but when one of their number limped off after a minute the ref had to abandon the match, as the rules state that teams must field at least seven players.**

• An abandoned match effectively decided the outcome of the 1904/05 league title. Everton were 3-1 up at Woolwich Arsenal in November 1904 before heavy fog led to the match being called off after 76 minutes. When the match was replayed towards the end of the season Everton lost 2-1 – a vital setback for the Merseysiders, who eventually finished just one point behind title winners Newcastle United.

ABERDEEN

Year founded: 1903
Ground: Pittodrie Stadium (22,199)
Nickname: The Dons
Biggest win: 13-0 v Peterhead (1923)
Heaviest defeat: 0-9 v Celtic (2010)

Aberdeen were founded in 1903, following the amalgamation of three city clubs, Aberdeen, Orion and Victoria United. The following year the club joined the Scottish Second Division, and in 1905 the Dons were elected to an expanded First Division. Aberdeen have remained in the top flight ever since, a record shared with just Rangers and Celtic.

• **The club was originally known as the Whites and later as the Wasps or the Black and Golds after their early strips, but in 1913 became known as the Dons. This nickname is sometimes said to derive from the involvement of professors at Aberdeen University in the foundation of the club, but is more likely to be a contraction of the word 'Aberdonians', the term used to describe people from Aberdeen.**

• Aberdeen first won the Scottish title in 1955, before enjoying a trio of championship successes in the 1980s under manager Alex Ferguson. Before he moved on to even greater triumphs at Old Trafford, Fergie also led the Dons to four victories in five years in the Scottish Cup, which included a record run of 20 cup games without defeat between 1982 and 1985.

• **The club's finest hour, though, came in 1983 when the Dons became only the second Scottish club (after Rangers in 1972) to win the European Cup Winners' Cup, beating Real Madrid 2-1 in the final. Later that year Aberdeen defeated Hamburg over two legs to claim the European Super Cup and remain** the only Scottish side to win two European trophies.

• In 1984 Aberdeen became the first club outside the 'Old Firm' to win the Double, after finishing seven points clear at the top of the league and beating Celtic 2-1 in the Scottish Cup final.

• **Aberdeen have the best record in the Scottish League Cup outside of the Old Firm, winning the trophy on six occasions. The Dons' most recent success in the competition came in 2014 when they beat Inverness Caledonian Thistle on penalties in the final after a 0-0 draw.**

• Scottish international defender Willie Miller has made more appearances for the club than any other player, an impressive 556 games between 1973 and 1990. Hotshot striker Joe Harper is the Dons' record goalscorer, with 205 during two spells at Pittodrie (1969-72 and 1976-81).

• **Aberdeen's most capped player is Miller's long-time defensive partner and former Birmingham and Aston Villa boss Alex McLeish, who made 77 appearances for Scotland between 1977 and 1990.**

• The Dons suffered their worst ever defeat in November 2010 when they were hammered 9-0 by Celtic, the biggest ever thrashing in the history of the SPL.

HONOURS
Division 1 Champions 1955
Premier Division champions 1980, 1984, 1985
Scottish Cup 1947, 1970, 1982, 1983, 1984, 1986, 1990
League Cup 1956, 1977, 1986, 1990, 1996, 2014
European Cup Winners' Cup 1983
European Super Cup 1983

ROMAN ABRAMOVICH

Born: Saratov, Russia, 24th October 1966

Chelsea owner Roman Abramovich has a fortune estimated at £8.5 billion and, since buying the Blues from previous owner Ken Bates in July 2003, he has invested hundreds of millions in the club – including nearly £800 million in transfer fees – in an attempt to establish the west Londoners as a dominant force in the English and European game.

IS THAT A FACT?
The most significant abandonment of the 2013/14 season saw Doncaster's match at Charlton called off at half-time due to a waterlogged pitch, with the visitors leading 3-1. When the match was replayed two months later Doncaster lost 2-0, and they ended up being relegated from the Championship on goal difference.

• Abramovich's massive spending spree has been rewarded with three league titles and six domestic cups, including the Double in 2010. For many years his burning ambition to see Chelsea win the Champions League was frustrated – a failure which led Abramovich to sack a number of his managers – but the Blues finally managed to lift the biggest prize of all in 2012 following a dramatic penalty shoot-out against Bayern Munich.

• After starting out selling retread car tyres, Abramovich's business career took off when he began trading oil products out of Russia's largest refinery in western Siberia. He gradually acquired a controlling interest in Sibneft, the country's main oil company, before selling his share to the Russian government-controlled Gazprom for an eye-watering £7.4 billion in 2005.

• Abramovich enjoys a lifestyle befitting his billionaire status, owning a number of luxury homes, three yachts, a private Boeing 767 jet and three helicopters.

AC MILAN

Year founded: 1899
Ground: San Siro (80,018)
Nickname: Rossoneri
League titles: 18
Domestic cups: 5
European cups: 14
International cups: 4

One of the giants of European football, the club was founded by British expatriates as the Milan Cricket and Football Club in 1899. Apart from a period during the fascist dictatorship of Benito Mussolini, the club has always been known as 'Milan' rather than the Italian 'Milano'.

• Milan were the first Italian side to win the European Cup, beating Benfica in the final at Wembley in 1963, and have gone on to win the trophy seven times – a record surpassed only by Real Madrid, with 10 victories.

• In 1986 the club was acquired by the businessman and future Italian President Silvio Berlusconi, who invested in star players like Marco van Basten, Ruud Gullit and Frank Rijkaard. Milan went on to enjoy a golden era under coaches Arrigo Sacchi and Fabio Capello, winning three European Cups and four Serie A titles between 1988 and 1994. Incredibly, the club were undefeated for 58 games between 1991 and 1993, the third longest such run in top-flight European football history behind Celtic (62 games) and Steaua Bucharest (104 games).

• Milan's San Siro Stadium, which they share with city rivals Inter, is the largest in Italy, with a capacity of over 80,000. As well as football, the stadium has hosted many pop concerts and in November 2009 was the venue for a rugby international between Italy and the All Blacks which attracted a crowd of 81,018 – a record for Italian rugby.

• Legendary defender Paolo Maldini made a Serie A record 647 league appearances for Milan between 1985 and 2009, and also played in a record 175 European club games.

HONOURS
Serie A champions *1901, 1906, 1907, 1951, 1955, 1957, 1959, 1962, 1968, 1979, 1988, 1992, 1993, 1994, 1996, 1999, 2004, 2011*
Italian Cup *1967, 1972, 1973, 1977, 2003*
European Cup/Champions League *1963, 1969, 1989, 1990, 1994, 2003, 2007*
European Cup Winners' Cup *1968, 1973*
European Super Cup *1989, 1990, 1994, 2003, 2007*
Intercontinental Cup *1969, 1989, 1990*
Club World Cup *2007*

ACCRINGTON STANLEY

Year founded: 1968
Ground: Crown Ground (5,057)
Nickname: The Stans
Biggest win: 10-1 v Lincoln United (1999)
Heaviest defeat: 2-8 v Peterborough (2008)

Accrington Stanley were founded at a meeting in a working men's club in Accrington in 1968, as a successor to the former Football League club of the same name which had folded two years earlier.

AC Milan's Keisuke Honda

• Conference champions in 2006, Stanley were promoted to the Football League in place of relegated Oxford United. Ironically, when a financial crisis forced the old Accrington Stanley to resign from the League in March 1962, the club that replaced them the following season was Oxford!

• In 2011 the club finished a best ever fifth in League Two, but their hopes of promotion were dashed by Stevenage who beat them 3-0 on aggregate in the play-off semi-final.

• **The original town club, Accrington, were one of the 12 founder members of the Football League in 1888, but resigned from the League after just five years.**

• The club's tiny Crown Ground has the second smallest capacity in the Football League, just over 5,000. Mind you, it's very rarely full and the Stans' match against Bristol Rovers on 22nd October 2013 was watched by just 1,101 fans – the lowest attendance of the 2013/14 season.

> HONOURS
> **Conference champions** *2006*

AFC WIMBLEDON

Year founded: 2002
Ground: Kingsmeadow (4,850)
Nickname: The Dons
Biggest win: 9-0 v Chessington United (2004) and v Slough Town (2007)
Heaviest defeat: 0-5 v York City (2010)

AFC Wimbledon were founded in 2002 by supporters of the former Premiership club Wimbledon, who opposed the decision of the FA to sanction the 'franchising' of their club when they allowed it to move 56 miles north from their south London base to Milton Keynes in Buckinghamshire (the club later becoming the MK Dons).

• **In October 2006 an agreement was reached with the MK Dons that the honours won by the old Wimbledon would return to the London Borough of Merton. This was an important victory for the AFC fans, who view their club as the true successors to Wimbledon FC.**

• In their former incarnation as Wimbledon the club won the FA Cup in 1988, beating hot favourites Liverpool 1-0 at Wembley. Incredibly, the Dons had only been elected to the Football League just 12 years earlier, but enjoyed a remarkable rise through the divisions, winning promotion to the top flight in 1986. Dubbed the 'Crazy Gang' for their physical approach on the pitch and madcap antics off it, Wimbledon remained in the Premiership until 2000.

• **While rising through the non-league pyramid AFC went 78 matches undefeated between February 2003 and December 2004 – the longest unbeaten run in English senior football. Then, in 2011, AFC beat Luton Town on penalties in the Conference play-off final at Eastlands, securing a place in the Football League just nine years after their formation.**

• With a capacity of just 4,850, the club's tiny Kingsmeadow Stadium is the smallest in the Football League.

> HONOURS
> **Division 4 champions** 1983 (As Wimbledon FC)
> *FA Cup* 1988 **(As Wimbledon FC)**
> **FA Amateur Cup** 1963 (As Wimbledon FC)

Libya won the Africa Cup of Nations for the first time in 2014

AFRICA CUP OF NATIONS

The Africa Cup of Nations was founded in 1957. The first tournament was a decidedly small affair consisting of just three competing teams (Egypt, Ethiopia and hosts Sudan) after South Africa's invitation was withdrawn when they refused to send a multi-racial squad to the finals. Egypt were the first winners, beating Ethiopia 4-0 in the final in Khartoum.

• **With seven victories, Egypt are the most successful side in the history of the competition. After triumphing in Angola in 2010 following a 1-0 victory over Ghana in the final, the north Africans claimed a record three consecutive trophies. However, Ghana were the first country to win the tournament three times and, following their third success in 1978, were allowed to keep the original Abdel Abdullah Salem Trophy, named after the first president of the Confederation of African Football.**

• The final has been decided on penalties on seven occasions, with Ivory Coast winning the longest shoot-out 11-10 against Ghana in 1992.

• **The top scorer in the history of the**

competition is Cameroon striker Samuel Eto'o, who has hit a total of 18 goals in the tournament. Mulamba Ndaye of Zaire holds the record for the most goals in a single tournament, with nine in 1974.

• Libya won the Africa Cup of Nations for the first ever time in 2014

AFRICAN FOOTBALLER OF THE YEAR

The African Footballer of the Year award was established by the Confederation of African Football in 1992, Nigerian striker Rashidi Yekini topping the first poll the following year.

• Cameroon legend Samuel Eto'o has won the award a record four times, including a hat-trick between 2003 and 2005. Manchester City midfielder Yaya Toure is the only other player to win the award three times on the trot, following his third consecutive triumph in 2014.

• The first Premier League-based player to win the award was Arsenal striker Kanu in 1999. Altogether, players at English clubs have won the award a record eight times.

• Players from eight different African countries have won the award, with Nigeria, Cameroon and Ivory Coast (five wins each) enjoying the most success.

AGE

Legendary winger Sir Stanley Matthews is the oldest player to appear in the top flight of English football. 'The Ageless Wonder' had celebrated his 50th birthday five days before playing his last match for Stoke against Fulham in February 1965.

• Matthews, though, was something of a spring chicken compared to Neil McBain, the New Brighton manager, who had to go in goal for his side's Division Three (North) match against Hartlepool during an injury crisis in 1947. He was 51 and 120 days at the time, the oldest player in the history of English football.

• Manchester City goalkeeper John Burridge became the oldest player in the Premier League when he came off the bench at half-time in City's match against Newcastle in April 1995, aged 43. The youngest player is Fulham's Matthew Briggs, who was aged 16 years and 65 days when he made his debut for the Cottagers against Middlesbrough in May 2007.

• The oldest international in British football is Wales' Billy Meredith, who played against England in 1920 at the age of 45. The youngest is Gareth Bale, who was aged just 16 and 315 days when he made his debut for Wales against Trinidad and Tobago in 2006.

• The youngest goalscorer in the history of the Football League is Bristol Rovers' Ronnie Dix, who was aged just 15 years and 180 days when he netted in a 3-0 win against Norwich City in 1928. The oldest goalscorer in Premier League history is Teddy Sheringham, who was aged 40 and 268 days when he hit the target for West Ham against Portsmouth on Boxing Day 2006.

• The oldest player to appear at the World Cup is Colombia goalkeeper Faryd Mondragon, who played the last five minutes of his side's 4-1 victory against Japan at the 2014 tournament three days after his 43rd birthday.

• The youngest player to appear for a professional team anywhere in the world is Mauricio Baldivieso, who was three days short of his 13th birthday when he came on as a substitute in the

TOP 10

OLDEST OUTFIELD PREMIER LEAGUE PLAYERS

1. Teddy Sheringham (West Ham, 2006)   40 years and 272 days
2. Ryan Giggs (Manchester United, 2014)   40 years and 158 days
3. Kevin Phillips (Crystal Palace, 2013)   40 years and 89 days
4. Gordon Strachan (Coventry City, 1997)   40 years and 83 days
5. Bryan Robson (Middlesbrough, 1997)   39 years and 355 days
6. Dean Windass (Hull City, 2008)   39 years and 269 days
7. Ray Wilkins (QPR, 1996)   39 years and 233 days
8. Trevor Francis (Sheffield Wednesday, 1993)   39 years and 215 days
9. Colin Cooper (Middlesbrough, 2006)   39 years and 68 days
10. Nigel Winterburn (West Ham, 2003)   39 years and 53 days

Bolivian First Division for Aurora FC on 19th July 2009. "I am the happiest man in the world," he said after his nine-minute cameo against La Paz FC.

• In 2014 54-year-old Bolivian President Evo Morales signed for First Division club Sport Boys. The club said that Morales, an enthusiastic midfielder, would play 20 minutes in every game unless he was occupied with presidential business.

SERGIO AGUERO

Born: Quilmes, Argentina, 2nd June 1988
Position: Striker
Club career:
2003-06 Independiente 54 (23)
2006-11 Atletico Madrid 175 (74)
2011- Manchester City 87 (52)
International record:
2006- Argentina 55 (21)

Prolific Manchester City striker Sergio Aguero has the best goals/minutes ratio of any player in Premier League history, on average banging in a goal every 115 minutes he has spent on the pitch.

• Known as 'El Kun' because of his resemblance to a Japanese cartoon character, Aguero became the

youngest ever player to appear in Argentina's top flight when he made his debut for Independiente in 2003 aged just 15 years and 35 days. The previous record was set by the legendary Diego Maradona, Aguero's former father-in-law.

• Aguero moved on to Atletico Madrid in 2006 aged 17, helping the Spanish club win the inaugural Europa League in 2010. The following year he joined Manchester City for £38 million, to become the second most expensive player in British football history at the time. The fee proved to be a bargain as Aguero banged in 23 Premier League goals – including a dramatic title-clinching winner against QPR on the last day of the season – as City topped the table for the first time since 1968. Two years later he contributed another 17 goals as City won the title again.

• A quicksilver attacker who possesses excellent close control, Aguero made his international debut for Argentina in a 2006 friendly against Brazil at Arsenal's Emirates Stadium. In 2008 he was a key figure in the Argentina team that won gold at the Beijing Olympics, but he endured heartache at the 2014 World Cup when he finished on the losing side in the final against Germany.

AIR CRASHES

On 6th February 1958 eight members of the Manchester United 'Busby Babes' team, including England internationals Roger Byrne, Duncan Edwards and Tommy Taylor, were killed in the Munich Air Crash. Their plane crashed while attempting to take off in a snowstorm at Munich Airport, where it had stopped to refuel after a European Cup tie in Belgrade. In total, 23 people died in the crash, although manager Matt Busby and Bobby Charlton were among the survivors. Amazingly, United still managed to reach the FA Cup final that year, but lost at Wembley to Bolton Wanderers.

• The entire first team of Torino, the strongest Italian club at the time, were wiped out in an air disaster on 4th May 1949. Returning from a testimonial match in Portugal, the team's plane crashed into the Basilica of Superga outside Turin. Among the 31 dead were 10 members of the Italian national side and the club's English manager, Leslie Lievesley. Torino fielded their youth team in their four remaining fixtures and, with their opponents doing the same as a mark of respect, won a fifth consecutive league title at the end of the season.

• 17 players and staff members from Pakhtakor Tashkent, the only team from Uzbekistan to reach the top flight of Russian football in the Soviet era, were killed in a mid-air collision over the Ukraine in 1979 while on their way to a match against Dinamo Minsk. All 178 people on board the two planes involved in the accident perished.

AJAX

Year founded: 1900
Ground: Ajax ArenA (52,342)
Nickname: De Godenzonen (the sons of the Gods)
League titles: 33
Domestic cups: 18
European cups: 8
International cups: 2

Founded in 1900 in Amsterdam, Ajax are named after the Greek mythological hero. The club is the most successful in Holland, having won the league a record 33 times, most recently in 2014, and the Dutch Cup a record 18 times.

• Ajax's white shirts with a broad vertical red stripe are among the most iconic in world football. However, the club's original kit was very different – an all-black outfit with a red sash tied around the players' waists.

• The Dutch side's most glorious decade was in the 1970s when, with a team featuring legends like Johan Cruyff, Johan Neeskens and Johnny Rep, Ajax won the European Cup three times on the trot, playing a fluid system known as 'Total Football'. In 1995 a young Ajax team won the trophy for a fourth time, Patrick Kluivert scoring the winner in the final against AC Milan.

• When Ajax beat Torino in the final of the UEFA Cup in 1992 they became only the second team, after Juventus, to win all three major European trophies.

• Ajax moved into a brand new all-seater stadium, the Amsterdam ArenA, in 1996. With a capacity in excess of 50,000, it is the largest football stadium in Holland. The stadium hosted the 1998 Champions League final between Real Madrid and Juventus, and the 2013

Sergio Aguero's 'robot dance' is much admired at the Etihad

Europa League final between Chelsea and Benfica.

DANI ALVES

Attacking right-back Dani Alves became the second most expensive defender in the world – behind Manchester United's Rio Ferdinand – in 2008 when he joined Barcelona from Sevilla for around £23 million. At the time he was the third most expensive signing in the Catalans' history, although he has subsequently dropped to seventh in the list.

• Alves won the UEFA Cup twice during a six-year stay in Seville, before adding many more trophies after moving to the Nou Camp. In his first season at Barca in 2008/09 he won the Treble, and in the years since he has accumulated three more Spanish league titles and another Champions League winners' medal.

• The Barca full-back hit the headlines in April 2014 when he picked up a banana thrown at him from the stands at Villarreal, peeled it and then took a big bite out of the fruit. Footballers around the world responded by posting pictures of themselves eating bananas on social media to show their support for Alves and their intolerance of any form of racism.

• He made his international debut for Brazil in a friendly against Ecuador in 2006, and the following year scored a goal in his country's 3-0 thrashing of Argentina in the Copa America final.

ANIMALS

Football fans around the globe were amused when a giant green grasshopper landed on James Rodriguez's arm as he prepared to take a penalty for Colombia against hosts Brazil in the quarter-finals of the 2014 World Cup. Seemingly unaware of the gigantic insect, Rodriguez calmly slotted his spot-kick into the net in his country's 2-1 defeat.

• The most famous dog in football, Pickles, never appeared on the pitch but, to the relief of fans around the globe, discovered the World Cup trophy which was stolen while on display at an exhibition in Central Hall, Westminster, on 20th March 1966. A black and white mongrel, Pickles found the trophy under a bush while out for a walk on Beulah Hill in south London with his owner. He was hailed as a national hero but, sadly, later that same year he was strangled by his lead while chasing after a cat.

• The World Cup also made an international celebrity of Paul, an octopus based at the Sea Life Aquarium in Oberhausen, Germany. During the 2010 finals in South Africa, the two-year-old cephalopod correctly predicted the result of all seven of Germany's games by choosing his favourite food, mussels, from one of two boxes marked with the national flag of the competing teams. Before the final between Holland and Spain, Paul's choice of breakfast snack suggested that the trophy would be heading to Madrid rather than Amsterdam... and, yet again, the amazing 'psychic' octopus was spot on!

• The championship match between QPR and Leicester City at Loftus Road in December 2013 was held up for five minutes after a squirrel ran onto the pitch. The match eventually resumed after Leicester striker David Nugent shepherded the creature towards the touchline.

• On the final day of the 1986/87 season a police dog inadvertently played a part in saving Torquay from relegation from the Football League. With minutes to go, the Gulls were losing 2-1 at home to Crewe when the dog, named Bryn, ran onto the pitch and

bit Torquay player Jim McNichol. In the time added on for treatment to his injury, Torquay launched a desperate last attack and scored an equaliser. As a show of gratitude to the dog, chairman Lew Pope gave him a juicy steak.

APPEARANCES

Goalkeeping legend Peter Shilton holds the record for the most Football League appearances, playing 1,005 games between 1966 and 1997. His total was made up as follows: Leicester City (286 games), Stoke City (110), Nottingham Forest (202), Southampton (188), Derby County (175), Plymouth (34), Bolton (1) and Leyton Orient (9). Shilton is followed in the all-time list by Tony Ford (931 appearances, 1975-2001) and Graham Alexander (833, 1991-2012).

• Manchester United assistant manager Ryan Giggs holds the Premier League appearance record, with a total of 632 appearances between 1992 and 2014. Brad Friedel holds the consecutive games record with 310 for Blackburn, Aston Villa and Tottenham between August 2004 and October 2012.

• The record for most League games with one club is held by Swindon Town's stalwart defender John Trollope, who appeared 770 times for the Robins between 1960 and 1980.

• Since making his debut in 1992 Sao Paulo goalkeeper Rogerio Ceni has played an incredible 1,149 games for the Brazilian outfit. No other player in the world has made as many competitive appearances for the same team.

• Giggs holds the record for the most appearances in the Champions League with 151. He is followed by a trio of Spanish stars: Xavi (147), Raul (144) and Iker Casillas (142).

IS THAT A FACT?
The start of the Brazilian league game between Ponte Preta and Atletico Sorocaba in March 2013 was delayed for 15 minutes after a swarm of bees settled on one of the crossbars. The invaders were eventually disposed of by two beekeepers who blasted them with a fire extinguisher.

To the delight of the Argentina players, the ref awarded them a throw on the halfway line

ARGENTINA

First international: Uruguay 2 Argentina 3, 1901
Most capped player: Javier Zanetti, 145 caps (1994-2011)
Leading goalscorer: Gabriel Batistuta, 56 goals (1991-2002)
First World Cup appearance: Argentina 1 France 0, 1930
Biggest win: 12-0 v Ecuador, 1942
Heaviest defeat: 1-6 v Czechoslovakia (1958) and v Bolivia (2009)

Outside Britain, Argentina is the oldest football nation on the planet. The roots of the game in this football-obsessed country go back to 1865, when the Buenos Aires Football Club was founded by British residents in the Argentine capital. Six clubs formed the first league in 1891, making it the oldest anywhere in the world outside Britain.

• Losing finalists in the first World Cup final in 1930, Argentina had to wait until 1978 before winning the competition for the first time, defeating Holland 3-1 on home soil. Another success, inspired by brilliant captain Diego Maradona, followed in 1986 and Argentina came close to retaining their trophy four years later, losing in the final to West Germany. After a 24-year wait they reached the final again in 2014, but narrowly lost to Germany.

• Argentina's oldest rivals are neighbours Uruguay. The two countries first met in 1901, in the first official international to be played outside Britain, with Argentina winning 3-2 in Montevideo. In the ensuing years the two sides have played each other 179 times, making the Argentina-Uruguay fixture the most played in the history of international football.

• **With an impressive 56 goals in 78 matches, former Fiorentina striker Gabriel Batistuta is Argentina's highest ever goalscorer. 'Batigol' is followed in the list by current superstar Lionel Messi on 42 goals.**

HONOURS
World Cup *1978, 1986*
Copa America *1921, 1925, 1927, 1929, 1937, 1941, 1945, 1946, 1947, 1955, 1957, 1959, 1991, 1993*
World Cup record
1930 Runners-up
1934 Round 1
1938 Did not enter
1950 Did not enter
1954 Did not enter
1958 Round 1
1962 Round 1
1966 Quarter-finals
1970 Did not qualify
1974 Round 2
1978 Winners
1982 Round 2
1986 Winners
1990 Runners-up
1994 Round 2
1998 Quarter-finals
2002 Round 1
2006 Quarter-finals
2010 Quarter-finals
2014 Runners-up

ARSENAL

Year founded: 1886
Ground: Emirates Stadium (60,361)
Previous name: Dial Square, Royal Arsenal, Woolwich Arsenal
Nickname: The Gunners
Biggest win: 12-0 v Ashford United (1893) and v Loughborough Town (1900)
Heaviest defeat: 0-8 v Loughborough Town (1896)

Founded as Dial Square in 1886 by workers at the Royal Arsenal in Woolwich, the club was renamed Royal Arsenal soon afterwards. Another name change, to Woolwich Arsenal, followed in 1891 when the club turned professional. Then, a year after moving north of the river to the Arsenal Stadium in 1913, the club became simply 'Arsenal'.

• One of the most successful clubs in the history of English football, Arsenal enjoyed a first golden period in the 1930s under innovative manager Herbert Chapman. The Gunners won the FA Cup for the first time in 1930 and later in the decade became only the second club to win three league titles on the trot. The first was the club Chapman managed in the 1920s, Huddersfield Town.

• Arsenal were the first club from London to win the league, topping the table in 1931 after scoring an incredible 60 goals in 21 away matches – an all-time record for the Football League.

• More recently, Arsenal have experienced enormous success under French manager Arsène Wenger. In 1998, just two years after Wenger arrived in England, the Gunners won the Double, a feat they repeated in 2002 while winning a top-flight record 14 consecutive league games. The club had previously won the league and FA Cup in the same season for the first time in 1971, and their total of three Doubles is only matched by Manchester United. In 2014 Wenger ended a nine-year trophyless run by leading Arsenal to victory in the FA Cup after a 3-2 win against Hull City in the final – the Gunners' 11th success in the competition, equalling Manchester United's record tally.

• Wenger's greatest triumph, though, came in the 2003/04 season when his team were crowned Premier League champions after going through the entire campaign undefeated. Only Preston North End had previously matched this feat, way back in 1888/89, but they had only played 22 league games compared to the 38 of Wenger's 'Invincibles'.

• The following season Arsenal extended their unbeaten run to 49 matches – setting an English league record in the process – before crashing to a bad-tempered 2-0 defeat against Manchester United at Old Trafford on 24th October 2004.

• One of the stars of that great Arsenal side was striker Thierry Henry, who is the Gunners' all-time leading scorer with 228 goals in all competitions in two spells at the club between 1999 and 2012.

Jack Wilshere and Aaron Ramsey: just two of Arsenal's huge collection of pint-sized midfielders

ASTON VILLA

ASTON VILLA

IS THAT A FACT?

Arsenal have played more games (429) in the FA Cup than any other club, and along with Manchester United have won the most games (227) in the history of the competition.

The former fans' favourite is also the most capped Arsenal player, appearing 81 times for France during his time with the club.

• In 1989 Arsenal won the closest ever title race by beating Liverpool 2-0 at Anfield in the final match of the season to pip the Reds to the championship on goals scored (the two sides had the same goal difference). But for a last-minute goal by Gunners midfielder Michael Thomas, after Alan Smith had scored with a second-half header, the title would have stayed on Merseyside.

• Irish international defender David O'Leary made a club record 722 first-team appearances for Arsenal between 1975 and 1993.

• Arsenal endured a nightmare season in 1912/13, finishing bottom of Division One and winning just one home game during the campaign – an all-time record. However, the Gunners returned to the top flight in 1919 and have stayed there ever since – the longest unbroken run in the top tier.

• Arsenal tube station on the Piccadilly Line is the only train station in Britain to be named after a football club. It used to be called Gillespie Road, until Herbert Chapman successfully lobbied for the name change in 1932.

• Three years later, on 14th December 1935, Arsenal thrashed Aston Villa 7-1 at Villa Park. Incredibly, centre-forward Ted Drake grabbed all seven of the Gunners' goals to set a top-flight record that still stands to this day.

• Arsenal spent 93 years at their old ground, Highbury, before moving to the state-of-the-art Emirates Stadium in 2006. With a capacity of 60,361, the Emirates is the second biggest club stadium in England after Old Trafford.

• Arsenal's most expensive signing is German midfielder Mesut Ozil, who cost the Gunners £42.4 million when he joined them from Real Madrid in September 2013. The club's record sale is Cesc Fabregas, who boosted the Gunners' coffers by £25.4 million when he signed for Barcelona in 2011.

• Previously famed for being a rather dull team who specialised in 1-0 victories, Arsenal have become the great entertainers in the Wenger era. Proof of the Gunners' attacking prowess came when they established an English league record by scoring in 55 consecutive matches between 2001 and 2002.

• The Gunners have a host of celebrity supporters, including athletics star Mo Farah, rapper Jay-Z and journalist Piers Morgan. Prince Harry is also a fan, as, apparently, is his grandmother. In 2007 a Buckingham Palace spokesman surprised the football world by revealing that "Her Majesty has been fond of Arsenal for over 50 years".

HONOURS
Division 1 champions 1931, 1933, 1934, 1935, 1948, 1953, 1971, 1989, 1991
Premier League champions 1998, 2002, 2004
FA Cup 1930, 1936, 1950, 1971, 1979, 1993, 1998, 2002, 2003, 2005, 2014
League Cup 1987, 1993
Double 1971, 1998, 2002
Fairs Cup 1970
European Cup Winners' Cup 1994

ASTON VILLA

Year founded: 1874
Ground: Villa Park (42,788)
Nickname: The Villans
Biggest win: 13-0 v Wednesbury Old Athletic (1886)
Heaviest defeat: 0-8 v Chelsea (2012)

One of England's most famous and distinguished clubs, Aston Villa were founded in 1874 by members of the Villa Cross Wesleyan Chapel in Aston,

Birmingham. The club were founder members of the Football League in 1888, winning their first title six years later.

• The most successful team of the Victorian era, Villa became only the second club to win the league and FA Cup Double in 1897 (Preston North End were the first in 1889). Villa's manager at the time was the legendary George Ramsay, who went on to guide the Villans to six league titles and six FA Cups – a trophy haul which has only been surpassed by Liverpool's Bob Paisley and, more recently, former Manchester United boss Sir Alex Ferguson.

• Ramsay is also the second longest serving manager in the history of English football, taking charge of the Villans for an incredible 42 years between 1884 and 1926. Only West Brom's Fred Everiss has managed a club for longer, racking up 46 years' service at the Hawthorns.

• Although they slipped as low as the old Third Division in the early 1970s, Villa have spent more time in the top flight than any other club apart from Everton (104 seasons compared to the Toffees' 112). The two clubs have played each other 198 times to date, making Aston Villa v Everton the most played fixture in the history of league football.

• Villa won the last of their seven league titles in 1980/81, when manager Ron Saunders used just 14 players throughout the whole campaign – equalling Liverpool's record set in 1965/66. The following season Villa became only the fourth English club to win the European Cup when they beat Bayern Munich 1-0 in the final in Rotterdam.

• In 1961 Villa won the League Cup in the competition's inaugural season, beating Rotherham 3-2 in a two-legged final. The Villans are the second most successful side in the tournament behind Liverpool with five triumphs, and have won more games (135) and scored more goals (454) in the competition than any other club.

• Aston Villa have provided a record 72 internationals for England, the first being Arthur Brown and Howard Vaughton who between them scored nine goals for England in a 13-0 trouncing of Ireland in 1882.

• Stalwart defender Charlie Aitken made more appearances for the club than any other player, turning out in

Aston Villa's Fabian Delph in action

Cameron, who is a nephew of former club chairman Sir William Dugdale.

ATLETICO MADRID

Year founded: 1903
Ground: Estadio Vicente Calderon (54,960)
Previous names: Athletic Club de Madrid, Athletic Aviacion de Madrid
Nickname: El Atleti
League titles: 10
Domestic cups: 10
European cups: 5
International cups: 1

The club was founded in 1903 by breakaway members of Madrid FC (later Real Madrid). In 1939, following a merger with the Spanish air force team, the club became known as Athletic Aviacion de Madrid before becoming plain Atletico Madrid eight years later.

• **Atletico are the third most successful club in Spanish football history with 10 La Liga triumphs under their belt. The most recent of these came in 2014 when Atleti drew 1-1 at runners-up Barcelona on the last day of the season to become the first side for a decade to break the Barca/Real Madrid duopoly.**

• The season promised to get even better for Atleti when they led city rivals Real Madrid 1-0 in the Champions League final in Lisbon with just seconds remaining, only to concede from a corner before falling apart in extra-time and losing 4-1. Nevertheless, Atletico have enjoyed European success in recent years, winning the Europa League in both 2010 and 2012 to become the first club to claim European football's newest competition on two occasions.

657 games between 1959 and 1976. Villa's all-time top goalscorer is Billy Walker, who found the back of the net an incredible 244 times between 1919 and 1933.

• Walker helped Villa bang in 128 league goals in the 1930/31 season, a record for the top flight which is unlikely ever to be broken. In the same campaign Tom 'Pongo' Waring scored a club record 49 league goals.

• **Before FA Cup semi-finals moved to Wembley, Villa Park staged a record 55 of these fixtures. The stadium has also hosted 16 England internationals and was the first venue to be used by the national team in three different centuries.**

• Villa's biggest league win came back in 1892 when they thrashed Accrington Stanley 12-2 in Division One – no side has scored more goals in a top-flight fixture. Six years earlier, though, the club recorded their biggest ever victory in the FA Cup, humiliating Wednesbury Old Athletic 13-0. In total Villa have scored 832 goals in the cup, a record unmatched by any other club.

• **Villa splashed out a club record £18 million on Sunderland striker Darren Bent in 2011. The previous year the Villans made their record sale when they offloaded winger James Milner to Manchester City for £26 million.**

• Famous Villa fans include punk violinist Nigel Kennedy, Prince William and David

• Four-time Atletico manager Luis Aragones, who famously led Spain to victory at Euro 2008, was the club's all-time leading scorer with 172 goals between 1964 and 1974.

HONOURS
Spanish League *1940, 1941, 1950, 1951, 1966, 1970, 1973, 1977, 1996, 2014*
Spanish Cup *1960, 1961, 1965, 1972, 1976, 1985, 1991, 1992, 1996, 2013*
European Cup Winners' Cup *1962*
Europa League *2010, 2012*
European Super Cup *2010, 2012*
Intercontinental Cup *1974*

ATTENDANCES

The Maracana Stadium in Rio de Janeiro holds the world record for a football match attendance, 199,854 spectators having watched the final match of the 1950 World Cup between Brazil and Uruguay. Most of the fans, though, went home in tears after Uruguay came from behind to win 2-1 and claim the trophy

TOP 10
PREMIER LEAGUE AVERAGE ATTENDANCES 2013/14

1.	Manchester United	75,207
2.	Arsenal	60,013
3.	Newcastle United	50,395
4.	Manchester City	47,080
5.	Liverpool	44,671
6.	Chelsea	41,482
7.	Sunderland	41,090
8.	Everton	37,732
9.	Aston Villa	36,081
10.	Tottenham	35,808

for a second time.

• **The biggest crowd at a match in Britain was for the first ever FA Cup final at Wembley in 1923. The official attendance for the match between Bolton and West Ham was 126,047, although, with thousands more fans gaining entry without paying, the actual crowd was estimated at**

150,000-200,000. The record official attendance for a match in Britain is 149,547, set in 1937 for Scotland's 3-1 victory over England in the Home International Championship at Hampden Park.

• In 1948 a crowd of 83,260 watched Manchester United entertain Arsenal at Maine Road (United's temporary home in the post-war years after Old Trafford suffered bomb damage), a record for the Football League. The following year, on 27th December 1949, the 44 Football League games played that day were watched by a record aggregate of 1,272,815 fans – an average of 28,913 per match.

• **On 15th April 1970 the biggest crowd ever to watch a European Cup tie, 135,826, crammed into Hampden Park in Glasgow to see Celtic beat Leeds United 2-1 in the semi-final second leg.**

• A record average crowd of 68,991 watched the matches at the 1994 World Cup in the USA.

A record attendance of 199,854 watched the final match of the 1950 World Cup between Brazil and Uruguay

LEIGHTON BAINES

Born: Kirkby, 11th December 1984
Position: Defender
Club career:
2002-07 Wigan Athletic 145 (4)
2007- Everton 231 (21)
International record:
2010- England 26 (1)

Everton left-back Leighton Baines has the best record from the penalty spot of any player in Premier League history. When he scored from 12 yards against Manchester United in April 2014, it was the 13th penalty out of 13 he had successfully converted in the league.

• **Baines began his career at Wigan, with whom he rose from the third tier to the Premier League in just three seasons between 2003 and 2005. A £6 million switch to Everton followed in 2007, and two years later Baines helped the Toffees reach the FA Cup final, but he had to settle for a runners-up medal after a 2-1 defeat by Chelsea.**

• In 2012 Baines became the first ever player from the Merseyside club to be included in the PFA Premier League Team of the Year since legendary goalkeeper Neville Southall in 1990. After another outstanding season in 2012/13, Baines was voted into the PFA team again by his fellow pros.

• **An attack-minded player who is known for his ability to whip in dangerous crosses from the left side, Baines won his first England cap in a 3-1 friendly win over Egypt at Wembley in March 2010. He scored his first international goal in a 5-0 rout of Moldova in September 2012 and was England's first-choice left-back at the 2014 World Cup in Brazil.**

GARETH BALE

Born: Cardiff, 16th July 1989
Position: Midfielder
Club career:
2006-07 Southampton 40 (5)
2007-13 Tottenham Hotspur 146 (42)
2013- Real Madrid 27 (15)
International record:
2006- Wales 44 (12)

Gareth Bale became the most expensive player in football history when he moved from Tottenham to Real Madrid for a world record transfer fee of £86 million in August 2013. The Welshman enjoyed a brilliant first season in the Spanish capital, scoring in Real's victories in both the Copa del Rey final and the Champions League final.

• **Bale began his career at Southampton, where he became the second youngest player to debut for the club (behind Theo Walcott) when he appeared in a 2-0 win against Millwall in the Championship in April 2006. The following season his** outstanding displays for the Saints earned him the Football League Young Player of the Year award.

• In the summer of 2007 Bale joined Tottenham for an initial fee of £5 million. Incredibly, he failed to feature on the winning side for Spurs in his first 24 league games – a Premier League record – but once he had buried that jinx his form rapidly improved, and he was soon being hailed as one of the most exciting talents in the game.

• **Now lauded as one of the best players in world football, Bale enjoyed an outstanding season with Spurs in 2010/11 and at the end of the campaign he was named PFA Player of the Year – only the fourth Welshman to receive this honour. He was also the only Premier League player to be voted into the UEFA Team of the Year for 2011. He had an even better season in 2012/13, picking up both Player of the Year gongs and the PFA Young Player of the Year award – only the second player, after Cristiano Ronaldo, to collect this individual treble.**

• Bale is the youngest player to appear for Wales, making his debut against Trinidad and Tobago on 27th May 2006 when he was aged 16 years and 315 days. Later that year he scored his first international goal, in a 5-1 home defeat by Slovakia, to become his country's youngest ever scorer.

Gareth Bale, the world's most expensive player

B
A
L
E

BALL BOYS

Ball boys developed from a gimmick employed by Chelsea in the 1905/06 season. To emphasise the extraordinary bulk of the team's 23-stone goalkeeper, William 'Fatty' Foulke, two young boys would stand behind his goal. They soon proved themselves useful in retrieving the ball when it went out of play, and so the concept of the ball boy was born.

• **Amazingly, a ball boy scored a goal in a match between Santacruzense and Atletico Sorocaba in Brazil in 2006. Santacruzense were trailing 1-0 when one of their players fired wide in the last minute. Instead of handing the ball back to the Atletico goalkeeper, the ball boy kicked it into the net and the goal was awarded by the female referee despite the angry protests of the Atletico players.**

• Almost as bizarrely, a ball girl was credited with an 'assist' during a Brazilian state championship match between Botafogo and Vasco de Gama in 2012. After the ball went out of play, 22-year-old Fernanda Maia quickly threw the ball she was carrying to a Botafogo player whose equally rapid throw-in was crossed for striker Maicosuel to score. Helped by her good looks, Maia became an instant celebrity in Brazil and cashed in on her newfound fame by baring all for *Playboy* magazine.

• **Sion's Serey Die hit the headlines in 2012 after slapping a ball boy in the face after his team's 1-0 defeat away to Laussane. The Ivory Coast midfielder was reported to be angry with the ball boy's time-wasting tactics during the match.**

• Seventeen-year-old Swansea ball boy Charlie Morgan helped his side reach the League Cup final in 2013 by falling on top of the ball when Chelsea's Eden

The 2014 World Cup ball also doubled as an unconventional hat

IS THAT A FACT?

Armenia striker Gevorg Ghazaryan was sent off in September 2012 after kicking a stray ball at a ball boy during a World Cup qualifier away to Bulgaria. The ball boy, Bozhidar Atanasov, was also dismissed for delivering a volley of abuse at Ghazaryan, but was unrepetant afterwards, saying, "The fourth official shouted, 'You, out!' But it was the coolest day of my life!"

Hazard wanted to take a corner kick. Frustrated at the lad's refusal to return the ball quickly, Hazard kicked it out from under him and was promptly shown a red card that pretty much ended Chelsea's chances of overhauling a two-goal deficit from the first leg.

BALLS

The laws of football specify that the ball must be an air-filled sphere with a circumference of 68-70cm and a weight before the start of the game of 410-450g. Before the first plastic footballs appeared in the 1950s, balls were made from leather and in wet conditions would become progressively heavier, sometimes actually doubling in weight.

• Most modern footballs are made in Pakistan, especially in the city of Sialkot, and are usually stitched from 32 panels of waterproofed leather or plastic. In the past child labour was often used in the production of the balls but, following pressure from UNICEF and the International Labour Organisation, manufacturers agreed in 1997 not to employ underage workers.

• Adidas have supplied the official ball for the World Cup since 1970. The ball for the 2014 tournament in Brazil, the Brazuca, was considered vastly superior to its predecessor, the Jabulani, which was widely thought to be the worst in the competition's history, its unpredictable trajectory attracting much criticism from players, managers and fans. FIFA, though, refused to bow to demands for the ball to be changed, although it later admitted that the Jabulani's ability to pick up 'incredible speed' may have been a factor in the numerous goalkeeping errors at the finals.

• Nike are the official supplier of balls for the Premier League, taking over the role from Mitre in 2000. A winter 'Hi-Vis' yellow ball has been used in the league since the 2004/05 season.

• Nike are also the official supplier of balls for the FA Cup, and in the 2013/14 season the company introduced a new 'mango' ball for the competition. York City's Ryan Jarvis was the first player to score with the new ball, netting in a 3-3 draw at Bristol Rovers in the first round.

• Remarkably, the ball burst during both the 1946 and 1947 FA Cup finals at Wembley – an unlikely coincidence which was probably caused by the poor quality of leather available after the Second World War.

MARIO BALOTELLI

Born: Palermo, Italy, 12th August 1990
Position: Striker
Club career:
2005-06 Lumezzane 2 (0)
2007-10 Inter Milan 59 (20)
2010-12 Manchester City 54 (20)
2013- 14 AC Milan 43 (26)
2014- Liverpool
International record:
2010- Italy 33 (13)

One of the most unpredictable players in world football, Liverpool striker Mario Balotelli joined the Reds from AC Milan in a £16 million deal in August 2014. Previously, Balotelli had played a big part in Manchester City's recent successes, being voted Man of the Match when they beat Stoke in the 2011 FA Cup final, and then helping the club win a first Premier League title the following year.

• Arguably, though, Balotelli is more famous for his madcap antics off the pitch than for anything he has done on the field of play. These include setting off fireworks in his bathroom, throwing darts at a youth team player and turning his garden into a quad bike course. If anything, however, his quirky behaviour has only endeared him even more to his teams' fans.

• The son of Ghanaian immigrants to Sicily who was cared for by foster parents as a child, Balotelli rose to prominence with Inter Milan. In November 2008 he became the club's youngest ever scorer in the Champions League when, aged 18 years and 85 days, he netted in a 3-3 draw against Cypriot outfit Anorthosis Famagusta. He helped Inter win consecutive Serie A titles between 2008 and 2010, but his lax attitude to training and volatile personality did not impress then Inter boss Jose Mourinho and he was sold to City for £23.5 million in the summer of 2010.

• In the same year Balotelli became the first black player to represent Italy at full international level when he played in a 1-0 friendly defeat against Ivory Coast. Two years later he starred for the Azzurri at Euro 2012, scoring both Italy's goals in their 2-1 semi-final defeat of Germany. However, Balotelli was less effective at the 2014 World Cup, despite scoring Italy's winner in their opening match against England.

"Look, ref, I promise I haven't got any fireworks with me today!"

BARCELONA

Year founded: 1899
Ground: Nou Camp (99,786)
Nickname: Barça
League titles: 22
Domestic cups: 26
European cups: 15
International cups: 2

One of the most famous and popular clubs in the world, Barcelona were founded in 1899 by bank worker Joan Gamper, a former captain of Swiss club Basel. The club were founder members and first winners of the Spanish championship, La Liga, in 1928 and have remained in the top flight of Spanish football ever since.

• For the people of Catalonia, **Barcelona is more like a national team than a mere club. As former manager Bobby Robson once succinctly put it, "Catalonia is a country and FC Barcelona is their army."**

• Along with Ajax, Juventus, Bayern Munich and Chelsea, Barcelona are one of just five clubs to have won three different European trophies: the European Cup/Champions League, the European Cup Winners' Cup (a record four times) and the Fairs Cup (Barça being the first winners of the competition in 1958).

• **With a capacity of 99,786, Barcelona's Nou Camp Stadium is the largest in Europe. Among the stadium's many facilities are a museum which attracts over one million visitors a year, mini training pitches and a chapel for the players.**

• For many years Barcelona played second fiddle to bitter rivals Real Madrid. Finally, in the 1990s, under former player-turned-coach Johan Cruyff, Barça turned the tables on the team from the Spanish capital, winning four La Liga titles on the trot between 1991 and 1994. Cruyff also led the Catalans to a first taste of glory in the European Cup, Barcelona beating Sampdoria at Wembley in 1992. The club have since won the Champions League on three more occasions, beating Arsenal 2-1 in the 2006 final and, under former manager Pep Guardiola, Manchester United 2-0 and 3-1 in 2009 and 2011 respectively.

• With 26 victories to their name, Barcelona have won the Copa del Rey (the Spanish version of the FA Cup) more times than any other club.

HONOURS

Spanish League *1929, 1945, 1948, 1949, 1952, 1953, 1959, 1960, 1974, 1985, 1991, 1992, 1993, 1994, 1998, 1999, 2005, 2006, 2009, 2010, 2011, 2013*
Spanish Cup *1910, 1912, 1913, 1920, 1922, 1925, 1926, 1928, 1942, 1951, 1952, 1953, 1957, 1959, 1963, 1968, 1971, 1978, 1981, 1983, 1988, 1990, 1997, 1998, 2009, 2012*
European Cup/Champions League *1992, 2006, 2009, 2011*
European Cup Winners' Cup *1979, 1982, 1989, 1997*
Fairs Cup *1958, 1960, 1961*
European Super Cup *1992, 1997, 2009, 2011*
Club World Cup *2009, 2011*

ROSS BARKLEY

Born: Liverpool, 5th December 1993
Position: Midfielder
Club career:
2010- Everton 47 (6)
2012 Sheffield Wednesday (loan) 13 (4)
2013 Leeds United (loan) 4 (0)
International record:
2013- England 9 (0)

Ross Barkley's eye-catching performances for Everton during the 2013/14 season saw him shortlisted for the PFA Young Player of the Year award, although he was eventually pipped to top spot by Chelsea's Eden Hazard.

• **Hailed by Everton manager Roberto Martinez as "a mix of Paul Gascoigne and Michael Ballack", Barkley joined the Toffees as an 11-year-old. He recovered from a triple leg fracture when he was 16 to make his debut against QPR in 2011, before spending much of the next year on loan at Sheffield Wednesday and Leeds United.**

• A strong player who loves to drive forward from midfield, Barkley scored his first goal for Everton in a 2-2 draw at Norwich on the opening day of the 2013/14 season with a long-range strike. He went on to hit other memorable goals against Manchester

City and Newcastle, the latter after a powerful run from inside his own half.

• Barkley played for England at all levels from Under-16 to Under-21, helping his country win the Under-17 European Championships in 2010 after a 2-1 victory over Spain in the final. He won his first full cap as a sub against Moldova in September 2013 and the following year was included in Roy Hodgson's England squad for the 2014 World Cup.

BARNSLEY

Year founded: 1887
Ground: Oakwell (23,009)
Previous name: Barnsley St Peter's
Nickname: The Tykes
Biggest win: 9-0 v Loughborough United (1899)
Heaviest defeat: 0-9 v Notts County (1927)

Founded as the church team Barnsley St Peter's in 1887 by the Rev Tiverton Preedy, the club changed to their present name a year after joining the Football League in 1898.

• **The Tykes have spent more seasons (73) in the second tier of English football than any other club and had to wait until 1997 before they had their first taste of life in the top flight. Unfortunately for their fans, it lasted just one season.**

• The Yorkshiremen's finest hour came in 1912 when they won the FA Cup, beating West Bromwich Albion 1-0 in a replay. The club were nicknamed 'Battling Barnsley' that season as they played a record 12 games during their cup run, including six 0-0 draws, before finally getting their hands on the trophy. Barnsley came close to repeating this feat in 2008, but were beaten in the semi-finals by fellow Championship side Cardiff City after they had sensationally knocked out Liverpool and cup holders Chelsea.

• **The youngest player to appear in the Football League is Barnsley striker Reuben Noble-Lazarus, who was 15 years and 45 days old when he faced Ipswich Town in September 2008. Afterwards, Barnsley boss Simon Davey joked Noble-Lazarus would be**

TOP 10

FEWEST EVER GAMES PLAYED IN TOP FLIGHT

1. Glossop North End (1899-1900)	34
2. Barnsley (1997/98)	38
3. Carlisle United (1974/75)	42
Leyton Orient (1962/63)	42
Northampton Town (1965/66)	42
Swindon Town (1993/94)	42
7. Darwen (1891/92 & 1893/94)	56
8. Millwall (1988-90)	76
9. Hull City (2008-10 & 2013/14)	114
Reading (2006-08 & 2012/13)	114

rewarded with a pizza as he was too young to be paid!

• Local boy Ernie Hine is Barnsley's leading goalscorer with 131 goals in two spells at the club in the 1920s and 1930s.

HONOURS
Division 3 (N) champions 1934, 1939, 1955
FA Cup 1912

BAYERN MUNICH

Year founded: 1900
Ground: Allianz Arena (71,137)
Nickname: The Bavarians
League titles: 24
Domestic cups: 17
European cups: 7

Bayern Munich players spend many hours perfecting their 'moody stare'

The biggest and most successful club in Germany, Bayern Munich were founded in 1900 by members of a Munich gymnastics club. Incredibly, when the Bundesliga was formed in 1963, Bayern's form was so poor they were not invited to become founder members of the league. But, thanks to the emergence in the mid-1960s of legendary players like goalkeeper Sepp Maier, sweeper Franz Beckenbauer and prolific goalscorer Gerd Muller, Bayern rapidly became the dominant force in German football. The club won the Bundesliga for the first time in 1969 and now have a record 24 German championships to their name.

• In 1974 Bayern became the first German club to win the European Cup, defeating Atletico Madrid 4-0 in the only final to go to a replay. Skippered by the imperious Beckenbauer, the club went on to complete a hat-trick of victories in the competition. However, Bayern had to wait another 25 years before winning the trophy again, beating Valencia on penalties in the Champions League final in 2001.

• In winning the Bundesliga title in 2012/13, Bayern set numerous records, including highest points total (91), most wins (29) and best goal difference (+80). They then beat Borussia Dortmund 2-1 at Wembley in the first all-German Champions League final, before becoming the first ever German team to win the Treble when they beat Stuttgart 3-2 in the final of the German Cup.

• With nearly 224,000 registered fans, Bayern have the second largest membership of any club in the world after Benfica.

• More than just a football club, Bayern also have departments devoted to a host of other sports, including basketball, chess, handball and table tennis, and can boast more than 1,000 active members.

HONOURS
German championship 1932, 1969, 1972, 1973, 1974, 1980, 1981, 1985, 1986, 1987, 1989, 1990, 1994, 1997, 1999, 2000, 2001, 2003, 2005, 2006, 2008, 2010, 2013, 2014
German Cup 1957, 1966, 1967, 1969, 1971, 1982, 1984, 1986, 1998, 2000, 2003, 2005, 2006, 2008, 2010, 2013, 2014
European Cup/Champions League 1974, 1975, 1976, 2001, 2013
European Cup Winners' Cup 1967
UEFA Cup 1996
Club World Cup 2013

FRANZ BECKENBAUER

Born: Munich, Germany,
11th September 1945
Position: Defender
Club career:
1964-77 Bayern Munich 427 (60)
1977-80 New York Cosmos 105 (19)
1980-82 Hamburg 28 (0)
1983 New York Cosmos 29 (2)
International record:
1965-77 West Germany 103 (14)

Germany's greatest ever player, Franz Beckenbauer's elegant playing style and outstanding leadership qualities earned him the nickname 'Der Kaiser' ('The Emperor'). Having started out as a midfielder, Beckenbauer created and defined the role of the offensive 'sweeper' in the late 1960s, turning defence into attack with surging runs from the back.

• **Beckenbauer enjoyed huge success at both club and international level. He captained Bayern Munich to three consecutive victories in the European Cup between 1974 and 1976, matching Ajax's treble earlier in the decade. As skipper of West Germany, Beckenbauer led his country to victory in the 1972 European Championships, and two years later he cemented his reputation as a national icon by collecting the World Cup trophy after a 2-1 defeat of the Netherlands in the 1974 final in Munich.**

• His consistent performances won him the European Footballer of the Year award in 1972 and 1976 – the first German player to win the award twice. He was also voted German Footballer of the Year a record four times: in 1966, 1968, 1974 and 1976.

• **More success followed for Beckenbauer in the late 1970s after he accepted a lucrative offer to play in America, his New York Cosmos side winning the NASL Soccer Bowl in 1977, 1978 and 1980.**

• Beckenbauer was appointed manager of West Germany in 1986 and when, four years later, his country triumphed at Italia '90 'Der Kaiser' became the first man to both captain and coach a World Cup-winning team. Later, in 1996, he led Bayern Munich to glory in the UEFA Cup, before becoming the driving force behind Germany's successful bid to host the 2006 World Cup.

David Beckham's desire to be the next James Bond was becoming a little too obvious

DAVID BECKHAM

Born: Leytonstone, 2nd May 1975
Position: Midfielder
Club career:
1993-2003 Manchester United 265 (62)
1995 Preston North End (loan) 5 (2)
2003-07 Real Madrid 116 (13)
2007-12 LA Galaxy 98 (18)
2009 AC Milan (loan) 18 (2)
2010 AC Milan (loan) 11 (0)
2013 Paris St Germain 10 (0)
International record:
1996-2009 England 115 (17)

One of the most famous names on the planet, David Beckham's fame extends far beyond the world of football. Yet, for all the interest in his marriage to Spice Girl Victoria Beckham, his fashion sense, his eye-catching haircuts and tattoos, it shouldn't be forgotten that his celebrity status stems primarily from his remarkable ability on the ball.

• **A superb crosser of the ball and free kick expert, at his peak Beckham was probably the best right-sided midfielder in the world. He twice came close to winning the World** Player of the Year award, finishing as runner-up in 1999 and 2001.

• Beckham enjoyed huge success with his first club Manchester United, winning six Premiership titles, two FA Cups and, as the final leg of the Treble, the Champions League in 1999. However, his glamorous lifestyle began to irritate United boss Sir Alex Ferguson, and the deteriorating relationship between the pair led to Beckham's departure to Spanish giants Real Madrid in 2003.

• **As one of Real's 'galacticos', Beckham was part of a team which was much hyped but frequently failed to deliver. He eventually won the Spanish title with Real in 2007, shortly before making a lucrative move to Major League Soccer in the USA with LA Galaxy, with whom he twice won the MLS championship. In 2013, shortly before announcing his retirement from the game, he enjoyed a brief spell with Paris St Germain, helping them to win the French league to become the first British player to win titles in four different countries.**

• One of just eight England centurions and the only England player to have scored at three different World Cups, Beckham captained his country from 2000 to 2006.

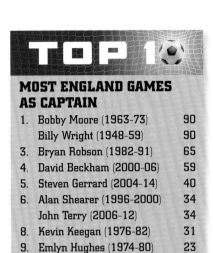

MOST ENGLAND GAMES AS CAPTAIN

1.	Bobby Moore (1963-73)	90
	Billy Wright (1948-59)	90
3.	Bryan Robson (1982-91)	65
4.	David Beckham (2000-06)	59
5.	Steven Gerrard (2004-14)	40
6.	Alan Shearer (1996-2000)	34
	John Terry (2006-12)	34
8.	Kevin Keegan (1976-82)	31
9.	Emlyn Hughes (1974-80)	23
10.	Bob Crompton (1903-14)	22
	Johnny Haynes (1960-62)	22

After being sent off against Argentina at the 1998 World Cup he was made the scapegoat for England's elimination from the competition, but famously bounced back to score the winning goal from the penalty spot against the same opposition at the 2002 tournament in Japan and South Korea.

• Beckham's England career appeared to be over when he was dropped from the squad by new manager Steve McClaren in 2006. However, he was recalled the following year and was rewarded with his 100th cap by McClaren's successor, his former Real boss Fabio Capello, against France in 2008. The following year he became England's most capped outfield player, beating the old record set by the great Bobby Moore, when he won his 109th cap against Slovakia. Sadly for Beckham, injury ruled him out of the 2010 World Cup, effectively ending his international career.

BELGIUM

First international: Belgium 3 France 3, 1904
Most capped player: Jan Ceulemans, 96 caps (1977-91)
Leading goalscorer: Bernard Voorhoof (1928-40) and Paul Van Himst (1960-74), 30 goals
First World Cup appearance: Belgium 2 Germany 5
Biggest win: Belgium 10 San Marino 1, 2001
Heaviest defeat: England amateurs 11 Belgium 2, 1909

A rising force in the world game, Belgium are yet to win a major trophy but they came mighty close in the 1980 European championships in Italy. After topping their group, ahead of the hosts, England and Spain, Belgium went straight through to the final against West Germany where they were unfortunate to go down 2-1 in a close encounter.

• **Belgium's best performance at the World Cup came in 1986 when, after beating the USSR and Spain in the earlier knock-out rounds, they lost 2-0 to a Diego Maradona-inspired Argentina in the semi-finals. After losing 4-2 in the third place match to France, Belgium had to be content with fourth spot at the tournament.**

• Following an impressive World Cup qualifying campaign, a young Belgian side featuring the likes of goalkeeper Thibaut Courtois, Manchester City skipper Vincent Kompany and Chelsea midfielder Eden Hazard, rose to a best-ever fifth place in the FIFA World Rankings in October 2013 and were given top-seed status in the draw for the 2014 World Cup. The Belgians lived up to their billing, reaching the last eight for only the second time in their history before bowing out to Argentina.

• **The Red Devils' current manager, Marc Wilmots, is Belgium's all-time leading goalscorer at the World Cup with five goals.**

• Midfielder Jan Ceulemans won a record 96 caps for Belgium, captaining his country on a record 48 occasions.

World Cup Record	
1930	Round 1
1934	Round 1
1938	Round 1
1950	Withdrew
1954	Round 1
1958	Did not qualify
1962	Did not qualify
1966	Did not qualify
1970	Round 1
1974	Did not qualify
1978	Did not qualify
1982	Round 2
1986	Fourth place
1990	Round 2
1994	Round 2
1998	Round 1
2002	Round 2
2006	Did not qualify
2010	Did not qualify
2014	Quarter-finals

Belgium's Marouane Fellaini loved playing against the All-star Midget XI

BENFICA

Year founded: 1904
Ground: Estadio Da Luz, Lisbon (65,647)
Nickname: The Eagles
League titles: 33
Domestic cups: 28
European cups: 2

Portugal's most successful club, Benfica were founded in 1904 at a meeting of 24 football enthusiasts in south Lisbon. The club were founder members of the Portuguese league in 1933 and have since won the title a record 33 times.

• **With 235,000 registered members, Benfica is officially the biggest club in the world, ahead of Bayern Munich and Barcelona.**

• Inspired by legendary striker Eusebio, Benfica enjoyed a golden era in the 1960s when the club won eight domestic championships. In 1961 Benfica became the first team to break Real Madrid's dominance in the European Cup when they beat Barcelona 3-2 in the final. The following year, the trophy stayed in Lisbon after the Eagles sensationally beat Real 5-3 in the final in Amsterdam.

• In 1972/73 Benfica went the whole season undefeated – the first Portuguese team to achieve this feat – winning a staggering 28 and drawing just two of their 30 league matches. The great Eusebio struck 40 goals that season to top the European scoring charts as Benfica were crowned champions once again.

• Benfica hold the unenviable record of losing in their last eight European finals they have appeared in, most recently being defeated in consecutive Europa League finals by Chelsea (2013) and Sevilla (2014).

HONOURS
***Portuguese championship** 1936, 1937, 1938, 1942, 1943, 1945, 1950, 1955, 1957,1960, 1961, 1963, 1964, 1965, 1967, 1968, 1969,1971, 1972, 1973, 1975,1976, 1977, 1981, 1983, 1984, 1987, 1989, 1991, 1994, 2005, 2010, 2014*
***Portuguese Cup** 1930, 1931, 1935, 1940, 1943, 1944, 1949, 1951, 1952, 1953, 1955, 1957, 1959, 1962, 1964,1969, 1970, 1972, 1980, 1981, 1983,1985, 1986, 1987, 1993, 1996, 2004, 2014*
***European Cup** 1961, 1962*

KARIM BENZEMA

Born: Lyon, France, 19th December 1987
Position: Striker
Club career:
2004-09 Lyon 112 (43)
2009- Real Madrid 159 (72)
International record:
2007- France 71 (24)

Real Madrid striker Karim Benzema is the highest-scoring French forward in La Liga, passing the previous best of the legendary Zinedine Zidane during the 2011/12 season.

• **A strong and powerful runner who can shoot accurately with both feet, Benzema rose to prominence with his hometown club, Lyon, enjoying a superb season in 2008/09 when he was voted Ligue 1 Player of the Year. He then moved on to Real for £30 million, but initially struggled in the Spanish capital, gaining weight and famously being described as 'listless' by then manager Jose Mourinho.**

• Benzema's form picked up, though, and in 2014 he played a key role in Real's record 10th Champions League success after they beat city rivals Atletico Madrid 4-1 in the final in Lisbon.

• After missing out on the 2010 World Cup due to his poor club form, Benzema was desperate to do well at the tournament four years later in Brazil. He didn't disappoint, finishing as France's top scorer with three goals.

GEORGE BEST

Born: Belfast, 22nd May 1946
Died: 25th November 2005
Position: Winger
Club career:
1963-74 Manchester United 361 (138)
1975 Stockport County 3 (2)
1975-76 Cork Celtic 3 (0)
1976-77 Fulham 33 (7)
1977-78 Los Angeles Aztecs 55 (27)
1978-79 Fort Lauderdale 26 (6)
1979-80 Hibernian 22 (3)
1980-81 San Jose Earthquakes 56 (28)
1983 Bournemouth 4 (0)
International record:
1964-78 Northern Ireland 37 (9)

Possibly the greatest natural talent in the history of the British game, George Best was a football genius who thrilled fans everywhere with his dazzling

Karim Benzema powers through the Atletico Madrid defence

Manchester United legend George Best in typical pose

dribbling skills, superb ball control and goalscoring ability.

• Best left his native Northern Ireland as a youngster to play for Manchester United, making his debut at Old Trafford in 1963 when aged just 17. His most memorable achievements were all packed into the next five years as he helped fire United to two league titles in 1965 and 1967 and to glory in the European Cup in 1968, Best scoring the vital second goal against Benfica at Wembley. In 1968 he was also named Footballer of the Year and European Footballer of the Year.

• Dubbed 'The Fifth Beatle' for his long hair and good looks, Best was the first footballer to become famous outside the game. He cashed in on his celebrity status by opening a chain of boutiques, appearing in a number of TV ads and dating a seemingly never-ending series of Miss World winners.

• In 1970 Best scored six goals to set a still-unbeaten United record as the Red Devils thrashed Northampton 8-2 in an FA Cup fifth-round tie at the Cobblers' old County Ground. "I was so embarrassed that I played the last 20 minutes at left-back," he said years later.

• There appeared to be no limit to what he might achieve, but Best's career nosedived in the 1970s as his hard-drinking, glamorous lifestyle inevitably took its toll. Sacked by Manchester United for repeatedly missing training sessions, Best played for a succession of lesser clubs in Britain and the USA, only occasionally showing flashes of his old brilliance. He eventually ended his playing career in the low-key environment of Dean Court, making four appearances for Bournemouth in 1983.

• Easily the finest player ever to represent Northern Ireland, Best never appeared in the final stages of the World Cup or European Championships. Yet he remains idolised in his home country, his standing summed up by the popular Belfast saying: "Maradona good, Pelé better, George Best".

• After a long battle with alcoholism, Best died in November 2005. His passing was marked by a minute's applause at grounds up and down the country – the first British player to receive this continental-style tribute.

IS THAT A FACT?

In 2006 Belfast City Airport was renamed George Best Belfast City Airport as a tribute to Northern Ireland's greatest ever footballer.

BIRMINGHAM CITY

Year founded: 1875
Ground: St Andrew's (30,016)
Previous name: Small Heath Alliance, Small Heath, Birmingham
Nickname: The Blues
Biggest win: 12-0 v Nottingham Forest (1899), Walsall Town Swifts (1892) and Doncaster Rovers (1903)
Heaviest defeat: 1-9 v Blackburn Rovers (1895) and Sheffield Wednesday (1930)

Founded in 1875 as Small Heath Alliance, the club were founder members and the first champions of the Second Division in 1892. Unfortunately, Small Heath were undone at the 'test match' stage (a 19th-century version of the play-offs) and failed to gain promotion to the top flight.

• The club had to wait until 2011 for the greatest day in their history, when the Blues beat hot favourites Arsenal 2-1 in the League Cup final at Wembley, on-loan striker Obafemi Martins grabbing the winner in the final minutes to spark ecstatic celebrations among Birmingham's long-suffering fans. City had previously won the competition back in 1963 after getting the better of arch-rivals Aston Villa over a two-legged final, although that achievement was hardly comparable as half the top-flight clubs hadn't even bothered to enter.

• However, on the final day of the 2010/11 season Birmingham were relegated from the Premier League, to become only the second club (after Norwich City in 1985) to win a major domestic trophy and suffer the drop in the same campaign. It was the 12th time in their history that the Blues had fallen through the top-flight trapdoor, a record of misery unmatched by any other club.

• In 1956 Birmingham became the first club to reach the FA Cup final without playing a single tie at home, the Midlanders winning at Torquay, Leyton Orient, West Brom and Arsenal before seeing off Sunderland in the semi-final at Hillsborough. Perhaps, though, their tricky route to Wembley caught up with them, as they lost in the final to Manchester City.

• On 15th May 1955 Birmingham became the first English club to compete in Europe when they drew 0-0 away to Inter Milan in the inaugural competition of the Fairs Cup. In 1960 the Blues went all the way to the final of the same tournament to set another first for English clubs in Europe, but lost 4-1 on aggregate to Barcelona. The following year Birmingham were runners-up in the Fairs Cup again, going down 4-2 on aggregate to Roma.

• England goalkeeper Gil Merrick played in a record 551 games for Birmingham in all competitions between 1946 and 1959.

• The Blues' youngest ever player is club legend Trevor Francis, who was aged just 16 and 139 days when he made his debut against Cardiff City in 1970. Francis went on to score 133 goals for the Brummies, a total only surpassed by pre-war striker Joe Bradford, who notched 267 in all competitions.

HONOURS
Division 2 champions 1893, 1921, 1948, 1955
Second Division champions 1995
League Cup 1963, 2011
Football League Trophy 1991, 1995

BLACKBURN ROVERS

Year founded: 1875
Ground: Ewood Park (31,367)
Nickname: Rovers
Biggest win: 11-0 v Rossendale United (1884)
Heaviest defeat: 0-8 v Arsenal (1933)

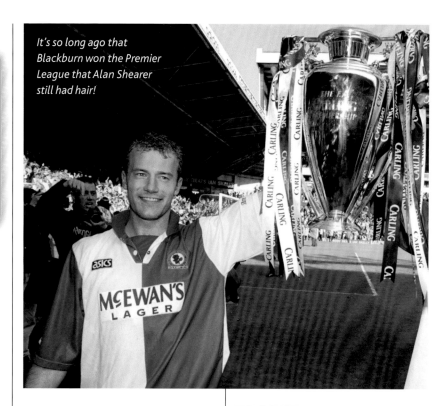

It's so long ago that Blackburn won the Premier League that Alan Shearer still had hair!

Founded in 1875 by a group of wealthy local residents and ex-public school boys, Blackburn Rovers joined the Football League as founder members in 1888. Two years later the club moved to a permanent home at Ewood Park, where they have remained ever since.

• Blackburn were a force to be reckoned with from the start, winning the FA Cup five times in the 1880s and 1890s. Of all league clubs Rovers were the first to win the trophy, beating Scottish side Queen's Park 2-1 in the final at Kennington Oval in 1884. The Lancashire side went on to win the cup in the two following years as well, setting a record which still stands by remaining undefeated in 24 consecutive games in the competition between 1884 and 1886.

• Rovers won the cup again in 1890, 1891 and 1928 to make a total of six triumphs in the competition. In the first of these victories they thrashed Sheffield Wednesday 6-1 in the final, with left winger William Townley scoring three times to become the first player to hit a hat-trick in the final.

• The club have won the league title three times: in 1912, 1914 and, most memorably, in 1995 when, funded by the millions of local steel

magnate Jack Walker and powered by the deadly 'SAS' strikeforce of Alan Shearer and Chris Sutton, Rovers pipped reigning champions Manchester United to the Premiership title. The team soon broke up, though, and Rovers were relegated from the top tier just four years later.

• Derek Fazackerley made the most appearances for Blackburn, turning out in 596 games between 1970 and 1986. The club's all-time leading scorer is Simon Garner, with 168 league goals between 1978 and 1992, although Alan Shearer's incredible record of 122 goals in just 138 games for the club is arguably more impressive.

• Rovers' most expensive signing is former England striker Andy Cole, who joined the club from Manchester United in 2001 for £8 million. The club made their record sale in 2009, when Paraguayan hitman Roque Santa Cruz left for Manchester City in an £18 million deal.

• In 1955 Rovers striker Tommy Briggs scored a club record seven goals in a single match in an 8-3 thrashing of Bristol Rovers at Ewood Park.

IS THAT A FACT?

Blackburn Rovers are the only club in Premier League history to clinch the title with a defeat. On the last day of the 1994/95 season Rovers lost 2-1 at Liverpool, but with closest challengers Manchester United only managing a 1-1 draw at West Ham the trophy still ended up at Ewood Park.

HONOURS

Division 1 champions *1912, 1914*
Premier League champions *1995*
Division 2 champions *1975*
FA Cup *1884, 1885, 1886, 1890, 1891, 1928*
League Cup *2002*

BLACKPOOL

Year founded: 1887
Ground: Bloomfield Road (17,338)
Nickname: The Seasiders
Biggest win: 10-0 v Lanerossi Vincenza (1972)
Heaviest defeat: 1-10 v Small Heath (1901)

Founded in 1887 by old boys of St John's School, Blackpool joined the Second Division of the Football League in 1896. The club merged with South Shore in 1899, the same year in which Blackpool lost their league status for a single season.

• Blackpool's heyday was in the late 1940s and early 1950s when the club reached three FA Cup finals in five years. The Seasiders lost in the finals of 1948 and 1951 but lifted the cup in 1953 after defeating Lancashire rivals Bolton 4-3 in one of the most exciting Wembley matches ever. Although centre-forward Stan Mortensen scored a hat-trick, the match was dubbed the 'Matthews Final' after veteran winger Stanley Matthews, who finally won a winners' medal at the grand old age of 38.

• An apprentice at the time of the 'Matthews Final', long-serving right-back Jimmy Armfield holds the record

for league appearances for Blackpool, with 569 between 1952 and 1971. Now a match summariser for BBC Radio Five Live, Armfield is also Blackpool's most capped player, having played for England 43 times. In 2011 a nine-foot-high statue of the Seasiders legend was unveiled outside Bloomfield Road.

• The club's record scorer is Jimmy Hampson, who hit 248 league goals between 1927 and 1938, including a season best 45 in the 1929/30 Second Division championship-winning campaign.

• The Seasiders were the first club to reach consecutive finals in the short-lived Anglo-Italian Cup, beating Bologna 2-1 in 1971 to lift the trophy before losing 3-1 to Roma in the following year's final.

• Blackpool conceded a top-flight record 125 goals in 1930/31 but, amazingly, just managed to avoid relegation to Division Two by finishing a point ahead of Leeds United (who only conceded 81 goals).

• Blackpool are the only club to have gained promotion from three different divisions via the play-offs, most recently rising from the Championship to the Premier League in 2010 after a thrilling 3-2 win over Cardiff City at Wembley. More than 30,000 ecstatic tangerine-clad fans celebrated the club's return to the top flight for the first time since 1971

by bringing the town's famous Golden Mile to a virtual standstill. However, the following year Blackpool dropped back down to the Championship, despite scoring 55 league goals – a record for a relegated Premier League club.

HONOURS
Division 2 champions 1930
FA Cup 1953
Football League Trophy 2002, 2004

BOLTON WANDERERS

Year founded: 1874
Ground: The Reebok Stadium (28,723)
Previous name: Christ Church
Nickname: The Trotters
Biggest win: 13-0 v Sheffield United (1890)
Heaviest defeat: 1-9 v Preston North End (1887)

The club was founded in 1874 as Christ Church, but three years later broke away from the church after a disagreement with the vicar and adopted their present name (the 'Wanderers' part stemmed from the fact that the club had no permanent

home until moving to their former stadium, Burnden Park, in 1895).

• Bolton were founder members of the Football League in 1888, finishing fifth at the end of the campaign. The Trotters have since gone on to play more seasons in the top flight without ever winning the title, 73, than any other club.

• The club, though, have had better luck in the FA Cup. After defeats in the final in 1894 and 1904, Bolton won the cup for the first time in 1923 after beating West Ham 2-0 in the first Wembley final. In the same match, Bolton centre-forward David Jack enjoyed the distinction of becoming the first player to score a goal at the new stadium. The Trotters went on to win the competition again in 1926 and 1929.

• In 1953 Bolton became the first, and so far only, team to score three goals in normal time in the FA Cup final yet finish as losers, going down 4-3 to a Stanley Matthews-inspired Blackpool. In 1958 Bolton won the cup for a fourth time, beating Manchester United 2-0 in the final at Wembley. Since then major honours have eluded the club, although the Trotters were runners-up in the League Cup in 1995 and 2004.

• In 1993, while they were in the third tier, Bolton became the last club from outside the top two flights to knock out the reigning FA Cup holders when they beat Liverpool 2-0 at Anfield in a third-round replay. The following season Wanderers, by then in the second tier, accounted for the holders again, beating Arsenal 3-1 in a fourth-round replay at Highbury.

• The club's top scorer is legendary centre-forward Nat Lofthouse, who notched 285 goals in all competitions between 1946 and 1960. The Trotters' appearance record is held by another England international of the same era, goalkeeper Eddie Hopkinson, who turned out 578 times for the club between 1952 and 1970.

• Popular winger Ricardo Gardner is Bolton's most-capped international, turning out 72 times for Jamaica between 1998 and 2012.

Blackpool legend Stanley Matthews goes on a trademark dribble

HONOURS
Division 2 champions 1909, 1978
First Division champions 1997
Division 3 champions 1973
FA Cup 1923, 1926, 1929, 1958
Football League Trophy 1989

BOOTS

The first record of a pair of football boots goes back to 1526 when Henry VIII, then aged 35, ordered "45 velvet pairs and one leather pair for football" from the Great Wardrobe. Whether he actually donned the boots for a royal kick-around in Hampton Court or Windsor Castle is not known.

• Early leather boots were very different to the synthetic ones worn by modern players, having hard toe-caps and protection around the ankles. Studs were originally prohibited, but were sanctioned after a change in the rules in 1891. Lighter boots without ankle protection were first worn in South America, but did not become the norm in Britain until the 1950s, following the example of England international Stanley Matthews who had a lightweight pair of boots made for him by a Yorkshire company.

• Herbert Chapman, later Arsenal's manager, is believed to be the first player to wear coloured boots, sporting a yellow pair in the 1900s. White boots first became fashionable in the 1970s when they were worn by the likes of Alan Ball (Everton), Terry Cooper (Leeds) and Alan Hinton (Derby County). In 1996, Liverpool's John Barnes was the first player to wear white boots in an FA Cup final.

• Boots, or rather the lack of them, became a major issue at the 1950 World Cup. After qualifying for the tournament for the first time, India pulled out of the finals after their players were refused permission to play barefoot!

• Today's top players all have individual boot sponsorship deals with the major manufacturers. Stars linked with the various boot companies include Cristiano Ronaldo (Nike), Lionel Messi (Adidas) and Sergio Aguero (Puma).

IS THAT A FACT?
Boot manufacturers Adidas have held a 9.1% share in German giants Bayern Munich since 2002.

BORUSSIA DORTMUND

Year founded: 1909
Ground: Signal Iduna Park (80,645)
Nickname: The Borussians
League titles: 8
Domestic cups: 3
European cups: 2
International cups: 1

Borussia Dortmund were founded by members of a church team in 1909 who decided to form their own club without the involvement of a strict local priest. They chose the name 'Borussia', which means 'Prussia' in Latin, after a nearby brewery.

• In 1966 Dortmund became the first German club to win a European trophy when they beat Liverpool 2-1 in the Cup Winners' Cup final. The greatest day in the club's history, though, came in 1997 when they defeated favourites Juventus 3-1 in the Champions League final. In the same year they lifted the Intercontinental Cup after beating Brazilian side Cruzeiro.

• The club's Signal Iduna Park Stadium (previously known as Westfalenstadion) is the largest in Germany, with a capacity of 80,645. The south terrace, nicknamed 'the Yellow Wall', is the largest terrace for standing in European football with a capacity of just under 25,000.

• In 2012 Dortmund clinched their first ever Double when they smashed Bayern Munich 5-2 in the German Cup final, three weeks after wrapping up the Bundesliga title for a second consecutive year. The following year they faced Bayern again in the first all-German Champions League final at Wembley, but ended up losing 2-1.

HONOURS
German championship 1956, 1957, 1963, 1995, 1996, 2002, 2011, 2012
German Cup 1965, 1989, 2012
Champions League 1997
European Cup Winners' Cup 1966
Intercontinental Cup 1997

It's a little-known fact that Spiderman plays for Borussia Dortmund!

BOURNEMOUTH

Year founded: 1899
Ground: Dean Court (12,000)
Previous name: Boscombe, Bournemouth and Boscombe Athletic
Nickname: The Cherries
Biggest win: 11-0 v Margate (1970)
Heaviest defeat: 0-9 v Lincoln City (1982)

The Cherries were founded as Boscombe FC in 1899, having their origins in the Boscombe St John's club, which was formed in 1890. The club's name changed to Bournemouth and Boscombe FC in 1923 and then to AFC Bournemouth in 1971, when the team's colours were altered to red-and-black stripes in imitation of AC Milan.

• However, any similarities with the Serie A giants end there, as much of Bournemouth's existence has been spent in the lower divisions struggling with financial difficulties. The Cherries, though, enjoyed a never-to-be-forgotten day in 1984 when they beat FA Cup holders Manchester United 2-0 in a third-round tie at Dean Court.

• Bournemouth recorded their biggest ever win in the same competition, smashing fellow seasiders Margate 11-0 at Dean Court in 1970. Cherries striker Ted MacDougall scored nine of the goals, an all-time record for an individual player in the competition.

• Bournemouth were the first ever winners of the Football League Trophy (then known as the Associate Members' Cup) in 1984, beating Hull City 2-1 in the final at Boothferry Park.

• The club's record scorer is Ron Eyre (202 goals between 1924 and 1933), while striker Steve Fletcher pulled on the Cherries' jersey an amazing 628 times in two spells at Dean Court between 1992 and 2013.

• Bournemouth achieved their highest ever league position in 2013/14, finishing a respectable 10th in the Championship.

HONOURS
Division 3 champions *1987*
Football League Trophy *1984*

The recent success of Bournemouth (in blue) has really annoyed their rivals!

BRADFORD CITY

Year founded: 1903
Ground: Valley Parade (25,136)
Nickname: The Bantams
Biggest win: 11-1 v Rotherham United (1928)
Heaviest defeat: 1-9 v Colchester United (1961)

Bradford City were founded in 1903 when a local rugby league side, Manningham FC, decided to switch codes. The club was elected to Division Two in the same year before they had played a single match – a swift ascent into the Football League which is only matched by Chelsea.

• City's finest hour was in 1911 when they won the FA Cup for the only time in the club's history, beating Newcastle 1-0 in a replayed final at Old Trafford. There were more celebrations in Bradford in 1929 when City won the Third Division (North) scoring 128 goals in the process – a record for the third tier.

• In 2013 Bradford City became the first club from the fourth tier of English football to reach a major final at Wembley, losing 5-0 to Swansea City in the League Cup. The Bantams bounced back to get to the League Two play-off final, which they enjoyed a lot more, comfortably beating Northampton Town 3-0 to earn promotion to League One.

• Sadly, City will forever be associated with the fire that broke out in the club's main stand on 11th May 1985 and killed 56 supporters. The official inquiry into the tragedy found that the inferno had probably been caused by a discarded cigarette butt which set fire to litter under the stand. As a permanent memorial to those who died Bradford added black trimming to their shirt collars and sleeves.

• Loyal right-back Ces Podd, an international player with Saint Kitts and Nevis, made a club record 502 league appearances for the Bantams between 1970 and 1984.

HONOURS
Division 2 champions 1908
Division 3 (N) champions *1929*
Division 3 champions 1985
FA Cup 1911

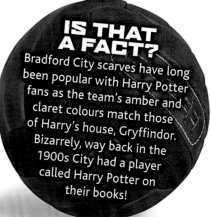

IS THAT A FACT?
Bradford City scarves have long been popular with Harry Potter fans as the team's amber and claret colours match those of Harry's house, Gryffindor. Bizarrely, way back in the 1900s City had a player called Harry Potter on their books!

BRADFORD CITY

BRAZIL

BRAZIL

First international:
Argentina 3 Brazil 0, 1914
Most capped player:
Cafu, 142 caps (1990-2006)
Leading goalscorer:
Pelé, 77 goals (1957-71)
First World Cup appearance: Brazil 1 Yugoslavia 2, 1930
Biggest win: Brazil 14 Nicaragua 0, 1975
Heaviest defeat: Brazil 1 Germany 7, 2014

The most successful country in the history of international football, Brazil are renowned for an exciting, flamboyant style of play which delights both their legions of drum-beating fans and neutrals alike.

To put it mildly, Brazil's elimination from the 2014 World Cup did not go down well with the fans

• Brazil is the only country to have won the World Cup five times. The South Americans first lifted the trophy in 1958 (beating hosts Sweden 5-2 in the final) and retained the prize four years later in Chile. In 1970, a great Brazilian side featuring legends such as Pelé, Jairzinho, Gerson and Rivelino thrashed Italy 4-1 to win the Jules Rimet trophy for a third time. Further triumphs followed in 1994 (3-2 on penalties against Italy after a dour 0-0 draw) and in 2002 (after beating Germany 2-0 in the final).

• Brazil is the only country to have appeared at every World Cup (a total of 20) since the tournament began in 1930. The South Americans have also recorded the most wins (70) at the finals. Less impressively, Brazil suffered the heaviest ever defeat by a host nation when they were trounced 7-1 by Germany in the semi-finals of the 2014 tournament.

• Brazil striker Jairzinho was the last player to score in every match at the World Cup, finding the net in all six games in 1970.

• With eight wins to their name, Brazil are the third most successful side in the history of the Copa

America (behind Uruguay and Argentina, who have won the trophy 15 and 14 times respectively). Brazil last won the tournament in Venezuela in 2007, beating neighbours Argentina 3-0 in the final.

• **Brazil have the best record of any nation in the Confederations Cup, winning the trophy four times – most recently in 2013, when they trounced Spain 3-0 in the final in Rio de Janeiro.**

HONOURS
World Cup *1958, 1962, 1970, 1994, 2002*
Copa America *1919, 1922, 1949, 1989, 1997, 1999, 2004, 2007*
Confederations Cup *1997, 2005, 2009, 2013*
World Cup record
1930 Round 1
1934 Round 1
1938 Semi-finals
1950 Runners-up
1954 Quarter-finals
1958 Winners
1962 Winners
1966 Round 1
1970 Winners
1974 Fourth place
1978 Third place
1982 Round 2
1986 Quarter-finals
1990 Round 2
1994 Winners
1998 Runners-up
2002 Winners
2006 Quarter-finals
2010 Quarter-finals
2014 Fourth place

BRENTFORD

Year founded: 1889
Ground: Griffin Park (12,300)
Nickname: The Bees
Biggest win: 9-0 v Wrexham (1963)
Heaviest defeat: 0-7 v Swansea Town (1926), v Walsall (1957) and v Peterborough (2007)

Brentford were founded in 1889 by members of a local rowing club. After playing at a number of different venues, the club settled at Griffin Park in 1904.

• **The club enjoyed its heyday in the decade before the Second World War. In 1929/30 Brentford won all 21 of their home games in the Third Division (South) to set a record which remains to this day. Promoted to the First Division in 1935, the Bees finished in the top six in the next three seasons before being relegated in the first post-war campaign.**

• Despite winning the League Two Championship in 2008/09 and gaining promotion to the Championship in 2014, Brentford have achieved little of note since those glory days. Supporters, though, have ample opportunity to drown their sorrows as the club's ground, Griffin Park, has a pub on all four corners – including one, The Princess Royal, which is owned by the club.

• **Brentford paid out a club record £1 million when they signed Leyton Orient midfielder Moses Odubajo in June 2014. The Bees received a record £2.5 million when they sold Icelandic defender Hermann Hreidarsson to Wimbledon in 1999.**

• Singer Rod Stewart had trials at Brentford in 1961 before concentrating on his music career, while TV presenter Bradley Walsh played for the club's reserve team in the late 1970s.

• **Defender Ken Coote played in a club record 514 league games for the Bees between 1949 and 1964.**

HONOURS
Division 2 champions 1935
Division 3 (S) champions 1933
Division 4 champions 1963
Third Division champions 1999
League Two champions 2009

Brighton striker Craig Mackail-Smith

BRIGHTON AND HOVE ALBION

Year founded: 1900
Ground: AMEX Stadium (30,750)
Previous name: Brighton and Hove Rangers
Nickname: The Seagulls
Biggest win: 10-1 v Wisbech (1965)
Heaviest defeat: 0-9 v Middlesbrough (1958)

Founded originally as Brighton and Hove Rangers in 1900, the club changed to its present name the following year. In 1920 Brighton joined Division Three as founder members, but had to wait another 38 years before gaining promotion to a higher level.

• **The club reached the final of the FA Cup for the only time in their history in 1983, holding favourites Manchester United to a 2-2 draw at Wembley. The Seagulls were unable to repeat their heroics in the replay, however, and crashed to a 4-0 defeat. In the same year Brighton were relegated from the old First Division, ending a four-season stint in the top flight.**

• A decade earlier, the Seagulls were briefly managed by the legendary Brian Clough. His time in charge of the club, though, was not a successful one and included an 8-2 thrashing by Bristol Rovers – the worst home defeat in Brighton's history.

• Brighton's record scorer is 1920s striker Tommy Cook, with 114 league goals. Cult hero Peter Ward, though, enjoyed the most prolific season in front of goal for the club, notching 32 times as the Seagulls gained promotion from the old Third Division in 1976/77. Ernie 'Tug' Wilson made the most appearances for the south coast outfit, with 509 between 1922 and 1936.

• Argentinian striker Leonardo Ulloa is both Brighton's record buy and sale, joining the Seagulls from Almeria for £2 million in 2013 before moving on to Leicester City a year later for £8 million.

• Famous fans of the club include TV presenters Des Lynam and Jamie Theakston, and DJ Norman Cook.

> **HONOURS**
> *Division 3 (S) champions* 1958
> *Second Division champions* 2002
> *League One champions* 2011
> *Division 4 champions* 1965
> *Third Division champions* 2001

BRISTOL CITY

Year founded: 1894
Ground: Ashton Gate (21,500)
Previous name: Bristol South End
Nickname: The Robins
Biggest win: 11-0 v Chichester City (1960)
Heaviest defeat: 0-9 v Coventry City (1934)

Founded as Bristol South End in 1894, the club took its present name when it turned professional three years later. In 1900 City merged with Bedminster, whose ground at Ashton Gate became the club's permanent home in 1904.

IS THAT A FACT?
For the first time since 1920, Bristol City are the only Football League club in Bristol following the relegation of Bristol Rovers to the Conference at the end of the 2013/14 campaign.

The colour has drained a little from Burnley's last league triumph in 1960

• The Robins enjoyed a golden decade in the 1900s, winning promotion to the top flight for the first time in 1906 after a campaign in which they won a joint record 14 consecutive games. The following season City finished second, and in 1909 they reached the FA Cup final for the first and only time in their history, losing 1-0 to Manchester United at Crystal Palace.

• Since then the followers of Bristol's biggest club have had to endure more downs than ups. The Robins returned to the top flight after a 65-year absence in 1976, but financial difficulties led to three consecutive relegations in the early 1980s (City being the first club ever to suffer this ghastly fate).

• City's strikers were on fire in 1962/63 as the Robins scored 100 goals in Division Three. Sadly for their fans, City could only finish 14th in the league – the lowest place ever by a club hitting three figures.

• With 315 goals in 597 league games for the club between 1951 and 1966, England international striker John Atyeo is both the Robins' top scorer and record appearance maker. In the history of league football only Dixie Dean (Everton) and George Camsell (Middlesbrough) scored more goals for the same club.

• England international Billy Wedlock, who has a stand named after him at Ashton Gate, won a club record 26 international caps while with Bristol City between 1907 and 1914.

> **HONOURS**
> *Division 2 champions* 1906
> *Division 3 (S) champions* 1923, 1927, 1955
> *Football League Trophy* 1986
> *Welsh Cup* 1934

BURNLEY

Year founded: 1882
Ground: Turf Moor (22,546)
Nickname: The Clarets
Biggest win: 9-0 v Darwen (1892), v New Brighton (1957) and v Penrith (1984)
Heaviest defeat: 0-11 v Darwen (1885)

One of England's most famous old clubs, Burnley were founded in 1882 when the Burnley Rovers rugby team decided to switch to the round ball game. The club was a founder member of the Football League in 1888 and has since won all four divisions of the league – a feat matched only by Preston and Wolves.

• Burnley have twice won the league championship, in 1921 and 1960. The first of these triumphs saw the Clarets go on a 30-match unbeaten run, the longest in a single season until Arsenal went through the whole of 2003/04 undefeated. In its own way, Burnley's 1960 title win was just as remarkable, as the Clarets only ever topped the league on the last day of the season after a 2-1 win at Manchester City.

• The club's only FA Cup triumph came in 1914 when they defeated Liverpool 1-0 in the last final at Crystal Palace. After the final whistle Burnley's captain Tommy Boyle became the first man to receive the cup from a reigning monarch, King George V.

• On 16th April 2011 Burnley defender Graham Alexander became only the second outfield player in the history of English football to make 1,000 professional appearances when he came on as a sub in the Clarets' 2-1 win over Swansea City. Alexander is also the most successful penalty taker ever in the domestic game, with 78 goals in 86 attempts from the spot.

• Burnley splashed out a club record £3 million on Hibs striker Steven Fletcher shortly after they gained promotion to the Premier League in 2009. Three years later the Clarets sold winger Jay Rodriguez to Southampton for a club record fee of £7 million.

• Charlie Austin set a new record for Burnley in the 2012/13 season when he reached 20 goals in only his 17th match of the campaign, a 1-0 win against Leeds United at Turf Moor on 6th November 2012.

• Burnley are the last club to score a century of goals in consecutive top-flight seasons, hitting the back of the net 102 times in 1960/61 and 101 in 1961/62.

• Famous Burnley fans include former Labour spin doctor Alastair Campbell, Radio Five Live presenter Tony Livesey and Prince Charles, who decided to adopt the club after his involvement with a number of charitable organisations in the town.

HONOURS
Division 1 champions 1921, 1960
Division 2 champions 1898, 1973
Division 3 champions 1982
Division 4 champions 1992
FA Cup 1914

BURTON ALBION

Year founded: 1950
Ground: Pirelli Stadium (6,912)
Nickname: The Brewers
Biggest win: 12-1 v Coalville Town (1954)
Heaviest defeat: 0-10 v Barnet (1970)

Burton Albion were founded at a public meeting at the Town Hall in 1950. The town had previously supported two Football League clubs, Burton Swifts and Burton Wanderers, who merged to form Burton United in 1901 before folding nine years later.

• The Brewers gained promotion to the Football League for the first time

in 2009, going up as Conference champions. Since then Burton have consolidated their position in the fourth tier, reaching the League Two play-off final in 2014. However, their hopes of promotion were dashed by Fleetwood Town, who beat them 1-0 at Wembley.

• DR Congo midfielder Jacques Maghoma played in a record 155 league games for Burton before joining Sheffield Wednesday in the summer of 2013. The club's leading scorer is striker Billy Kee, with 37 league goals since making his debut in 2011.

• In 2006 Burton achieved the greatest result in their history when they held mighty Manchester United to a 0-0 draw at home in the third round of the FA Cup. A record visiting contingent at Old Trafford of 11,000 Brewers fans attended the replay, but they had little to cheer about as United strolled to an emphatic 5-0 victory. Five years later the Brewers reached the fourth round of the cup for the first time, before their hopes of making further progress were dashed by Burnley.

HONOURS
Conference champions 2009

BURY

Year founded: 1885
Ground: Gigg Lane (11,840)
Nickname: The Shakers
Biggest win: 12-1 v Stockton (1897)
Heaviest defeat: 0-10 v Blackburn Rovers (1887) and West Ham (1982)

The club with the shortest name in the Football League, Bury were founded in 1885 at a meeting at the Old White Horse Hotel in Bury, as successors to two other teams in the town, the Bury Unitarians and the Bury Wesleyans. Bury were founder members of the Lancashire League in 1889, joining the Second Division of the Football League five years later.

• Bury have won the FA Cup on two occasions, in 1900 and 1903. In the second of these triumphs, the Shakers

Bury has the shortest name in the Football League

thrashed Derby County 6-0 at Crystal Palace to record the biggest ever victory in an FA Cup final.

• On 27th August 2005 Bury became the first club to score 1,000 goals in all four tiers of the Football League. The landmark was reached when Brian Barry-Murphy scored the first of the Shakers' goals in their 2-2 home draw with Wrexham in a League Two fixture.

• The following year Bury set a less happy record, when they became the first club to be thrown out of the FA Cup for fielding an ineligible player – Stephen Turnbull, a loan signing from Hartlepool United.

HONOURS
Division 2 champions 1895
Division 3 champions *1961*
Second Division champions 1997
FA Cup 1900, 1903

IS THAT A FACT?
Bury became the first Football League club to sign a player from the Indian sub-continent when striker Baichung Bhutia joined the Shakers from East Bengal in 1999.

GARY CAHILL

Born: Dronfield, 19th December 1985
Position: Defender
Club career:
2004-08 Aston Villa 28 (2)
2004-05 Burnley (loan) 27 (1)
2007-08 Sheffield United (loan) 16 (2)
2008-12 Bolton Wanderers 130 (13)
2012- Chelsea 66 (4)
International record:
2010- England 27 (3)

A resolute central defender who also has good technical skills, Gary Cahill enjoyed a tremendous start to his Chelsea career when he helped the Blues win the FA Cup and Champions League just four months after arriving in west London from Bolton Wanderers for a bargain £7 million in January 2012.

• The following year Cahill had more silverware to add to his collection, when he played in the Chelsea side that defeated Benfica 2-1 in the Europa League final in Amsterdam. In 2014 his consistent performances for the Blues were recognised by his peers when he was voted into the PFA Premier League Team of the Year.

• Cahill started out with Aston Villa, before joining Bolton in 2008 in a £5 million deal. In 2010 he became only the second Bolton player – after striker Michael Ricketts – to be capped by England in 48 years. Then, the following season, he became the first Wanderers player for 52 years to score for England when he netted in a 3-0 win over Bulgaria in a Euro 2012 qualifier in Sofia.

• At the 2014 World Cup in Brazil Cahill was the only England player to feature in all 270 minutes of the Three Lions' three group games.

"Look, ref, I'm not ticklish, so just stop it!"

CAMBRIDGE UNITED

Year founded: 1912
Ground: Abbey Stadium (10,847)
Previous name: Abbey United
Nickname: The U's
Biggest win: 7-0 v Weymouth (2007) and v Forest Green (2009)
Heaviest defeat: 0-7 v Sunderland (2002)

Conference play-off winners in 2014, Cambridge United were founded as Abbey United in 1912 before taking their current name two years after turning professional in 1949.

• The club was elected to the Football League in 1970 and rose to the second tier a decade later. However, the U's soon returned to the basement division after being relegated in 1984 (setting a then league record of 31 consecutive games without a win) and in 1985 (losing 35 matches to equal the league record).

• On a happier note, Cambridge won the first ever play-off final at Wembley, beating Chesterfield 1-0 in 1990 to earn promotion to the old Third Division.

• Loyal midfielder Steve Spriggs holds the club appearance record, turning out in 416 league games between 1975 and 1987.

ERIC CANTONA

Born: Paris, France, 24th May 1966
Position: Striker
Club career:
1983-88 Auxerre 81 (23)
1985-86 Martigues (loan) 15 (4)
1988-91 Marseille 40 (13)
1988-89 Bordeaux (loan) 11 (6)
1989-90 Montpellier (loan) 33 (10)
1991-92 Nimes 17 (2)
1992 Leeds United 28 (9)
1992-97 Manchester United 144 (64)
International record:
1987-95 France 45 (20)

Maverick Frenchman Eric Cantona is one of the most successful foreign players in Premiership history, winning the league championship in five of his six seasons in English football and landing the Double twice.

• **In 1993 Cantona became the first ever player to win back-to-back league titles with two different clubs when he fired Manchester United to the championship just 12 months after helping Leeds do the same. Amazingly for such an influential figure, Cantona's switch across the Pennines cost the Old Trafford side just £1.2 million in November 1992.**

• The signing of the inspirational Cantona proved to be the catalyst for a decade of dominance by United in the 1990s. In 1994 the former Marseille star was voted PFA Player of the Year as United won the Double for the first time in their history, Cantona coolly slotting home two penalties in his side's 4-0 thrashing of Chelsea in the FA Cup final to become the first Frenchman to win the trophy. Two years later, United won the Double for a second time and again Cantona was their match-winner in the FA Cup final, scoring the only goal of the game against Liverpool. Another PFA Player of the Year award duly followed.

• **However, the period in between these triumphs saw Cantona serve a nine-month ban – the longest in Premier League history – after he launched a 'kung fu' kick at an abusive Crystal Palace fan in a match at Selhurst Park in January 1995. The hot-headed Frenchman was also fined £10,000 by the FA and ordered to complete 120 hours of community service after being found guilty of assault.**

• Since his retirement from the game in 1997 when he was aged just 30, Cantona has pursued a successful career as an actor, starring as himself in the 2009 film, *Looking for Eric*.

CAPS

Legendary goalkeeper Peter Shilton has won more international caps than any other British player. 'Shilts' played for England 125 times between 1970 and 1990 and would have won many more caps if he had not faced stiff competition for the No. 1 shirt from his great rival Ray Clemence, who won 61 caps during the same period.

• **The first international caps were awarded by England in 1886, following a proposal put forward by the founder of the Corinthians, N.L. Jackson. To this day players actually receive a handmade 'cap' to mark the achievement of playing for their country. England caps are made by a Bedworth-based company called Toye, Kenning & Spencer, who also provide regalia for the freemasons.**

• The most capped player in the history of the game is Egypt midfielder Ahmed Hassan, who played an astonishing 184 times for his country between 1995 and 2012. The women's record is held by Kristine Lilly, who made 352 appearances for the USA between 1987 and 2010.

• **England lined up with three centurions for the first time ever in September 2013 when Steven Gerrard, Frank Lampard and Ashley Cole all played in a World Cup qualifier away to Ukraine.**

After playing his last game for Manchester United, Eric Cantona set off into the sun...

CARDIFF CITY

Year founded: 1899
Ground: Cardiff City Stadium (28,018)
Previous name: Riverside
Nickname: The Bluebirds
Biggest win: 16-0 v Knighton Town (1961)
Heaviest defeat: 2-11 v Sheffield United (1926)

Founded as the football branch of the Riverside Cricket Club, the club changed to its present name in 1908, three years after Cardiff was awarded city status.

• Cardiff are the only non-English club to have won the FA Cup, lifting the trophy in 1927 after a 1-0 victory over Arsenal at Wembley. They came close to repeating that feat in 2008, but were beaten 1-0 by Portsmouth in only the second FA Cup final staged at the new Wembley.

• On 7th April 1947 a crowd of 51,621 squeezed into Cardiff's old Ninian Park Stadium for the club's match against Bristol City – an all-time record attendance for the third tier of English football.

• Cardiff have won the Welsh Cup 22 times, just one short of Wrexham's record. The Bluebirds' domination of the tournament in the 1960s and 1970s earned them regular qualification for the European Cup Winners' Cup and in 1968 they reached the semi-finals of the competition before losing 4-3 on aggregate to Hamburg.

• Cardiff's record appearance maker is defender Phil Dwyer, who turned out 476 times for the club between 1972 and 1985. The Bluebirds' record scorer is Len Davies, who banged in 128 league goals in the 1920s.

• Chilean international midfielder Gary Medel, an £11 million recruit from Sevilla in August 2013, is the club's record signing. A year later Medel became the Bluebirds' record sale when he joined Inter Milan for £10 million.

• Cardiff's promotion to the Premier League meant that, for the first time ever in English football, Wales had two representatives in the top flight at the start of the 2013/14 season, the Bluebirds and their great rivals, Swansea City. Sadly for their fans, however, Cardiff finished rock bottom of the league and were relegated back to the Championship.

HONOURS
Championship champions 2013
Division 3 (S) champions 1947
Third Division champions 1993
FA Cup 1927
Welsh Cup 1912, 1920, 1922, 1923, 1927, 1928, 1930, 1956, 1959, 1964, 1965, 1967, 1968, 1969, 1970, 1971, 1973, 1974, 1976, 1988, 1992, 1993

CARLISLE UNITED

Year founded: 1903
Ground: Brunton Park (18,202)
Nickname: The Blues
Biggest win: 8-0 v Hartlepool (1928) and v Scunthorpe (1952)
Heaviest defeat: 1-11 v Hull City (1939)

Carlisle United were formed in 1903 following the merger of two local clubs, Shaddongate United and Carlisle Red Rose. The Blues joined the Third Division (North) in 1928 and were long-term residents of the bottom two divisions until 1965, when they won promotion to the second tier for the first time.

• The club's greatest moment came in 1974 when, in their one season in the top flight, they sat on top of the old First Division after the opening three games. The Cumbrians, though, were quickly knocked off their lofty perch and ended the campaign rock bottom.

• Following a long period of decline Carlisle were facing relegation from the Football League in 1999. However, needing a win against Plymouth on the last day of the season to stay up, United were saved when on-loan goalkeeper Jimmy Glass went up for a corner and scored a never-to-be-forgotten winner.

• Carlisle have appeared in the Football League Trophy final on a record six occasions, and in 1995 became the first and only team to lose an English trophy on the 'golden goal' rule when they conceded in extra-time in the final against Birmingham City.

• Striker Jimmy McConnell scored a record 126 league goals for Carlisle, including a club record 42 in the Blues' first ever season in the Football League in 1928/29.

HONOURS
Division 3 champions 1965
Third Division champions 1995
League Two champions 2006
Football League Trophy 1997, 2011

IKER CASILLAS

Born: Madrid, Spain, 20th May 1981
Position: Goalkeeper
Club career:
1999- Real Madrid 478
International record:
2000- Spain 156

Spain captain Iker Casillas is the only goalkeeper to have skippered his country to success in both the European Championships and the World Cup. The Real Madrid star pulled off the first leg of this double when Spain beat Germany in the Euro 2008 final in Vienna, before landing the biggest prize of all two years later after his country's 1-0 defeat of the Netherlands in the 2010 World Cup final in Johannesburg. He then made it a hat-trick as Spain retained the European Championships in 2012.

• In 2000 Casillas became the youngest goalkeeper to play in the Champions League final, appearing in Real's 3-0 victory over Valencia just four days after his 19th birthday. He won the competition again two years later, after coming on as a sub in Real's 2-1 defeat of Bayer Leverkusen in the final in Glasgow, and a third time in 2014. In the final against Atletico Madrid that year he played in his 430th victory for Real, a record for the club.

IS THAT A FACT?
In 1974/75 Carlisle became one of only six clubs to spend just a single season in the top flight, along with Glossop North End (1899/1900), Leyton Orient (1962/63), Northampton Town (1965/66), Swindon Town (1993/94) and Barnsley (1997/98).

• Casillas is the highest capped international in Spanish football history, passing fellow goalkeeper Andoni Zubizarreta's record of 126 games for Spain in 2011. The following year he set a new record of 73 international clean sheets when Spain beat Serbia 2-0 in a friendly, extending his total to an incredible 89 games by the end of August 2014.

• **Thanks in part to Spain's huge success in recent years, Casillas now holds the record for playing in the most international victories. He passed Lilian Thuram's record of 94 wins when he came on as a sub in Spain's 3-1 friendly defeat of South Korea in May 2012 and became the first player ever to win 100 internationals when Spain thrashed Italy 4-0 in the final of Euro 2012.**

EDINSON CAVANI

Born: Salto, Uruguay, 14th February 1987
Position: Striker
Club career:
2005-07 Danubio 25 (10)
2007-10 Palermo 109 (34)
2010-13 Napoli 104 (78)
2013- Paris St Germain 30 (16)
International record:
2008- Uruguay 63 (22)

Long-haired Uruguayan striker Edinson Cavani is the most expensive player in the history of French football, his £55 million move from Napoli to Paris St Germain in 2013 beating the previous record of Radamel Falcao when he joined Monaco from Atletico Madrid.

• **In his first season with PSG, Cavani helped his new club win the French title and reach the quarter-finals of the Champions League, where they went out to Chelsea on the away goals rule.**

• A powerfully-built centre-forward who finishes with aplomb on the ground and in the air, Cavani had to wait until 2012 before winning his first domestic silverware, the Coppa Italia with Napoli. The next season he was the top scorer in Serie A with 29 goals, sparking interest in his services all around Europe.

• **Cavani scored against Colombia on his international debut in 2008, and two years later his partnership with Luis Suarez was a key factor in**

Santi Cazorla, the only Spanish player to score in an FA Cup final

Uruguay's progress to the World Cup semi-finals. In 2011 he was part of the Uruguayan side which beat Paraguay in the final of the Copa America.

SANTI CAZORLA

Born: Llanera, Spain, 13th December 1984
Position: Midfielder
Club career:
2003-04 Villarreal B 40 (4)
2003-06 Villarreal 40 (4)
2006-07 Recreativo de Huelva 54 (2)
2007-11 Villarreal 127 (23)
2011-12 Malaga 38 (9)
2012- Arsenal 69 (16)
International record:
2008- Spain 66 (11)

Arsenal playmaker Santi Cazorla became the first ever Spanish player to score in the FA Cup final when he curled in a delightful free kick against Hull City at Wembley in 2014, triggering Arsenal's comeback from 2-0 down to eventual 3-2 winners. Cazorla had previously been instrumental in the Gunners reaching the final, scoring the winner in the penalty shoot-out in the semi-final against Championship outfit Wigan Athletic.

• **A skilful and perceptive midfielder, Cazorla began his career with Villarreal, before joining Recreativo de Huelva where his outstanding performances saw him voted Spanish Player of the Year in 2007. He returned to Villarreal that same year, then joined Malaga in 2011 for around £18 million. After helping Malaga qualify for the Champions League for the first time in their history, he moved on to Arsenal for £16 million in 2012.**

• Cazorla first played for Spain in 2008, going on to appear in his country's 1-0 victory over Germany later that year in the final of the European Championships. He missed out on the 2010 World Cup through injury, but returned to the national side to help Spain win Euro 2012.

PETR CECH

Born: Plzen, Czech Republic, 20th May 1982
Position: Goalkeeper
Club career:
1999-2001 Chmel Blsany 27
2001-02 Sparta Prague 27
2002-04 Rennes 70
2004- Chelsea 326
International record:
2002- Czech Republic 107

A brilliant shot-stopper who dominates his penalty area with his imposing physique, Cech joined Chelsea from French club Rennes for £10 million in 2004. During the Blues' title-winning season in 2004/05, Cech set two Premiership records by keeping 24 clean sheets and going 1,025 minutes without conceding a goal (the second record has since been beaten by Edwin van der Sar).

• The giant goalkeeper also holds the record for the most clean sheets, 161, in the Premier League era for a single club and is closing in on David James' all-time record of 173 shut-outs.

• Cech was a member of the Czech Republic side which reached the semi-finals of Euro 2004 before losing to eventual winners Greece. In March 2013 he became only the second Czech player, after Karel Poborsky, to play 100 times for his country.

• In October 2006 Cech suffered a depressed fracture of the skull following a challenge by Reading's Stephen Hunt. He returned to action after three months out of the game wearing a rugby-style headguard for protection, and has gone on to make 478 appearances in all competitions for Chelsea – a club record for an overseas player.

• In 2012 Cech became the first ever goalkeeper to win the FA Cup four times when he played in Chelsea's 2-1 defeat of Liverpool in the final at Wembley. Two weeks later he starred in the Blues' Champions League final victory over Bayern Munich, blocking a penalty from former team-mate Arjen Robben in extra-time and then saving two more in the shoot-out. The following year he added more silverware to his collection when he helped Chelsea win the Europa League after the Blues beat Benfica in the final.

Passionate fans with green-and-white scarves – it must be Celtic Park!

CELTIC

Year founded: 1888
Ground: Celtic Park (60,832)
Nickname: The Bhoys
Biggest win: 11-0 v Dundee (1895)
Heaviest defeat: 0-8 v Motherwell (1937)

The first British team to win the European Cup, Celtic were founded by an Irish priest in 1887 with the aim of raising funds for poor children in Glasgow's East End slums. The club were founder members of the Scottish League in 1890, and have gone on to spend a record 117 seasons in the top flight.

• Celtic have won the Scottish Cup more times than any other club, with 36 victories in the final. The Bhoys first won the cup in 1892, beating Queen's Park 5-1 in a replay.

• Under legendary manager Jock Stein Celtic won the Scottish league for nine

IS THAT A FACT?
In 1936 Celtic became the first European club to field an Indian player, winger Mohammed Salim.

consecutive seasons in the 1960s and 1970s, with a side featuring great names like Billy McNeill, Jimmy Johnstone, Bobby Lennox and Tommy Gemmell. This extraordinary run of success equalled a world record established by MTK Budapest of Hungary in the 1920s but, painfully for Celtic fans, was later matched by bitter rivals Rangers in the 1990s.

• The greatest ever Celtic side, managed by Stein and dubbed the 'Lisbon Lions', became the first British club to win the European Cup when they beat Inter Milan 2-1 in the Portuguese capital in 1967. Stein was central to the team's triumph, scoring an early point by sitting in Inter manager Helenio Herrera's seat and refusing to budge, and then urging his players forward after they went a goal down to the defensive-minded Italians. Sticking to their attacking game plan, Celtic fought back with goals by Gemmell and Steve Chalmers to spark jubilant celebrations at the end among the travelling fans. Remarkably, all the 'Lisbon Lions' were born and bred within a 30-mile radius of Celtic Park.

• That 1966/67 season was the most successful in the club's history as they won every competition they entered: the Scottish League, Scottish Cup and Scottish League Cup, as well as the European Cup. To this day, no other British side has won a similar 'Quadruple'.

• The skipper of the 'Lisbon Lions' was Billy McNeill, who went on to play in a record 790 games for Celtic in all competitions between 1957 and 1975. He later managed the club, leading Celtic to the Double in their centenary season in 1987/88.

TOP 10

APPEARANCES IN SCOTTISH CUP FINAL

1.	Celtic	54
2.	Rangers	50
3.	Aberdeen	15
4.	Hearts	14
5.	Hibernian	13
6.	Queen's Park	12
7.	Dundee United	10
8.	Kilmarnock	8
9.	Motherwell	7
	Vale of Leven	7

The club's most capped player is goalkeeper Pat Bonner, who made 80 appearances for the Republic of Ireland between 1981 and 1996.

• Jimmy McGrory, who played for the club between 1922 and 1938, scored a staggering 397 goals for Celtic – a British record by a player for a single club. His most prolific season for the Bhoys was in 1935/36 when he hit a club record 50 league goals.

• In 1957 Celtic won the Scottish League Cup for the first time, demolishing Rangers 7-1 in the final at Hampden Park. The victory stands as the biggest by either side in an Old Firm match and is also a record for a major Scottish cup final. Celtic went on to enjoy more success in the League Cup, appearing in a record 14 consecutive finals (winning six) between 1965 and 1978.

• Celtic hold the record for the longest unbeaten run in Scottish football, with 62 matches undefeated (49 wins, 13 draws) from 13th November 1915 until 21st April 1917 when Kilmarnock finally beat the men from Glasgow 2-0. The club also holds the record for the most points in a single league season, racking up 103 when winning the SPL in 2002.

• Two years later, during the 2003/04 season, Celtic won an incredible 25 SPL games on the trot. The run was a Scottish record and has only ever been bettered by three clubs worldwide.

• During the 2013/14 season Celtic goalkeeper Fraser Forster set a new clean sheet record for Scottish football by keeping the ball out of his net for an incredible 1,215 minutes.

• Celtic's Kris Commons scored the fastest goal in SPL history when he netted in a 4-3 victory against Aberdeen after just 12 seconds on 16th March 2013.

HONOURS

Division 1 champions 1893, 1884, 1896, 1898, 1905, 1906, 1907, 1908, 1909, 1910, 1914, 1915, 1916, 1917, 1919, 1922, 1926, 1936, 1938, 1954, 1966, 1967, 1968, 1969, 1970, 1971, 1972, 1973, 1974
Premier Division champions 1977, 1979, 1981, 1982, 1986, 1988, 1998
SPL champions 2001, 2002, 2004, 2006, 2007, 2008, 2012, 2013, 2014
Scottish Cup 1892, 1899, 1900, 1904, 1907, 1908, 1911, 1912, 1914, 1923, 1925, 1927, 1931, 1933, 1937, 1951, 1954, 1965, 1967, 1969, 1971, 1972, 1974, 1975, 1977, 1980, 1985, 1988, 1989, 1995, 2001, 2004, 2005, 2007, 2011, 2013
League Cup 1957, 1958, 1966, 1967, 1968, 1969, 1970, 1975, 1983, 1998, 2000, 2001, 2006
European Cup 1967

CHAMPIONS LEAGUE

The most prestigious competition in club football, the Champions League replaced the old European Cup in 1992. Previously a competition for domestic league champions only, runners-up from the main European nations were first admitted in 1997 and the tournament has subsequently expanded to include up to four entrants per country.

• Spanish giants Real Madrid won the first European Cup in 1956, defeating French side Reims 4-3 in the final in Paris. Real went on to win the competition the next four years as well, thanks largely to the brilliance of their star players Alfredo Di Stefano and Ferenc Puskas. With six wins in the European Cup and four in the Champions League, current holders Real have won the competition a record 10 times.

• The first British club to win the European Cup was Celtic, who famously beat Inter Milan in the final in Lisbon in 1967. The following year Manchester United became the first English club to

Real Madrid have won the Champions League a record 10 times, most recently in 2014

triumph, beating Benfica 4-1 at Wembley. The most successful British club in the tournament, though, are Liverpool, with five wins in 1977, 1978, 1981, 1984 and 2005 followed by Manchester United with three (1968, 1999 and 2008). Three other English clubs, Nottingham Forest (in 1979 and 1980), Aston Villa (in 1982) and Chelsea (in 2012) have also won the tournament.

• **Veteran Spanish striker Raul is the leading scorer in the competition, with an incredible 71 goals for Real Madrid and Schalke. He is followed by current stars Cristiano Ronaldo (68 goals, including a record 17 in the 2013/14 season) and Lionel Messi (67 goals). Meanwhile, former Manchester United midfielder Ryan Giggs has appeared in a record 151 games in the tournament.**

• Real Madrid winger Francisco Gento is the most successful player in the history of the competition with six winners' medals (1956-60 and 1966).

• **Former Ajax, Juventus and Manchester United goalkeeper Edwin van der Sar holds the record for the most clean sheets in the Champions League with 51.**

• Manchester United made a record 18 consecutive appearances in the Champions League between the 1996/97 and 2013/14 seasons, but will see this particular record equalled by Real Madrid in 2014/15.

• **Just two managers have won the competition a record three times:**

Bob Paisley with Liverpool in 1977, 1978 and 1981, and Carlo Ancelotti with AC Milan in 2003 and 2007 and Real Madrid in 2014.

• Feyenoord recorded the biggest win in the competition in 1969 when they thrashed KR Reykjavik 12-2 in the first round. Benfica hold the record for the biggest aggregate victory with an 18-0 first-round humiliation of Luxembourg no-hopers Stade Dudelange in 1965.

• **The first final between two teams from the same country was in 2000 when Real Madrid beat Valencia 3-0. Since then there have been four other one-country finals, most recently in 2014 when Real Madrid beat Atletico Madrid 4-1 after extra-time in Lisbon in the first final between two clubs from the same city.**

CHAMPIONS LEAGUE FINALS
1993 Marseille 1 AC Milan 0
1994 AC Milan 4 Barcelona 0
1995 Ajax 1 AC Milan 0
1996 Juventus 1* Ajax 1
1997 Borussia Dortmund 3 Juventus 1
1998 Real Madrid 1 Juventus 0
1999 Man United 2 Bayern Munich 1
2000 Real Madrid 3 Valencia 0
2001 Bayern Munich 1* Valencia 1
2002 Real Madrid 2 Bayer Leverkusen 1
2003 AC Milan 0* Juventus 0
2004 Porto 3 Monaco 0
2005 Liverpool 3* AC Milan 3
2006 Barcelona 2 Arsenal 1

2007 AC Milan 2 Liverpool 1
2008 Man United 1* Chelsea 1
2009 Barcelona 2 Man United 0
2010 Inter Milan 2 Bayern Munich 0
2011 Barcelona 3 Man United 1
2012 Bayern Munich 1 Chelsea 1*
2013 Bayern Munich 2
Borussia Dortmund 1
2014 Real Madrid 4 Atletico Madrid 1
* Won on penalties

CHANTS

A survey by www.fanchants.com during the 2010/11 season found that Liverpool fans were the loudest in the Premier League, their chants averaging an impressive 97 decibels. They were followed by fans of Manchester United and Aston Villa, while Fulham supporters were the quietest.

• **In 2004, in a competition sponsored by Barclaycard, Birmingham fan Jonny Hurst was chosen as England's first 'Chant Laureate' by a judging panel chaired by then Poet Laureate Andrew Motion. Bizarrely, Hurst's winning entry, set to the tune of the Barry Manilow song, Copacabana, was about Colombian striker Juan Pablo Angel – who, at the time, was playing for Brum's arch-rivals Aston Villa!**

• The loudest noise generated by a football crowd is 131.76 decibels by Galatasaray fans during their home derby against Istanbul rivals

Liverpool fans are officially the loudest in the Premier League

Fenerbahce on 18th March 2011. Despite the intimidating atmosphere created by the home fans, visitors Fenerbahce won the derby 2-1.

• Possibly the oldest football chant is 'Who ate all the pies?', which researchers at Oxford University have discovered dates back to 1894 when it was playfully directed by Sheffield United fans at their 22-stone goalkeeper William 'Fatty' Foulke. The chant stemmed from an incident when the tubby custodian got up early at the team hotel, sneaked down into the dining room and munched his way through all the players' breakfast pies.

CHARLTON ATHLETIC

Year founded: 1905
Ground: The Valley (27,111)
Nickname: The Addicks
Biggest win: 8-1 v Middlesbrough (1953)
Heaviest defeat: 1-11 v Aston Villa (1959)

Charlton Athletic were founded in 1905 when a number of youth clubs in the south-east London area, including East Street Mission and Blundell Mission, decided to merge. The club, whose nickname 'the Addicks' stemmed from the haddock served by a local chippy, graduated from minor leagues to join the Third Division (South) in 1921.

• Charlton's heyday was shortly before and just after the Second World War. After becoming the first club to win successive promotions from the Third to First Division in 1935/36, the Addicks finished runners-up, just three points behind league champions Manchester City, in 1937. After losing in the 1946 FA Cup final to Derby County, Charlton returned to Wembley the following year and this time lifted the cup thanks to a 1-0 victory over Burnley in the final.

• Charlton's home ground, The Valley, used to be one of the biggest in English football. In 1938 a then record crowd of 75,031 squeezed into the stadium to see the Addicks take on Aston Villa in a fifth-round FA Cup tie. In 1985, though, financial problems forced Charlton to

leave the Valley and the Addicks spent seven years as tenants of West Ham and Crystal Palace before making an emotional return to their ancestral home in 1992.

• When the play-offs were introduced in the 1986/87 season, Charlton figured among the first finalists, beating Leeds to preserve their First Division status. In 1998, during the long managerial reign of Alan Curbishley, the Addicks triumphed in the highest scoring Wembley play-off final, beating Sunderland 7-6 on penalties after a 4-4 draw to earn promotion to the Premiership.

• Sam Bartram, who was known as 'the finest keeper England never had', played a record 623 games for the club between 1934 and 1956. Bearded striker Derek Hales is Charlton's record goalscorer, notching 168 in two spells at the club in the 1970s and 1980s.

• Defender Radostin Kishishev is Charlton's most-capped player, turning out 43 times for Bulgaria while he was at The Valley between 2000 and 2007.

HONOURS
***First Division champions** 2000*
***Division 3 (S) champions** 1929, 1935*
***League One champions** 2012*
***FA Cup** 1947*

SIR BOBBY CHARLTON

Born: Ashington, 11th October 1937
Position: Midfielder
Club career:
1956-73 Manchester United 606 (199)
1973-74 Preston North End 38 (8)
1975 Waterford 31 (18)
International record:
1958-70 England 106 (49)

One of English football's greatest ever players, Sir Bobby Charlton had a magnificent career with Manchester United and England. He remains the highest scorer for both club and country, with 249 goals in all competitions for the Reds and 49 goals in 106 international appearances.

• Charlton broke into the United first team in 1956, scoring twice on his debut against Charlton Athletic. Two years later he was one of the

few United players to survive the Munich air crash, after being hauled from the burning wreckage by goalkeeper Harry Gregg.

• During the 1960s Charlton won everything the game had to offer, winning the league title twice (1965 and 1967), the FA Cup (1963), the European Cup (scoring twice in the final against Benfica at Wembley in 1968) and the World Cup with England in 1966 (along with his brother, Jack). Probably his best performance for his country came in the semi-final against Portugal at Wembley, when he scored both goals (including a trademark piledriver) in a 2-1 victory.

• European Footballer of the Year in 1966, Charlton eventually left United in 1973 to become player-manager of Preston. He returned to Old Trafford as a director in 1984 and was knighted a decade later.

CHEATING

The most famous instance of on-pitch cheating occurred at the 1986 World Cup in Mexico when Argentina's Diego Maradona punched the ball into the net to open the scoring in his side's quarter-final victory over England. Maradona was unrepentant afterwards, claiming the goal was scored by "the hand of God, and the head of Diego".

• In a similar incident in 2009 France captain Thierry Henry clearly handled the ball before crossing for William Gallas to score the decisive goal in a World Cup play-off against Ireland. "I will be honest, it was a handball – but I'm not the ref," a sheepish Henry admitted after the match.

IS THAT A FACT?
Shakhtar Donetsk striker Luiz Adriano caused a storm in a 2012 Champions League game when, following an injury, he collected a ball which his team-mate Willian was returning to the FC Nordsjaelland goalkeeper and slotted his shot into the net. The referee had no choice but to allow the goal to stand, but UEFA were unimpressed and promptly banned Adriano for one game for unsporting behaviour.

• In 2014 Gambia were banned from all African football competitions after fielding five over-age players in an under-20 match against Liberia. One of the players involved, Ali Sowe of Italian club Chievo Verona, was reported to be as old as 25.

• In September 2009 IFK Gothenburg goalkeeper Kim Christensen was caught by TV cameras using his feet to push the bottom of his posts a few centimetres inwards before a match against Orebro. The referee eventually spotted that the posts had been moved and pushed them back into the correct position. Christensen later admitted that he had moved the goalposts in several earlier matches.

• During the 2012/13 season Tottenham's Gareth Bale was booked a record seven times in all competitions for 'simulation' – more commonly known simply as 'diving'.

CHELSEA

Year founded: 1905
Ground: Stamford Bridge (41,837)
Nickname: The Blues
Biggest win: 13-0 v Jeunesse Hautcharage (1971)
Heaviest defeat: 1-8 v Wolves (1953)

Founded in 1905 by local businessmen Gus and Joseph Mears, Chelsea were elected to the Football League in that very same year. At the time of their election, the club had not played a single match – only Bradford City can claim a similarly swift ascent into league football.

• **Thanks to the staggering wealth of their Russian owner, Roman Abramovich, Chelsea are now one of the richest clubs in the world. Since taking over the Londoners in 2003, Abramovich has pumped hundreds of millions into the club and has been rewarded with back-to-back Premiership titles in 2005 and 2006, the FA Cup in 2007, 2009 and 2012, the Carling Cup in 2005 and 2007 and, under former manager Carlo Ancelotti, the league and cup Double in 2010. After watching his team come agonisingly close on numerous occasions, Abramovich finally saw Chelsea win the Champions League in**

No wonder Chelsea keep winning things, their team has 16 players!

2012 when, led by caretaker manager Roberto di Matteo, the Blues beat Bayern Munich on penalties in the final.

• The following year Chelsea won the Europa League after defeating Benfica 2-1 in the final in Amsterdam. That victory meant the Blues became the first British club to win all three historic UEFA trophies, as they had previously won the European Cup Winners' Cup in both 1971 and 1998. It was in the Cup Winners' Cup that Chelsea thrashed Luxembourg minnows Jeunesse Hautcharage 21-0 in 1971 to set a European record aggregate score.

• **The Blues' recent success is in marked contrast to their early history. For the first 50 years of their existence Chelsea won precisely nothing, finally breaking their duck by winning the league championship in 1955. After a succession of near misses, the club won the FA Cup for the first time in 1970, beating Leeds 2-1 at Old Trafford in the first post-war final to go to a replay. Flamboyant striker Peter Osgood scored in every round of the cup run and remains the last player to achieve this feat.**

• The club's fortunes declined sharply in the late 1970s and 1980s, the Blues spending much of the period in the Second Division while saddled with

large debts. However, an influx of veteran foreign stars in the mid-1990s, including Gianfranco Zola, Ruud Gullit and Gianluca Vialli, sparked an exciting revival capped when the Blues won the FA Cup in 1997, their first major trophy for 26 years.

• **In the final against Middlesbrough, Italian midfielder Di Matteo scored with a long-range shot after just 43 seconds – at the time the fastest ever goal in a Wembley final.**

• Chelsea's arrival as one of England's top clubs was finally confirmed when charismatic manager Jose Mourinho led the Blues to the Premiership title in 2005. The club's tally of 95 points and 29 wins set records for the competition, while goalkeeper Petr Cech went a then record 1,025 minutes during the season without conceding a goal. A second Premiership title followed in 2006, before Mourinho was sensationally sacked a year later. When the club first won the championship way back in 1955, they did so with a record low of just 52 points.

• **In 2007 Chelsea won the first ever FA Cup final at the new Wembley, Ivorian striker Didier Drogba scoring the only goal against Manchester United. In the same year the Blues won the League Cup, making them just the third English team after**

Arsenal (1993) and Liverpool (2001) to claim a domestic cup double. The Blues also won the FA Cup in 2009 and 2010, making them the first team to retain the trophy at the new Wembley.

• Hardman defender Ron 'Chopper' Harris is Chelsea's record appearance maker, turning out an incredible 795 times for the club in all competitions between 1962 and 1980. Popular midfielder Frank Lampard became the Blues' record scorer in 2013, taking his tally to 211 by the time he left the club the following year. Legendary striker Jimmy Greaves scored the most goals in a single season, with 41 in 1960/61.

• Between 2004 and 2008 the Blues were unbeaten in 86 consecutive home league matches, a record for both the Premiership and the Football League. The impressive run was eventually ended by Liverpool, who won 1-0 at Stamford Bridge on 26th October 2008.

• Chelsea clinched the title in 2010 with an 8-0 thrashing of Wigan, a resounding victory that meant the Blues finished the season with a Premier League record 103 goals and a top-flight best ever goal difference of 71.

• The club's record signing is Fernando Torres, who cost a British record £50 million when he moved to west London from Liverpool in January 2011. Three years later the Blues sold Brazilian defender David Luiz to PSG for a club record £50 million.

HONOURS
Division 1 champions 1955
Premier League champions 2005, 2006, 2010
Division 2 champions 1984, 1989
FA Cup 1970, 1997, 2000, 2007, 2009, 2010, 2012
Double 2010
League Cup 1965, 1998, 2005, 2007
Champions League 2012
European Cup Winners' Cup 1971, 1998
Europa League 2013
European Super Cup 1998

CHELTENHAM TOWN

Year founded: 1892
Ground: Whaddon Road (7,266)
Nickname: The Robins
Biggest win: 12-0 v Chippenham Rovers (1935)
Heaviest defeat: 1-10 v Merthyr Tydfil (1952)

Cheltenham were founded in 1892 but didn't play in the Football League until 1999, the year that the club won the Conference under manager Steve Cotterill. The star of the Robins' promotion-winning side was 41-year-old winger Clive Walker, a former favourite at Chelsea, Sunderland and Fulham.

• The Robins have since twice gained promotion to the third tier via the play-offs, defeating Rushden 3-1 in the final at the Millennium Stadium in 2002 and Grimsby 1-0 four years later at the same venue, but missed out on a hat-trick when they lost 2-0 to Crewe in the 2012 final. The club also won the FA Trophy in 1998, beating Southport 1-0 at Wembley Stadium.

• Cheltenham reached the fifth round of the FA Cup for the first and only time to date in 2002, when they narrowly lost 1-0 away to West Bromwich Albion.

• Midfielder Dave Bird made a record 289 league appearances for Cheltenham between 2002 and 2012.

• A record crowd of 8,326 turned up at Whaddon Road to watch Cheltenham's first round FA Cup tie against Reading in 1956. Sadly for the home fans, their team lost 2-1.

HONOURS
Conference champions 1999

CHESTERFIELD

Year founded: 1866
Ground: Proact Stadium (10,504)
Previous name: Chesterfield Town
Nickname: The Spireites
Biggest win: 10-0 v Glossop North End (1903)
Heaviest defeat: 0-10 v Gillingham (1987)

The fourth oldest club in the UK, Chesterfield were founded in 1866. The club was elected to the Second Division in 1899 as Chesterfield Town but lost its league status a decade later, only to return as plain Chesterfield when Division Three (North) was created in 1921.

• Chesterfield fans still complain about a refereeing decision in the 1997 FA Cup semi-final against Middlesbrough which they believe denied their team a place in the final at Wembley. TV replays showed that Jonathan Howard's shot had crossed the Boro line, but referee David Elleray thought otherwise. The game went to a replay in which the Spireites were eventually beaten.

• In the 1923/24 campaign Chesterfield goalkeeper Arthur Birch scored five goals for the club, all of them penalties – a record tally by a keeper in a single season.

• Chesterfield's best ever season was back in 1946/47 when they came fourth in the old Second Division, finishing above such stellar names as Tottenham, Newcastle United and West Ham United.

HONOURS
Division 3 (N) champions 1931, 1936
Division 4 champions 1970, 1985
League Two champions 2011, 2014
Football League Trophy 2012

CLEAN SHEETS

Former Manchester United goalkeeper Edwin van der Sar holds the British record for consecutive league clean sheets, keeping the ball out of his net for 14 Premier League games and a total of 1,311 minutes in the 2008/09 season. He was finally beaten on 4th March 2009 by Newcastle's Peter Lovenkrands in United's 2-1 victory at St James' Park.

• The world record for clean sheets is held by Brazilian goalkeeper Mazaropi of Vasco de Gama who went 1,816 minutes without conceding in 1977/78, while the European record belongs to Dany Verlinden of Bruges (1,390 minutes in 1990).

• Italy's long-serving goalkeeper Dino Zoff holds the international record, going 1,142 minutes without having to pick the ball out of his net between September 1972 and June 1974. Another Italian goalkeeper, Walter Zenga, holds the record for clean sheets at the World Cup, with a run of 518 minutes at the 1990 tournament.

• England's overall clean sheet record is held by Peter Shilton, who shut out the opposition in 66 of his 125 international appearances between 1970 and 1990. The international record is held by Spain's Iker Casillas with 89 in 156 appearances.

TOP 10

WORLD CUP CLEAN SHEETS

1.	Brazil	43
2.	Germany	41
3.	England	32
4.	Italy	29
5.	Argentina	28
6.	France	19
	Netherlands	19
8.	Spain	18
9.	Uruguay	16
10.	Russia	14

• Chelsea hold the Premier League record for clean sheets in a season, with 25 in 2004/05. Less impressively, Blackburn Rovers went a record 27 games at the start of the 2011/12 season without managing to keep a single clean sheet.

CLUB WORLD CUP

A competition contested between the champion clubs of all six continental confederations of FIFA, the Club World Cup was first played in Brazil in 2000 but has only been an annual tournament since 2005 when it replaced the old Intercontinental Cup.

• Manchester United's participation in the first Club World Cup led to the Red Devils pulling out of the FA Cup in 2000, a tournament they had won the previous season. United's decision attracted a lot of criticism at the time, not least from many of their own fans.

• Barcelona have the best record in the competition, having won two finals – 2-1 against Estudiantes in 2009 and 4-0 against Santos in 2011 – as well as finishing as runners-up to Brazilian club Internacional in 2006.

• Manchester United became the first British winners of the tournament when a goal by Wayne Rooney saw off Ecuadorian side Quito in the 2008 final in Yokohama. Chelsea missed a chance to match United's feat when they lost 1-0 in the 2012 final to Brazilian side Corinthians.

• The 2013 champions were Bayern Munich, who beat Moroccan side Raja Casablanca 2-0 in the final in Marrakesh.

Bayern Munich celebrate their 2013 Club World Cup triumph

COLCHESTER UNITED

Year founded: 1937
Ground: The Colchester Community Stadium (10,084)
Nickname: The U's
Biggest win: 9-1 v Bradford City (1961) and v Leamington (2005)
Heaviest defeat: 0-8 v Leyton Orient (1989)

Founded as the successors to amateur club Colchester Town in 1937, Colchester United joined the Football League in 1950. The club lost its league status in 1990, but regained it just two years later after topping the Conference.

• **The greatest day in the club's history, though, was in 1971 when the U's sensationally beat Leeds United, then the most powerful side in the country, 3-2 in an epic fifth-round FA Cup tie at their old Layer Road ground. Even a 5-0 defeat at Everton in the next round failed to wipe the smiles off the faces of the Colchester fans.**

• The first brothers to be sent off in the same match while playing for the same team were Colchester's Tom and Tony English against Crewe in 1986.

• **In 1971, the U's became the first English club to win a tournament in a penalty shoot-out after defeating West Brom 4-3 on penalties in the final of the Watney Cup at the Hawthorns.**

• Defender Micky Cook made a record 614 league appearances for Colchester between 1969 and 1984.

HONOURS
Conference champions 1992

ASHLEY COLE

Born: Stepney, 20th December 1980
Position: Defender
Club career:
2000-06 Arsenal 156 (8)
2000 Crystal Palace (loan) 14 (1)
2006-14 Chelsea 229 (7)
2014- Roma
International record:
2001-14 England 107 (0)

Veteran left-back Ashley Cole is the most successful player ever in the history of the FA Cup, having won the competition seven times in total with Arsenal and Chelsea.

• **When Cole helped Chelsea triumph in the FA Cup a week after the Blues' 2009/10 Premier League title success, he became the first English player ever to win the Double with two different clubs, having previously achieved the same feat with Arsenal in 2002.**

Ashley Cole has won the FA Cup a record seven times

• One of just eight players to win 100 caps for England, Cole is the highest capped full-back in his country's history and played in more games at tournament finals (22) than any other Three Lions player. Somewhat less impressively, he holds the record for the most games played by an England outfield player without once scoring a goal.

• **Before joining Roma in 2014, Cole was often in the newspapers for his on/off relationship with singer and former X-Factor panellist Cheryl Tweedy. He made the headlines for the wrong reasons again in 2011 when he accidentally shot a young Chelsea staff member with an air rifle he had taken to the club's training ground.**

CHRIS COLEMAN

Born: Swansea, 10th June 1970
Managerial career:
2003-07 Fulham
2007-08 Real Sociedad
2008-10 Coventry City
2011-12 Larissa
2012- Wales

Chris Coleman was appointed manager of Wales in January 2012 following the tragic death of his predecessor, Gary Speed. The Swansea-born boss lost his first four matches in charge, but has since seen his team gain some much better results, including two World Cup qualifying victories over Scotland and a creditable draw in Belgium.

• **Coleman's first experience of management came at Fulham, where he was the youngest ever Premier League manager when he was put in charge of the Cottagers, aged 32 and 10 months, in April 2003.**

• After parting company with the west Londoners in 2007, Coleman managed Spanish side Real Sociedad and Coventry, where he was sacked after leading the Midlanders to their lowest position – 19th in the Championship – for 45 years in 2010.

• **A tough centre-back in his playing days with Swansea, Crystal Palace, Blackburn and Fulham, Coleman won 32 caps for Wales before his career was ended by a bad car crash in 2002.**

IS THAT A FACT?

In 2013 Cardiff City became the first Premier League club to change the colour of their home shirt, when they switched from blue to red shirts at the instigation of club owner, Vincent Tan.

COLOURS

In the 19th century, players originally wore different coloured caps, socks and armbands – but not shirts – to distinguish between the two sides. The first standardised kits were introduced in the 1870s, with many clubs opting for the colours of the schools or other sporting organisations from which they had emerged.

• In the period after the Second World War, clothing restrictions forced many teams in Britain to wear unusual kits. For instance, Oldham Athletic, who traditionally wore blue and white, spent two seasons in red-and-white shirts borrowed from a local rugby league club while Scottish club Clyde turned out in khaki.

• Thanks largely to the longstanding success of Arsenal, Liverpool and Manchester United, teams wearing red have won more trophies in England than those sporting any other colour. Teams wearing stripes have fared less well, their last FA Cup success coming in 1987 (Coventry City) and their last league triumph way back in 1936 (Sunderland).

• Until 1989 both teams regularly changed colours in FA Cup ties where there was a kit clash. The last final in which both teams wore change kits was in 1982 when Tottenham (yellow) beat QPR (red) 1-0 in a replay at Wembley.

COMMUNITY SHIELD

The Community Shield was originally known as the Charity Shield and since 1928 has been an annual fixture usually played at the start of the season between the reigning league champions and the FA Cup winners. Founded in 1908 to provide funds for various charities, the Charity Shield was initially played between the league champions and the Southern League champions, developing into a game between select teams of amateurs and professionals in the early 1920s.

• Manchester United were the first club to win the Charity Shield, defeating QPR 4-0 in a replay at Stamford Bridge. With 16 outright wins and four shared, United are also the most successful side in the history of the competition.

• United were also involved in the highest scoring Charity Shield match, beating Swindon Town 8-4 in 1911.

• In the first Charity Shield played at Wembley in 1974, Liverpool's Kevin Keegan and Leeds' Billy Bremner were sent off for fighting, becoming the first British players to be dismissed at the national stadium. To make matters worse, they tore their shirts off as they left the pitch and both were subsequently banned for five weeks.

• Manchester United's Ryan Giggs is the most successful player in the history of the Shield, with nine wins in 15 appearances (another record).

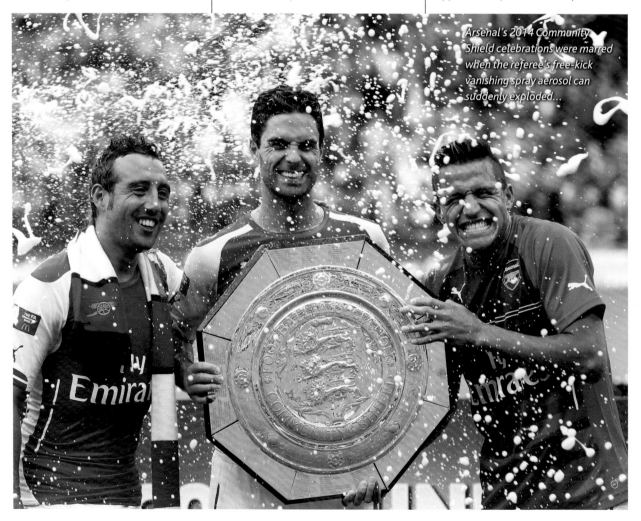

Arsenal's 2014 Community Shield celebrations were marred when the referee's free-kick vanishing spray aerosol can suddenly exploded...

Winning the Conference meant a lot to Luton and their mascot, The Mad Hatter!

COMPUTER GAMES

FIFA 13 sold more than 4.5 million copies worldwide in the first five days after its launch in 2012, leading publishers EA to claim it was the biggest selling sports video launch of all time. The FIFA series as a whole has sold over 100 million copies since it launched in 1993, making it the best selling football video game of all time.

• The first football video game was created in 1973 by Tomohiro Nishikado, who later designed *Space Invaders*. Called simply *Soccer*, the ball-and-paddle game allowed two players to each control a goalkeeper and a striker.

• In August 2014 Reading winger Royston Drenthe invited a group of fans over to his house to play in a *FIFA 13* tournament. The Dutch star rewarded the winner by giving him a signed Reading shirt and a cash prize.

• In November 2012 Vugar Huseynzade was appointed manager of Azerbaijan side Baku FC after impressing club officials with his skills on *Football Manager*. The 21-year-old student landed the job ahead of a number of experienced coaches and ex-pros, including former France star Jean-Pierre Papin.

CONFEDERATIONS CUP

The Confederations Cup is a competition held every four years contested by the holders of each of the six FIFA confederation championships – such as the European Championships and the Copa America – plus the World Cup holders and host nation.

• Since 2005 the Confederations Cup has been held in the country that will host the following year's World Cup, acting as a dress rehearsal for the larger and more prestigious tournament.

• Brazil have the best record in the tournament with four victories to their name: in 1997 (after a 6-0 win over Australia in the final), in 2005 (4-1 against Argentina), 2009 (3-2 against the USA) and 2013 (3-0 against Spain). The only other countries to win the Confederations Cup are France (in 2001 and 2003) and Mexico (in 1999).

• Spain recorded the biggest ever win at the Confederations Cup when they hammered minnows Tahiti 10-0 in 2013. Spanish striker Fernando Torres scored four of the goals to set a new individual record for the tournament – and if hadn't missed a penalty it would have been five.

CONFERENCE

Formed in 1979 as the Alliance Premier League, the Football Conference is the pinnacle of the non-league National League System which feeds into the Football League. The Conference itself has been divided into three sections – National, North and South – since 2004.

• Promotion and relegation between the Football League and the Conference became automatic in 1987, when Scarborough United replaced Lincoln City.

• However, clubs have to satisfy the Football League's minimal ground requirements before their promotion can be confirmed and Kidderminster Harriers, Macclesfield Town and Stevenage Borough all failed on this count in the mid-1990s after topping the Conference table.

• The league is known as the Vanarama Conference after its sponsors. Previously, it was sponsored by Gola (1984-86), Vauxhall (1986-98), Nationwide Building Society (1998-2007), Blue Square (2007-13) and Skrill (2013-14).

• Crawley Town won the Conference with a record total of 105 points in 2011, while Luton Town were crowned champions in 2014 after finishing a record 19 points ahead of runners-up Cambridge United.

COPA AMERICA

The oldest surviving international football tournament in the world, the Copa America was founded in 1916. The first championships were held in Argentina as part of the country's independence centenary commemorations, with Uruguay emerging as the winners from a four-team field. Originally known as the South American Championship, the tournament was renamed in 1975. Previously, the Copa America was held every two years, but in 2007 it was decided to stage future tournaments at four-year intervals.

• **Uruguay have won the tournament a record 15 times and hold the trophy after their victory in 2011, while Argentina are second in the winners' list, lifting the trophy on 14 occasions.**

• Norberto Mendez of Argentina and Zizinho of Brazil share the tournament record of 17 goals. Three players have scored a record nine goals in a single tournament: Jair Pinto (Brazil, 1949), Humberto Maschio (Argentina, 1957) and Javier Ambrois (Uruguay, 1957).

TOP 10

COPA LIBERTADORES CLUB RECORDS

1. Independiente (Argentina)   7 wins
2. Boca Juniors (Argentina)   6 wins, 4 times runners-up
3. Penarol (Uruguay)   4 wins, once runners-up
   Estudiantes (Argentina)   4 wins, once runners-up
5. Club Olimpia (Paraguay)   3 wins, 4 times runners-up
6. Nacional (Uruguay)   3 wins, 3 times runners-up
   Sao Paulo (Brazil)   3 wins, 3 times runners-up
8. Santos (Brazil)   3 wins, once runners-up
9. Cruzeiro (Brazil)   2 wins, twice runners-up
   Gremio (Brazil)   2 wins, twice runners-up
   River Plate (Argentina)   2 wins, twice runners-up

COPA LIBERTADORES

The Copa Libertadores is the South American equivalent of the Champions League, played annually between top clubs from all the countries in the continent (in recent years, leading clubs

Angel Di Maria, the world's most expensive corner-taker

from Mexico have also participated). Argentine club Independiente have the best record in the competition, winning the trophy seven times, including four in a row between 1972 and 1975.

• **Ecuadorian striker Albert Spencer is the leading scorer in the history of the competition with 54 goals (48 for Uruguayan club Penarol, helping them to win the first two tournaments in 1960 and 1961, and six for Ecuadorian outfit Barcelona de Guayaquil).**

• In a first-round match in 1970, Penarol thrashed Venezuelan club Valencia 11-2 to record the biggest ever win in the competition.

• **Argentinian clubs have won the trophy a record 22 times, six more than those from Brazil. The most successful player in the Copa Libertadores is Argentinian defender Francisco Sa, who won the tournament six times in the 1970s with Independiente and Boca Juniors.**

CORNERS

Corner kicks were first introduced in 1872, but goals direct from a corner were not allowed until 1924. The first player to score from a corner in league football was Billy Smith of Huddersfield in the 1924/25 season. On 2nd October 1924 Argentina's Cesareo Onzari scored direct from a corner against reigning Olympic champions Uruguay in Buenos Aires, the first goal of this sort in an international fixture.

• **The first Premier League match to feature no corners was between Wigan Athletic and Chelsea on 21st August 2010. Despite the lack of action on the wings, Chelsea still won 6-0.**

• A corner count has been proposed as an alternative to penalty shoot-outs as a way of deciding drawn cup ties. This method was used to determine the result of the 1965 All-African Games football tournament, with Congo beating Mali 7-2 on corners after a 0-0 draw.

• Former Yugoslav international Dejan Petkovic holds the world record for the most goals scored direct from a corner with eight, his last effort coming for Brazilian side Flamengo in 2009.

• Marcos Coll of Colombia is the only player to score direct from a corner at the World Cup, in a 4-4 draw against the USSR in 1962.

DIEGO COSTA

Born: Lagarto, Brazil, 7th October 1988
Position: Striker
Club career:
2006 Braga 0 (0)
2006 Penafiel (loan) 13 (5)
2007-09 Atletico Madrid 0 (0)
2007 Braga (loan) 7 (0)
2007-08 Celta (loan) 30 (5)
2008-09 Albacete (loan) 34 (9)
2009-10 Valladolid 34 (8)
2010-14 Atletico Madrid 94 (43)
2012 Rayo Vallecano (loan) 16 (10)
2014- Chelsea
International record:
2013 Brazil 2 (0)
2014- Spain 4 (0)

Fiery striker Diego Costa became the most hated man in Brazil when he turned his back on his birth nation, opting instead to play for Spain at the 2014 World Cup.

• **After a fairly undistinguished start to his career, Costa gradually developed into one of Europe's deadliest forwards after rejoining Atletico from Valladolid in 2010. Three years later he scored a vital goal in the Copa del Rey final as Atleti beat Real Madrid 2-1 to record their first victory over their glitzy city rivals since 1999.**

• The following season Costa was third-top scorer in La Liga with 27 goals – only Cristiano Ronaldo and Lionel Messi were more prolific – as Atletico surprised everyone by lifting the title. Costa also helped Atleti reach the final of the Champions League for the first time, but had to limp out of the showpiece event against Real with a hamstring injury after just eight minutes. In the close season he joined Chelsea for £32 million.

• **Costa won the first of two caps for Brazil in 2013, but later that year gained Spanish citizenship** and declared his intention to play for his adopted nation. He made his debut for Spain in a 1-0 friendly win over Italy in March 2014.

Diego Costa's fetching pink-and-blue boots are the envy of his Chelsea team-mates

C

COSTA

COURTOIS

"I'm so good, I only need two defenders!"

THIBAUT COURTOIS

Born: Bree, Belgium, 11th May 1992
Position: Goalkeeper
Club career:
2009-2011 Genk 41
2011- Chelsea
2011-14 Atletico Madrid (loan) 111
International record:
2011- Belgium 22

Now back at Chelsea after a three-year loan spell at Atletico Madrid, Thibaut Courtois is the youngest ever goalkeeper to have played for Belgium after making his debut as a 19 year old in a 0-0 friendly draw with France in 2011.
· Courtois came through the youth ranks at Genk to help the Belgian outfit win the league title in 2011, a season in which he was voted Goalkeeper of the Year.
· A tall and muscular goalkeeper who specialises in confidently plucking high crosses from the skies, Courtois joined Chelsea for around £5 million in summer 2011, but was swiftly moved out on loan to Spain. He enjoyed three magnificent years with Atletico, helping the Madrid side win the Europa League in 2012, the Copa del Rey in 2013 and the league title in 2014. In addition, he became the first Atletico goalkeeper ever to retain the Ricardo Zampora trophy – awarded to the goalkeeper with the best goals-to-games ratio – when he topped the poll in both 2013 and 2014.
· **Widely rated as one of the best goalkeepers in the world despite still only being 22, Courtois played in all of Belgium's 10 qualifying games for the 2014 World Cup, keeping an impressive six clean sheets. His good form continued at the tournament proper, where he helped Belgium reach the quarter-finals before a 1-0 defeat to Argentina ended their hopes of glory.**

PHILIPPE COUTINHO

Born: Rio de Janeiro, Brazil, 12th June 1992
Position: Midfielder
Club career:
2009-10 Vasco de Gama 19 (1)
2010-13 Inter Milan 28 (3)
2012 Espanyol (loan) 16 (5)
2013- Liverpool 46 (8)
International record:
2010- Brazil 1 (0)

A tricky midfielder who has been compared to South American superstars Lionel Messi and Ronaldinho, Philippe Coutinho was one of Liverpool's stand-out players as they challenged for the league title in 2013/14. Indeed, it was the Brazilian's well-taken winner in a 3-2 victory against Manchester City late on in the campaign which made the Reds the odds-on favourites for the

Silky Liverpool midfielder Philippe Coutinho

COVENTRY CITY

Year founded: 1883
Ground: Ricoh Arena (32,609)
Previous name: Singers FC
Nickname: The Sky Blues
Biggest win: 9-0 v Bristol City (1934)
Heaviest defeat: 2-11 v Berwick Rangers (1901)

Coventry were founded in 1883 by workers from the local Singer's bicycle factory and were named after the company until 1898. The club was elected to the Second Division in 1919, but their league career started unpromisingly with a 5-0 home defeat to Tottenham Hotspur.

• A club with a history of ups and downs, Coventry were the first team to play in seven different divisions: Premier, Division One, Two, Three, Four, Three (North) and Three (South). They have also played in the Championship and, from 2012, League One.

• Coventry's greatest moment came in 1987 when the club won the FA Cup for the only time, beating Tottenham 3-2 in an exciting Wembley final. Two years later, though, the Sky Blues were dumped out of the cup by non-league Sutton United in one of the competition's biggest ever upsets.

IS THAT A FACT?

When Coventry City were relegated from the Premiership in 2001 only Arsenal, Everton and Liverpool could boast longer tenures in the top flight.

trophy before they eventually had to be satisfied with second place.

• Coutinho moved to Italian giants Inter Milan from Vasco de Gama when he was just 18, but struggled to establish himself in Serie A. However, a loan spell at Spanish outfit Espanyol in 2012 proved more fruitful and the following January he joined Liverpool in a £8.5 million deal.

• A typical Brazilian number 10 who combines vision, flair and creativity in equal measure, Coutinho made his debut for his country in a 3-0 friendly win against Iran in 2010 when he was aged just 18. He missed out on Brazil boss Luis Felipe Scolari's squad for the 2014 World Cup, but was called up afterwards by new boss Dunga.

• Under innovative manager Jimmy Hill, Coventry rose from the Third to the First Division in the mid-1960s and remained there for 34 years until dropping out of the Premiership at the end of the 2000/01 season.

• Long-serving goalkeeper Steve Ogrizovic played in a club record 504 league games between 1984 and 2000.

• After falling into administration, Coventry moved out of their 32,000-capacity Ricoh Arena in July 2013 to ground-share with Northampton Town at the considerably smaller Sixfields Stadium. Happily for their fans, the Sky Blues returned to the Ricoh in September 2014.

HONOURS
Division 2 champions 1967
Division 3 champions 1964
Division 3 (S) champions 1936
FA Cup 1987

CRAWLEY TOWN

Year founded: 1896
Ground: Broadfield Stadium (6,134)
Nickname: The Red Devils
Biggest win: 8-0 v Droylsden (2008)
Heaviest defeat: 0-7 v Bath City (2000)

Founded in 1896, Crawley Town started out in the West Sussex League, eventually rising to the Conference in 2004. Dubbed 'the Manchester City of non-league', Crawley splashed out more than £500,000 on new players at the start of the 2010/11 season, an investment which paid off when the club won promotion to the Football League at the end of the campaign.

• Runaway Conference champions, Crawley's haul of 105 points set a new record for the division, while they also equalled the records for fewest defeats (3), most wins (31) and best goal difference (63). The following season Crawley enjoyed a second successive promotion, after finishing third in League Two behind Swindon and Shrewsbury.

• Crawley reached the fifth round of the FA Cup for the first time in their history

in 2011 after knocking out Swindon, Derby and Torquay. To their fans' delight they were then paired with Manchester United, and their team did them proud, only losing 1-0 at Old Trafford.

• Five players, including two from Crawley, were sent off following a post-match brawl after the Red Devils won 2-1 at Bradford City on 27th March 2012, equalling the record for the most dismissals in an English league game.

HONOURS
Conference champions *2011*

CREWE ALEXANDRA

Year founded: 1877
Ground: Alexandra Stadium (10,153)
Nickname: The Railwaymen
Biggest win: 8-0 v Rotherham (1932)
Heaviest defeat: 2-13 v Tottenham Hotspur (1960)

Founded by railway workers in 1877, the Crewe Football Club added 'Alexandra' to their name in honour of Princess Alexandra, wife of the future king, Edward VII. The club were founder members of the Second Division in 1892,

although they lost their league status four years later before rejoining the newly formed Third Division (North) in 1921.

• Helped by a club record 19-match unbeaten run Crewe were League Two play-off winners in 2012, but they had to wait until the following year before landing their first piece of major silverware, the Football League Trophy. During Alex's 2-0 win over Southend United, 19-year-old sub George Ray became the first player ever to make his club debut at Wembley.

• Alex fans endured a miserable spell in the mid-1950s when their club failed to win away from home for a record 56 consecutive matches. The depressing run finally ended with a 1-0 win at Southport in April 1957.

• Club legend Herbert Swindells scored a record 126 goals for Crewe between 1927 and 1937. Crewe's appearance record is held by Tommy Lowry who turned out in 475 games between 1966 and 1977.

• John Pearson is the only Crewe player to represent England, making one appearance in 1892. He later became a referee, taking charge of the 1911 FA Cup final between Bradford City and Newcastle United.

HONOURS
Football League Trophy 2013
Welsh Cup 1936, 1937

CASH / CARDS

Match Day Ticket Office

"What time's the Crawley match on?" "Er, when can you get here?"

A goalkeepers' eye view of Crystal Palace's Selhurst Park

JOHAN CRUYFF

Born: Amsterdam, Netherlands, 5th April 1947
Position: Midfielder/striker
Club career:
1964-73 Ajax 240 (190)
1973-78 Barcelona 142 (48)
1979-80 Los Angeles Aztecs 27 (16)
1980-81 Washington Diplomats 32 (12)
1981 Levante 10 (2)
1981-83 Ajax 36 (14)
1983-84 Feyenoord 33 (11)
International record:
1966-78 Netherlands 48 (33)

Arguably the greatest European player ever, Johan Cruyff was captain of the brilliant Netherlands side which reached the final of the 1974 World Cup and of the outstanding Ajax team which won the European Cup three times on the trot in the early 1970s.

• Unquestionably the best player in the world at the time, Cruyff became the first man to win the European Player of the Year award three times, topping the poll in 1971, 1973 and 1974.
• Fast, skilful, creative and a prolific scorer, Cruyff was also a superb organiser on the pitch. His talents prompted Barcelona to shell out a world record £922,000 fee to bring him to the Nou Camp in 1973 and the following year Cruyff helped the Catalans win their first title for 14 years.
• After his retirement, Cruyff coached both Ajax and Barcelona. He led the Spanish giants to four consecutive league titles between 1991 and 1994 and, in 1992, guided them to their first ever European Cup success, with a 1-0 victory over Sampdoria at Wembley.
• Cruyff's magnificent contribution to football in Holland was recognised in a 2004 poll when he was voted the sixth greatest Dutch person ever, ahead of two of the world's finest painters, Rembrandt and Vincent Van Gogh.

CRYSTAL PALACE

Year founded: 1905
Ground: Selhurst Park (26,255)
Nickname: The Eagles
Biggest win: 9-0 v Barrow (1959)
Heaviest defeat: 0-9 v Burnley (1909) and v Liverpool (1989)

The club was founded in 1905 by workers at the then cup final venue at Crystal Palace, and was an entirely separate entity to the amateur club of the same name which was made up of groundkeepers at the Great Exhibition and reached the first ever semi-finals of the FA Cup in 1871.
• After spending their early years in the Southern League, Palace were founder members of the Third Division

Crystal Palace fans aren't that bothered if they turn up late – their team didn't score a single goal in the first 15 minutes in 2013/14!

"FAMOUS RED AND BLUE"

(South) in 1920. The club had a great start to their league career, going up to the Second Division as champions in their first season.

• Palace's greatest moment came in 1990 when they reached the FA Cup final. In the final at Wembley against Manchester United, Ian Wright came off the bench to score twice in a thrilling 3-3 draw before the Eagles went down 1-0 in the replay.

• Pre-war striker Peter Simpson is the club's all-time leading scorer with 153 league goals between 1930 and 1936. Rugged defender Jim Cannon holds the club appearance record, making 660 appearances between 1973 and 1988.

• Palace are the only club to have been promoted to the top flight four times via the play-offs, most recently in 2013. The Eagles are also the only club to have won play-off finals at four different venues:

Selhurst Park (1989), old Wembley (1997), Millennium Stadium (2004) and new Wembley (2013).

• Less happily for their fans, Palace have been relegated a record four times from the Premier League, including a particularly unfortunate occasion in 1993 when they went down with a record 49 points (from 42 games). In 2013/14, though, the Eagles avoided relegation back to the Championship for the first time in five Premier League campaigns.

• The club made their record signing in September 2014, when Scottish midfielder James McArthur signed from Wigan for £7 million. The Eagles' record sale is pacy winger Wilfried Zaha, who joined Manchester United for £15 million in 2013.

• Kevin Phillips became the oldest player ever to score for Palace when he slotted home from the penalty spot in the 2013 Championship play-off final against Watford at Wembley aged 39 and 306 days.

• Palace's famous fans include comedians Eddie Izzard and Jo Brand, and rapper Dizzee Rascal.

IS THAT A FACT?
Crystal Palace were the only Premier League side who failed to score a single goal in the first 15 minutes of any of their matches in the 2013/14 season.

HONOURS
Division 2 champions 1979
First Division champions 1994
Division 3 (S) champions 1921

CUP WINNERS' CUP

A competition for the domestic cup winners of all European countries, the European Cup Winners' Cup ran for 39 seasons from 1960/61 until 1998/99. The first winners were Italian club Fiorentina, who beat Rangers 4-1 on aggregate in a two-legged final.

• In 1963 Tottenham Hotspur became the first British club to win the competition and the first to win a major European trophy, when they thrashed Atletico Madrid 5-1 in Rotterdam – a record score for a European final.

• English clubs won the cup eight times – a figure unmatched by any other country. England's successful teams were Tottenham (1963), West Ham (1965), Manchester City (1970), Chelsea (1971 and 1998), Everton (1985), Manchester United (1991) and Arsenal (1994).

• In 1963 Sporting Lisbon tonked APOEL Nicosia 16-1 in a second-round, first-leg tie to record the biggest ever win in any European fixture. Chelsea hold the competition record for the biggest aggregate win, smashing Luxembourg side Jeunesse Hautcharage 21-0 in 1971.

• The top scorer in the competition is former Netherlands international Rob Resenbrink, who banged in an impressive 25 goals in total for Belgian clubs Bruges and Anderlecht between 1970 and 1978.

DAGENHAM & REDBRIDGE

Year founded: 1992
Ground: Victoria Road (6,078)
Previous name: Dagenham
Nickname: The Daggers
Biggest win: 8-1 v Woking (1994)
Heaviest defeat: 0-9 v Hereford United (2004)

The self-styled 'pub team from Essex' were formed in 1992 following the merger of local rivals Dagenham and Redbridge Forest, the latter having previously incorporated the once-famous amateur clubs Ilford, Leytonstone and Walthamstow Avenue.

• In 2007 Dagenham & Redbridge were promoted to the Football League for the first time in their history after winning the Conference. Just three years later the Daggers went up to League One via the play-offs, only to come back down the following season. Nonetheless, the club's 6-0 win over Morecambe in the semi-final set a new record for the biggest ever play-off win.

• Dagenham's record appearance maker, Tony Roberts, is the only goalkeeper to have scored in the FA Cup from open play, netting in a fourth qualifying round tie against Basingstoke in 2001. Less impressively, the Welsh international is the only keeper to have been sent off in the competition while in the opposition penalty area. The bizarre incident happened late on in the Daggers' 5-2 loss to Southend in 2008 when Roberts went up for a corner and was red carded for headbutting a Shrimpers defender.

• **The Daggers' coffers received a welcome boost in January 2013 when they sold striker Dwight Gayle to Peterborough United for a club record £700,000.**

• In 2003 the Daggers reached the FA Cup fourth round for the first, and so far only, time in their history before losing 1-0 to Norwich City.

> HONOURS
> *Conference champions* 2007

KENNY DALGLISH

Born: Glasgow, 4th March 1951
Position: Striker
Club career:
1968-77 Celtic 204 (112)
1977-90 Liverpool 354 (118)
International record:
1971-87 Scotland 102 (30)

A smiling Kenny Dalglish was a familiar sight in the 1980s

The last player to score 100 league goals in both the Scottish and English leagues, Kenny Dalglish began his career at Celtic, winning nine major trophies before moving to Liverpool in 1977 for a then British record fee of £440,000. A true Anfield legend, Dalglish won nine championships, two FA Cups and four League Cups with the Reds, plus the European Cup in 1978, 1981 and 1984. He was voted Footballer of the Year in 1979 and 1983.

• **A clever striker with a superb first touch, Dalglish won a record 102 caps for Scotland and scored 30 goals – a figure matched only by Denis Law. He represented his country at three World Cups in 1974, 1978 and 1982.**

• In 1986 he became the first player-manager to lead a club to the title when he won the championship with Liverpool, and he secured two more titles in 1988 and 1990 before suddenly resigning in 1991.

• **Eight months later he took over at Blackburn and in 1995 steered Rovers to the Premiership title, becoming only the third manager to win the title with two different clubs. In 1997 Dalglish became Newcastle manager, but was sacked after a poor start to the 1998/99 season.**

• He was briefly manager of Celtic but was out of the game for nine years before going back to Liverpool in 2009, initially as youth academy coach. In January 2011 Dalglish replaced Roy Hodgson as manager but, despite winning the Carling Cup the following year and guiding the Reds to the 2012 FA Cup final, the Kop legend was sacked at the end of the 2011/12 season after a poor league campaign.

DEATHS

The first recorded death as a direct result of a football match came in 1889 when William Cropper of Derbyshire side Staveley FC died of a ruptured bowel sustained in a collision with an opponent.

• **In 1931 Celtic's brilliant young international goalkeeper John Thompson died in hospital after fracturing his skull in a collision with Rangers forward Sam English. Some 40,000 fans attended his funeral, many of them walking the 55 miles from Glasgow to Thompson's home**

DEBUTS

village in Fife. In the same decade two other goalkeepers, Jimmy Utterson of Wolves and Sunderland's Jimmy Thorpe, also died from injuries sustained on the pitch. Their deaths led the Football Association to change the rules so that goalkeepers could not be tackled while they had the ball in their hands.

• In 1998 11 players were killed by a bolt of lightning which struck the pitch during a game in the Democratic Republic of Congo. Oddly, all those who died were members of the visiting team while the players from the home side, Busanga, survived unscathed.

• **In May 2010 Goran Tunjic collapsed and died from a heart attack while playing for Croatian county level side Mladost FC. Unfortunately, the referee completely failed to comprehend the unfolding tragedy… and gave Tunjic a yellow card for diving.**

• British players to collapse on the pitch and subsequently die in recent years include Robbie James (Llanelli, 2000) and Phil O'Donnell (Motherwell, 2007).

• **In August 2014 Cameroonian player Albert Ebosse of Algerian side JS Kabylie was killed by a stone thrown from the stands at the end of his side's 2-1 defeat to USM Alger.**

DEBUTS

The best debut by an England player was probably that of Blackpool striker Stan Mortensen who scored four times in a 10-0 rout of Portugal in Lisbon in 1947. The 'Blackpool Bombshell' went on to notch an impressive 24 goals for his country in just 25 appearances.

• **The worst ever international debut was by American Samoa goalkeeper Nicky Salapu against Fiji in 2001. He conceded 13 goals in that game, and** then another 44 within a week in three matches against Samoa, Tonga and Australia.

• Freddy Eastwood scored the fastest goal on debut, netting after just seven seconds for Southend against Swansea in 2004. Almost as impressively, goalkeeper Tony Coton was just 83 seconds into his debut with Birmingham City in 1980 when he saved a penalty with his first touch in top-flight football.

• **Legendary striker Jimmy Greaves famously scored on his debut for Chelsea (1957), AC Milan (1961), Tottenham (1962), West Ham (1970), England under-23s (1957) and England (1959).**

• The only player to score a hat-trick on his Premier League debut is Middlesbrough's Italian striker Fabrizio Ravenelli, who scored all of his team's goals in a 3-3 draw with Liverpool on the opening day of the 1996/97 season.

DERBIES

So called because they matched the popularity of the Epsom Derby horserace, 'derby' matches between local sides provoke intense passions among fans and players alike.

• **Probably the most intense derby match in Britain, and possibly the whole world, is between bitter Glasgow rivals Rangers and Celtic. In the 2010/11 season the two teams met a record seven times, the clashes provoking so many violent incidents in Glasgow that the chairman of the Scottish Police Federation called for future Old Firm matches to be banned. Although Rangers have since tumbled down the divisions, Celtic v Rangers remains the most played derby in world football – the two teams having met an incredible 399 times.**

• Other famous derbies include Liverpool v Everton, Arsenal v Tottenham, Manchester City v Manchester United, Newcastle v Sunderland and, on mainland Europe, Inter v AC Milan, Sporting Lisbon v Benfica and Lazio v Roma. Strangely, the match often described as 'the world's greatest derby', the 'El Clasico' clash between Barcelona and Real Madrid, is not a derby in the strict sense.

• Manchester derbies have produced many dramatic moments, notably in 1974 when former United legend Denis Law scored for City with a cheeky backheel in the closing stages at Old Trafford. The goal doomed United to relegation from the First Division and prompted thousands of their fans to invade the pitch in an attempt to get the match abandoned. They succeeded in their aim, but the result (a 1-0 win for City) stood. More recently, City triumphed by the same score in the first ever Wembley meeting between the sides in the 2011 FA Cup semi-final and in a virtual title decider at Eastlands the following year thanks to Vincent Kompany's header.

• Possibly the most important goal in an English derby game, though, came at Tottenham's White Hart Lane in 1971 when Arsenal's Ray Kennedy scored with a last-minute header to win his side the league championship and the first leg of a famous Double.

• **Arsenal have won a record 107 London derbies since the Premier League began in 1992.**

DERBY COUNTY

Year founded: 1884
Ground: Pride Park (33,597)
Nickname: The Rams
Biggest win: 12-0 v Finn Harps (1976)
Heaviest defeat: 2-11 v Everton (1890)

Derby were formed in 1884 as an offshoot of Derbyshire Cricket Club and originally wore an amber, chocolate and blue strip based on the cricket club's colours. Perhaps wisely, they changed to their traditional black-and-white colours in the 1890s.

• **The club were founder members of the Football League in 1888 and seven years later moved from the ground they shared with the cricketers to the Baseball Ground (so named because baseball was regularly played there in the 1890s). Derby had to oust a band of gypsies before they could move in, one of whom is said to have laid a curse on the place as he left. No doubt, then, the club was pleased to leave the Baseball Ground for Pride Park in 1997… although when Derby's first game at the new stadium had to be**

IS THAT A FACT?

Paul Goddard (1982, against Iceland), Danny Wallace (1986, against Egypt), Francis Jeffers (2003, against Australia) and David Nugent (2007, against Andorra) are the last four players to score on their debut for England, but never play for their country again.

abandoned due to floodlight failure, there were fears that the curse had followed them!

· Runners-up in the FA Cup final in 1898, 1899 and 1903, Derby reached their last final in 1946. Before the match the club's captain, Jack Nicholas, visited a gypsy encampment and paid for the old curse to be lifted. It worked, as Derby beat Charlton 4-1 after extra-time.

· **Under charismatic manager Brian Clough, Derby took the top flight by storm after winning promotion to the First Division in 1969. Three years later they won the league in one of the closest title races ever. Having played all their fixtures ahead of their title contenders, Derby's players were actually sitting on a beach in Majorca when they heard news of their victory. The following season Derby reached the semi-finals of the European Cup and, in 1975 under the management of former skipper Dave Mackay, they won the championship again.**

· Sadly, the club have failed to live up to those glory days in the decades since. By the early 1980s the Rams had sunk as low as the Third Division and were only saved from extinction when publisher Robert Maxwell bailed them out. The club enjoyed a reasonable spell in the Premiership in the late 1990s, but their most recent season in the top flight in 2007/08 was an utter disaster – the Rams managing just one win in the whole campaign, equalling a Football League record set by Loughborough in 1900.

· **Mason Bennett is the youngest player to appear for Derby, making his debut aged 15 and 99 days against Middlesbrough in October 2011. The following season he became the club's youngest ever scorer when he notched against Tranmere Rovers in the FA Cup.**

· Derby's best ever goalscorer was one of the true greats of the game in the late 19th and early 20th centuries, Steve Bloomer. He netted an incredible 332 goals in two spells at the club between 1892 and 1914. Striker Kevin Hector, a two-time title winner with the club in the 1970s, played in a record 485 league games for the Rams during two spells at the Baseball Ground.

> **HONOURS**
> *Division 1 champions 1972, 1975*
> *Division 2 champions 1912, 1915, 1969, 1987*
> *FA Cup 1946*

ANGEL DI MARIA

> **Born:** Rosario, Argentina, 14th February 1988
> **Position:** Winger
> **Club career:**
> 2005-07 Rosario Central 35 (6)
> 2007-10 Benfica 76 (7)
> 2010-2014 Real Madrid 122 (22)
> 2014– Manchester United
> **International record**
> 2008– Argentina 52 (10)

Argentina winger Angel Di Maria became the most expensive footballer in British transfer history when he joined Manchester United from Real Madrid for an incredible £59.7 million in August 2014.

· **After beginning his career with his hometown club Rosario, Di Maria came to prominence during a three-year stay with Benfica where he was hailed as "Argentina's next superstar" by the legendary Diego Maradona.**

· He joined Real Madrid for around £20 million in 2010 and helped the Spanish titans win the Copa del Rey in 2011 and the league title the following year. In 2014 he scored the opening goal in the Copa del Rey final as Real beat arch rivals Barcelona 2-1 in Valencia.

· **A tricky player who loves to take on opposition defenders, Di Maria scored the winning goal in the final of the 2008 Olympic Games in Beijing as Argentina beat Nigeria 1-0 to claim the Gold medal. Later that year he was capped at full level for the first time and has gone on to represent his country at both the 2010 and 2014 World Cups.**

DISCIPLINE

Yellow and red cards were introduced into English league football on 2nd October 1976, and on the same day Blackburn's David Wagstaffe received the first red card during his side's match with Leyton Orient. Five years later cards were withdrawn by the Football Association as referees were getting 'too flashy', but the system was re-introduced in 1987.

· **A stormy last 16 match between the Netherlands and Portugal in 2006 was the most ill-disciplined in the history of the World Cup. Russian referee Valentin Ivanov was the busiest man on the pitch as he pulled out his yellow card 16 times and his red one four times, with the match ending as a nine-a-side affair.**

Angel Di Maria is the most expensive player ever in British football

• West Ham collected a Premier League record eight yellow cards against QPR in October 2012.

• **Roy McDonough, a journeyman striker for Walsall, Colchester, Southend and Exeter in the 1970s and 1980s, was sent off a record 21 times during his career, earning himself the nickname 'Red Card Roy'.**

• Richard Dunne, Duncan Ferguson and Patrick Vieira share the record for receiving the most red cards in Premier League matches, with eight each. Former Bolton striker Kevin Davies was shown the yellow card on a record 100 occasions and also committed a record 782 fouls.

• **When a mass brawl erupted in the middle of the pitch during a match between Argentinian sides Victoriano Arenas and Claypole on 26th February 2011, referee Damian Rubino showed red cards to all 22 players and 14 substitutes as well as coaches and technical staff. The total of 36 players sent off set a new world record, smashing the previous 'best' of 20!**

• David Beckham picked up a record total of 17 yellow cards during his England career between 1996 and 2013.

• In March 2014 referee Andre Marriner mistakenly sent of Arsenal's Kieran Gibbs against Chelsea at Stamford Bridge after team-mate Alex Oxlade-Chamberlain had handled on the line. One man short, the Gunners went down to a 6-0 defeat in manager Arsène Wenger's 1,000th match in charge.

TOP 10

WORST PREMIER LEAGUE DISCIPLINARY RECORDS 1992-2014

		Total yellow cards	Total red cards
1.	Chelsea	1,294	67
2.	Everton	1,234	75
3.	Arsenal	1,204	73
4.	Aston Villa	1,200	47
5.	Tottenham	1,171	58
6.	West Ham	1,142	65
7.	Manchester United	1,111	55
8.	Blackburn Rovers	1,090	75
9.	Newcastle United	1,081	68
10.	Liverpool	1,031	48

DONCASTER ROVERS

Year founded: 1879
Ground: Keepmoat Stadium (15,231)
Nickname: The Rovers
Biggest win: 10-0 v Darlington (1964)
Heaviest defeat: 0-12 v Small Heath (1903)

Founded in 1879 by Albert Jenkins, a fitter at Doncaster's Great Northern Railway works, Doncaster turned professional in 1885 and joined the Second Division of the Football League in 1901.

• **Remarkably, Doncaster hold the record for the most wins in a league season (33 in 1946/47) and for the most defeats (34 in 1997/98).**

• Doncaster's leading scorer is Tom Keetley, who banged in 180 league goals for Rovers, including a club record six in a single game against Ashington in 1929.

• **In 1946 Doncaster were involved in the longest ever football match, a Third Division (North) cup tie against Stockport County at Edgeley Park which the referee ruled could extend beyond extra-time in an attempt to find a winner. Eventually, the game was abandoned after 203 minutes due to poor light.**

• One Direction singer Louis Tomlinson was signed by Doncaster as a non-contract player in the 2013/14 season, making his debut for the club in a reserve game against Rotherham on 26th February 2014. More than 4,000 supporters – many of them teenage girls – turned up to see him come on as a sub in a 0-0 draw.

HONOURS
League One champions 2013
Division 3 (North) champions 1935, 1947, 1950
Division 4 champions 1966, 1969
Third Division champions 2004
Football League Trophy 2007

DOUBLES

The first club to win the Double of league championship and FA Cup were Preston North End, in the very first season of the Football League in 1888/89. The Lancashire side achieved this feat in fine style, remaining undefeated in the league and keeping a clean sheet in all their matches in the FA Cup.

• **Arsenal and Manchester United have both won the Double a record three times. The Reds' trio of successes all came within a five-year period in the 1990s (1994, 1996 and 1999), with the last of their Doubles comprising two-thirds of a legendary Treble which also included the Champions League. Arsenal first won the Double in 1971 and since then the Gunners have twice repeated the feat under manager Arsène Wenger in 1998 and 2002.**

• Perhaps, though, the most famous Double of all was achieved by Tottenham Hotspur in 1961 as it was the first such success in the 20th century. Under legendary manager Bill Nicholson, Spurs clinched the most prized honour in the domestic game with a 2-0 victory over Leicester City in the FA Cup final. The other English clubs to win the Double are Aston Villa (1897), Liverpool (1986) and Chelsea (2010).

• **Northern Ireland side Linfield have won a world record 23 Doubles. Rangers, with 18 Doubles, lie in second place, while Greek outfit Olympiacos (16 Doubles) are in third place.**

DRAWS

Everton have drawn more matches in the top flight than any other club, having finished on level terms in 1,081 out of 4,328 matches. Even the Toffees, though, can't match Norwich City's record of 23 draws in a single season, set in the First Division in 1978/79.

• **The highest scoring draw in the top division of English football was 6-6, in a match between Leicester City and Arsenal in 1930. That bizarre scoreline was matched in a Second Division encounter between Charlton**

IS THAT A FACT?
AEK Athens are the only club to draw all six of their group games in the Champions League, twice finishing on level terms with Real Madrid, Roma and Genk in the 2002/03 season.

and Middlesbrough at The Valley in 1960, with a certain Brian Clough grabbing a hat-trick for the visitors.

• The highest scoring draw in Premier League history came on the last day of the 2012/13 season at the Hawthorns when West Brom and Manchester United drew 5-5 in Sir Alex Ferguson's last game in charge of the Red Devils.

• The fourth qualifying round of the FA Cup between Alvechurch and Oxford United in 1971 went to five replays before Alvechurch finally won 1-0 in the sixth game between the clubs. The total playing time of 11 hours is a record for an FA Cup tie.

• Stockport County drew a record six consecutive games in the old Division Four at the start of the 1973/74 season – a run matched by Leicester City in the old Division One at the start of the 1976/77 campaign.

Didier Drogba, the only man to score in four FA Cup finals

DIDIER DROGBA

Born: Abidjan, Ivory Coast, 11th March 1978
Position: Striker
Club career:
1998-2002 Le Mans 63 (12)
2002-03 En Avant Guingamp 45 (20)
2003-04 Marseille 35 (18)
2004-12 Chelsea 226 (100)
2012-13 Shanghai Shenhua 11 (8)
2013-14 Galatasaray 37 (15)
2014 - Chelsea
International record:
2002-14 Ivory Coast 104 (65)

Chelsea legend Didier Drogba is the only player to have scored in four FA Cup finals, his goals helping the Blues win the trophy in 2007, 2009, 2010 and 2012. In the last of those years he also played a vital part in the Londoners' first ever Champions League success, heading the equaliser against Bayern Munich in the final and then calmly scoring in the penalty shoot-out to secure the Blues' historic triumph.

• After rising to prominence with Marseille, Drogba moved to Chelsea for a then club record fee of £24 million in the summer of 2004. In his first season at the Bridge he helped the Londoners win their first ever Premier League title and also scored in the Blues' Carling Cup final victory over Liverpool.

• The following year Drogba won a second league title, but was widely criticised by opposition fans and the media for falling over too easily around the penalty box. He responded to the critics in fine style, topping the Premiership scoring charts in 2006/07 and scoring Chelsea's winning goals in both the Carling Cup final victory over Arsenal and the Blues' FA Cup final defeat of Manchester United in the first final played at the new Wembley.

• Drogba enjoyed his best season with the Blues in 2009/10, scoring the winner in the FA Cup final against Portsmouth. He also fired in a career-best 29 league goals to win the Golden Boot for a second time. His record of 38 goals in the Champions League is the best in the competition by an African player.

• The all-time leading goalscorer for the Ivory Coast by some distance, Drogba was voted African Footballer of the Year in 2006.

Dundee v Dundee United – it's the match of the season if you happen to live in Dundee!

DUNDEE

Year founded: 1893
Ground: Dens Park (11,850)
Nickname: The Dee
Biggest win: 10-0 v Alloa (1947), v Dunfermline (1947) and v Queen of the South (1962)
Heaviest defeat: 0-11 v Celtic (1895)

Dundee were founded in 1893 after the merger of two local clubs, Dundee Our Boys and Dundee East End.

• **The club's greatest ever moment was in 1962 when The Dee won the Scottish title under the managership of Bob Shankly, brother of the legendary Bill. The following season Dundee reached the semi-finals of the European Cup, before bowing out to eventual winners AC Milan.**

• Dundee were the first club to retain the Scottish League Cup, following victories in the final over Rangers in 1952 and Kilmarnock in 1953.

• **Dundee have become a yo-yo club in recent seasons, gaining two promotions to the Scottish top flight** in 2012 and 2014. On the second of these occasions, The Dee went up as the first winners of the newly formed Championship division.

• On 9th November 2013 novice striker Craig Wighton became Dundee's youngest ever scorer when he netted in a 2-0 win against Raith Rovers, aged 16 years, three months and 19 days.

HONOURS
Division 1 champions 1962
Division 2 champions 1947
First Division champions 1979, 1992
Championship champions 2014
Scottish Cup 1910
Scottish League Cup 1952, 1953, 1974

DUNDEE UNITED

Year founded: 1909
Ground: Tannadice Park (14,209)
Previous name: Dundee Hibernian
Nickname: The Terrors
Biggest win: 14-0 v Nithsdale Wanderers (1931)
Heaviest defeat: 1-12 v Motherwell (1954)

Originally founded as Dundee Hibernian by members of the city's Irish community in 1909, the club changed to its present name in 1923 to attract support from a wider population.

• **The club emerged from relative obscurity to become one of the leading clubs in Scotland under long-serving manager Jim McLean in the 1970s and 1980s, winning the Scottish Premier Division in 1983. The club's success, allied to that of Aberdeen, led to talk of a 'New Firm' capable of challenging the 'Old Firm' of Rangers and Celtic for major honours.**

• United reached the semi-finals of the European Cup in 1984 and the final of the UEFA Cup in 1987, where they lost to Gothenburg. The club's European exploits also include four victories over Barcelona – a 100 per cent record against the Catalans which no other British team can match.

• **After being losing finalists on six previous occasions, Dundee United finally won the Scottish Cup in 1994 when they beat Rangers 1-0 in the final. They won the trophy for a second time in 2010, following a comfortable 3-0 win against shock finalists Ross County, but went down in the 2014 final to surprise winners St Johnstone.**

• Dundee United are known as the Terrors because of the lion in the club's badge. Their supporters, though, are called 'The Arabs', the name possibly stemming from a game the club won on a heavily sanded pitch in the early 1960s.

• **United's top scorer is Peter McKay, who knocked in 158 league goals between 1947 and 1954.**

• In a BBC poll in 2006 Dundee United fan Zippy from Rainbow was voted Britain's favourite celebrity football fan. The show's presenter, Geoffrey Hayes, a longstanding Terrors' fan, had previously insisted on the puppet's bright orange colour to reflect United's famous tangerine shirts.

• **Tannadice Park, Dundee United's home since their foundation, is situated just a few hundred yards from Dundee's Dens Park, making the two clubs the closest neighbours in British football.**

> HONOURS
> *Premier League champions 1983*
> *Division 2 champions 1925, 1929*
> *Scottish Cup 1994, 2010*
> *Scottish League Cup 1980, 1981*

EDIN DZEKO

> **Born:** Sarajevo, Bosnia & Herzegovina, 17th March 1986
> **Position:** Striker
> **Club career:**
> 2003-05 Zeljeznicar 40 (5)
> 2005-07 Teplice 43 (16)
> 2005 Usti nad Labem (loan) 15 (6)
> 2007-11 Wolfsburg 111 (66)
> 2011- Manchester City 108 (46)
> **International record:**
> 2007- Bosnia & Herzegovina 65 (36)

Manchester City striker Edin Dzeko is the leading scorer in the history of his country, Bosnia & Herzegovina, with a total of 36 goals since making his international debut in 2007. He was on target 10 times during his team's successful World Cup 2014 qualification campaign, making him the second-highest goalscorer in the UEFA section behind Robin van Persie.

• **Known as 'The Bosnian Diamond' in his home country, Dzeko made his name with Wolfsburg, winning the Bundesliga title in 2009 after contributing 26 goals. The following season he was the league's top scorer with 22 goals.**

The Leaning Tower of Pisa? No, it's the 'Bosnian Diamond', Edin Dzeko

• In January 2011 Dzeko moved to Manchester City for £27 million, in the process becoming the most expensive ever export from a German club. He helped City win the FA Cup in 2011, the Premier League in 2012 and, two years later, the league title again. During the 2013/14 campaign, Dzeko scored the fastest ever Premier League goal by an away side at Old Trafford when he netted in City's 3-0 win over rivals Manchester United after just 43 seconds.

• **A powerfully-built striker who is especially strong in the air, Dzeko's achievements with club and country have seen him voted Bosnian Footballer of the Year on three occasions.**

• At the 2014 World Cup in Brazil, Dzeko scored Bosnia's opening goal in their 3-1 defeat of Iran – their first ever win at the finals. However, it was not enough to see them progress to the knock-out stage of the competition after Bosnia lost to both Argentina and Nigeria.

TOP 10

ENGLAND GOALSCORERS

1.	Bobby Charlton (1958-70)	49
2.	Gary Lineker (1984-92)	48
3.	Jimmy Greaves (1959-67)	44
4.	Michael Owen (1998-2008)	40
	Wayne Rooney (2003-)	40
6.	Tom Finney (1946-58)	30
	Nat Lofthouse (1950-58)	30
	Alan Shearer (1992-2000)	30
9.	Vivian Woodward (1903-11)	29
	Frank Lampard (1999-14)	29

ENGLAND

First international: Scotland 0 England 0, 1872

Most capped player: Peter Shilton, 125 caps (1971-90)

Leading goalscorer: Bobby Charlton, 49 goals (1958-70)

First World Cup appearance: England 2 Chile 0, 1950

Biggest win: England 13 Ireland 0, 1882

Heaviest defeat: Hungary 7 England 1, 1954

England, along with their first opponents Scotland, are the oldest international team in world football. The two countries met in the first official international in Glasgow in 1872, with honours being shared after a 0-0 draw. The following year William Kenyon-Slaney of Wanderers FC scored England's first ever goal in a 4-2 victory over Scotland at the Kennington Oval.

• **With a team entirely composed of players from England, Great Britain won the first Olympic Games football tournament in 1908 and repeated the feat in 1912.**

• England did not lose a match on home soil against a team from outside the British Isles until 1953 when they were thrashed 6-3 by Hungary at Wembley. The following year England went down to their worst ever defeat to the same opposition, crashing 7-1 in Budapest.

• **Although Walter Winterbottom was appointed as England's first full-time manager in 1946, the squad was picked by a committee until Alf Ramsey took over in 1963. Three years later England hosted and won the World Cup – the greatest moment in the country's football history by some considerable margin.**

• There were many heroes in that 1966 team, including goalkeeper Gordon Banks, skipper Bobby Moore and striker Geoff Hurst, who scored a hat-trick in the 4-2 victory over West Germany in the final at Wembley. Ramsey, too, was hailed for his part in the success and was knighted soon afterwards.

• **Since then, however, England fans have experienced more than their fair share of disappointment. A second appearance in the World Cup final was within the grasp of Bobby Robson's team in 1990 but, agonisingly, they lost on penalties in the semi-final to the eventual winners, West Germany.**

• In 1996 England hosted the European Championships and were again knocked out on penalties by Germany at the semi-final stage. England have lost four more times on penalties at major tournaments, most recently going out of Euro 2012 on spot-kicks to Italy, to leave them with the worst shoot-out record (one win in seven) of any country in the world.

• **With 49 goals for England, Bobby Charlton is England's leading scorer. His 1960s team-mate Jimmy Greaves scored a record six hat-tricks for the Three Lions.**

• Derby legend Steve Bloomer scored in a record 10 consecutive games for England between 1895 and 1899, and also holds the record for most goals in the Home Internationals with 28.

• **Billy Wright, the first player to appear 100 times for England, also played in a**

Despite Daniel Sturridge's goal against Italy, England's showing at the 2014 World Cup was their worst ever

record 70 consecutive internationals between 1951 and 1959.

• Tommy Lawton scored the fastest ever England goal, netting after just 17 seconds in a 10-0 rout of Portugal in 1947.

• England's worst ever World Cup showing came at the 2014 tournament in Brazil when they failed to win a single one of their three group games against Italy, Uruguay and Costa Rica.

HONOURS
World Cup *1966*
World Cup record
1930 Did not enter
1934 Did not enter
1938 Did not enter
1950 Round 1
1954 Quarter-finals
1958 Round 1
1962 Quarter-finals
1966 Winners
1970 Quarter-finals
1974 Did not qualify
1978 Did not qualify
1982 Round 1
1986 Quarter-finals
1990 Semi-finals
1994 Did not qualify
1998 Round 2
2002 Quarter-finals
2006 Quarter-finals
2010 Round 2
2014 Round 1

CHRISTIAN ERIKSEN

Born: Middelfart, Denmark, 14th February 1992
Position: Midfielder
Club career:
2010-13 Ajax 113 (25)
2013- Tottenham Hotspur 25 (7)
International record:
2010- Denmark 44 (5)

Tottenham midfielder Christian Eriksen enjoyed an excellent first season at White Hart Lane in 2013/14, being voted the club's Player of the Year after scoring seven Premier League goals and making a number of valuable assists.

• As a youth player with OB Copenhagen Eriksen was a transfer target for numerous top European clubs, but after trials with Chelsea, Manchester United, Barcelona and Real Madrid, he decided to join Ajax as a 16-year-old in 2008. It proved to be

Sevilla's 2014 Europa League-winning squad included quite a few chubby, middle-aged men

a wise move, as the youngster soon cemented a place in the Dutch giants' side and went on to win three league titles before joining Spurs for £11 million in 2013.

• When he made his international debut in 2010 against Austria, aged 18, Eriksen became the fourth youngest Danish player ever to appear for the national team. He then became the youngest Danish player ever to score in a European championship qualifier when he netted in a 2-0 win against Iceland the following year.

• Aged just 18 and four months, Eriksen was the youngest player to appear at the 2010 World Cup in South Africa.

EUROPA LEAGUE

The inaugural Europa League final was played between Atletico Madrid and Fulham in Hamburg in 2010, the Spanish side winning 2-1 thanks to a late winner by Uruguayan striker Diego Forlan. Two years later Atletico won the competition for a second time after beating Athletic Bilbao 3-0 in the final in Bucharest.

• In 2011 Porto beat Braga 1-0 in Dublin in the first ever all-Portuguese European final. Porto's match-winner was Colombian striker Radamel Falcao, whose goal in the final was his 17th in the competition that season – a record for the tournament.

• The competition is now in its third incarnation, having previously been known as the Fairs Cup (1955-71) and the UEFA Cup (1971-2009). The tournament was originally established in 1955 as a competition between cities,

rather than clubs. The first winners were Barcelona, who beat London 8-2 on aggregate in a final which, bizarrely, did not take place until 1958!

• The first team to win the newly named UEFA Cup were Tottenham Hotspur in 1972, who beat Wolves 3-2 on aggregate in the only all-English final. Following Chelsea's triumph in the 2013 Europa League, English clubs have won the competition 11 times... an impressive record, although Spanish teams lead the way with 14 victories.

• Swedish striker Henrik Larsson is the leading scorer in the history of the UEFA Cup with 40 goals for Feyenoord, Celtic and Helsingborg between 1993 and 2009.

EUROPEAN CHAMPIONSHIPS

Originally called the European Nations Cup, the idea for the European Championships came from Henri Delaunay, the then secretary of the French FA. The first championships in 1960 featured just 17 countries (the four British nations, Italy and West Germany were among those who declined to take part). The first winners of the tournament were the Soviet Union, who beat Yugoslavia 2-1 in the final in Paris.

• Germany have the best record in the tournament, having won the trophy three times (in 1972, 1980 and 1996) and been runners-up on a further three occasions. Spain have also won the championships three times (1964, 2008 and 2012) and are the only country to retain the trophy

Spain celebrated their 2012 European Championship success in the customary low-key style

la roja

following a 4-0 demolition of Italy in the final at Euro 2012 – the biggest win in any European Championships or World Cup final.

• Germany also hold a number of minor records, having played the most games in the finals (43), won the most matches (23) and scored the most goals (65).

• **French legend Michel Platini is the leading scorer in the finals of the European Championships with nine goals. England's Alan Shearer is in second place with a total of seven goals at the 1996 and 2000 tournaments.**

• Platini is also the only player to score two hat-tricks at the finals, notching trebles against both Belgium and Yugoslavia in 1984.

• **In the qualifying tournament for the 2008 finals Germany recorded the biggest ever win in the history of the competition, thrashing minnows San Marino 13-0 on their home patch.**

• Holland's Edwin van der Sar and France's Lilian Thuram share the appearance record at the finals, having both played in 16 games. The pair are also among the eight players to have played in a record four tournaments, both featuring between 1996 and 2008.

EUROPEAN CHAMPIONSHIPS FINALS

1960 USSR 2 Yugoslavia 1 (Paris)
1964 Spain 2 USSR 1 (Madrid)
1968 Italy 2 Yugoslavia 0• (Rome)
1972 West Germany 3 USSR 0 (Brussels)
1976 Czechoslovakia 2*
West Germany 2 (Belgrade)
1980 West Germany 2 Belgium 1 (Rome)
1984 France 2 Spain 0 (Paris)
1988 Netherlands 2 USSR 0 (Munich)
1992 Denmark 2 Germany 0 (Gothenburg)
1996 Germany 2 Czech Republic 1 (London)
2000 France 2 Italy 1 (Rotterdam)
2004 Greece 1 Portugal 0 (Lisbon)
2008 Spain 1 Germany 0 (Vienna)
2012 Spain 4 Italy 0 (Kiev)
• After 1-1 draw   * Won on penalties

EUROPEAN GOLDEN BOOT

Now officially known as the European Golden Shoe, the European Golden Boot has been awarded since 1968 to the leading scorer in league matches in the top division of every European league.

Since 1997 the award has been based on a points system which gives greater weight to goals scored in the leading European leagues.

• **The first winner of the award was the legendary Portuguese international Eusebio, who picked up the trophy after knocking in an incredible 43 goals for Benfica. He topped the poll again in 1973, aged 30, with a total of 40 goals.**

• The first British winner of the award was Liverpool's Ian Rush in 1984, and the most recent was Sunderland's Kevin Phillips in 2000. Since then, Thierry Henry

IS THAT A FACT?
The first non-European winner of the European Golden Boot was Argentinian striker Hector Yazalde, who banged in 46 goals for Sporting Lisbon in 1973/74. As a prize for topping the scoring charts, Yazalde was presented with a Toyota car, which he then sold before splitting the cash he received with his team-mates.

(in 2004 and 2005), Cristiano Ronaldo (in 2008) and Luis Suarez (jointly with Cristiano Ronaldo in 2014) have won the Golden Shoe after topping both the Premiership and European goalscoring charts. Ronaldo also won the Golden Shoe with Real Madrid in 2011, to become the first player to win the award in two different countries.

• **The most controversial winner of the award was Rumania's Rodion Camataru, who scored 20 of his 44 goals for Dynamo Bucharest in the last six games of the 1986/87 season. Suspicions that some of these matches had not been played in a wholly competitive spirit were confirmed by evidence that emerged in the post-Communist era and in 2007 the runner-up in the 1987 list, Austria Vienna striker Toni Polster, was also granted a Golden Boot.**

• Lionel Messi and his great rival Cristiano Ronaldo are the only players to win the award three times. Messi also holds the record for the most goals scored by a Golden Boot winner, with an incredible 50 in 2011/12.

EVERTON

Year founded: 1878
Ground: Goodison Park (40,157)
Previous name: St Domingo
Nickname: The Toffees
Biggest win: 11-2 v Derby County (1890)
Heaviest defeat: 0-7 v Sunderland (1934), v Wolves (1939) and v Arsenal (2005)

The club was formed as the church team St Domingo in 1878, adopting the name Everton (after the surrounding area) the following year. In 1888 Everton joined the Football League as founder members, winning the first of nine league titles three years later.

• **One of the most famous names in English football, Everton hold the proud record of spending more seasons, 113, in the top flight than any other club. Relegated only twice, in 1930 and 1951, they have spent just four seasons in total outside the top tier.**

• The club's unusual nickname, the Toffees, stems from a local business called Ye Ancient Everton Toffee House which was situated near Goodison Park. In the early 1930s Everton's precise style of play earned the club the tag 'The School of Science', a nickname which lingers to this day.

• **The club's record goalscorer is the legendary Dixie Dean, who notched an incredible total of 383 goals in all competitions between 1925 and 1937. Dean's best season for the club was in the Toffees' title-winning campaign in 1927/28 when his 60 league goals set a Football League record that is unlikely ever to be beaten. His total of 349 league goals is a record for a player with the same club.**

• Everton's most capped player is long-serving goalkeeper Neville Southall, who made 93 appearances for Wales in the 1980s and 1990s. He is also the club's record appearance maker, turning out in 578 league games.

• In 1931 Everton won the Second Division title, scoring 121 goals in the process. The following season the Toffees banged in 116 goals on their way to lifting the First Division title, becoming the first club to find the net 100 times in consecutive seasons.

• The club's most successful decade, though, was in the 1980s when, under manager Howard Kendall, they won the league championship (1985 and 1987), FA Cup (1984) and the European Cup Winners' Cup (in 1985, following a 3-1 win over Austria Vienna in the final). Since those glory days Everton have had to play second fiddle to city rivals Liverpool, although the Toffees did manage to win the FA Cup for a fifth time in 1995, beating Manchester United in the final thanks to a single goal by striker Paul Rideout.

• The club's record signing is Belgian striker Romelu Lukaku, who moved to Merseyside from Chelsea for £28 million in July 2014 after spending the previous season on loan at Goodison Park. The Toffees' previous most expensive player, afro-haired midfielder Marouane Fellaini, became the club's record sale when he joined Manchester United for £27.5 million in August 2013.

• In 1893 Everton's Jack Southworth became the first player in Football League history to score six goals in a match when he fired a double hat-trick in a 7-1 victory against West Bromwich Albion.

• Everton's Louis Saha scored the fastest ever goal in the FA Cup final, when he netted after just 25 seconds against Chelsea at Wembley in 2009. However, the Toffees were unable to hold onto their lead and were eventually beaten 2-1 – one of a record eight times Everton have lost in the final.

• The oldest ground in the Premier League, Goodison Park is the only stadium in the world to have a church, St Luke the Evangelist, inside its grounds. The stadium was the first club ground in England to host the FA Cup final (1894) and the only one in the UK to have staged a World Cup semi-final – the clash between West Germany and Russia in 1966.

• Everton's James Vaughan holds the record for the youngest player to score in the Premier League, coming off the bench to net in a 4-0 thrashing of Crystal Palace at Goodison Park in 2005 when he was aged just 16 and 271 days.

• Everton were the first club to win the FA Cup after falling 2-0 down in the final, fighting back to beat Sheffield Wednesday 3-2 in 1966.

> **HONOURS**
> *Division 1 champions 1891, 1915, 1928, 1932, 1939, 1963, 1970, 1985, 1987*
> *Division 2 champions 1931*
> *FA Cup 1906, 1933, 1966, 1984, 1995*
> *European Cup Winners' Cup 1985*

EXETER CITY

Year founded: 1904
Ground: St James Park (8,541)
Nickname: The Grecians
Biggest win: 14-0 v Weymouth (1908)
Heaviest defeat: 0-9 v Notts County (1948) and v Northampton Town (1958)

Exeter City were founded in 1904 following the amalgamation of two local sides, Exeter United and St Sidwell's United. The club were founder members

In July 2014 Exeter City played a re-match of their game against Fluminense 100 years before, in 1914, which was the first ever 'international' football match in Brazil!

Extra-time in the 2014 World Cup final and Germany's players couldn't resist a quick game of 'bundle'

of the Third Division (South) in 1920 and remained in the two lower divisions until they were relegated to the Conference in 2003. Now owned by the Exeter City Supporters' Trust, the club rejoined the Football League in 2008.

• **The club recorded their best ever win in 1908, smashing Weymouth 14-0 in the FA Cup. Striker James 'Daisy' Bell contributed six of the goals, a club best.**

• In the 1973/74 season Exeter only played 45 of their 46 league games after failing to turn up for a fixture at Scunthorpe, who were awarded the points.

• **On a tour of South America in 1914 Exeter became the first club side to play the Brazilian national team. The Grecians lost 2-0 but the occasion**

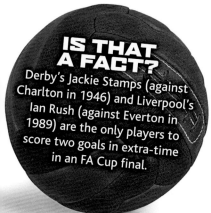

IS THAT A FACT?
Derby's Jackie Stamps (against Charlton in 1946) and Liverpool's Ian Rush (against Everton in 1989) are the only players to score two goals in extra-time in an FA Cup final.

has gone into club folklore, with Exeter fans delighting in taunting their opponents by chanting, "Have you ever, have you ever, have you ever played Brazil?"

HONOURS
Division 4 champions 1990

EXTRA-TIME

Normally consisting of two halves of 15 minutes each, extra-time has been played to produce a winner in knock-out tournaments since the earliest days of football, although to begin with the playing of the additional time had to be agreed by the two captains. Extra-time was first played in an FA Cup final in 1875, Royal Engineers and the Old Etonians drawing 1-1 (Royal Engineers won the replay 2-0). In all, extra-time has been played in 19 finals, the most recent in 2014 when Arsenal eventually beat Hull City 3-2.

• **The first World Cup final to go to extra-time was in 1934, when hosts Italy and Czechoslovakia were tied 1-1 at the end of 90 minutes. Seven minutes into the additional period, Angelo Schiavio scored the winner for Italy. Since then, six other finals have gone to extra-time, most recently in 2014 when Germany's Mario Gotze**

scored the winner against Argentina with just seven minutes to play.

• In an attempt to encourage attacking football and reduce the number of matches settled by penalty shoot-outs, FIFA ruled in 1993 that the first goal scored in extra-time would win the match. The first major tournament to be decided by the so-called 'golden goal' rule was the 1996 European Championships, Germany defeating the Czech Republic in the final thanks to a 94th-minute strike by Oliver Bierhoff. The 2000 final of the same competition was also decided in the same manner, David Trezeguet scoring a stunning winner for France against Italy in the 103rd minute.

• **Concerns that the 'golden goal' put too much pressure on referees led UEFA to replace it with the 'silver goal' in 2002. Under this rule, which was used at Euro 2004 but scrapped afterwards, only the first half of extra-time was played if either team led at the interval.**

• The first European Cup final to require extra-time was between Real Madrid and AC Milan in 1962, Real eventually winning 3-2. In all, 16 finals have gone to extra-time, but only five produced a winner inside the additional 30 minutes – the most recent in 2014, when Real Madrid beat city rivals Atletico 4-1 in Lisbon.

CESC FABREGAS

Born: Arenys de Mar, Spain,
4th May 1987
Position: Midfielder
Club career:
2003-11 Arsenal 212 (35)
2011-14 Barcelona 96 (28)
2014- Chelsea
International record:
2006- Spain 91 (13)

Cesc Fabregas became the third most expensive Spanish player in the Premier League (after team-mate Fernando Torres and former Blue Juan Mata) when he joined Chelsea from Barcelona in May 2014 for £30 million.

• Fabregas came through the Barca youth system before signing for Arsenal in September 2003. A month later he became the Gunners' youngest ever player when he made his debut in a League Cup tie against Rotherham United, aged just 16 and 177 days. In 2008 he was named PFA Young Player of the Year and in the same year he was made Arsenal captain by boss Arsene Wenger.

• To the dismay of Gunners fans, Fabregas returned to Barcelona in 2011 for £25.4 million, making him the most expensive player ever to leave the Emirates. In three years at the Nou Camp, the midfielder helped the Catalans win both the Spanish Cup (in 2012) and La Liga (in 2013).

• When Fabregas made his debut for Spain against Ivory Coast in 2006, he was the youngest player to represent his country for 70 years. A magnificent passer of the ball who can unpick the tightest of defences, he has gone on to enjoy huge success with the Spanish national team, helping them to win the European Championships in 2008 and 2012, and the World Cup in 2010 when his clever pass set up Andres Iniesta for the winning goal in the final against the Netherlands.

FA CUP

The oldest knock-out competition in the world, the FA Cup dates back to 1871 when it was established under the control of the Football Association. The first round of the first FA Cup was played on 11th November 1871, Clapham Rovers' Jarvis Kenrick scoring the very first goal in the competition in a 3-0 win over Upton Park.

• The following year Wanderers beat Royal Engineers at Kennington Oval in the first ever FA Cup final. The only goal of the game was scored by Morton Peto Betts, who played under the pseudonym A.H. Chequer. Uniquely, Wanderers, as holders, were given a bye all the way through to the following year's final, and they took full advantage by beating Oxford University 2-1.

• Unlike the League Cup, the FA Challenge Cup – the competition's full title – has always retained the same name despite being sponsored in recent years by Littlewoods (1994-98), AXA (1998-2002), E.ON (2006-11) and Budweiser (2011-14).

• There have, however, been five different trophies. The first trophy – known as the 'little tin idol' – was stolen from a Birmingham shop window in September 1895 where it was on display, having been won by Aston Villa a few months earlier. Sixty years later the thief revealed that the trophy was melted down and turned into counterfeit coins. A second trophy was used until 1910

Arsenal have won the FA Cup a joint-record 11 times, most recently in 2014

when it was presented to the FA's long-serving President and former five-time cup winner, Lord Kinnaird. A new, larger trophy was commissioned by the FA from Fattorini and Sons Silversmiths in Bradford – and, by a remarkable coincidence, was won in its first year by Bradford City in 1911. This trophy was used until 1992, when it was replaced with an exact replica. In 2014 a new trophy, with an identical design to the 1911 one, was presented to that year's winners, Arsenal.

• The only league team to have won the FA Cup in three consecutive years are Blackburn Rovers, who lifted the trophy in 1884, 1885 and 1886. The most successful clubs in the competition are Arsenal and Manchester United, who have both won the FA Cup a record 11 times.

• In 2000 Manchester United became the first holders not to defend their title when they failed to enter the FA Cup, opting instead to take part in the inaugural FIFA Club World Championship in Brazil.

• Five years later United were involved in the first FA Cup final to be decided by penalties, losing 5-4 to Arsenal after a 0-0 draw at the Millennium Stadium, Cardiff. In 2007 the final returned to Wembley, Chelsea becoming the first club to lift the trophy at the new national stadium after a 1-0 victory over Manchester United.

• Tottenham Hotspur are the only non-league side to win the competition, lifting the trophy for the first time in 1901 while members of the Southern League. West Ham were the last team from outside the top flight to win the cup, beating Arsenal 1-0 in the 1980 final.

• Leicester City are the most unfortunate club in FA Cup history, losing all four of the finals they have appeared in.

• In 1887 Preston North End recorded the biggest win in the history of the competition when they thrashed Hyde 26-0 in a first-round tie. In the same season, Preston's Jimmy Ross scored a record 19 goals in the competition.

• Ashley Cole has won the FA Cup a record seven times. Three of his triumphs came with Arsenal (in 2002,

TOP 10

BIGGEST FA CUP WINS

1. Preston North End 26 Hyde 0, 1887
2. Preston North End 18 Reading 0, 1894
3. Wanderers 16 Farningham 0, 1874
4. Royal Engineers 15 High Wycombe 0, 1875
   Clapham Rovers 15 Finchley 0, 1880
   Darwen 15 Romford 0, 1881
   Queen's Park 15 Manchester 0, 1883
   Notts County 15 Rotherham Town 0, 1885
9. Wolverhampton Wanderers 14 Crosswell's Brewery 0, 1886
   Clapton 0 Nottingham Forest 14, 1891

2003 and 2005), and he has also enjoyed four successes with Chelsea (in 2007, 2009, 2010 and 2012).

• The leading scorer in the FA Cup is Notts County's Henry Cursham, who banged in 49 goals between 1877 and 1888. Liverpool's Ian Rush scored a record five goals in three appearances in the final in 1986, 1989 and 1992, but Chelsea's Didier Drogba is the only player to have scored in four finals (2007, 2009, 2010 and 2012).

• A record 763 clubs entered the FA Cup in the 2011/12 season.

RADAMEL FALCAO

Born: Santa Maria, Colombia, 10th February 1986
Position: Striker
Club career:
2005-09 River Plate 90 (34)
2009-11 FC Porto 51 (41)
2011-13 Atletico Madrid 67 (52)
2013- Monaco 20 (11)
2014- Manchester United (loan)
International record:
2007- Colombia 51 (20)

Prolific Colombian striker Radamel Falcao was arguably the most high-profile signing of the summer 2014 transfer window when he joined Manchester United on deadline day for a £6 million loan fee, with an option for making the

Manchester United's Radamel Falcao

deal a permanent one at the end of the season.

• The brilliant South American is the all-time leading scorer in the Europa League with 30 goals, including 17 in the 2010/11 campaign with Porto – a record tally for an individual player in any European competition. He scored the winner in the 2011 final against fellow Portuguese outfit Braga, and repeated the trick with Atletico a year later with two goals in his side's 3-0 thrashing of Athletic Bilbao. In the process, Falcao became the first man ever to win consecutive European trophies with two different clubs.

• 'El Tigre' (The Tiger), as he is sometimes called, went on to break another record at the start of the 2012/13 season, becoming the first player to score a hat-trick in the UEFA Super Cup as Atletico beat Champions League holders Chelsea 4-1 in Monaco.

• Falcao, who cost Atletico a club record £30 million when they bought him from Porto in 2011, has also torn up the record books in domestic football, becoming the first player for over a decade to score five goals in a La Liga match when he went mad against Deportivo de La Coruna in December 2012. The following summer he joined free-spending Monaco for a then record French transfer fee of around £50 million.

• Falcao made his debut for Colombia in 2007, and was his country's leading scorer in qualification for the 2014 World Cup with an impressive total of nine goals. Unfortunately for the star striker he missed the finals in Brazil with a cruciate ligament injury.

RIO FERDINAND

Born: Peckham, 7th November 1978
Position: Defender
Club career:
1996-2000 West Ham United 127 (2)
1996 Bournemouth (loan) 10 (0)
2000-02 Leeds United 54 (2)
2002-14 Manchester United 312 (7)
2014- QPR
International record:
1997-2011 England 81 (3)

Although he no longer holds the honour, Rio Ferdinand has twice been the most expensive defender in the world: first, when he moved from West Ham to Leeds United for £18 million in 2000, and then when he joined Manchester United for £29.1 million two years later.

• A composed and commanding centre-half who likes to bring the ball out from the back to launch attacking moves, Ferdinand won the Premier League title in his first season at Old Trafford. He has since won the title on five further occasions and in 2008 he skippered United when the Reds won the Champions League after beating Chelsea on penalties in the final in Moscow.

• A mainstay of the England defence throughout the first decade of the new millennium, Ferdinand was first capped against Cameroon in 1997, just one week after his 19th birthday. At the time he was the youngest ever defender to play for England – although this record has since been beaten by Micah Richards. In 2008 Ferdinand captained his country for the first time as then England manager Fabio Capello tried out a number of players in the role before finally handing the armband to the United star's defensive partner, John Terry. When Terry was stripped of the captaincy in 2010 after allegations about his private life, Capello handed Ferdinand the armband on a permanent basis, only for the Chelsea man to regain the captaincy the following year.

• Ferdinand has played in more games for England, 81, without once appearing at the European Championships. He wasn't selected for the 2000 tournament, was banned in 2004 after missing a drugs test and, after England failed to qualify in 2008, he was controversially omitted from Roy Hodgson's squad for Euro 2012. He played his last game for England in 2011 before retiring from international football two years later.

• Peckham-born Ferdinand hails from a football family. His younger brother Anton played in the Premier League for West Ham, Sunderland and QPR while older cousin Les was a prolific striker with QPR, Newcastle, Tottenham and England.

SIR ALEX FERGUSON

Born: Govan, 31st December 1942
Managerial career: 1974 East Stirling
1974-78 St Mirren
1978-86 Aberdeen
1985-86 Scotland (caretaker)
1986-2013 Manchester United

The legendary Sir Alex Ferguson is the most successful British manager in the history of the game. Over his long career he won 38 major trophies and is the only manager from these shores

A nervous-looking official gets the full Fergie 'hairdryer' treatment

IS THAT A FACT?

Sir Alex Ferguson won the Premier League Manager of the Month award a record 27 times – more than twice as often as his nearest rival Arsène Wenger, who has topped the poll 13 times.

to win the Champions League on two occasions.

• Ferguson's reputation was forged at Aberdeen between 1978 and 1986 where he transformed the Dons into Scotland's leading club, breaking the domination of the Glasgow Old Firm in the process. Under Fergie, Aberdeen won three Premier Division titles, four Scottish Cups, one League Cup and the European Cup Winners' Cup in 1983, making him easily the most successful boss in the club's history.

• He moved to Manchester United in 1986 and, after some difficult early years, established the Reds as the dominant force of the 1990s and the new millennium. With United Ferguson won a record 13 Premier League titles, five FA Cups (another record), three League Cups, the European Cup Winners' Cup and the Champions League in both 1999 and 2008.

• Fergie's 26-year and 1,500-game tenure at Old Trafford from November 1986 until his retirement in May 2013 included a record 625 top-flight wins and made him the Premier League's and Manchester United's longest serving manager, ahead of the 24-year stint of another Scot, Sir Matt Busby.

• Ferguson is the only man to guide both Scottish and English clubs to success in all three domestic competitions and in Europe. He is also the only manager to win the English championship in three consecutive seasons with the same club twice, achieving this feat with United between 1999 and 2001 and 2007 and 2009. In the first of those years Fergie also won the FA Cup and Champions League to pull off an unprecedented Treble.

• A committed but not especially skilful striker in his playing days in the 1960s and early 1970s, Ferguson scored over 150 goals for a number of Scottish clubs including Dunfermline, Rangers and Falkirk.

• Knighted for services to football in 1999, Ferguson was named Premier League Manager of the Year on a record 11 occasions, claiming the award for the last time at the end of the 2012/13 season. Following the announcement of his retirement from the game, tributes flooded in from far and wide, with Prime Minister David Cameron describing Ferguson as "a remarkable man in British football".

Fleetwood's fans' fave look is based on Sir Elton John, circa 1974

FIFA

FIFA, the Federation Internationale de Football Association, is the most important administrative body in world football. It is responsible for the organisation of major international tournaments, notably the World Cup, and enacts law changes in the game.

• **Founded in Paris in 1904, FIFA is now based in Zurich and has 209 members, 16 more than the United Nations. The President is Sepp Blatter (elected in 1998), while his predecessors include Jules Rimet (1921-54), Sir Stanley Rous (1961-74) and Joao Havelange (1974-98). In 2011 Blatter was re-elected unopposed as President after his rival for the job, Mohammed bin Hammam, withdrew his candidacy following allegations that he offered bribes for votes.**

• Law changes that FIFA have introduced into the World Cup include the use of substitutes (1970), penalty shoot-outs to settle drawn games (1982) and the banning of the professional foul (1990).

• **The British football associations have twice pulled out of FIFA. First, in 1918 when they were opposed to playing matches against Germany after the end of the First World War, and again in 1928 over the issue of payments to amateurs. This second dispute meant that none of the British teams were represented at the first World Cup in 1930.**

• In 1992 FIFA decided to introduce a ranking index for all its member countries. As of August 2014 the three top-ranked nations were Germany, Argentina and Netherlands, reflecting their finishing positions at the 2014 World Cup.

FLEETWOOD TOWN

Year founded: 1997
Ground: Highbury Stadium (5,327)
Previous names: Fleetwood Wanderers, Fleetwood Freeport
Nickname: The Trawlermen
Biggest win: 13-0 v Oldham Town (1998)
Heaviest defeat: 0-7 v Billingham Town (2001)

Established in 1997 as the third incarnation of a club which dates back to 1908, Fleetwood Town have enjoyed a remarkable rise in recent years. In 2012 the Trawlermen were promoted to the Football League as Conference champions, and just two years later they went up to the third tier after beating Burton Albion 1-0 in the League Two play-off final

• **The Trawlermen's points tally of 103 in 2011/12 was just two short of Crawley Town's Conference record of 105, set in the previous season. Fleetwood's superb campaign also saw them reach the third round of the FA Cup for the first time in their history.**

• Fleetwood's climb through the divisions – they were playing in the Conference North as recently as 2010 – has seen their home attendances soar over the past decade. In 2003/04 they were playing in front of an average crowd of just 134, but by 2013/14 that figure had risen 21 times to 2,819.

HONOURS
Conference champions 2012

If it wasn't for floodlights, evening football would be a pretty gloomy affair...

THIS IS LOFTUS ROAD   WE ARE QPR

FLOODLIGHTS

The first ever floodlit match was played at Bramall Lane between two representative Sheffield sides on 14th October 1876 in front of a crowd of 10,000 people (around 8,000 of whom used the cover of darkness to get in without paying). The pitch was illuminated by four lamps, powered by dynamos driven by engines located behind the goals.

• **For many years the Football Association banned floodlight football, so the first league match played under lights did not take place until 1956, when Newcastle beat Portsmouth 2-0 at Fratton Park. It was hardly the most auspicious of occasions, though, as floodlight failure meant the kick-off was delayed for 30 minutes.**

• Arsenal became the first top-flight club in England to install floodlights in 1951 – some 20 years after legendary Gunners manager Herbert Chapman had advocated their use. Chesterfield were the last Football League club to install floodlights, finally putting up a set in 1967.

• **In the winter of 1997 two Premier League games, at West Ham and Wimbledon, were abandoned because of floodlight failure. What seemed to be an unfortunate coincidence was eventually revealed to be the work of a shadowy Far Eastern betting syndicate, four members of whom were eventually arrested and sentenced to three years each in prison.**

• England first played under floodlights on 8th June 1953 when they beat the USA 6-3 at the Yankee Stadium in New York.

FOOTBALL ASSOCIATION

Founded in 1863 at a meeting at the Freemasons' Tavern in central London, the Football Association is the oldest football organisation in the world and the only national association with no mention of the country in its name.

• **The first secretary of the FA was Ebenezer Cobb Morley of Barnes FC, nicknamed 'The Father of Football', who went on to draft the first set of laws of the game. The most controversial of the 14 laws he suggested outlawed kicking an opponent, known as 'hacking'. The first match to be played under the new laws was between Barnes and Richmond in 1863.**

• In 1871 the then secretary of the FA, Charles Alcock, suggested playing a

• Among the innovations the FA has fought against before finally accepting are the formation of an international tournament, the use of substitutes and the use of floodlights.

FOOTBALL LEAGUE

The Football League was founded at a meeting at the Royal Hotel, Piccadilly, Manchester in April 1888. The prime mover behind the new body was Aston Villa director William McGregor, who became the league's first President.

• **The 12 founder members were Accrington, Aston Villa, Blackburn Rovers, Bolton Wanderers, Burnley, Derby County, Everton, Notts County, Preston North End, Stoke City, West Bromwich Albion and Wolverhampton Wanderers. At the end of the inaugural 1888/89 season, Preston were crowned champions.**

• In 1892 a new Second Division, absorbing clubs from the rival Football Alliance, was added to the League and by 1905 the two divisions were made up of a total of 40 clubs. After the First World War, the League was expanded again to include a Third Division (later split between North and South sections).

• **A further expansion after 1945 took the number of clubs playing in the league to its long-time total of 92.**

The formation of the Premier League in 1992 reduced the Football League to three divisions – now known as the Championship, League One and League Two.

• As well as being the governing body for the three divisions, the Football League also organises two knock-out competitions: the League Cup (known as the Capital One Cup for sponsorship reasons) and the Football League Trophy (aka the Johnstone's Paint Trophy).

• **Liverpool are the most successful club in the history of the Football League, with 18 First Division titles to their name.**

FOOTBALLER OF THE YEAR

Confusingly, there are two Footballer of the Year awards in England and Scotland. The Football Writers' Association award was inaugurated in 1948, and the first winner was England winger Stanley Matthews. In 1974 the Professional Footballers' Association (PFA) set up their own award, Leeds hard man Norman 'Bites Yer Legs' Hunter being the first to be honoured by his peers.

• **Liverpool midfielder Terry McDermott was the first player to win both awards in the same season after helping Liverpool retain the title in 1980. A total of 16 different players have won both Footballer of the Year awards in the same season,**

Luis Suarez was delighted to be named double Footballer of the Year in 2014

national knock-out tournament similar to the competition he had enjoyed as a schoolboy at Harrow School. The idea was accepted by the FA and the competition, named the FA Challenge Cup, has been running ever since. The FA Cup, as it is usually called, has long been the most famous national club competition in world football.

• **Since 1992, the FA has run the English game's top division, the Premier League, which was formed when the old First Division broke away from the then four-division Football League.**

• The FA is also responsible for the appointment of the management of the England men's and women's football teams. The FA's main asset is the new Wembley Stadium, which it owns via its subsidiary, Wembley National Stadium Limited.

FRANCE

most recently Liverpool striker Luis Suarez in 2014. Former Arsenal striker Thierry Henry won a record five awards, landing the 'double' in both 2003 and 2004, and also carrying off the Football Writers' award in 2006.

• In 1977 Aston Villa striker Andy Gray became the first player to win both the main PFA award and the Young Player of the Year trophy. Only Cristiano Ronaldo in 2007 and Gareth Bale in 2013 have since matched this achievement.

Football Writers' Player of the Year
(since 1990)
1990 John Barnes (Liverpool)
1991 Gordon Strachan (Leeds United)
1992 Gary Lineker (Tottenham)
1993 Chris Waddle (Sheffield Wednesday)
1994 Alan Shearer (Blackburn Rovers)
1995 Jurgen Klinsmann (Tottenham)
1996 Eric Cantona (Manchester United)
1997 Gianfranco Zola (Chelsea)
1998 Dennis Bergkamp (Arsenal)
1999 David Ginola (Tottenham)
2000 Roy Keane (Manchester United)
2001 Teddy Sheringham (Manchester United)
2002 Robert Pires (Arsenal)
2003 Thierry Henry (Arsenal)
2004 Thierry Henry (Arsenal)
2005 Frank Lampard (Chelsea)
2006 Thierry Henry (Arsenal)
2007 Cristiano Ronaldo (Manchester United)
2008 Cristiano Ronaldo (Manchester United)
2009 Steven Gerrard (Liverpool)
2010 Wayne Rooney (Manchester United)
2011 Scott Parker (West Ham United)
2012 Robin van Persie (Arsenal)
2013 Gareth Bale (Tottenham)
2014 Luis Suarez (Liverpool)
PFA Footballer of the Year (since 1990)
1990 David Platt (Aston Villa)
1991 Mark Hughes (Manchester United)
1992 Gary Pallister (Manchester United)
1993 Paul McGrath (Aston Villa)
1994 Eric Cantona (Manchester United)
1995 Alan Shearer (Blackburn Rovers)
1996 Les Ferdinand (Newcastle United)
1997 Alan Shearer (Newcastle United)
1998 Dennis Bergkamp (Arsenal)
1999 David Ginola (Tottenham)

2000 Roy Keane (Manchester United)
2001 Teddy Sheringham (Manchester United)
2002 Ruud van Nistelrooy (Manchester United)
2003 Thierry Henry (Arsenal)
2004 Thierry Henry (Arsenal)
2005 John Terry (Chelsea)
2006 Steven Gerrard (Liverpool)
2007 Cristiano Ronaldo (Manchester United)
2008 Cristiano Ronaldo (Manchester United)
2009 Ryan Giggs (Manchester United)
2010 Wayne Rooney (Manchester United)
2011 Gareth Bale (Tottenham)
2012 Robin van Persie (Arsenal)
2013 Gareth Bale (Tottenham)
2014 Luis Suarez (Liverpool)

FRANCE

First international: Belgium 3 France 3, 1904
Most capped player: Lilian Thuram, 142 caps (1994-2008)
Leading goalscorer: Thierry Henry, 51 goals (1997-2010)
First World Cup appearance: France 4 Mexico 1, 1930
Biggest win: France 10 Azerbaijan 0, 1995
Heaviest defeat: France 1 Denmark 17, 1908

One of the most successful football nations of recent years, France won the World Cup for the first and only time on home soil in 1998 with a stunning 3-0 victory over Brazil in the final in Paris. Midfield genius Zinedine Zidane was the star of the show, scoring two goals.

• Two years later France became the first World Cup holders to go on to win the European Championships when they overcame Italy in the final in Rotterdam. This, though, was a much closer affair with the French requiring a 'golden goal' by striker David Trezeguet in extra-time to claim the trophy.

• France had won the European Championships once before, in 1984. Inspired by the legendary Michel Platini, who scored a record nine goals in the tournament, Les Bleus beat Spain 2-0 in the final in Paris.

FRENCH PREMIER LEAGUE PLAYERS
1. Eric Cantona (Leeds United & Manchester United, 1992-97)
2. Thierry Henry (Arsenal, 1999-2012)
3. Patrick Vieira (Arsenal & Manchester City, 1996-2011)
4. David Ginola (Newcastle, Tottenham, Aston Villa & Everton, 1995-2002)
5. Claude Makelele (Chelsea, 2003-08)
6. Robert Pires (Arsenal & Aston Villa, 2000-11)
7. Nicolas Anelka (Arsenal, Liverpool, Manchester City, Bolton, Chelsea & West Brom, 1997-2014)
8. Patrice Evra (Manchester United, 2006-)
9. Marcel Desailly (Chelsea, 1998-2004)
10. William Gallas (Chelsea, Arsenal & Tottenham, 2001-13)

Source: www.talksport.com

• French striker Just Fontaine scored an all-time record 13 goals at the 1958 World Cup finals in Sweden. His remarkable strike rate helped his country finish third in the tournament.

• When World Cup holders France were beaten 1-0 by Senegal in the 2002 World Cup, it was one of the biggest shocks in the history of the tournament. Les Bleus slumped out of the competition in the first round on that occasion, but bounced back to reach the final again in 2006... only to suffer the agony of a penalty shoot-out defeat at the hands of Italy. In 2010, though, the French endured another nightmare campaign, internal disputes between leading players and coach Raymond Domenech contributing to a humiliating first-round exit in South Africa.

• In 1908 France suffered one of the biggest ever defeats in international football when they were hammered 17-1 by Denmark in the semi-finals of the Olympic Games tournament in London. The French team were so depressed afterwards that they declined to play for the bronze medal against Holland.

• On 13th July 1930 France's Lucien Laurent scored the first ever goal at the World Cup finals, netting with a 19th-minute volley in his side's 4-1 defeat of

Free kicks offer a great opportunity to score – especially if Alexis Sanchez is taking one!

Mexico in the Estadio Pocitos in Montevideo, Uruguay. "Everyone was pleased but we didn't all roll around on the ground," he recalled many years later. "Nobody realised that history was being made."

HONOURS
World Cup *1998*
European Championships *1984, 2000*
Confederations Cup *2001, 2003*
World Cup record
1930 Round 1
1934 Round 1
1938 Round 2
1950 Did not qualify
1954 Round 1
1958 Third place
1962 Did not qualify
1966 Round 1
1970 Did not qualify
1974 Did not qualify
1978 Round 1
1982 Fourth place
1986 Third place
1990 Did not qualify
1994 Did not qualify
1998 Winners
2002 Round 1
2006 Runners-up
2010 Round 1
2014 Quarter-finals

FREE KICKS

A method for restarting the game after an infringement, free kicks may either be direct (meaning a goal may be scored directly) or indirect (in which case a second player must touch the ball before a goal may be scored).

• In 2000 a new rule was introduced which allowed the referee to punish dissent by moving a free kick 10 yards nearer the defenders' goal. The rule change, though, was deemed not to be a success and was unceremoniously scrapped five years later.

• One of the most memorable free kicks ever was taken by England captain David Beckham in a vital World Cup qualifier against Greece at Old Trafford in 2001. With the last kick of the match Beckham curled a superb free kick over the Greek wall and into the corner of the net to earn England a draw which booked the team's passage to the finals of the tournament in Japan and Korea.

• Brazilian midfielder Juninho Pernambucano holds the world record for the most goals scored direct from a free kick with 76, most of them coming during his time at French club Lyon between 2001 and 2009.

• Vanishing spray from an aerosol can to mark the 10 yards defenders must retreat from an attacking free kick was introduced to the Premier League at the start of the 2014/15 season. The spray was first used at an international tournament in the 2011 Copa America and was first used at the World Cup in Brazil in 2014.

IS THAT A FACT?
Maynor Figueroa scored the longest-range free kick in Premier League history when he slammed one in from an incredible 88 metres for Wigan against Stoke City on 12th December 2009.

FRIENDLIES

The first official international friendly took place on 30th November 1872 between Scotland and England at the West of Scotland Cricket Ground, Partick, Glasgow. The Scottish side for the match, which ended in a 0-0 draw, was made up entirely of players from the country's leading club, Queen's Park.

• England's first ever friendly against continental opposition was on 6th June 1908 against Austria in Vienna. England won that match 6-1 and two days later they did even better against the same opposition, winning 11-1.

• On 6th February 2007 London played host to a record four international friendlies on the same night – and England weren't even one of the eight teams in action! At the Emirates Stadium Portugal beat Brazil 2-0, Ghana thrashed Nigeria 4-1 at Brentford's Griffin Park, South Korea beat European champions Greece 1-0 at Craven Cottage, while at Loftus Road Denmark were 3-1 winners over Australia.

• Possibly the most bizarre friendly ever took place between Athletic Bilbao and a 200-strong 'team' of local schoolchildren in May 2010. The youngsters' side consisted of 197 outfield players and three goalkeepers, but despite their huge numerical advantage they were defeated 5-3 by their heroes.

• Then England manager Sven-Goran Eriksson became the first Three Lions boss to substitute all 11 starters in a 2-1 friendly defeat to Italy in 2002. However, two years later FIFA ruled that the maximum number of substitutes that could be used in an international friendly would be limited to six per team.

FULHAM

Year founded: 1879
Ground: Craven Cottage (25,700)
Previous name: Fulham St Andrew's
Nickname: The Cottagers
Biggest win: 10-1 v Ipswich Town (1963)
Heaviest defeat: 0-10 v Liverpool (1986)

London's oldest club, Fulham were founded in 1879 by two clergymen. Originally known as Fulham St Andrew's, the club adopted its present name nine years later. After winning the Southern League in two consecutive seasons Fulham were elected to the Football League in 1907.

• Before moving to Craven Cottage in 1896, Fulham had played at no fewer than 11 different grounds.

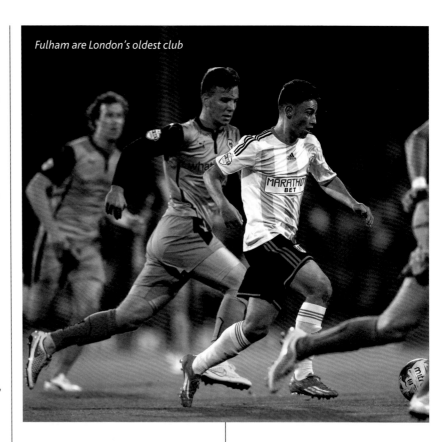

Fulham are London's oldest club

Including a stay at Loftus Road from 2002-04 while the Cottage was being redeveloped, Fulham have played at 13 venues, a total only exceeded by QPR.

• The proudest moment in the club's history came as recently as May 2010 when Fulham met Atletico Madrid in Hamburg in the first Europa League final. Sadly for their fans and their inspirational manager Roy Hodgson, the Cottagers lost 2-1 in extra-time despite putting up a spirited fight.

• In 1975 Fulham reached the FA Cup final for the first (and so far only) time, losing 2-0 to West Ham. The Cottagers have appeared in the semi-final six times, including a forgettable occasion in 1908 when they were hammered 6-0 by Newcastle, to this day the biggest ever winning margin at that stage of the competition.

• Midfield legend Johnny Haynes holds the club's appearance record, turning out in 594 league games between 1952 and 1970. 'The Maestro', as he was known to Fulham fans, is also the club's most honoured player at international level, with 56 England caps. Welsh international striker Gordon Davies is Fulham's top scorer with 159 league goals in two spells at the club between 1978 and 1991.

• In 1997 Fulham missed out on the Third Division title on 'goals scored' after finishing level on points with Wigan Athletic, despite having a superior goal difference. Ironically, then Fulham chairman Jimmy Hill had advocated the change to using goals scored, rather than goal difference, to separate teams who were equal on points.

• Bankrolled by then owner Mohamed Al-Fayed, Fulham climbed from the basement division to the Premiership in just four years between 1997 and 2001 – a year less than the then Harrods boss had predicted. Only Swansea City have made a quicker rise through the divisions, taking just three years between 1978 and 1981. However, Fulham's 13-year stay in the top flight ended in 2014 after a season in which they used 39 different players – a record for a Premier League campaign.

• Fulham's biggest ever win, 10-1 against Ipswich on Boxing Day 1963, was the last time a team scored double figures in the English top flight.

• Cottagers' midfielder Scott Parker is the first player to have appeared for five London clubs in the Premier League, after previous spells at Charlton, Chelsea, West Ham and Tottenham.

HONOURS
Division 2 champions 1949
First Division champions 2001
Division 3 (S) champions 1932
Second Division champions 1999

PAUL GASCOIGNE

Born: Gateshead, 25th May 1967
Position: Midfielder
Club career:
1985-88 Newcastle United 92 (21)
1988-92 Tottenham Hotspur 92 (19)
1992-95 Lazio 43 (6)
1995-98 Rangers 74 (30)
1998-2000 Middlesbrough 41 (4)
2000-02 Everton 32 (1)
2002 Burnley 6 (0)
2003 Gansu Tianma 4 (2)
2004 Boston United 5 (0)
International record:
1988-98 England 57 (10)

The most talented English midfielder of his generation, Paul Gascoigne could unlock the tightest of defences with a clever pass or a trademark dribble past a couple of opponents. His prodigious skills prompted Tottenham to sign him for £2 million from Newcastle in 1988, making him the most expensive British player at the time.

• Troubled by injuries throughout his career, Gascoigne was at his peak at the 1990 World Cup in Italy when his brilliant performances powered England to the last four. 'Gazzamania' completely swept the country after his tears during the England-Germany semi-final (after he picked up a yellow card which meant he would miss the final) perfectly summed up the mood of disappointment that swept the nation as England went on to lose a penalty shoot-out. A few months later he was voted BBC Sports Personality of the Year – only the second footballer, after Bobby Moore in 1966, to receive the award.

• Gazza also starred at Euro '96, scoring a superb solo goal in the local derby with Scotland at Wembley that many rate as the best England goal ever. However, he was controversially left out of England's 1998 World Cup squad after a series of drunken incidents and never added to his 57 caps.

• At club level, Gascoigne is one of a select band of players to have won both the FA Cup (with Spurs in 1991) and the Scottish Cup (with Rangers in 1996). While at Ibrox he also won two league titles and the League Cup.

• A fun-loving character who was once described as being "as daft as a brush" by then England manager Bobby Robson, Gazza has sadly struggled with alcohol addiction and mental health problems since quitting the game in 2004.

DAVID DE GEA

Born: Madrid, 7th November 1990
Position: Goalkeeper
Club career:
2008-09 Atletico Madrid B 35
2009-11 Atletico Madrid 57
2011- Manchester United 95
International record:
2014- Spain 1

David De Gea is the most expensive goalkeeper in the history of the British game, costing Manchester United around £18 million when he moved from Atletico Madrid in June 2011.

• After coming through the youth ranks at Atletico, De Gea enjoyed a great first season with the Madrid club, helping them win the Europa League following a 2-1 victory against Fulham in the final in Hamburg. At the start of the following campaign he starred in Atletico's UEFA Super Cup victory over Champions League holders Inter Milan, saving a late penalty from Uruguayan striker Diego Milito.

• De Gea confirmed his reputation as one of Europe's most promising young goalkeepers with a string of outstanding performances for the Spain Under-21 side which won the 2011 European Championships in Denmark. Shortly after this triumph De Gea signed for Manchester United, then manager Sir Alex Ferguson having targeted the Spaniard for some time as his first-choice replacement for the retired Edwin van der Sar.

• After some unconvincing early performances for United De Gea

David De Gea, the most expensive goalkeeper in British football

was dropped by Ferguson, but after winning back his place in the side his form was much improved. In 2013 he helped United win the Premier League title and his individual contribution to that success was recognised when he was voted into the PFA Team of the Year.

TOP 10

HIGHEST SCORING COUNTRIES AT THE WORLD CUP

1.	Germany	224 goals
2.	Brazil	221 goals
3.	Argentina	131 goals
4.	Italy	128 goals
5.	France	106 goals
6.	Spain	92 goals
7.	Hungary	87 goals
8.	Netherlands	86 goals
9.	Uruguay	80 goals
10.	England	79 goals

GERMANY

First international: Switzerland 5 Germany 3, 1908
Most capped player: Lothar Matthaus, 150 caps (1980-2000)
Leading goalscorer: Miroslav Klose, 71 goals (2001-14)
First World Cup appearance: Germany 5 Belgium 2, 1934
Biggest win: Germany 16 Russia 0, 1912
Heaviest defeat: Austria 6 Germany 0, 1931

Germany (formerly West Germany) have the joint second best record in the World Cup behind Brazil, having won the tournament four times and reached the final on a record eight occasions. They have also won the European Championships a joint-record three times and been losing finalists on another three occasions.

• The Germans recorded their fourth World Cup triumph in Brazil in 2014, when they beat Argentina 1-0 in the final thanks to Mario Gotze's extra-time goal. Perhaps more remarkable, though, was their performance in the

semi-final when they massacred the hosts 7-1 – the biggest ever win at that late stage of the competition. Germany's other victories came in 1954 (against Hungary), on home soil in 1974 (against the Netherlands) and at Italia '90 (against Argentina).

• Lothar Matthaus, a powerhouse in the German midfield for two decades, played in a record 25 matches at the World Cup in five tournaments between 1982 and 1998. His total of 150 caps for Germany is also a national record.

• Germany striker Miroslav Klose is the all-time leading scorer at the World Cup with a total of 16 goals, one ahead of Brazil's Ronaldo and two better than fellow countryman Gerd 'the Bomber' Muller.

• Germany's Oliver Kahn is the only goalkeeper to win the Player of the Tournament award at a World Cup, topping the poll for his performances in 2002 in Japan and Korea.

• Germany have played in a record 106 games at the World Cup and scored a tournament best 224 goals.

HONOURS

World Cup *1954, 1974, 1990, 2014*
European Championships *1972, 1980, 1996*
World Cup record
1930 Did not enter
1934 Third place
1938 Round 1
1950 Did not enter
1954 Winners
1958 Fourth place
1962 Quarter-finals
1966 Runners-up
1970 Third place
1974 Winners
1978 Round 1
1982 Runners-up
1986 Runners-up
1990 Winners
1994 Quarter-finals
1998 Quarter-finals
2002 Runners-up
2006 Third place
2010 Third place
2014 Winners

STEVEN GERRARD

Born: Whiston, 30th May 1980
Position: Midfielder
Club career:
1998- Liverpool 475 (111)
International record:
2000-14 England 114 (21)

Liverpool captain Steven Gerrard is the only player to have scored in the FA Cup final, the League Cup final, the UEFA Cup final and the Champions League final. He achieved this feat between 2001 and 2006 while winning all four competitions with the Reds (and, indeed, earning winners' medals in the FA Cup and League Cup on two occasions).

• Once a dynamic midfielder who was famed for his surging runs and thunderous shooting, Gerrard is now a deep-lying playmaker at his boyhood club. He made his Liverpool debut in 1998 and, five years later, then Anfield boss Gerard Houllier made the Kop idol his skipper – he has retained the armband ever since. A Red to his very core, Gerrard has twice turned down lucrative moves to Chelsea.

• In the 2006 FA Cup final Gerrard scored two stunning goals against West Ham, including a last-minute equaliser which many rate as the best ever goal in the final. Liverpool went on to win the match on penalties and Gerrard's heroics were rewarded with the 2006 PFA Player of the Year award – the first Liverpool player to top the poll since John Barnes in 1988. Three years later he was voted Footballer of the Year by the football writers.

• Gerrard made his international debut for England against Ukraine in 2000 and scored his first goal for his country with a superb 20-yarder in the famous 5-1 thrashing of Germany in Berlin in 2001. In the absence of regular skipper Rio Ferdinand, he captained England at the 2010 World Cup and, after being appointed the permanent captain by new boss Roy Hodgson, he led his country at the 2012 European

IS THAT A FACT?
Steven Gerrard has been voted into the PFA Premier League Team of the Year a record eight times, most recently in 2014 after a superb campaign in which he led Liverpool to within a whisker of the league title.

Championships and the 2014 World Cup.

• With 114 caps to his name before he announced his retirement from international football in July 2014, Gerrard is third on the list of England's all-time appearance makers behind Peter Shilton and David Beckham.

Liverpool great Steven Gerrard

GIANT-KILLING

Many of the most remarkable instances of giant-killing have occurred in the FA Cup, with a number of non-league clubs claiming the scalps of top-flight opposition. One of the biggest such shocks came in 1989 when Coventry City, who had won the FA Cup just two years earlier, were knocked out of the competition by non-league Sutton United in the third round.

• **In 2013 Luton Town became the first non-league side to knock a Premier League team out of the FA Cup when they sensationally beat Norwich City 1-0 at Carrow Road in the fourth round.**

• In their non-league days Yeovil Town beat a record 20 league teams in the FA Cup. The Glovers' most famous win came in the fourth round in 1949 against First Division Sunderland, who they defeated 2-1 on their notorious sloping pitch at Huish Park.

• **There have been a number of famous giant-killings in the League Cup final, including Swindon's shock 3-1 win over Arsenal in 1969, Stoke's 2-1 win against Chelsea in 1972 and Luton's 3-2 win over the Gunners in 1988.**

• Giant-killings also happen occasionally at international level. At the 1950 World Cup in Brazil, for instance, England sensationally lost 1-0 to an unheralded United States team. The result was so unexpected that many people assumed it was a misprint when they saw it in the newspapers and that the true score was 10-1 to England! Other major World Cup shocks include Cameroon's 1-0 defeat of holders Argentina in 1990, Senegal's 1-0 win over holders France in 2002 and Costa Rica's surprise 1-0 win over Italy in 2014.

RYAN GIGGS

Born: Cardiff, 29th November 1973
Position: Winger/midfielder
Club career:
1991-2014 Manchester United 672 (114)
International record:
1991-2007 Wales 64 (12)

In a glorious career with Manchester United, Ryan Giggs became the most decorated player in English football history. Between 1991 and 2014, when he announced his retirement from the game, he won 22 major honours: a record 13 Premier League titles, four FA Cups, three League Cups and two Champions League trophies. In 2009 he was voted PFA Player of the Year by his fellow professionals.

• Now Manchester United's assistant manager after a brief spell as the club's caretaker manager in 2014, Giggs scored at least one goal in a record 21 Premier League seasons before drawing a blank in the 2013/14 campaign. He also holds the Premier League appearance record, 632 games, and has also played more games in the top flight for the same club, 672, than any other player.

• A one-club man throughout his stellar career, Giggs made a record 963 appearances for United in all competitions – 205 more than the previous record holder, Bobby Charlton.

• Giggs enjoyed his best ever year in 1999 when he won the Premiership, FA Cup and Champions League with United. His goal against Arsenal in that season's FA Cup semi-final, when he dribbled past four defenders before smashing the ball into the roof of the net from a tight angle, is often recalled

as one of the greatest ever and was voted Goal of the Season.

• The oldest goalscorer ever in the Champions League, Giggs has also played more games in the competition (151) than any other player.

• Once Wales' youngest ever player, Giggs previously played for England Schoolboys under the name Ryan Wilson (the surname being that of his father, a former Welsh rugby league player). However, having no English grandparents, Giggs was ineligible to play for the England national team and was proud to represent Wales on 64 occasions before retiring from international football in 2007.

GILLINGHAM

Year founded: 1893
Ground: Priestfield Stadium (11,582)
Previous name: New Brompton
Nickname: The Gills
Biggest win: 12-1 v Gloucester City (1946)
Heaviest defeat: 2-9 v Nottingham Forest (1950)

Founded by a group of local businessmen as New Brompton in 1893, the club changed to its present name in 1913. Seven years later Gillingham joined the new Third Division but in 1938 were voted out of the league in favour of Ipswich Town. They eventually returned in 1950.

• The only Kent-based team in the Football League, Gillingham recovered from a financial crisis in the mid-1990s to enjoy a first spell in the second tier between 2000 and 2005. After dropping back into the basement division, they are now in the third tier after winning the 2013 League Two championship.

• In 1952 the Gills' Jimmy Scarth notched three goals in just two minutes and 30 seconds against Leyton Orient to set a record for the fastest Football League hat-trick which stood until 2004.

• In their 1995/96 promotion campaign Gillingham only conceded 20 goals – a record for a 46-game season in the Football League.

• Winger Luke Freeman became the youngest ever player in the FA Cup

proper when he came on as a sub for Gillingham against Barnet in 2007 when aged just 15 years and 233 days.

HONOURS
Division 4 champions 1964
League Two champions 2013

OLIVIER GIROUD

Born: Chambery, France, 30th September 1986
Position: Striker
Club career:
2005-08 Grenoble 23 (2)
2007-08 Istres (loan) 33 (14)
2008-10 Tours 44 (24)
2010-12 Montpellier 73 (33)
2010 Tours (loan) 17 (6)
2012- Arsenal 70 (27)
International record:
2011- France 34 (9)

Arsenal striker Olivier Giroud enjoyed his best season yet for Arsenal in 2013/14, scoring 16 Premier League goals and setting up the winner for Aaron Ramsey in the FA Cup final against Hull City with a clever backheel.

• A tall, powerful striker who finishes well on the ground and in the air, Giroud first came to the fore when he was top scorer in the French second division with Tours in 2009/10, his goalscoring feats also earning him the Ligue 2 Player of the Year award.

• A move to Montpellier followed, and in only his second season with the club Giroud helped the southern French side win the league for the first time in their history. The striker's 21 goals during the campaign made him the league's joint-top scorer and were instrumental in Montpellier's surprise success. Later that summer he joined Arsenal for £9.6 million.

• Giroud won his first cap for France in a 1-0 friendly win over the USA in 2011. He represented his country at the 2014 World Cup, scoring France's 100th goal at the tournament in a 5-2 thrashing of Switzerland.

TOP 10

PREMIER LEAGUE APPEARANCES

1.	Ryan Giggs (1992-2014)	632
2.	Frank Lampard (1996-)	577
3.	David James (1992-2010)	572
4.	Gary Speed (1992-2008)	532
5.	Gareth Barry (1998-)	531
6.	Emile Heskey (1996-2012)	516
7.	Jamie Carragher (1997-2013)	508
	Mark Schwarzer (1996-)	508
9.	Phil Neville (1995-2013)	505
10.	Sol Campbell (1992-2011)	503

• In February 2014 Giroud issued a grovelling apology on Twitter after a picture of him in his underpants, taken by a pin-up model, appeared in a national newspaper. "I now have to fight for my family and my club and obtain their forgiveness," Giroud said. "Nothing else matters at the moment."

GOAL CELEBRATIONS

Elaborate and sometimes spectacular goal celebrations have been a feature of English football since the mid-1990s when the Premier League started opening its doors to large numbers of overseas players. Middlesbrough striker Fabrizio Ravanelli, for instance, was famed for pulling his shirt over his head after scoring, and soon players were removing their shirts altogether, sometimes to reveal personal, political or religious messages written on a t-shirt.

• **In 2003 FIFA decided that the craze had got out of hand and ruled that any player removing his shirt would be booked. The first player to be sent off after falling foul of this new law was Everton's Tim Cahill, who was shown a second yellow against Manchester City in 2004.**

• In 2013 West Brom striker Nicolas Anelka was fined a record £80,000 by the FA and banned for five matches after celebrating a goal at West Ham by placing his arm across his chest in a gesture known as the 'quenelle' which, especially in Anelka's native France, carries anti-semitic connotations. The former France star was subsequently sacked by his club for gross misconduct.

• **In one of the most bizarre goal celebrations ever, Manchester United star Carlos Tevez produced a baby's dummy from his shorts and sucked on it after scoring against Birmingham at Old Trafford in 2008. He later explained that the routine was a tribute to his young daughter, Florencia. Earlier in his career, Tevez was sent off while playing for Boca Juniors against arch-rivals River Plate when he celebrated a goal in front of the opposition fans by imitating a chicken.**

• In 2004 Servette midfielder Paulo Diogo celebrated a goal he had created against FC Schaffhausen by jumping on a metal perimeter fence. Unfortunately, his wedding ring caught in the fence and when he jumped down he left much of his finger behind. To add insult to injury, Diogo was then shown a yellow card by the referee for leaving the pitch without permission.

• **In possibly the most costly goal celebration ever, AEK Athens midfielder Giorgos Katidis was**

Olivier Giroud, proud to be a Gunner

Colombia's players spent many hours practising their goal celebrations before the 2014 World Cup

fined £40,000, banned for the rest of the season and given a lifetime ban from representing Greece for making a Nazi salute after scoring the winner against FC Veria in March 2013. The Greek football federation described Katidis' action as "a severe provocation which insulted all the victims of Nazi bestiality", while the player himself pleaded innocence saying, "I would not have done it if I had known what it meant".

GOAL OF THE SEASON

The Goal of the Season award has been awarded by BBC TV's flagship football programme *Match of the Day* since 1971 (apart from the years 2001-04 when, for broadcasting rights reasons, the award was given by ITV). The first winner was Coventry City's Ernie Hunt, whose spectacular volley against Everton at Highfield Road topped the poll.

• **Liverpool's John Aldridge is the only player to win Goal of the Season in consecutive seasons, taking the award in 1988 and 1989 for his FA Cup strikes against Nottingham Forest and Everton respectively, the second of these goals coming in the final itself.** Manchester United striker Wayne

Rooney is the only player to win the award three times, most recently in 2011 for an acrobatic overhead kick against local rivals Manchester City.

• Only two players have won the award for goals scored for their countries rather than their clubs: Scotland's Kenny Dalglish in 1983 and England's Bryan Robson in 1986.

• **Liverpool players have won the Goal of the Season award a record six times, most recently in 2006 when Steven Gerrard's 30-yarder in the FA Cup final against West Ham topped the list. Arsenal have conceded the Goal of the Season a record five times, most recently in 1999 when Ryan Giggs dribbled through the Gunners' defence to score the winner in the FA Cup semi-final for Manchester United.**

GOALKEEPERS

• On 27th March 2011 Sao Paulo's Rogerio Ceni became the first goalkeeper in the history of football to score 100 career goals when he netted with a free kick in a 2-1 win against Corinthians. His unlikely century was made up of 56 free kicks and 44 penalties. He has since added a further 17 goals to his record-breaking tally.

• Just five goalkeepers have scored in the Premier League: Peter Schmeichel (Aston Villa), Brad Friedel (Blackburn Rovers), Paul Robinson (Tottenham), Tim Howard (Everton) and Asmir Begovic (Stoke City). Begovic's goal after just 13 seconds against Southampton in November 2013 is the fastest ever by a goalkeeper in English football history and was scored at a greater distance (91.9 metres) than any goal ever.

• Amazingly, East Stirling used four goalkeepers in their Scottish Third Division match away to Albion Rovers on 10th May 2003. After first-choice goalkeeper Chris Todd was injured early on, he was replaced by Scott Findlay, who was sent off just before half-time. His replacement, Graham McLaren, also saw red following a foul in the penalty area. Kevin McCann took over the gloves and saved the penalty, but couldn't prevent East Stirling going down to a 3-1 defeat.

• **Gianluigi Buffon is the world's most expensive goalkeeper after moving to Juventus from Parma in 2001 for a cool £32.6 million.**

• David James holds the record for both Premier League appearances by a goalkeeper (573) and for clean sheets (173).

GOAL-LINE TECHNOLOGY

Goal-line technology was introduced to the Premier League for the first time for the 2013/14 season after the league agreed to adopt the Hawk-Eye system, which uses seven cameras per goal and notifies the match officials whether or not the ball has crossed the line via a vibration and optical signal sent to the officials' watches within one second of the incident.

• In July 2012 FIFA's International Football Association Board, which determines the laws of the game, agreed to the principle of using goal-line technology at future FIFA tournaments. The following year Goal Control, a similar system to Hawk-Eye, was used at the 2013 Confederations Cup and again at the 2014 World Cup in Brazil.

• For many years FIFA President Sepp Blatter was opposed to the introduction of goal-line technology, believing that it would undermine the authority of the match officials. However, he changed his mind after the 2010 World Cup, during which a number of questionable goal-line decisions were made, most notably the denying of a goal to England when Frank Lampard's shot clearly crossed the line in his country's last 16 match with Germany. "I was so shocked that the goal was not allowed," Blatter said later.

"The next day, when I gathered myself, I made the declaration that we should start to consider the technology and look for a simple way to implement it."

• **The first Premier League goal to be decisively awarded using goal-line technology was scored by Edin Dzeko for Manchester City against Cardiff City on 18th January 2014.**

GOALS

Manchester United have scored more league goals than any other English club. Up to the start of the 2014/15 season, the Red Devils had managed 7,647 goals. Liverpool, though, have scored the most goals at home (4,596), while Notts County have conceded the most in total (6,935).

• **Peterborough United hold the record for the most league goals in a season, banging in 134 in 1960/61 on their way to claiming the Fourth Division title. Less impressively, Darwen conceded a record 141 goals in the Second Division in 1898/99.**

• Aston Villa hold the top-flight record, with 128 goals in 1930/31. Despite their prolific attack, the Villans were pipped to the First Division title by Arsenal (amazingly, the Gunners managed 127 goals themselves). Title-winners Chelsea became the first team to score a century of goals in the Premier League era in 2009/10, the Blues taking their tally to 103 with an 8-0 thrashing of Wigan on the final day of the season. Premier League winners Manchester City (102) and runners-up Liverpool (101) both notched a century of league goals in 2013/14 – the first time since 1961 that two teams had hit three figures in the top flight – while City set a new record by hitting an incredible 156 goals in all competitions.

• Arthur Rowley scored a record 434 Football League goals between 1946 and 1965, notching four for West Brom, 27 for Fulham, 251 for Leicester City and 152 for Shrewsbury. Former Republic of Ireland international John Aldridge is the overall leading scorer in post-war English football, with an

IS THAT A FACT?
Manchester United have scored a record 1,691 goals since the formation of the Premier League in 1992, while Tottenham have conceded the most goals (1,117).

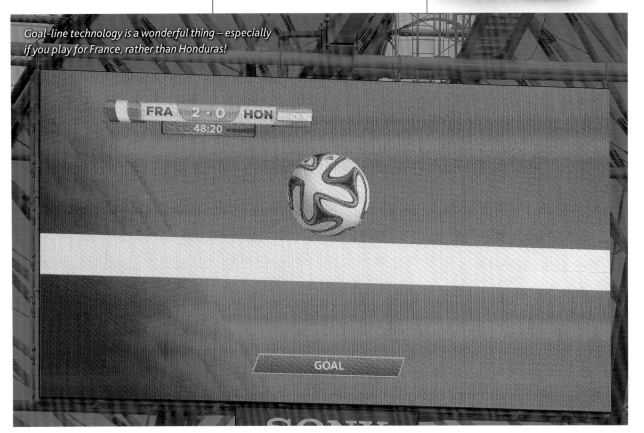

Goal-line technology is a wonderful thing – especially if you play for France, rather than Honduras!

Goal! Germany's Mats Hummels heads beyond France goalkeeper Hugo Lloris at the 2014 World Cup

JIMMY GREAVES

Born: East Ham, 20th February 1940
Position: Striker
Club career:
1957-61 Chelsea 157 (124)
1961-62 AC Milan 14 (9)
1962-70 Tottenham 321 (220)
1970-71 West Ham United 38 (13)
International record:
1959-67 England 57 (44)

With 44 goals for England, Jimmy Greaves is his country's third highest ever goalscorer behind Bobby Charlton and Gary Lineker. He scored on his international debut in 1959 in a 4-1 defeat by Peru, and went on to bag a record six hat-tricks for his country. Famously, Greaves also scored on his debut for all the clubs he played for.

• **A quicksilver striker who always carefully picked his spot when shooting, Greaves began his career at Chelsea. In the 1960/61 season he hit an incredible 41 league goals for the Blues – a post-war record for the top flight – and also scored a record 13 goals for England.**

• After a brief spell with AC Milan, Greaves moved to Tottenham where he helped the club claim two major trophies, the European Cup Winners' Cup in 1963 and the FA Cup in 1967. His haul of 220 league goals for Spurs remains a club record.

• **At 21, Greaves was the youngest player to score 100 league goals. He netted his 200th aged 23 years and 290 days, coincidentally exactly**

impressive total of 476 goals in all competitions for Newport County, Oxford United, Liverpool and Tranmere between 1979 and 1998.

• Joe Payne set an English Football League record for goals in a game by scoring 10 times for Luton against Bristol Rovers on 13th April 1936.

• **A record 209 league goals were scored in the Football League on 1st February 1936, while the most prolific day in top-flight history was on Boxing Day 1963 when 66 goals hit the back of the net in just 10 games – the highest score was at**

Craven Cottage where Fulham stuffed Ipswich 10-1.

• When he scored for Cardiff in a 2-1 win against Norwich on 1st February 2014, Craig Bellamy became the first player ever to score for seven different Premier League clubs. The veteran Welsh striker had previously notched for Coventry, Newcastle, Blackburn, Liverpool, West Ham and Manchester City.

• Iranian striker Ali Daei is the leading scorer in international football with an incredible 109 goals, including a record 35 in World Cup qualifiers, between 1993 and 2006.

Jimmy Greaves shoots – and (probably) scores

the same age at which Dixie Dean reached the same landmark with Everton.

• Arguably English football's most consistent ever striker, Greaves was top scorer in the First Division six times and notched a total of 357 league goals – both top-flight records that are unlikely to be broken.

• **He experienced the lowest point of his career in 1966 when, after starting in England's opening matches at the World Cup, he was left out of the team for the triumphant final against West Germany. Bitterly disappointed, he was the only member of the squad not to attend the victory bash in a London hotel.**

• After hanging up his boots Greaves overcame alcoholism to launch a new career as a TV personality, his double act with former Liverpool star Ian St John being especially popular with viewers.

PEP GUARDIOLA

Born Santpedor, Spain, 18th January 1971

Managerial career:
2007-08 Barcelona B
2008-12 Barcelona
2013- Bayern Munich

Bayern Munich manager Pep Guardiola is the only coach to lead a club to six trophies in a calendar year, claiming an amazing sextuple in 2009 when his former charges Barcelona won the Spanish title, the Copa del Rey, the Champions League, the Spanish Super Cup, the UEFA Super Cup and, finally, the FIFA Club World Cup.

• **When Barcelona won the Champions League in 2009, following a 2-0 win over Manchester United in the final in Rome, the 38-year-old Guardiola became the youngest coach ever to win the trophy.**

• After winning 14 trophies in four years – an impressive haul unmatched by any other Barcelona manager – Guardiola quit

the Catalan club in 2012, citing "tiredness" as the main reason for his decision. A year later he took over the reins at Bayern Munich and in his first season with the German giants in 2013/14 won the league and cup Double. However, Bayern fans were disappointed to see their side lose their grip on the Champions League following a 5-0 aggregate trouncing by Real Madrid in the semi-finals.

• **A defensive midfielder in his playing days, Guardiola was a key member of Johan Cruyff's attack-minded 'Dream Team' which won Barcelona's first European Cup in 1992 and four La Liga titles in the early 1990s.**

"Listen lads, heading is a lot easier when you're bald!"

HAMILTON ACADEMICAL

Year founded: 1874
Ground: New Douglas Park (6,078)
Nickname: The Accies
Biggest win: 11-1 v Chryston, 1885
Heaviest defeat: 1-11 v Hibernian, 1965

Founded in 1874 by the Rector and pupils of Hamilton Academy, Hamilton Academical is the only professional club in Britain to have originated from a school team. Shortly after the start of the 1897/98 season, the Accies joined the Scottish League in place of Renton, who were forced to resign for financial reasons.

• Hamilton fans have had little to cheer over the years, but the club did reach the Scottish Cup final in 1911 (losing to Celtic after a replay) and again in 1935 (losing to Rangers).

• English striker David Wilson scored a club record 246 goals for the Accies between 1928 and 1939.

• With a capacity of just 6,078, Hamilton's New Douglas Park stadium is the smallest in the SPL.

• In 2014 Hamilton became the first club to be promoted to the Scottish Premier League via the new play-off system, defeating Hibernian on penalties to send the Edinburgh side down to the second tier. Towards the end of their promotion season, the Accies hammered Morton 10-2 to record their biggest ever league win.

> HONOURS
> **First Division champions** 1986, 1988, 2008
> **Division 2 champions** 1904
> **Third Division champions** 2001

JOE HART

Born: Shrewsbury, 19th April 1987
Position: Goalkeeper
Club career:
2003-06 Shrewsbury Town 54
2006- Manchester City 195
2007 Tranmere Rovers (loan) 6
2007 Blackpool (loan) 5
2009-10 Birmingham City (loan) 36
International record:
2008- England 43

Joe Hart is only the second goalkeeper (after Liverpool's Pepe Reina) to win the Premier League Golden Gloves award for keeping the most clean sheets in the division three years on the trot, claiming the honour in 2011, 2012 and 2013. In the second of those years Hart was a pivotal figure for his club, Manchester City, as they won their first ever Premier League title. In 2014 he went one better, helping City win both the title and the League Cup despite suffering a dip in form which saw him relegated to the bench earlier in the season.

• Hart began his career with his hometown club, Shrewsbury Town. His assured performances with the Shrews soon attracted the attention of bigger clubs and in 2006 he moved to City for an initial £600,000 fee. After loan spells at Tranmere Rovers, Blackpool and Birmingham City, where his superb displays earned him a place in the 2010 PFA Team of the Year, he returned to Eastlands to claim the keeper's jersey ahead of Shay Given.

• While a regular between the sticks for the England Under-21 side, Hart moved up to the senior squad and in June 2008 made his full debut as a sub in a 3-0 win over Trinidad and Tobago.

• Hart became a regular for England during the Euro 2012 qualifiers and since then he has become established as his country's No 1. In 2013 he saved a penalty from Brazil legend Ronaldinho at Wembley to help his country record their first victory over the South Americans for 23 years.

This incident gave Joe Hart the idea of launching his own sandwich chain...

HARTLEPOOL UNITED

Year founded: 1908
Ground: Victoria Ground (7,856)
Previous name: Hartlepools United, Hartlepool
Nickname: The Pool
Biggest win: 10-1 v Barrow (1959)
Heaviest defeat: 1-10 v Wrexham (1962)

The club were founded as Hartlepools United in 1908 as a professional team to emulate the success of West Hartlepools, winners of the FA Amateur Cup three years earlier. In 1968 they became 'Hartlepool', adding the word 'United' in 1977.

• The Pool, as they are nicknamed, had to apply for re-election to the Football League a record 11 times, including five times between 1960 and 1964 when they finished bottom or second bottom of the old Fourth Division in five consecutive seasons. On each occasion, though, they earned a reprieve and in recent years they have twice climbed out of the bottom tier into League One.

• Hartlepool's Victoria Ground was the first ever football stadium to be bombed, its wooden stand being destroyed by a bomb dropped from a German Zeppelin airship in 1917, during the First World War. The ground is also notable for being one of just two (along with Old Trafford) which has staged two football league matches on the same day, hosting both Hartlepool v Cardiff and Middlesbrough v Port Vale on 23rd August 1983 (Boro's Ayresome Park ground having been shut after the club went into liquidation).

• Hartlepool have the worst overall goal difference of any Football League club (-998).

• Hartlepool's youngest player is diminutive winger David Foley, who was aged just 16 and 44 days when he made his debut as a sub in a 2-0 win against Port Vale on 25th August 2003.

HAT-TRICKS

Geoff Hurst is the only player to have scored a hat-trick in a World Cup final, hitting three goals in England's 4-2 defeat of West Germany at Wembley in 1966.

• Eighteen-year-old Tony Ross scored the fastest hat-trick in football history

MOST IMPORTANT HAT-TRICKS

1. Geoff Hurst (England 4 West Germany 2, 1966 World Cup final)
2. Stan Mortensen (Blackpool 4 Bolton 3, 1953 FA Cup final)
3. Michael Owen (Germany 1 England 5, 2001)
4. Clive Mendonca (Charlton 4 Sunderland 4, 1998 Play-off final)
5. Thierry Henry (Arsenal 4 Liverpool 2, 2004)
6. Paul Gascoigne (Rangers 3 Aberdeen 1, 1996)
7. Andrey Arshavin (Liverpool 4 Arsenal 4, 2009)
8. Scott Sinclair (Swansea 4 Reading 2, 2011 Play-off final)
9. Gary Lineker (England 3 Poland 0, 1986 World Cup)
10. Ally McCoist (Rangers 3 Celtic 2, 1986 Scottish League Cup final)

Source: www.dailymail.co.uk

in 1964, taking just 90 seconds to complete a treble for Ross County in a Highland League match against Nairn County.

• In 2004 Bournemouth's James Hayter struck the fastest hat-trick in English football league history, finding the net three times in just two minutes and 20 seconds against Wrexham. Incredibly, he was only on the pitch for six minutes after coming on as a late substitute! Ten years earlier, Liverpool's Robbie Fowler hit the fastest hat-trick in Premier League history, grabbing three goals in under five minutes against Arsenal at Anfield.

• The legendary Dixie Dean scored a record 37 hat-tricks during his career, while his contemporary George Camsell scored a record nine hat-tricks for Middlesbrough in the 1925/26 season.

• Paraguayan international Jose Luis Chilavert is the only goalkeeper to have notched a hat-trick, scoring three penalties for Argentinean side Velez Sarsfield in their 6-1 win over Ferro Carril Oeste in 1999.

• A total of 273 hat-tricks have been scored in the Premier League, with a

record three being notched on 23rd September 1995 when Liverpool's Robbie Fowler, Blackburn's Alan Shearer and Leeds' Tony Yeboah all hit trebles.

• Lionel Messi has scored a record four hat-tricks in the Champions League, filling his boots against Arsenal (2010), Viktoria Plzen (2011), Bayer Leverkusen (2012) and Ajax (2013).

EDEN HAZARD

Born: Louviere, Belgium, 7th January 1991
Position: Midfielder
Club career:
2007-12 Lille 147 (36)
2012- Chelsea 69 (23)
International record:
2008- Belgium 50 (6)

A creative midfielder who possesses wonderful dribbling skills, Eden Hazard was voted PFA Young Player of the Year and finished second behind Luis Suarez for the main Player of the Year award after an exceptional 2013/14 campaign with Chelsea.

"Dear God, please make me as good as my hero, Zinedine Zidane!"

• The son of footballers – his father played in the Belgian second tier, while his mother was a striker in the women's league – Hazard joined Lille when he was 14, making his debut for the first team just two years later. In his first full season, 2008/09, he became the first non-French player to win the Young Player of the Year award. He scooped the award again the following season to become the first player to win it twice.

• In 2011, after completing a league and cup double with Lille, Hazard was voted Player of the Year – aged 20, he was the youngest player to win the award. He topped the poll again the following year to become only the second player to retain the trophy.

• After signing for Chelsea for £32 million in May 2012, Hazard's eye-catching performances in his first season at Stamford Bridge saw him voted into the PFA Team of the Year. However, his temperament was questioned by some pundits after he was stupidly sent off in the League Cup semi-final against Swansea for kicking the ball from underneath the body of a time-wasting ball boy.

• Hazard was first capped by Belgium, aged 17, against Luxembourg in 2008. He hasn't always been able to transfer his scintillating club form to the international stage, however, and in 2011 he was criticised for leaving the stadium after being substituted against Turkey, choosing to eat a burger with his family rather than watch the rest of the match.

HEADERS

In 2011 Ryujiro Ueda, a defender with Fagiano Okayama, scored with a header from 58.6 metres in a J-League match against Yokohama to set a record for the longest distance headed goal. He was helped, though, by some dodgy goalkeeping, the Yokohama keeper allowing the ball to bounce over his head and dribble into the net.

• **Huddersfield striker Jordan Rhodes scored the fastest headed hat-trick in Football League history in 2009, nodding in three goals against Exeter City in eight minutes and 23 seconds to smash a record previously held by Everton legend Dixie Dean.**

• Alan Shearer holds the Premier League record for headed goals with 46 for Blackburn Rovers and Newcastle. At the opposite end of the scale, Fulham's Damien Duff has scored the most Premier League goals, 53, without once netting with his head.

• **A record 26 out of a total 76 goals were scored from headers at the 2012 European Championships in Poland and Ukraine.**

HEART OF MIDLOTHIAN

Year founded: 1874
Ground: Tynecastle (17,529)
Nickname: Hearts
Biggest win: 21-0 v Anchor (1880)
Heaviest defeat: 1-8 v Vale of Leven (1883)

Hearts were founded in 1874, taking their unusual and romantic-sounding name from a popular local dance hall which, in turn, was named after the famous novel *The Heart of the Midlothian* by Sir Walter Scott. The club were founder members of the Scottish league in 1890, winning their first title just five years later.

IS THAT A FACT?
The only post-war FA Cup final to feature three headed goals was in 1964 when Geoff Hurst and Ronnie Boyce nodded in for West Ham, with Alex Dawson replying for Preston in the Hammers' 3-2 victory.

Robin van Persie's brilliant header against Spain at the 2014 World Cup went so high it disappeared off this page!

• Now slumming it in the Scottish Championship following relegation from the SPL in 2014, the club enjoyed a golden era in the late 1950s and early 1960s, when they won two league championships and five cups. In the first of those title triumphs in 1958 Hearts scored 132 goals, many of them coming from the so-called 'Terrible Trio' of Alfie Conn, Willie Bauld and Jimmy Wardhaugh. The total is still a record for the top flight in Scotland. In the same year Hearts conceded just 29 goals, giving them the best ever goal difference in British football, an incredible 103.

• In 1965 Hearts came agonisingly close to winning the championship again when they were pipped by Kilmarnock on goal average after losing 2-0 at home to their title rivals on the last day of the season. Twenty-one years later they suffered a similar fate, losing the title on goal difference to Celtic after a surprise last-day defeat against Dundee. Annoyingly for their fans, on both occasions Hearts would have won the title if the alternative method for separating teams level on points had been in use.

• The club's record goalscorer is **John Robertson with 214 goals between 1983 and 1998. Midfielder Gary Mackay made a record 640 appearances for Hearts between 1980 and 1997.**

• Hearts won the Scottish Cup in 2012, thrashing local rivals Hibs 5-1 in the final at Hampden Park – the biggest victory in the final since Hearts themselves were tonked by the same score by Rangers in 1996. It was the eighth time that Hearts had won the Scottish Cup, making them the fourth most successful club in the competition after Celtic, Rangers and Queen's Park.

• Hearts' Scott Robinson is the youngest player ever to appear in the SPL, making his debut as a sub against Inverness Caledonian Thistle on 26th April 2008 when aged just 16 and 45 days.

HONOURS
Division 1 champions 1895, 1897, 1958, 1960
First Division champions 1980
Scottish Cup 1891, 1896, 1901, 1906, 1956, 1998, 2006, 2012
League Cup 1955, 1959, 1960, 1963

THIERRY HENRY

Born: Paris, 17th August 1977
Position: Striker
Club career:
1994-98 Monaco 105 (20)
1999 Juventus 16 (3)
1999-2007 Arsenal 254 (174)
2007-10 Barcelona 80 (35)
2010- New York Red Bulls 113 (48)
2012 Arsenal (loan) 4 (2)
International record:
1997-2010 France 123 (51)

Arguably Arsenal's greatest ever player, Thierry Henry is the Gunners' all-time top goalscorer. During an eight-year stay in north London after signing from Juventus for a bargain £10.5 million in 1999 he scored 224 goals, many of them memorable ones. He briefly returned to Arsenal on loan from New York Red Bulls in 2012, adding two more goals to his Gunners account.

• **Frighteningly quick and a reliably clinical finisher, Henry started out with Monaco and helped the club win the French title in 1997. He was even more successful at Arsenal, winning two league titles and three FA Cups, and in 2006 become the first ever player to win the Footballer of the Year award three times. The following year he joined Barcelona, with whom he won the Spanish league title and the Champions League in 2009.**

• Henry's total of 175 league goals for Arsenal puts him third in the list of all-time Premier League scorers behind Alan Shearer and Andy Cole. In both 2004 and 2005 he won the European Golden Boot, sharing the award with Villarreal's Diego Forlan in 2005.

• **A member of the French squad that won the World Cup in 1998, Henry collected a European Championships winners' medal two years later. In 2006 he had to settle for a runners'-up medal in the World Cup final.**

• With 51 international goals to his name, Henry is easily France's record scorer. Capped 123 times, he stands second behind Lilian Thuram in France's all-time top appearance makers.

Thierry Henry, Arsenal's record goalscorer

ANDER HERRERA

Born: Bilbao, Spain, 14th August 1989
Position: Midfielder
Club career:
2008-09 Zaragoza B 10 (2)
2009-11 Zaragoza 82 (6)
2011-14 Athletic Bilbao 94 (7)
2014- Manchester United

Manchester United ended a year-long quest to sign Ander Herrera when Athletic Bilbao finally accepted a £29 million bid from the Red Devils in July 2014. The tenacious midfielder had previously been a transfer target for former United boss David Moyes after impressing against the Premier League club in the Europa League in 2012.
• **After starting out with Zaragoza,**

Herrera joined his hometown club Athletic Bilbao in 2011. In his first season with the Basque outfit he helped them reach the final of the Europa League and the Copa del Rey, where they were beaten by Atletico Madrid and Barcelona respectively.
• Although uncapped at senior level, Herrera has played for Spain's Under-20, Under-21 and Under-23 teams. In 2011

Ander Herrera is finally in a Manchester United shirt, a year after the club first took a shine to him!

he scored in the final of the European Under-21 championship against Switzerland in a 2-0 victory.

• Herrera's father, Pedro, was also a footballer, playing as a midfielder for Zaragoza in the 1980s.

HIBERNIAN

Year founded: 1875
Ground: Easter Road (20,421)
Previous name: Hibernians
Nickname: Hibs
Biggest win: 22-1 v 42nd Highlanders (1881)
Heaviest defeat: 0-10 v Rangers (1898)

Hibs hope to be flying out of the Scottish Championship in 2015

Founded in 1875 by Irish immigrants, the club took its name from the Roman word for Ireland, Hibernia. After losing many players to Celtic the club disbanded in 1891, but reformed and joined the Scottish League two years later.

• Hibs won the Scottish Cup for the first time in 1887 and lifted the same trophy again in 1902. Since then, however, the club have reached the final on a further 10 occasions, most recently in 2013 when they lost to Celtic, but failed to win once.

• The club enjoyed a golden era after the Second World War, winning the league championship in three out of five seasons between 1948 and 1952 with a side managed by Hugh Shaw that included the 'Famous Five' forward line of Bobby Johnstone, Willie Ormond, Lawrie Reilly, Gordon Smith and Willie Turnbull. All of the Famous Five went on to score 100 league goals for Hibs, a feat only achieved for the club since by Joe Baker.

• In 1955 Hibs became the first British side to enter the European Cup, having been invited to participate in the new competition partly because their Easter Road ground had floodlights. They did Scotland proud, reaching the semi-finals of the competition before falling 3-0 on aggregate to French side Rheims.

• Hibs hold the British record for the biggest away win, thrashing Airdrie 11-1 on their own patch on 24th October 1959. As if to prove that astonishing result was no fluke, they also hit double figures at Partick later that season, winning 10-2.

• When Joe Baker made his international debut against Northern Ireland in 1959 he became the first man to represent England while playing for a Scottish club. In the same season Baker scored an incredible 42 goals in just 33 league games to set a club record.

• In 2014 Hibs became the first club to drop into the Championship under the new promotion/relegation play-off system after losing on penalties to Hamilton Academical.

HONOURS
Division 1 champions *1903, 1948, 1951, 1952*
Division 2 champions *1894, 1895, 1933*
First Division champions *1981, 1999*
Scottish Cup *1887, 1902*
League Cup *1972, 1991, 2007*

GLENN HODDLE

Born: Hayes, 27th October 1957
Position: Midfielder
Club career:
1975-87 Tottenham Hotspur 377 (88)
1987-90 Monaco 69 (27)
1991-93 Swindon Town 64 (1)
1993-95 Chelsea 31 (1)
International record:
1979-88 England 53 (8)

An extravagantly gifted midfielder, Glenn Hoddle gained 53 caps for England and might have won many more but for doubts about his work-rate and tackling ability.

• During a 12-year playing career with Tottenham Hotspur, Hoddle won the FA Cup twice (in 1981 and 1982) and the UEFA Cup (in 1984). He joined Monaco in 1987, where he played under Arsène Wenger, and the following year became the first Englishman to be part of a championship-winning side in France. "I couldn't understand why he hadn't been appreciated in England," Wenger said of him. "Perhaps he was a star in the wrong period, years ahead of his time."

• As player-manager of Swindon, Hoddle led the Wiltshire club into the top flight for the first time in their history in 1993. In the same role at Chelsea the following year he guided the Blues to their first FA Cup final for nearly a quarter of a century.

• In May 1996 Hoddle was appointed England manager, succeeding Terry Venables after Euro '96. Aged 38, he was the youngest man to fill the position since Walter Winterbottom.

• Hoddle led England to the 1998 World Cup in France, where they were unlucky to lose to Argentina in a penalty shoot-out. The following year, though, he was dismissed from the job after suggesting in a newspaper interview that disabled people were somehow paying for sins committed in a previous life. He has subsequently managed Southampton, Tottenham and Wolves, and in August 2014 was appointed first-team coach at QPR.

ROY HODGSON

Born: Croydon, 9th August 1947
Managerial career:
1976-80 Halmstads
1982 Bristol City
1983-85 Orebro
1985-90 Malmo
1990-92 Neuchatel Xamax
1992-95 Switzerland
1995-97 Inter Milan
1997-98 Blackburn Rovers
1999 Inter Milan
1999-2000 Grasshoppers
2000-01 Copenhagen
2001 Udinese
2002-04 United Arab Emirates
2004-05 Viking
2006-07 Finland
2007-2010 Fulham
2010-11 Liverpool
2011-12 West Bromwich Albion
2012- England

England boss Roy Hodgson holds the unwanted record of overseeing the Three Lions' worst ever World Cup showing after his side failed to win any of their three group games at the 2014 tournament in Brazil.

• Hodgson is the oldest man to be appointed England manager, taking charge of the Three Lions in May 2012 at the age of 64 and then leading them to the quarter-finals of the European Championships. He is also the first England boss to have international experience, having previously managed Switzerland, United Arab Emirates and Finland.

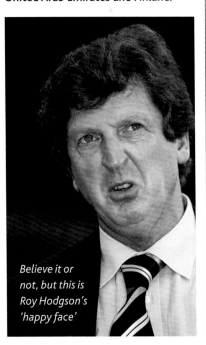

Believe it or not, but this is Roy Hodgson's 'happy face'

• After failing to make the grade as a player at Crystal Palace, Hodgson spent much of his early managerial career in Sweden. He won the title with Halmstads in 1979 before leading Malmo to a Swedish record five consecutive championships between 1985 and 1989.

• Hodgson has enjoyed mixed fortunes with Premier League clubs, being sacked by both Blackburn and Liverpool after brief spells at the helm of those clubs, but doing much better with Fulham and West Brom. His time at Liverpool in the 2010/11 season was particularly forgettable, as he led the Reds to their worst start in 82 years and was eventually shown the door after just 31 games in charge, making his the shortest managerial reign in the history of the Anfield club.

• His three-year stint at his previous club, Fulham, on the other hand, was much happier. In his first season at Craven Cottage Hodgson guided his team to an unlikely escape from relegation after the west Londoners won their final three Premier League fixtures. Two years later, in 2010, he easily topped that achievement by taking Fulham to the Europa League final. Although the Cottagers lost out to Atletico Madrid, Hodgson picked up the League Managers' Association Manager of the Year award for his efforts.

• His other great success came with Switzerland, who he took to the last 16 of the World Cup in 1994 – the country's best performance for 40 years. Hodgson also earned plaudits during two spells with Inter Milan, taking the Italian giants to the UEFA Cup final in 1997, where they were beaten on penalties by Schalke.

HOME AND AWAY

Brentford hold the all-time record for home wins in a season. In 1929/30 the Bees won all 21 of their home games at Griffin Park in Division Three (South). However, their away form was so poor they missed out on promotion to champions Plymouth.

• Chelsea hold the record for the longest unbeaten home run in the league, remaining undefeated at Stamford Bridge between February 2004 and October 2008. Ironically, the Blues' 86-game run was eventually broken by Liverpool, the previous holders of the same record.

• Arsenal hold the record for the most consecutive away wins, with 12 in the Premier League in 2013. The highest number of straight home wins is 25, a record set by Bradford Park Avenue in the Third Division (North) in 1926/27.

• Manchester United hold the record for both the biggest home and away Premier League victories, beating Ipswich 9-0 at Old Trafford in 1995 and winning 8-1 at Nottingham Forest in 1999.

• Millwall scored a record 87 goals at home in 1927/28, a total which helped the London club top the Third Division (South) table that season. The away record is held by Arsenal, who scored 60 goals on their travels in their 1930/31 championship-winning campaign.

• Manchester United conceded a record low of four goals in the Premier League in 1994/95, while Chelsea let in just nine goals on their travels in 2004/05.

HUDDERSFIELD TOWN

Year founded: 1908
Ground: John Smith's Stadium (24,500)
Nickname: The Terriers
Biggest win: 11-0 v Heckmondwike (1909)
Heaviest defeat: 1-10 v Manchester City (1987)

Huddersfield Town were founded in 1908 following a meeting held at the local Imperial Hotel some two years earlier – it took the club that long to find a ground to play at! The club were elected to the Second Division of the Football League two years later.

• The Terriers enjoyed a golden era in the 1920s when, under the

IS THAT A FACT?
Liverpool scored a Premier League record 48 away goals in the 2013/14 season. Chelsea hold the home record after banging in an impressive 68 goals at Stamford Bridge in their 2009/10 Double-winning season.

shrewd management of the legendary Herbert Chapman, they won three consecutive league titles between 1924 and 1926 – no other club had matched this feat at the time and only three have done so since. The Terriers also won the FA Cup in 1922.

• Huddersfield won the first of their league titles in 1924 by pipping Cardiff City on goal average, the first time the champions had been decided by this method.

• **The early 1970s were a desperate time for Huddersfield, who slumped from the First to the Fourth Division in just four seasons, becoming the first league champions to be relegated to the bottom tier.**

• However, recent seasons have been happier for the Terriers, who made it back into the Championship in 2012 after a dramatic penalty shoot-out play-off victory over Yorkshire rivals Sheffield United at Wembley. With both sides taking 11 spot-kicks it was the longest shoot-out in play-off history. Huddersfield's promotion push was helped by a Football League record unbeaten run of 43 games during most of 2011.

• **Outside left Billy Smith made a record 521 appearances, scoring 114 goals, for Huddersfield between 1913 and 1934. Smith and his son, Conway,** who started out with the Terriers before playing for QPR and Halifax, were the first father and son to both hit a century of goals in league football.

• The Terriers smashed their transfer record in January 2014 when they forked out £5 million for Bradford City's Bermudan international striker Nahki Wells. The club's coffers were boosted by a record £8 million in 2012 when prolific striker Jordan Rhodes joined Blackburn.

> **HONOURS**
> *Division 1 champions 1924, 1925, 1926*
> *Division 2 champions 1970*
> *Division 4 champions 1980*
> *FA Cup 1922*

HULL CITY

Year founded: 1904
Ground: KC Stadium (25,586)
Nickname: The Tigers
Biggest win: 11-1 v Carlisle United (1939)
Heaviest defeat: 0-8 v Wolves (1911)

Hull City were formed in 1904, originally sharing a ground with the local rugby league club. The club joined the Football League in 1905 but failed to achieve promotion to the top flight until 2008.

• Hull enjoyed their best ever moment when they reached their first ever cup final in 2014 after a thrilling 5-3 victory over Sheffield United in the FA Cup semi-final. In the final against Arsenal at Wembley the Tigers roared into a shock 2-0 lead, but eventually went down 3-2 after extra-time. Nonetheless, Hull's cup exploits meant they competed in European competition for the first time in their history in 2014/15.

• **The 2013/14 season was a great one all round for Hull fans, as their team finished a best ever 16th in the Premier League. The Tigers first made it into the top flight in 2008 thanks to a play-off final victory over Bristol City, with local boy Dean Windass scoring the vital goal. The triumph meant that Hull had climbed from the bottom tier to the top in just five seasons – a meteoric rise only bettered in the past by Swansea City and Wimbledon.**

• The club's record goalscorer is Chris Chilton, who banged in 193 league goals in the 1960s and 1970s. His sometime team-mate Andy Davidson has pulled on a Hull shirt more than any other player,

Hull fans had to settle for this replica of the FA Cup after their team lost the 2014 final to Arsenal

HURST

making 520 league appearances between 1952 and 1968.

• In his first spell at Hull between 1991 and 1996, goalkeeper Alan Fettis played a number of games as a striker during an injury crisis. He did pretty well too, scoring two goals!

• In September 2014 Hull splashed a club record £10 million on Palermo striker Abel Hernandez. A month earlier the Tigers received a club record £12 million when striker Shane Long moved to Southampton.

• **Hull were the first team in the world to lose in a penalty shoot-out, Manchester United beating them 4-3 on spot-kicks in the semi-final of the Watney Cup in 1970.**

• The club's record attendance is 55,019 for the visit of Manchester United to Boothferry Park in the sixth round of the FA Cup in 1949. In 2002 Hull moved to the much more compact KC Stadium (which they share with rugby league side Hull FC), so it's a record that's unlikely to be beaten.

Was it over the line? Geoff Hurst's second goal in the 1966 World Cup final still annoys Germans to this day

SIR GEOFF HURST

Born: Ashton-under-Lyme, 8th December 1941
Position: Striker
Club career:
1959-72 West Ham United 410 (180)
1972-75 Stoke City 108 (30)
1975-76 West Bromwich Albion 10 (2)
1976 Seattle Sounders 24 (9)
International record:
1966-72 England 49 (24)

Geoff Hurst is the only player to have scored a hat-trick in the World Cup final. His famous treble against West Germany at Wembley helped England to a legendary 4-2 triumph in 1966, although his second goal remains one of the most controversial of all time as the Germans claimed the ball didn't cross the line after Hurst's shot bounced down off the underside of the crossbar.

• Along with Ian Rush, Hurst is the leading scorer in the history of the League Cup with an impressive total of 49 goals. He is also the last player to hit six goals in a top-flight league match, netting a double hat-trick in West Ham's 8-0 thrashing of Sunderland at Upton Park in 1968.

• A well-built centre-forward who was strong in the air and possessed a powerful shot, Hurst won an FA Cup winners' medal with West Ham in 1964 and, the following year, helped the Hammers win the European Cup Winners' Cup.

• **In 1979 he was appointed manager of Second Division side Chelsea, but was sacked two years later after a dismal run of results. However, Hurst's great achievements on the pitch remain part of English folklore and earned him a knighthood in 1998.**

ZLATAN IBRAHIMOVIC

Born: Malmo, Sweden, 3rd October 1981
Position: Striker
Club career:
1999-2001 Malmo 40 (16)
2001-04 Ajax 74 (35)
2004-06 Juventus 70 (23)
2006-09 Inter Milan 88 (57)
2009-11 Barcelona 29 (16)
2010-11 AC Milan (loan) 29 (14)
2011-12 AC Milan 32 (28)
2012- Paris St Germain 67 (56)
International record:
2001- Sweden 98 (48)

An exceptionally gifted striker with an individualistic style of play, Sweden captain Zlatan Ibrahimovic is the only player to have won league titles with six different European clubs.

• His incredible run began with Ajax, who he had joined from his first club Malmo in 2001, when the Amsterdam giants won the Dutch league in 2004. Ibrahomivic's golden touch continued with his next club, Juventus, where he won back-to-back Serie A titles, although these were later scrubbed from the record books following Juve's involvement in a match-fixing scandal.

• At his next club, Inter Milan, Ibrahimovic fared even better, helping the Nerazzurri win a hat-trick of titles in 2007, 2008 and 2009. He then moved to Barcelona, with Samuel Eto'o joining Inter as part of the deal, and, despite failing to see eye-to-eye with Barca boss Pep Guardiola, won a La Liga title medal in 2010. Returning to Italy, his astonishing run of success continued with AC Milan, who were crowned Serie A champions in 2011.

• In the summer of 2012 Ibrahimovic was transferred to newly moneyed Paris St Germain for £31 million, taking his combined transfer fee up to a world record £150 million, the highest for any player ever. In a tremendous first season with PSG he won the league title and was voted Ligue 1 Player of the Year. He repeated these feats in 2013/14, scoring 40 goals in all competitions to set a new club record.

• With 48 international goals to his name, Ibrahimovic is just one behind his country's all-time top scorer, Sven Rydell.

• In November 2012 he became the first player ever to score four goals in a match against England, when he starred in his country's 4-2 friendly win over Roy Hodgson's side. His fourth goal, a spectacular 35-yard overhead kick, was one of his greatest ever and won the 2013 FIFA Puskas Award for Goal of the Year.

"Now, let me think. Who is the only player to score four goals in a game against England..."

Andres Iniesta on the ball – as usual!

ANDRES INIESTA

Born: Albacete, Spain, 11th May 1984
Position: Midfielder
Club career:
2001–03 Barcelona B 54 (5)
2002– Barcelona 337 (33)
International record:
2006– Spain 100 (11)

Attacking midfielder Andres Iniesta became an iconic figure for the whole Spanish nation when he scored the winning goal in the 2010 World Cup final against Holland at Soccer City Stadium in Johannesburg. To cap a great day for the Barcelona star, he also picked up the Man of the Match award and was shortlisted for the Golden Ball.

• Nicknamed 'El Cerebro' ('The Brain') for his brilliant reading of the game,

Iniesta made his debut for Spain in 2006 and scored his first goal for his country the following year in a 1-0 friendly win against England at Old Trafford. In 2008 he helped Spain win their first major honour for 44 years, the European Championships in Austria and Switzerland, and four years later he picked up the Player of the Tournament award as Spain retained the trophy in Poland and the Ukraine. However, he failed to shine at the 2014 World Cup, although he did collect his 100th cap in a 3-0 defeat of Australia.

• A product of the Barcelona youth system, La Masia, he is now revered as one of the great Spanish players of his generation. As well as his international honours, Iniesta has won six league titles with Barca, plus a hat-trick of Champions League titles in 2006, 2009 and 2011.

• Iniesta is the fifth highest appearance maker in Barcelona's illustrious history, playing in 508 matches in all competitions for the Catalan giants.

INTER MILAN

Year founded: 1908
Ground: San Siro (80,018)
Nickname: Nerazzurri (The black and blues)
League titles: 18
Domestic cups: 7
European cups: 6
International cups: 3

Founded in 1908 as a breakaway club from AC Milan, Internazionale (as they are known locally) are the only Italian team never to have been relegated from Serie A. The dominant force in Italian football in the last decade, Inter have 18 title wins to their name – a total only bettered by Juventus.

• Inter were the first Italian club to win the European Cup twice, beating the mighty Real Madrid 3-1 in the 1964 final before recording a 1-0 defeat of Benfica the following year. They had to wait 45 years, though, before making it a hat-trick with a 2-0 defeat of Bayern Munich in Madrid in 2010 – a victory that, with the domestic league and cup already in the bag, secured Inter their first ever treble.

• Under legendary manager Helenio Herrera, Inter introduced the 'catenaccio' defensive system to world football in the 1960s. Playing with a sweeper behind two man-markers, Inter conceded very few goals as they powered to three league titles between 1963 and 1966.

• The club endured a barren period domestically until they were awarded their first Serie A title for 17 years in 2006 after Juventus and AC Milan, who had both finished above them in the league table, had points deducted for their roles in a match-fixing scandal. Inter went on to win the championship in more conventional style in the following four years – the last two of these triumphs coming under Jose Mourinho – to equal Juventus' record of five consecutive triumphs in the 1930s.

• On their way to claiming the title in 2005/06 Inter won 17 consecutive matches to set a new Serie A record.

HONORS

HONOURS
Italian champions 1910, 1920, 1930, 1938, 1940, 1953, 1954, 1963, 1965, 1966, 1971, 1980, 1989, 2006, 2007, 2008, 2009, 2010
Italian Cup 1939, 1978, 1982, 2005, 2006, 2010, 2011
European Cup/Champions League 1964, 1965, 2010
UEFA Cup 1991, 1994, 1998
Intercontinental Cup/Club World Cup 1964, 1965, 2010

INVERNESS CALEDONIAN THISTLE

Year founded: 1994
Ground: Caledonian Stadium (7,800)
Previous name: Caledonian Thistle
Nickname: Caley Thistle
Biggest win: 8-1 v Annan Athletic (1998)
Heaviest defeat: 0-6 v Airdrie (2001), v Celtic (2010 and 2014)

Founded as Caledonian Thistle in 1994 following the amalgamation of Highland league sides Caledonian and Inverness Thistle, the club was elected to the Scottish Third Division in the same year. In 1996, at the request of Inverness District Council, the club added 'Inverness' to its name.
• **The club has steadily climbed up the league ladder in the years since, eventually gaining promotion to the SPL in 2004 after winning the First Division title. Caley were relegated from the SPL in 2009, but bounced back the following season – the first club for a decade to make such a swift return.**
• In February 2000 Thistle pulled off one of the biggest ever shocks in the Scottish Cup when they beat Celtic 3-1 in the third round at Parkhead. *The Sun* newspaper reported this famous giant-killing under the witty headline "Super Caley go ballistic, Celtic are atrocious".
• **Incredibly, Caley went 'ballistic' again in 2003 when they knocked Celtic out of the cup for a second time, winning 1-0 at their tiny Caledonian Stadium. The club went on to reach the semi-**

final of the Scottish Cup for the first time in their history, before losing to Dundee. The following season they got to the semi-finals again, only to be beaten by Dunfermline in a replay.
• Caley finally reached a major cup final in 2014, but it wasn't a great day for their fans as they lost on penalties to Aberdeen in the League Cup final at Celtic Park.

HONOURS
First Division champions 2004, 2010
Third Division champions 1997

IPSWICH TOWN

Year founded: 1878
Ground: Portman Road (30,311)
Nickname: The Blues
Biggest win: 10-0 v Floriana (1962)
Heaviest defeat: 1-10 v Fulham (1963)

The club was founded at a meeting at the town hall in 1878 but did not join the Football League until 1938, two years after turning professional.
• **Ipswich were the last of just four clubs to win the old Second and First Division titles in consecutive seasons, pulling off this remarkable feat in 1962 under future England manager Alf Ramsey. The team's success owed much to the strike partnership of Ray Crawford and Ted Phillips, who together scored 61 of the club's 93 goals during the title-winning campaign.**
• Two years after that title win, though,

Ipswich were relegated after conceding 121 goals – only Blackpool in 1930/31 (125 goals against) have had a worse defensive record in the top flight. The Blues' worst defeat in a season to forget was a 10-1 hammering at Fulham, the last time a team has conceded double figures in a top-flight match.
• **However, the club enjoyed more success under Bobby Robson, another man who went on to manage England, in the following two decades. In 1978 Ipswich won the FA Cup, beating favourites Arsenal 1-0 in the final at Wembley, and three years later they won the UEFA Cup with attacking midfielder John Wark contributing a then record 14 goals during the club's continental campaign.**
• Ipswich have the best home record in European competition of any club, remaining undefeated at Portman Road in 31 games since making their debut in the European Cup in 1962 with a 10-0 hammering of Maltese side Floriana – the Blues' biggest win in their history.
• **With 203 goals for the Tractor Boys between 1958 and 1969, Ray Crawford is the club's record goalscorer. Mick Mills is the club's record appearance maker, turning out 591 times between 1966 and 1982. Another defender from that era, Allan Hunter, is Ipswich's most capped international, winning 47 of his 53 caps for Northern Ireland while at Portman Road.**

HONOURS
Division 1 champions 1962
Division 2 champions 1961
Division 3 (S) champions 1954, 1957
FA Cup 1978
UEFA Cup 1981

Long hair was still all the rage in Ipswich when they won the FA Cup in 1978

Hopefully, Italy fans' scary mask craze won't be coming to the Premier League any time soon

ITALY

First international: Italy 6 France 2, 1910
Most capped player: Gianluigi Buffon, 142 caps (1997-)
Leading goalscorer: Luigi Riva, 35 goals (1965-74)
First World Cup appearance: Italy 7 USA 1, 1934
Biggest win: Italy 11 Egypt 3, 1928
Heaviest defeat: Hungary 7 Italy 1, 1924

Italy have the joint best record of any European nation at the World Cup, having won the tournament four times (in 1934, 1938, 1982 and 2006). Only Brazil, with five wins, have done better in the competition.

• The Azzurri, as they are known to their passionate fans, are the only country to have been involved in two World Cup final penalty shoot-outs. In 1994 they lost out to Brazil, but in 2006 they beat France on penalties after a 1-1 draw in the final in Berlin.

• When Italy won 1-0 at Wembley in 1997 in a World Cup qualifier, they became the first country to beat England on home soil in a World Cup match.

• The most humiliating moment in Italy's sporting history came in 1966 when they lost 1-0 to minnows North Korea at the World Cup in England. The Italians had a remarkably similar embarrassment at the 2002 tournament when they were knocked out by hosts South Korea after a 2-1 defeat. Fortunately for the Azzurri, neither 'East Korea' or 'West Korea' exist as independent countries!

• To the dismay of their fans, Italy had another World Cup to forget in 2010 when they defended their trophy in lamentable style, finishing bottom of their group behind Paraguay, Slovakia and, most embarrassingly, New Zealand.

IS THAT A FACT?

Italy have the best record of any country in the world against Germany, having won 16 and drawn 12 of the nations' 36 meetings. The Italians' wins in these encounters included three memorable ones at the World Cup: in the 1982 final and the 1970 and 2006 semi-finals.

• Italy have won the European Championships just once, beating Yugoslavia 2-0 in the final in Rome in 1968. They reached the final again in 2000 but lost to France, and endured more disappointment in 2012 when they were hammered 4-0 by Spain in the final in Kiev.

HONOURS
World Cup *1934, 1938, 1982, 2006*
European Championships *1968*
World Cup record
1930 Did not enter
1934 Winners
1938 Winners
1950 Round 1
1954 Round 1
1958 Did not qualify
1962 Round 1
1966 Round 1
1970 Runners-up
1974 Round 1
1978 Fourth place
1982 Winners
1986 Round 2
1990 Third place
1994 Runners-up
1998 Quarter-finals
2002 Round 2
2006 Winners
2010 Round 1
2014 Round 1

ADNAN JANUZAJ

Born: Brussels, Belgium, 5th February 1995
Position: Midfielder
Club career:
2013- Manchester United 27 (4)
International record:
2014- Belgium 2 (0)

After an excellent first season in Manchester United's senior team in 2013/14, Adnan Januzaj has emerged as one of the most talented young players in the Premier League.

• Born in Brussels, Januzaj started his career in Anderlecht's youth academy before moving to Old Trafford aged 16. He made his debut for the Red Devils as a sub in the 2013 Community Shield against Wigan Athletic, before scoring two goals in a 2-1 win at Sunderland in his first Premier League start.

• Januzaj's eye-catching performances in United's midfield saw him nominated for the BBC's Young Sports Personality of the Year award. Less impressively, three bookings for 'simulation' saw him earn an unwanted reputation for diving in the opponents' penalty area.

• A cosmopolitan family background meant that Januzaj was eligible to play for Albania, Belgium, Serbia and Turkey at international level. He would even have been eligible to play for England in 2018 after residing in the country for five years and was strongly courted by the FA. But, after turning down a number of approaches from Belgium, he finally committed himself to his birth nation in April 2014 and made his debut as a sub the following month in a World Cup warm-up against Tunisia.

GLEN JOHNSON

Born: Dartford, 23rd August 1984
Position: Defender
Club career:
2001-03 West Ham United 15 (0)
2002 Millwall (loan) 8 (0)
2003-07 Chelsea 42 (3)
2006-07 Portsmouth (loan) 26 (0)
2007-09 Portsmouth 68 (5)
2009- Liverpool 141 (7)
International record:
2003- England 54 (1)

An attacking right-back who spends as much time in the opposition half as his own team's, Glen Johnson became the first ever defender to win the BBC's Goal of the Season award, topping the poll in 2009 for a stunning 35-yard strike for Portsmouth against Hull City.

• Johnson started his career with West Ham, before becoming the first player to be signed by Chelsea during the Roman Abramovich era in the summer of 2003. He won the League Cup with the Blues in 2005 but, after losing his place in the team, he was allowed to join Portsmouth, initially on loan.

• He helped Pompey win the FA Cup in 2008, but the following year was on the move again, joining Liverpool for a cool £17 million. He collected his first medal with the Reds in 2012 when Liverpool beat Cardiff in the League Cup final, Johnson scoring from the spot in the penalty shoot-out.

• Johnson made his debut for England as a substitute against Denmark in November 2003. He took some time to establish himself in the team, but is now recognised as his country's first-choice right-back. Despite not performing brilliantly at the 2014 World Cup, Johnson had the satisfaction of setting up Wayne Rooney's goal against Uruguay in a 2-1 group stage loss.

JUVENTUS

Year founded: 1897
Ground: Juventus Stadium (41,000)
Nickname: The Zebras
League titles: 30
Domestic cups: 9
European cups: 8
International cups: 2

The most famous and the most successful club in Italy, Juventus were founded in 1897 by pupils at a school in Turin – hence the team's name, which means 'youth' in Latin. Six years later the club binned their original pink shirts and adopted their distinctive black-and-white-striped kit after an English member of the team had a set of Notts County shirts shipped out to Italy.

• Juventus emerged as the dominant force in Italian football in the 1930s when they won five titles in a row. They have a record 30 titles to their name and are the only team in Italy allowed to wear two gold stars on their shirts, signifying 20 Serie A victories. Juve won the league in 2013/14 with an incredible 102 points – the highest points tally ever in any of Europe's top 10 leagues.

Andrea Pirlo of Juventus, the most successful club in Italy

IS THAT A FACT?
Juventus have won more Serie A matches (1,408) and scored more goals (4,577) than any other Italian club.

• When, thanks to a single goal by their star player Michel Platini, Juventus beat Liverpool in the European Cup final in 1985 they became the first ever club to win all three European trophies. However, their triumph at the Heysel Stadium in Brussels was overshadowed by the death of 39 of their fans, who were crushed to death as they tried to flee from crowd trouble before the kick-off.

• **Juventus have won the Italian Cup nine times, a record matched only by Roma, although they haven't raised the trophy for nearly a decade since their last success in 1995.**

• Juventus legend Alessandro del Piero is the club's leading scorer with an incredible 208 goals in Serie A in 513 matches (also a club record) between 1993 and 2012.

• **Juventus striker Enrique Omar Sivori holds the record for the most goals by a player in a Serie A match, with six in an incredible 9-1 thrashing of Inter Milan in 1961.**

• Players from the British Isles to wear Juve's famous black-and-white stripes include Welsh legends John Charles and Ian Rush, and Republic of Ireland midfielder Liam Brady.

HONOURS
Italian champions 1905, 1926, 1931, 1932, 1933, 1934, 1935, 1950, 1952, 1958, 1960, 1961, 1967, 1972, 1973, 1975, 1977, 1978, 1981, 1982, 1984, 1986, 1995, 1997, 1998, 2002, 2003, 2012, 2013, 2014
Italian Cup 1938, 1942, 1959, 1960, 1965, 1979, 1983, 1990, 1995
European Cup/Champions League 1985, 1996
European Cup Winners' Cup 1984
UEFA Cup 1977, 1990, 1993
European Super Cup 1984, 1996
Club World Cup 1985, 1996

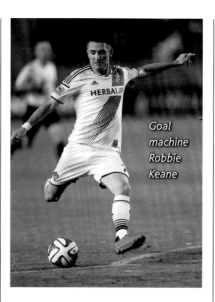

Goal machine Robbie Keane

ROBBIE KEANE

Born: Dublin, 8th July 1980
Position: Striker
Club career:
1997-99 Wolves 74 (24)
1999-2000 Coventry City 31 (12)
2000-01 Inter Milan 6 (0)
2001 Leeds United (loan) 18 (9)
2001-02 Leeds United 28 (4)
2002-08 Tottenham Hotspur 197 (80)
2008-09 Liverpool 19 (5)
2009-11 Tottenham Hotspur 41 (11)
2010 Celtic (loan) 16 (12)
2011 West Ham United (loan) 9 (2)
2011- LA Galaxy 81 (49)
2012 Aston Villa (loan) 6 (3)
International record:
1998- Republic of Ireland 133 (62)

Livewire striker Robbie Keane is the Republic of Ireland's all-time top scorer and highest appearance maker. His record of 62 goals for his country since making his debut in 1998 puts him in fifth place in the all-time list of European international goalscorers.

• **Keane began his club career with Wolves, for whom he scored twice on his debut against Norwich in 1997. Two years later, aged 19, he joined Coventry City for £6 million – then a record fee for a teenager.**

• After brief spells with Inter Milan and Leeds, Keane moved to Tottenham in 2002. While at White Hart Lane he finally won the first trophy of his career, the Carling Cup in 2007/08 – a season in which he hit a personal best 23 goals in all competitions.

• **His goals record prompted Liverpool to pay £20 million for him in the summer of 2008. It was a dream move**

for Keane, a childhood fan of the Reds, but he was used irregularly by then Liverpool boss Rafa Benitez and, in the January 2009 transfer window, he returned to Tottenham for £15 million. However, he soon found himself surplus to requirements at White Hart Lane and, after loan spells at Celtic and West Ham, Keane signed for LA Galaxy in a £3.5 million deal in the summer of 2011. He briefly returned from America to play on loan at Aston Villa during the second half of the 2011/12 season.

ROY KEANE

Born: Cork, 10th August 1971
Position: Midfielder
Club career:
1989-90 Cobh Ramblers 12 (1)
1990-93 Nottingham Forest 114 (22)
1993-2005 Manchester United 323 (33)
2005-06 Celtic 10 (1)
International record:
1991-2005 Republic of Ireland 66 (9)

Manchester United legend Roy Keane is the club's most successful captain ever, leading the Reds to nine major trophies while wearing the armband between 1997 and 2005.

• **The driving force in United's midfield for over a decade after arriving from Nottingham Forest for a then British record fee of £3.75 million in 1993, Keane won seven league titles and four FA Cups while at Old Trafford but he missed out on the Reds' 1999 Champions League triumph through suspension.**

• A fiery, volatile character, Keane was sent off 13 times during his career – a record for the top flight. He set another unwanted record in 2002 when he was fined £150,000 by the FA for bringing the game into disrepute when he admitted in his autobiography that he had intended to hurt an opponent, Manchester City's Alf-Inge Haaland.

• **Keane starred for the Republic of Ireland at the 1994 World Cup, being named his country's best player. However, before the 2002 tournament in Japan and Korea he stormed out of Ireland's training camp on the Pacific island of Saipan after a furious row with manager Mick McCarthy. Despite the intervention of Irish Prime Minister**

Roy Keane now has two jobs with the Republic of Ireland and Aston Villa (below) – that's a helluva lot of shouting!

with *Head Over Heels* in 1979. The single fared less well in the UK, stalling at number 31.

• Keegan finished his playing days at Newcastle in the early 1980s, returning to St James' Park a decade later as manager. But, after five years in charge, he dramatically quit the club a few months after his entertaining Toon team had narrowly missed out on the Premiership title. A brief second spell in charge of the Geordies ended in similar fashion in 2008 following a long-running disagreement with owner Mike Ashley about the club's management structure.

• **Keegan also walked out on the England job in October 2000 just a few minutes after his team had lost a vital World Cup qualifier to Germany in the last ever match played at the old Wembley. He had only been in charge for 18 months, but had increasingly come under fire after a poor England showing at Euro 2000.**

KICK-OFF

Scottish club Queen's Park claim to have been the first to adopt the traditional kick-off time of 3pm on a Saturday, which allowed those people who worked in the morning time to get to the match.

• **The fastest ever goal from a kick-off was scored in just two seconds by Nawaf Al Abed, a 21-year-old striker for Saudi Arabian side Al Hilal in a cup match against Al Shoalah in 2009. After a team-mate tapped the ball to him, Al Abed struck a fierce left-foot shot from the halfway line which sailed over the opposition keeper and into the net.**

• Ledley King scored the fastest goal in Premier League history, striking just 9.9 seconds after the kick-off for Tottenham against Bradford City on 9th December 2000.

Bertie Ahern, Keane refused to return, although he later played for his country again under new boss Brian Kerr.

• After retiring in 2006 he moved into management with Sunderland and then Ipswich. In 2013 he became assistant manager of the Republic of Ireland, and the following year he took up a similar role at Aston Villa.

KEVIN KEEGAN

Born: Doncaster, 14th February 1951
Position: Striker
Club career:
1968-71 Scunthorpe United 124 (18)
1971-77 Liverpool 230 (68)
1977-80 Hamburg 90 (32)
1980-82 Southampton 68 (37)
1982-84 Newcastle United 78 (48)
International record:
1972-82 England 63 (21)

A busy, all-action striker with a sharp eye for goal, Kevin Keegan is the only British player to have twice been voted European Footballer of the Year and he was only the second player – after the great Johan Cruyff – to win the award in consecutive seasons (1978 and 1979).

• **Keegan was also the first English player to appear in the European Cup final with two different clubs. In 1977 he was a winner with Liverpool against Borussia Monchengladbach, but three years later he had to settle for a runners-up medal after Hamburg were beaten by Nottingham Forest.**

• Uniquely, Keegan's first three England appearances were all against the same opposition, Wales. He went on to win 63 caps, 31 of them as captain.

• Nicknamed 'Mighty Mouse' during his spell with Hamburg, Keegan had a top 10 hit in Germany

IS THAT A FACT?

In a bid to allow their overseas stars to play before jetting off on international duty, Barcelona kicked off their midweek home match against Sevilla in September 2005 at five past midnight. In spite of the ridiculously late start, more than 80,000 fans turned up at the Nou Camp to watch a 1-1 draw.

• The fastest goal in Football League history was scored after just four seconds by Jim Fryatt for Bradford Park Avenue against Tranmere Rovers on 25th April 1964.

• The earliest kick-off in an English match was the FA Cup tie between Burton Swifts and Singers FC (later Coventry City) in 1892. Bizarrely, the match started at 8am at Burton's request, as they wanted to minimise disruption to their league programme.

KILMARNOCK

Year founded: 1869
Ground: Rugby Park (18,128)
Nickname: Killie
Biggest win: 13-2 v Saltcoats Victoria (1896)
Heaviest defeat: 1-9 v Celtic (1938)

The oldest professional club in Scotland, Kilmarnock were founded in 1869 by a group of local cricketers who were keen to play another sport during the winter months. Originally, the club played rugby (hence the name of Kilmarnock's stadium, Rugby Park) before switching to football in 1873.

• That same year Kilmarnock entered the inaugural Scottish Cup and on 18th October 1873 the club took part in the first ever match in the competition, losing 2-0 in the first round to Renton.

• Kilmarnock's greatest moment was back in 1965 when they travelled to championship rivals Hearts on the last day of the season requiring a two-goal win to pip the Edinburgh side to the title on goal average. To the joy of their travelling fans, Killie won 2-0 to claim the title by 0.04 of a goal.

• Kilmarnock have won the Scottish Cup three times, and claimed their first ever League Cup in 2012 when they beat Celtic 1-0 in the final at Hampden Park, Belgian striker Dieter van Tornhout scoring the winning goal six minutes from time.

• Full-back Joe Nibloe, one of a select band of players to win cup medals both north and south of the border, is Kilmarnock's most-capped player with 11 appearances for Scotland between 1929 and 1932.

• With 88 goals for Kilmarnock and 101

Toni Kroos gives Real Madrid's new kit deal the thumbs up

for Rangers, former Killie striker Kris Boyd is the leading goalscorer in the history of the SPL.

HONOURS
Division 1 champions 1965
Division 2 champions 1898, 1899
Scottish Cup 1920, 1929, 1997
Scottish League Cup 2012

KIT DEALS

In July 2014 Manchester United signed the biggest ever kit deal in football history with German company Adidas. The deal, which starts at the beginning of the 2015/16 campaign, will see United paid £750 million over 10 seasons in return for wearing Adidas supplied training and playing kit.

TOP 1

KIT DEALS
1. Manchester United (Adidas) £75 million/year
2. Arsenal (Puma) £34 million/year
3. Real Madrid (Adidas) £31 million/year
4. Chelsea (Adidas) £30 million/year
5. Barcelona (Nike) £27 million/year
6. Liverpool (Warrior) £25 million/year
7. Bayern Munich (Adidas) £21 million/year
8. Juventus (Adidas) £18 million/year
9. AC Milan (Adidas) £14 million/year
10. Manchester City (Nike) £12 million/year

• Outside the Premier League, Real Madrid have the most lucrative kit deal in Europe, pulling in £31 million per year from Adidas – £4 million more than deadly rivals Barcelona receive from Nike.

• Adidas are the biggest spending kit supliers, paying out a colossal £189 million per year for the privilege of providing kit for just six leading European clubs.

VINCENT KOMPANY

Born: Brussels, Belgium, 10th April 1986
Position: Defender
Club career:
2003-06 Anderlecht 73 (6)
2006-08 Hamburg 29 (1)
2008- Manchester City 181 (11)
International record:
2004- Belgium 60 (4)

In 2012 Vincent Kompany became the first Manchester City captain to lift the Premier League title when his team pipped local rivals Manchester United to top spot on the last day of the season. Two years later he repeated the feat, scoring in his side's 2-0 defeat of West Ham which secured the 2014 title on the final day of the season. In the same campaign, he also skippered City to their first triumph in the League Cup for 38 years when they beat Sunderland 3-1 in the final at Wembley.

• **In 2011 Kompany became the first City captain since Tony Book in 1969 to raise the FA Cup, when City beat Stoke City 1-0 in the final at Wembley. His consistent performances in both campaigns earned him a place in the PFA Premier League Team of the Season.**

• Kompany began his career with Anderlecht, with whom he won the Belgian league in both 2004 and 2006. He moved on to Hamburg after that second triumph, before joining City for around £6 million in 2008. In July 2012 City awarded him a six-year contract, the longest in the club's history.

• **Kompany was just 17 when he made his debut for Belgium against France in 2004, one of the youngest ever players to represent his country. He was appointed captain in 2011 and led his country to the last eight at the 2014 World Cup.**

You get the impression that Vincent Kompany quite enjoyed lifting the Premier League trophy in 2014

Philipp Lahm, or 'The Magic Dwarf' as he's known to his friends

PHILIPP LAHM

Born: Munich, Germany, 11th November 1983
Position: Defender/midfielder
Club career:
2001-03 Bayern Munich II 63 (4)
2002- Bayern Munich 260 (8)
2003-05 Stuttgart (loan) 53 (2)
International record:
2004-14 Germany 113 (5)

In 2014 Philipp Lahm became the first ever European to lead his country to World Cup glory on South American soil when he skippered Germany in their 1-0 victory over Argentina in the final in Rio de Janeiro, Brazil. It turned out to be his last match for Germany, as he announced his retirement from international football soon afterwards.

• Equally at home playing at full-back or in a defensive midfield role, Lahm became Germany's youngest ever captain at the World Cup when he led the side at the 2010 tournament in South Africa, aged 26. On that occasion, he had to settle for third place.
• In 2013 Lahm became the first German player to lead his club to the Treble, when he helped Bayern win the Bundesliga, the German Cup and the Champions League, the latter trophy after a narrow 2-1 victory over Borussia Dortmund in the final at Wembley.
• 'The Magic Dwarf', as the pint-sized Lahm has been dubbed by fans, has won an impressive total of six Bundesliga titles – just two short of the record held by former Bayern players Mehmet Scholl and Oliver Kahn – since making his debut for the German giants back in 2002.

ADAM LALLANA

Born: St Albans, 10th May 1988
Position: Midfielder
Club career:
2006-14 Southampton 235 (48)
2007 Bournemouth (loan) 3 (0)
2014- Liverpool
International record:
2013- England 9 (0)

Liverpool midfielder Adam Lallana is the only player to have been voted into the PFA Team of the Year for the three current top divisions: League One, the Championship and the Premier League.
• An intelligent player who can spot a killer pass while also carrying a goal threat himself, Lallana came through the ranks at Southampton to make his debut as an 18 year old in a 5-2 defeat of Yeovil Town in the League Cup in August 2006. He became a regular for the Saints in the 2009/10 season, during which he became the first Southampton midfielder since club legend Matt Le Tissier in 1994/95 to score 20 goals in a season in all competitions.
• After enjoying successive promotions with Southampton in 2011 and 2012, and being made captain in 2012, Lallana quickly demonstrated that he was more than comfortable playing at the highest level, with his dynamic displays earning him a nomination for the PFA Player of the Year in 2014. That summer he moved on to Liverpool for £25 million, becoming the most expensive player ever to leave St Mary's.

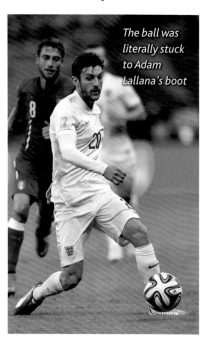

The ball was literally stuck to Adam Lallana's boot

• Lallana won his first England cap in November 2013, gaining rave reviews for his vibrant performance in a friendly against Chile at Wembley. He went on to be selected for Roy Hodgson's 2014 World Cup squad, featuring in all three group games.

RICKIE LAMBERT

Born: Kirkby, 16th February 1982
Position: Striker
Club career:
1998-2000 Blackpool 3 (0)
2001-02 Macclesfield Town 44 (8)
2002-05 Stockport County 98 (18)
2005-06 Rochdale 64 (28)
2006-09 Bristol Rovers 128 (51)
2009-14 Southampton 207 (106)
2014- Liverpool
International record:
2013- England 7 (3)

When Rickie Lambert scored with his first touch in international football just three minutes after coming off the bench against Scotland in August 2013, it was one of the fastest goals ever by an England player on his debut – but still some way short of the 19-second record set by Bill Nicholson against Portugal in 1951.

"Overall, I think I prefer this to working in a beetroot bottling factory"

• After failing to make the grade at local club Liverpool, Lambert joined Blackpool but only made three appearances for the Seasiders before being released. He worked for a while in a beetroot bottling plant before being signed by Macclesfield in 2001.
• Following spells with Stockport County and Rochdale, Lambert moved on to Bristol Rovers in 2006, enjoying a fine season with the club in 2008/09 when his 29 league goals made him the League One joint-top scorer. Suitably impressed, Southampton signed him for £1 million.
• **In his first season with the Saints Lambert scored 31 league goals, a tally which made him the top scorer in all four divisions. He was also the club's top scorer over the next two seasons as Southampton won successive promotions to the Premier League.**
• After another successful season in 2013/14, during which he scored 13 Premier League goals and took his penalty record for Southampton to an incredible 34 goals from the same number of spot-kicks, Lambert returned to Liverpool in a £4 million deal.

FRANK LAMPARD

Born: Romford, 20th June 1978
Position: Midfielder
Club career:
1996-2001 West Ham United 148 (24)
1995-96 Swansea City (loan) 9 (1)
2001-14 Chelsea 429 (147)
2014- New York City
2014- Manchester City (loan)
International record:
1999-2014 England 106 (29)

With 171 goals to his name, Frank Lampard is the highest scoring midfielder in Premier League history and, along with Wayne Rooney, one of just two players to hit double figures in the league in 10 consecutive seasons (2004-13). The vast majority of those strikes have come for Chelsea, who Lampard joined from West Ham in an £11 million deal back in 2001.
• **Lampard is the highest goalscorer in the Blues' history with an impressive total of 211 goals in all competitions for the club, who he served for 13 years before Chelsea released him in the summer of 2014.**
• Lampard won the league three times and the FA Cup four times during his time with the Blues, including the Double in 2010. After numerous near misses, he finally won the Champions League with Chelsea in 2012, scoring one of his team's penalties in the shoot-out victory over Bayern Munich in the final. The following year he skippered the Blues to success in the Europa League after the Londoners beat Benfica in the final.
• **A model of consistency, Lampard played in a then record 164 consecutive Premier League games until illness forced him out of Chelsea's visit to Manchester City in December 2005. Goalkeepers David James and Brad Friedel have since passed his total, but Lampard still holds the Premier League record for an outfield player.**
• The son of former England and West Ham defender Frank senior, Lampard made his international debut in 1999 against Belgium, but took a while to

establish himself in the England team. He starred at the European Championships in 2004, scoring in three of his country's four games, but fared less well at the 2006 World Cup where he was one of three England players to miss a penalty in the quarter-final shoot-out defeat at the hands of Portugal. His luck was also out at the 2010 tournament in South Africa, when the officials failed to spot that his shot in England's second-round defeat by Germany had clearly crossed the line after bouncing down off the crossbar. His total of 29 goals for his country is a record for an England midfielder, while his total of nine converted penalties is also a Three Lions record.

DENIS LAW

Born: Aberdeen, 24th February 1940
Position: Striker
Club career:
1956-60 Huddersfield Town 81 (16)
1960-61 Manchester City 44 (21)
1961-62 Torino 27 (10)
1962-73 Manchester United 309 (171)
1973-74 Manchester City 24 (9)
International record:
1958-74 Scotland 55 (30)

Along with Kenny Dalglish, Denis Law is Scotland's leading scorer with 30 international goals. Law, though, scored his goals in roughly half the number of games as 'King Kenny'.
• Law made his international debut in 1958, scoring in a 3-0 win against Wales. Aged 18, he was the youngest player to appear for Scotland since before the war. He went on to represent Scotland for 16 years,

taking his bow at the 1974 World Cup in Germany.
• On two occasions Law was sold for fees that broke the existing British transfer record. In 1960 he moved from Huddersfield to Manchester City for a record £55,000, and two years later his £115,000 transfer from Torino to Manchester United set a new benchmark figure.
• With United, Law won two league titles and the FA Cup in 1963, but he missed out on the club's European Cup triumph in 1968 through a knee injury. He remains the only Scottish player to have been voted European Footballer of the Year, an award he won in 1964.
• The last goal Law scored, a clever backheel for Manchester City against United at Old Trafford in 1974, gave him no pleasure at all as it condemned his old club to relegation to the Second Division. "I have seldom felt so depressed as I did that weekend," he remarked later.
• In 2002 a statue of Law was unveiled at Old Trafford, scene of many of his greatest triumphs. The following year the Scottish Football Association marked UEFA's Jubilee by naming him as Scotland's 'Golden Player' of the previous 50 years.

LAWS

Thirteen original laws of association football were adopted at a meeting of the Football Association in 1863, although these had their roots in the 'Cambridge Rules' established at Cambridge University as far back as 1848.
• No copy of those 1848 rules now exists, but they are thought to have included laws relating to throw-ins, goal-kicks, fouls and offside. They even allowed for a length of string to be used as a crossbar.
• Perhaps the most significant rule change occurred in 1925 when the offside law was altered so that an attacking player receiving the ball would need to be behind two opponents, rather than three. The effect of this rule change was dramatic, with the average number of goals per game in the Football League rising from 2.55 in 1924/25 to 3.44 in 1925/26.
• The laws of the game are governed by the International Football Association Board, which was founded in 1886 by the four football associations of the United Kingdom. Each of these associations still has one vote on

the IFAB, with FIFA having four votes. Any changes to the laws of the game require a minimum of six votes.
• In recent years the most important change to the laws of the game was the introduction of the 'back pass' rule in 1992, which prevented goalkeepers from handling passes from their own team-mates. The rule was introduced to discourage time-wasting and overly defensive play, following criticisms of widespread negative tactics at the 1990 World Cup.

TOP 10

BIGGEST LEAGUE CUP WINS

1. West Ham United 10 Bury 0, 1983
   Liverpool 10 Fulham 0, 1986
3. Workington 9 Barrow 1, 1964
4. Leyton Orient 9 Chester 2, 1962
5. Northampton Town 8
   Brighton & Hove Albion 0, 1966
   Everton 8 Wimbledon 0, 1978
   Watford 8 Darlington 0, 1987
   Aldershot 0
   Sheffield Wednesday 8, 1989
   Crystal Palace 8
   Southend United 0, 1990
   Doncaster 0 Nottingham Forest 8, 1997
   Stoke City 0 Liverpool 8, 2000
   Coventry City 8
   Rushden & Diamonds 0, 2002

LEAGUE CUP

With eight wins to their name, most recently in the 2012 final against Cardiff, Liverpool have won the League Cup more often than any other club. The Reds have also appeared in the most finals, 11.
• The competition has been known by more names than any other in British football. Originally called the Football League Cup (1960-81), it has subsequently been rebranded through sponsorship deals as the Milk Cup (1981-86), Littlewoods Cup (1986-90), Rumbelows Cup (1990-92), Coca-Cola Cup (1992-98), Worthington Cup (1998-2003), Carling Cup (2003-12) and, since 2012, the Capital One Cup.
• Ian Rush won a record five winners' medals in the competition with Liverpool (1981-84 and 1995) and, along with Geoff Hurst, is also the leading scorer in the history of the League Cup with 49 goals. In the 1986/87 season Tottenham's Clive Allen scored a record

"Altogether lads, we're the Capital One Cup Kings. That rolls off the tongue nicely, doesn't it?"

12 goals in the competition.

• Oldham's Frankie Bunn scored a record six goals in a League Cup match when Oldham thrashed Scarborough 7-0 on 25th October 1989.

• Liverpool won the competition a record four times in a row between 1981 and 1984, going undefeated for an unprecedented 25 League Cup matches.

• Swansea City recorded the biggest win in the final, when they crushed Bradford City 5-0 at Wembley in 2013. Manchester City's 9-0 aggregate thashing of West Ham the following year is the biggest semi-final win.

• Norman Whiteside, the youngest player ever to score in an FA Cup final (for Manchester United v Brighton in 1983), is also the youngest man ever to score in the League Cup final (for Manchester United v Liverpool, also in 1983), aged 17 years and 324 days.

• Liverpool's John Arne Riise scored the fastest goal in the League Cup final, after just 45 seconds against Chelsea in 2005.

• The first League Cup final to be played at Wembley was between West Brom and QPR in 1967. QPR were then a Third Division side and pulled off a major shock by winning 3-2. Prior to 1967, the final was played on a home and away basis over two legs.

• The highest scoring match in the history of the competition was the 2012 meeting between Reading and Arsenal at the Madejski Stadium, which the Gunners won 7-5 after trailing 4-0 at one point.

• Chelsea striker Didier Drogba scored a record four goals in League Cup finals,

finding the target against Liverpool in 2005, Arsenal in 2007 (two goals) and Tottenham in 2008.

• In 1983 West Ham walloped Bury 10-0 to record the biggest ever victory in the history of the League Cup. Three years later Liverpool equalled the Hammers' tally with an identical thrashing of Fulham.

LEEDS UNITED

Year founded: 1919
Ground: Elland Road (37,890)
Nickname: United
Biggest win: 10-0 v Lyn Oslo (1969)
Heaviest defeat: 1-8 v Stoke City (1934)

Leeds United were formed in 1919 as successors to Leeds City, who had been expelled from the Football League after making illegal payments to their players. United initially joined the Midland League before being elected to the Second Division in 1920.

• **Leeds' greatest years were in the 1960s and early 1970s under legendary manager Don Revie. The club were struggling in the Second Division when he arrived at Elland Road in 1961 but, building his side around the likes of Jack Charlton, Billy Bremner and Johnny Giles, Revie soon turned Leeds into a formidable force.**

• During the Revie years Leeds won two league titles in 1969 and 1974, the FA Cup in 1972, the League Cup in 1968, and two Fairs Cup in 1968 and 1971. In the last of those triumphs Leeds became the first club to win a European trophy on the away goals rule after they drew 2-2 on aggregate with Italian giants Juventus.

• **Leeds also reached the final of the European Cup in 1975, losing 2-0 to Bayern Munich. Sadly, rioting by the club's fans resulted in Leeds becoming the first English club to be suspended from European competition. The ban lasted three years.**

• Peter Lorimer, another Revie-era stalwart, is the club's leading scorer, hitting 168 league goals in two spells at Elland Road: 1962-79 and 1983-86. Jack Charlton holds the club appearance record, turning out in 773 games in total between 1952 and 1973. Significantly, the next six players on the list behind 'Big Jack' are all his old team-mates from the 1960s and 1970s.

• **Former South Africa captain Lucas Radebe won a record 61 caps while at Leeds between 1994 and 2005.**

• In 1992 Leeds pipped Manchester United to the title to make history as the last club to win the old First Division before it became the Premiership. Ironically, Leeds' star player at the time, Eric Cantona, joined the Red Devils the following season. The club remained a force over the next decade, even reaching the Champions League semi-final in 2001, but financial mismanagement saw them plummet to League One in 2007 before they climbed back into the Championship three years later.

• **Incredibly, Leeds failed to win a single FA Cup tie between 1952 and 1963 – the worst ever run by a league club in the post-war era.**

• Rio Ferdinand is both Leeds' record buy and record sale, joining the club from West Ham for £18 million in 2000 before leaving for Manchester United for a then British record £29.1 million two years later.

HONOURS
Division 1 champions 1969, 1974, 1992
Division 2 champions 1924, 1964, 1990
FA Cup 1972
League Cup 1968
Fairs Cup 1968, 1971

After years in the doldrums, Leicester City are back in the top flight

LEICESTER CITY

Year founded: 1884
Ground: King Power Stadium (32,262)
Previous name: Leicester Fosse
Nickname: The Foxes
Biggest win: 13-0 v Notts Olympic (1894)
Heaviest defeat: 0-12 v Nottingham Forest (1909)

Founded in 1884 as Leicester Fosse by old boys from Wyggeston School, the club were elected to the Second Division a decade later. In 1919 they changed their name to Leicester City, shortly after Leicester was given city status.

• The Foxes have enjoyed great success in the League Cup, winning the trophy three times. Their first victory came against Stoke in 1964 and more recently they won the trophy twice under then manager Martin O'Neill, against Middlesbrough in 1997 and Tranmere Rovers in 2000.

• Leicester have won the second-tier championship seven times – a record only matched by Manchester City. On the last of these occasions in 2013/14 the Foxes set a number of significant club records, including highest number of points (102) and most league games won (33).

• In 1909, while still known as Leicester Fosse, the club suffered their worst ever defeat, losing 12-0 to East Midlands neighbours Nottingham Forest – still a record score for a top-flight match. It later emerged that the Leicester players had been celebrating the wedding of a team-mate for two full days before the game, which might have contributed to their pitiful performance!

• Leicester City are the only club to have played in four FA Cup finals and lost them all. Beaten in 1949, 1961 and 1963, they were defeated again by Manchester City in 1969 – the same season that they were relegated from the First Division. Only four other teams, most recently Portsmouth in 2010, have suffered a similar double blow.

• Leicester made their record sale in 2000, when England striker Emile Heskey moved to Liverpool for £11 million. In June 2014 the Foxes made their record signing, bringing Argentinian striker Leonardo Ulloa to the King Power from Brighton for £8 million.

• Arthur Chandler holds the club goalscoring record, netting 259 times between 1923 and 1935. Remarkably, he scored in a record 16 consecutive matches during the 1924/25 season. The club's appearance record is held by defender and ex-Leicestershire county cricketer Graham Cross, who turned out 599 times in all competitions for the Foxes between 1960 and 1976.

• Former *Dr Who* actor Matt Smith played for Leicester at Under-16 level before a back injury forced him to give up his football dreams and concentrate on acting instead.

HONOURS
Division 2 champions 1925, 1937, 1954, 1957, 1971, 1980
Championship champions 2014
League One champions 2009
League Cup 1964, 1997, 2000

ROBERT LEWANDOWSKI

Born: Warsaw, Poland, 21st August 1988
Position: Striker
Club career:
2006 Delta Warsaw 10 (4)
2005-06 Legia Warsaw II 5 (2)
2006-08 Znicz Pruszków 59 (36)
2008-10 Lech Poznań 55 (32)
2010-14 Borussia Dortmund 131 (74)
2014- Bayern Munich
International record:
2008- Poland 61 (19)

Robert Lewandowski, probably the only player whose favourite opponents are Real Madrid!

Pacy Polish striker Robert Lewandowski is the only player to have scored four goals in a Champions League semi-final, achieving this record in Borussia Dortmund's 4-1 defeat of Real Madrid in 2013. His sensational performance powered Borussia into the final, where they lost 2-1 at Wembley to German rivals Bayern Munich.

• After starting out in the Polish lower leagues, Lewandowski made his name at Lech Poznan. In only his second season in the top flight, in 2009/10, he led the scoring charts with 18 goals as Poznan won the title.

• In the summer of 2010 Lewandowski moved on to Dortmund for around £4 million. The fee proved to be a bargain as Lewandowski's goals helped his club win two league titles and the German Cup in 2012, the Pole scoring a hat-trick in Borussia's 5-2 demolition of Bayern in the final. The following season Lewandowski set a new club record when he scored in 12 consecutive league games. After topping the Bundesliga scoring charts in 2013/14 he moved on to Bayern Munich.

• Lewandowski first played for Poland aged 20 in 2008, coming off the bench to score in a World Cup qualifier against San Marino to become his country's second ever youngest goalscorer on his debut. By the time the Euro 2012 championships were played in Poland and Ukraine, he was very much his country's star player and didn't disappoint his adoring fans by scoring the first goal of the tournament against Greece.

LEYTON ORIENT

Year founded: 1881
Ground: The Matchroom Stadium (9,271)
Previous name: Eagle FC, Clapton Road, Orient
Nickname: The O's
Biggest win: 9-2 v Aldershot (1934) and v Chester (1962)
Heaviest defeat: 0-8 v Aston Villa (1929)

Originally founded by members of a local cricket team, the club chose the name 'Orient' in 1888 following a suggestion by one of the players who worked for the Orient Shipping Company.

• Over 40 Orient players and staff fought in the First World War, three of them dying in the conflict. In recognition of this sacrifice, the Prince of Wales (later King Edward VIII) watched an Orient match in 1921 – the first time a member of the Royal Family had attended a Football League fixture.

• Orient are the only club to have played league matches at the old Wembley Stadium. During the 1931/32 season, while still named Clapton Orient, the club played matches against Brentford and Southend at 'the home of football' after their own Lea Bridge ground was temporarily closed for failing to meet official standards.

• The club have not broken their transfer fee record since October 1989, when defender Paul Beesley signed from Wigan Athletic for £175,000.

• Orient's record scorer is Tommy Johnston, who banged in 121 goals in two spells at the club between 1956 and 1961. In 2009 the South Stand at Brisbane Road was named after the prolific striker.

• In the Third Division play-off final in 2001, Orient's Chris Tate scored against Blackpool after just 27 seconds – the fastest ever goal at the Millennium Stadium. Sadly for the O's, they lost the game 4-2.

HONOURS
Division 3 (S) champions 1956
Division 3 champions 1970

GARY LINEKER

Born: Leicester, 30th November 1960
Position: Striker
Club career:
1978-85 Leicester City 194 (95)
1985-86 Everton 41 (30)
1986-89 Barcelona 103 (43)
1989-92 Tottenham Hotspur 105 (67)
1992-94 Nagoya Grampus 8 23 (9)
International record:
1984-92 England 80 (48)

Now a popular BBC sports presenter known for his excruciating puns, Gary Lineker is England's second highest scorer, with 48 goals, just one behind the legendary Bobby Charlton. He had a great chance to beat the record, but failed to score in any of his final six matches and even missed a penalty to equal Charlton's tally against Brazil.

• He is, though, England's leading scorer at the finals of the World Cup with 10 goals. At the 1986 tournament in Mexico Lineker scored six goals to win the Golden Boot, and he added another four at Italia '90.

• Lineker is the only player to have twice scored all four England goals in a match, grabbing all his side's goals in 4-2 away wins over Spain in 1987 and Malaysia in 1991. In all, he hit five hat-tricks in his 80 international appearances.

• At club level Lineker won the European Cup Winners' Cup with Barcelona in 1989 and the FA Cup with Spurs two years later. He was also voted PFA Player of the Year in 1986 after a single goal-filled season with Everton.

• In his last international, against Sweden at the 1992 European Championships, Lineker was controversially substituted by England boss Graham Taylor. The move backfired as England lost the match and were eliminated.

• A revered figure in his hometown, Lineker has a stand named after him at Leicester's King Power Stadium.

LIVERPOOL

Year founded: 1892
Ground: Anfield (45,522)
Nickname: The Reds
Biggest win: 11-0 v Stromsgodset (1974)
Heaviest defeat: 1-9 v Birmingham City (1954)

Liverpool were founded as a splinter club from local rivals Everton following a dispute between the Toffees and the landlord of their original ground at Anfield, John Houlding. When the majority of Evertonians decided to decamp to Goodison Park in 1892, Houlding set up Liverpool FC after his attempts to retain the name 'Everton' had failed.

• With 18 league titles to their name, Liverpool are the second most successful club in the history of English football behind deadly rivals Manchester United. However, the Reds have failed to lift the championship trophy for over two decades, their last title coming way back in 1990.

Love is in the air at Liverpool, England's most successful club in Europe

• Liverpool dominated English football in the 1970s and 1980s after the foundations of the club's success were laid by legendary manager Bill Shankly in the previous decade. Under Shankly's successor, Bob Paisley, the Reds won 13 major trophies – a haul only surpassed by Sir Alex Ferguson.

• **Liverpool are the most successful English side in Europe, having won the European Cup/Champions League on five occasions. The Reds first won the trophy in 1977, beating Borussia Monchengladbach 3-1 in Rome, and the following year became the first British team to retain the cup (after a 1-0 win in the final against Bruges at Wembley, club legend Kenny Dalglish grabbing the all-important goal).**

• In 1984 Liverpool became the first club to win the European Cup on penalties when they beat Roma by this method after a 1-1 draw. In 2005 the Reds won the trophy on spot-kicks again, this time against AC Milan, and remain the only club to have twice triumphed in the competition after a penalty shoot-out.

• **Liverpool have won the League Cup a record eight times, including four times in a row between 1981 and 1984, and are the only club to win the trophy twice on penalties (in 2001 and 2012). Reds striker Ian Rush is the joint leading scorer in the history of the competition with 49 goals, hitting all but one of these for Liverpool in** two spells at the club in the 1980s and 1990s.

• Rush also scored a record five goals in three FA Cup finals for Liverpool in 1986, 1989 and 1992 – all of which were won by the Reds. In all, the Merseysiders have won the trophy seven times, most recently in 2006 when they became only the second team (after Arsenal the previous year) to claim the cup on penalties.

• **When the Reds recorded their biggest ever victory, 11-0 against Norwegian no-hopers Stromsgodset in the Cup Winners' Cup in 1974, no fewer than nine different Liverpool players got on the scoresheet to set a British record for the most scoring players in a competitive match.**

• In 1986 Liverpool became only the third English side in the 20th century to win the Double, pipping rivals Everton to the league title and then beating the Toffees 3-1 in the FA Cup final at Wembley with a line-up that featured not a single English player – a first for the final.

• **England international striker Roger Hunt is the club's leading scorer in league games, with 245 goals between 1958 and 1969. His team-mate Ian Callaghan holds the Liverpool appearance record, turning out in 640 league games between 1960 and 1978.**

• Pony-tailed striker Andy Carroll is the club's record signing, joining the Reds from Newcastle for £35 million in January 2011. In the summer of 2014 Uruguayan striker Luis Suarez left Anfield for Barcelona for a club record £75 million.

• **In 2001 Liverpool became only the second English club to win the League Cup and FA Cup in the same season. For good measure, the Reds made it a 'Treble' by lifting the UEFA Cup as well after a thrilling 5-4 victory over Spanish club Alaves in the final.**

• Liverpool have the best overall goal difference of any Football League club, +2,106.

• Famous Liverpool fans include Spice Girl Mel C, comedian John Bishop and TV presenter Matt Smith.

HONOURS

Division 1 champions 1901, 1906, 1922, 1923, 1947, 1964, 1966, 1973, 1976, 1977, 1979, 1980, 1982, 1983, 1984, 1986, 1988, 1990

Division 2 champions 1894, 1896, 1905, 1962

FA Cup 1965, 1974, 1986, 1989, 1992, 2001, 2006

League Cup 1981, 1982, 1983, 1984, 1995, 2001, 2003, 2012

Double 1986

European Cup/Champions League 1977, 1978, 1981, 1984, 2005

UEFA Cup 1973, 1976, 2001

European Super Cup 1977, 2001, 2005

HUGO LLORIS

Born: Nice, France, 26th December 1986
Position: Goalkeeper
Club career:
2004-06 Nice B 20
2005-08 Nice 72
2008-12 Lyon 146
2012- Tottenham Hotspur 64
International record:
2008- France 61

When Hugo Lloris made his Premier League debut in the Tottenham goal against Aston Villa on 7th October 2012, he brought to an end his team-mate Brad Friedel's record run of 310 consecutive appearances in the league stretching back eight years.

• After starting out with his hometown club Nice, Lloris made his name with Lyon. During a four-year stint with the French giants, Lloris was voted Ligue 1 Goalkeeper of the Year three times, but only managed to win one piece of silverware – the French Cup in 2012, following a 1-0 victory in the final over third-tier Quevilly.

• Famed for his superb reflexes and his ability to rush out to the edge of his box to snuff out dangerous opposition attacks, Lloris won the European Under-19 championship with France in 2005. He was awarded his first senior cap in 2008, keeping a clean sheet in a 0-0 draw with Uruguay, and he skippered his country for the first time in a 2-1 friendly win against England at Wembley in November 2010.

• At the 2014 World Cup in Brazil Lloris was in fine form, keeping three clean sheets in five games as France reached the quarter-final stage before losing to eventual winners Germany.

DAVID LUIZ

Born: Diadema, Brazil, 22nd April 1987
Position: Defender
Club career:
2006-07 Vitoria 26 (1)
2007 Benfica (loan) 10 (0)
2007-11 Benfica 72 (4)
2011-14 Chelsea 81 (6)
2014- Paris St Germain
International record:
2010- Brazil 43 (2)

David Luiz, the world's most expensive defender

Flamboyant centre-back David Luiz joined Paris St Germain from Chelsea in June 2014 for £50 million, making him the world's most expensive ever defensive purchase.

• The frizzy-haired Brazilian's skills on the ball made him a cult figure at Stamford Bridge, with stallholders outside the stadium doing a roaring trade in 'David Luiz wigs'. However, his occasionally erratic approach to the basics of defending led to some criticism, notably from *Sky Sports* pundit Gary Neville who, after one haphazard display by Luiz, said that he played as though "controlled by a 10 year old on a PlayStation".

• Luiz answered his critics in the best possible manner by playing a starring role in Chelsea's run to the 2012 Champions League final and then bravely stepping up to score one of his team's penalties in the shoot-out victory over Bayern Munich which brought the trophy to London for the first time. The following year he helped the Blues become the first British side to win the Europa League, after victory over his former club Benfica in the final.

• In 2010 Luiz made his debut for Brazil in a 2-0 friendly win over the USA, and two years later he captained his country for the first time in a 1-0 win against South Africa. He had mixed fortunes at the World Cup in 2014, playing well in the early games and scoring a thunderous free kick in the quarter-final against Colombia, but he ended the tournament in tears after Brazil were hammered 7-1 by Germany in the semi-final.

LUTON TOWN

Year founded: 1885
Ground: Kenilworth Road (10,226)
Nickname: The Hatters
Biggest win: 15-0 v Great Yarmouth Town (1914)
Heaviest defeat: 0-9 v Small Heath (1898)

Founded in 1885 following the merger of two local sides, Luton Town Wanderers and Excelsior, Luton Town became the first professional club in the south of England five years later.

• The club's greatest moment came in 1988 when they beat Arsenal 3-2 in the League Cup final. The Hatters returned to Wembley for the final the following year, but lost to Nottingham Forest – the same club which beat them in their only FA Cup final appearance in 1959.

• In 1936 Luton striker Joe Payne scored a Football League record 10 goals in a Third Division (South) fixture against Bristol Rovers. The Hatters won the match 12-0 to record their biggest ever league victory

• Luton were docked a record 30 points by the Football League for financial irregularities at the start of the 2008/09 season. At the end of the campaign the club was relegated from League Two, despite a brave battle to make up the lost ground. Having suffered the drop in the previous two seasons as well, Luton became the first club to be relegated from the Championship to the Conference in consecutive seasons.

• In 2014, however, Luton bounced back to the Football League after topping the Conference table. The previous year the Hatters became the first non-league club to beat a Premier League side in the FA Cup when they won 1-0 at Norwich in the fourth round.

HONOURS

Division 2 champions 1982
Division 3 (South) champions 1937
League One champions 2005
Division 4 champions 1968
Conference champions 2014
League Cup 1988
Football League Trophy 2009

ALLY McCOIST

Born: Bellshill, 24th September 1962
Position: Striker
Club career:
1979-81 St Johnstone 57 (22)
1981-83 Sunderland 56 (8)
1983-98 Rangers 418 (251)
1998-2001 Kilmarnock 59 (12)
International record:
1986-98 Scotland 61 (19)

Rangers legend Ally McCoist is the highest scorer in the Gers' history with an incredible 355 goals for the Ibrox outfit in all competitions. His tally of 251 league goals is also a club record.

• During a 15-year career with Rangers, McCoist won no fewer than 10 league titles (including nine in a row between 1989 and 1997), nine Scottish League Cups and one Scottish Cup. His haul of medals is unmatched by any other Scottish player in the last quarter of a century.

• In 1992 McCoist hit a personal best 34 goals and won the European Golden Boot. In the same year he was voted Scottish Player of the Year. A Scotland international for over a decade, his total of 19 goals for his country is only bettered by four players.

• In 2007 McCoist became assistant manager of Rangers and was promoted to the top job in 2011 following Walter Smith's retirement. His first season in charge of the Glasgow giants was an extremely difficult one as Rangers were plunged into an ever-deepening financial catastrophe, a crisis which eventually resulted in the club's liquidation and relegation to the Scottish fourth tier. The following season, though, he led Rangers to the Scottish Third Division title and in 2013/14 he guided the club back into the second tier after an unbeaten league campaign.

MANAGER OF THE YEAR

Former Manchester United boss Sir Alex Ferguson won the FA Premier League Manager of the Year award a record 11 times, once more than all the other winning managers put together. He also won the old Manager of the Year award in 1993, giving him a total of 12 triumphs.

• Arsène Wenger (in 1998, 2002 and 2004) and Jose Mourinho (2005 and 2006) are the only other managers to win the award more than once since it was introduced in the 1993/94 season.

• The first manager to win the award despite not guiding his team to the title was George Burley, who was honoured in 2001 after leading Ipswich to fifth place in the Premiership a year after winning promotion.

• Tony Pulis topped the poll in 2014 despite his club, Crystal Palace, finishing only 11th in the Premier League – the lowest ever placing for a manager collecting the award.

MANCHESTER CITY

Year founded: 1887
Ground: Etihad Stadium (47,405)
Previous name: Ardwick
Nickname: The Citizens
Biggest win: 12-0 v Liverpool Stanley (1890)
Heaviest defeat: 1-9 v Everton (1906)

City have their roots in a church team which was renamed Ardwick in 1887 and became founder members of the Second Division five years later. In 1894, after suffering financial difficulties, the club was reformed under its present name.

• Now owned by Sheikh Mansour of the Abu Dhabi Royal Family, City are one of the richest clubs in the world. Following a massive spending spree on the likes of Edin Dzeko, David Silva and Yaya Toure, the Sheikh received the first return on his huge investment in 2011 when City won the FA Cup, their first trophy for 35 years, after beating Stoke City 1-0 in the final at Wembley. More silverware followed the next season as City won the Premier League, their first league title since 1968, after pipping arch rivals Manchester United on goal difference. In 2014 City won the Premier League for a second time, banging in an impressive 102 goals in the process – just one behind Chelsea's record haul. For good measure, City also won the League Cup after beating Sunderland 3-1 in the final.

• Prior to the modern era, the late 1960s were the most successful period in City's history, a side featuring the likes of Colin Bell, Francis Lee and Mike Summerbee winning the league title (1968), the FA Cup (1969), the League Cup (1970) and the European Cup Winners' Cup (also in 1970) and for a short time usurping Manchester United as the city's premier club.

• City also won the league title in 1937. Incredibly, the following season they were relegated to the Second Division despite scoring more goals than any other side in the division. To this day they remain the only league champions to suffer the drop in the following campaign.

• Eric Brook, an ever-present in that initial title-winning season, is City's joint leading scorer (along with 1920s marksman Tommy Johnson) with 158 league goals between 1928 and 1940. The club's record appearance maker is Alan Oakes, who turned out 564 times in the sky blue shirt between 1958 and 1976.

• Apart from their most recent triumph City have won the FA Cup four other times and, in 1926, were the first club to reach the final and be relegated in the same season. A 1-0 defeat by Bolton at Wembley ensured a grim season ended on a depressing note.

• The 1957/58 season was more enjoyable, especially for fans who like goals, as City scored 104 times while conceding 100 – the first and only time this 'double century' has been achieved. City finished fifth in the old First Division that season, the highest ever position by a team conceding 100 or more goals.

• City have won the title for the second tier of English football a joint record seven times, most recently in 2002 when they returned to the Premiership under then manager Kevin Keegan. Four years earlier the club experienced their lowest ever moment when they dropped into the third tier for the first and only time in their history – the first European trophy winners to sink this low.

• The highest attendance ever at an English club ground, 84,569, saw City beat Stoke 1-0 at their old Maine Road Stadium in the sixth round of the FA Cup in 1934.

• The club's most expensive purchase is Argentinian striker Sergio Aguero, who signed from Atletico Madrid for around £38 million in July 2011. Shaun Wright-Phillips, now with QPR, boosted the club's coffers by a record £21 million when he joined Chelsea in 2005.

"So, who's the top team in Manchester now?" asks Edin Dzeko

• City are the last club to have hit double figures in a Football League game, smashing Huddersfield 10-1 in a Division Two fixture in November 1987.

HONOURS
Division 1 champions 1937, 1968
Premier League champions *2012, 2014*
Division 2 champions 1899, 1903, 1910, 1928, 1947, 1966
First Division champions 2002
FA Cup 1904, 1934, 1956, 1969, 2011
League Cup 1970, 1976, 2014
European Cup Winners' Cup 1970

MANCHESTER UNITED

Year founded: 1878
Ground: Old Trafford (75,731)
Previous name: Newton Heath
Nickname: Red Devils
Biggest win: 10-0 v Anderlecht (1956)
Heaviest defeat: 0-7 v Blackburn (1926), v Aston Villa (1930) and v Wolverhampton Wanderers (1931)

The club was founded in 1878 as Newton Heath, a works team for employees of the Lancashire and Yorkshire Railway. In 1892 Newton Heath (who played in yellow-and-green-halved shirts) were elected to the Football League but a decade later went bankrupt, only to be immediately reformed as Manchester United with the help of a local brewer, John Davies.

• **United are the most successful club in the history of English football, having won the league title a record 20 times and the FA Cup a joint-record 11 times. The Red Devils have been the dominant force of the Premier League era, winning the title a record 13 times under former manager Sir Alex Ferguson.**

• United were the first English club to win the Double on three separate occasions, in 1994, 1996 and 1999. The last of these triumphs was particularly memorable as the club also went on to win the Champions League, beating Bayern Munich 2-1 in the final in Barcelona thanks to two late goals by Teddy Sheringham and Ole Gunner Solskjaer, to record English football's first ever Treble.

• **Under legendary manager Sir Matt Busby United became the first ever English club to win the European Cup in 1968, when they beat Benfica 4-1 in the final at Wembley. Victory was especially sweet for Sir Matt who, a decade earlier, had narrowly survived the Munich air crash which claimed the lives of eight of his players as the team returned from a European Cup fixture in Belgrade. United also won European football's top club prize in 2008, beating Chelsea in the Champions League final on penalties in Moscow.**

• United won the FA Cup for the first time in 1909, beating Bristol City 1-0 in the final. The club's total of 18 appearances in the final (11 wins, seven defeats) is a record for the competition shared with Arsenal.

• **The club's history, though, has not always been glorious. The 1930s were a particularly grim decade for United, who were threatened with relegation to the old Third Division on the final day of the 1933/34 season. In a bid to change their luck, United swapped their red shirts for cherry and white hoops for the first and only time, and beat Millwall 2-0 away to stay in the Second Division.**

• Old Trafford has the highest capacity of any club ground in Britain but, strangely, when United set an all-time Football League attendance record of 83,260 for

TOP 1⚽

LEAGUE TITLE WINNERS

1.	Manchester United	20
2.	Liverpool	18
3.	Arsenal	13
4.	Everton	9
5.	Aston Villa	7
6.	Sunderland	6
7.	Chelsea	4
	Manchester City	4
	Newcastle United	4
	Sheffield Wednesday	4

their home game against Arsenal on 17th January 1948 they were playing at Maine Road, home of local rivals Manchester City. This was because Old Trafford was badly damaged by German bombs during the Second World War, forcing United to use their neighbours' ground in the immediate post-war period.

• **United's leading appearance maker is Ryan Giggs, who played in an incredible 963 games in all competitions for the club between 1991 and 2014.**

• The club's highest goalscorer is Sir Bobby Charlton, who banged in 199 league goals for the club between 1956 and 1973. Charlton is also United's most capped international, playing 106 times for England in an illustrious career. Denis Law, another 1960s United legend, scored a record 18 hat-tricks for the club.

• **United recorded the biggest ever victory in Premier League history on 4th March 1995 when they thrashed Ipswich 9-0 at Old Trafford, with striker Andy Cole scoring five of the goals to set another Premiership record.**

• No fewer than 20 different players found the net for United in their most recent title-winning season in 2012/13 – a record for the Premier League era.

• **Known for many years as a big-spending club, United's record signing is Argentinian Angel Di Maria, who cost £59.7 million when he moved from Real Madrid in August 2014. The club's most expensive sale is former Old Trafford hero Cristiano Ronaldo, who joined Real Madrid for a then world record £80 million in 2009.**

• Manchester United have more fans than any other club in the world. A 2012 survey across 39 different countries by market research firm Kantar discovered that the Red Devils have a staggering 659 million fans worldwide.

HONOURS

Division 1 champions 1908, 1911, 1952, 1956, 1957, 1965, 1967
Premier League champions 1993, 1994, 1996, 1997, 1999, 2000, 2001, 2003, 2007, 2008, 2009, 2011, 2013
Division 2 champions 1936, 1975
FA Cup 1909, 1948, 1963, 1977, 1983, 1985, 1990, 1994, 1996, 1999, 2004
League Cup 1992, 2006, 2009, 2010
Double 1994, 1996, 1999
European Cup/Champions League 1968, 1999, 2008
European Cup Winners' Cup 1991
European Super Cup 1991
Intercontinental Cup/Club World Cup 1999, 2008

MANSFIELD TOWN

Year founded: 1897
Ground: Field Mill (8,186)
Previous names: Mansfield Wesleyans, Mansfield Wesley
Nickname: The Stags
Biggest win: 9-2 v Rotherham United (1932)
Heaviest defeat: 1-7 v Reading (1932), v Peterborough United (1966) and v QPR (1966)

The club was founded as Mansfield Wesleyans, a boys brigade team, in 1897, before becoming Mansfield Town in 1910. The Stags eventually joined the Football League in 1931, remaining there until relegation to the Conference in 2008. Five years later the club bounced back to League Two as Conference champions.

• **In the 1950/51 season Mansfield were the first club ever to remain unbeaten at home in a 23-game fixture schedule, but just missed out on promotion to the old Second Division. The Stags finally reached the second tier in 1977, but were relegated at the end of the campaign.**

• Club legend Ted Harston scored an amazing 55 goals in the 1936/37 season – a record for the Third Division (North) – including a Stags' record seven goals in a game in an 8-2 drubbing of Hartlepool United .

• **Goalkeeper Rod Arnold made a record 440 league appearances for the Stags**

between 1970 and 1984. The club's top scorer is Harry Johnson, who hit an incredible 104 goals in just three seasons at Field Mill from 1932-35.

HONOURS

Division 3 champions 1977
Division 4 champions 1975
Conference champions 2013
Football League Trophy 1987

DIEGO MARADONA

Born: Buenos Aires, 30th October 1960
Position: Striker/midfielder
Club career:
1976-80 Argentinos Juniors 167 (115)
1980-82 Boca Juniors 40 (28)
1982-84 Barcelona 36 (22)
1984-91 Napoli 186 (83)
1992-93 Sevilla 25 (4)
1995-97 Boca Juniors 29 (7)
International record:
1977-94 Argentina 91 (34)

The best player in the world in the 1980s, Diego Maradona is considered by many to be the greatest footballer ever.

• **During his career in his native Argentina, then in Spain and Italy, he smashed three transfer records. First, his £1 million move from Argentinos Juniors to Boca Juniors in 1980 was a world record for a teenager. Then he broke the world transfer record when he joined Barcelona from Boca for £4.2 million in 1982, and again when he signed for Napoli for £6.9 million in 1984.**

• A superb dribbler who used his low centre of gravity to great effect, Maradona was almost impossible to mark. He was idolised at Napoli, who he led to a first ever Italian title in 1987 and a first European trophy two years later, when they won the UEFA Cup.

• **He made his international debut aged 16 in 1977 and went on to play at four World Cups, captaining his country in a record 16 games at the finals. His greatest triumph came in 1986 when, after scoring the goals that beat England (including the infamous 'Hand of God' goal which he punched into the net) and Belgium in the quarter and semi-finals, he skippered Argentina to victory in the final against West Germany. He also led his side to the 1990 final against the same opponents.**

• However, Maradona's international career ended in disgrace when he was thrown out of the 1994 World Cup in the USA after failing a drugs test. He had previously been hit with a worldwide 15-month ban from football in 1991 after testing positive for cocaine.

• Despite these blots on his reputation, Maradona was voted 'The Player of the Century' by more than half of those who took part in a worldwide FIFA internet poll in 2000. In 2008 he became head coach of Argentina, but resigned two years later after his side were thrashed 4-0 by Germany in the World Cup quarter-finals.

ROBERTO MARTINEZ

Born: Balaguer, Spain, 13th July 1973
Managerial career:
2007-09 Swansea City
2009-13 Wigan Athletic
2013- Everton

Everton boss Roberto Martinez is the only manager ever to lead a club to FA Cup glory and relegation in the same season, achieving this unique double with his former club, Wigan Athletic, in 2013 shortly before he moved to Merseyside.

• Martinez began his managerial career with Swansea City in 2007, a club he had played for a short while earlier. He was an instant success in south Wales, guiding the Swans to the League One title in 2008. The following year, however, Martinez shocked the club's fans when he agreed to join Premier League outfit Wigan Athletic, another of his former teams from his playing days.

• In his first season in Lancashire, Martinez managed to keep Wigan up even though they suffered two of the worst defeats in Premier League history – 9-1 at Tottenham and 8-0 at Chelsea. The Latics, though, looked doomed during the 2011/12 campaign when they were rooted to the bottom of the table. However, an incredible late-season run of seven wins in nine games – including famous victories over Manchester United and Arsenal – saw them climb to safety.

• The first Everton manager ever to not hail from the British Isles, Martinez enjoyed a fine first season with the Toffees in 2013/14, guiding them to fifth place in the Premier League and qualification for the Europa League. He also became the first Everton manager since Harry Catterick in 1969/70 to oversee a league double over Manchester United.

Roberto Martinez is Everton's first foreign manager

Peter Burrow, Peterborough United's giant rabbit mascot, is probably the scariest in the Football League

MASCOTS

In 2013 Lenny Berry, who had played the role of Bradford City's mascot 'City Gent' for 20 years, was forced to stand down from his role as he was no longer tubby enough to fill the costume.

• Swansea mascot Cyril the Swan was fined a record £1,000 in 1999 for celebrating a goal against Millwall in the FA Cup by running onto the pitch and pushing the referee. Two years later Cyril was in trouble again when he pulled off the head of Millwall's Zampa the Lion mascot and drop-kicked it into the crowd.

IS THAT A FACT?

Mother-of-three Tracy Chandler was sacked as Doncaster Rovers mascot Donny the Dog in 2011 after she posed in revealing lingerie alongside the head of Donny to raise money for charity. The club later relented and gave Tracy her job back.

• In one of the most bizarre football sights ever, Wolves mascot Wolfie traded punches with his Bristol City counterpart City Cat during a half-time penalty shoot-out competition at Ashton Gate in 2002. City Cat, who was backed up by three little piggies representing a local company, got the better of the fracas which had to be broken up by stewards.

• **The Mascot Grand National, an annual race over hurdles between football and other sporting mascots, has been held at Huntingdon Racecourse since 1999. The first winner was Birmingham's Beau Brummie Bulldog, while Oldham's Chaddy the Owl was the first mascot to retain the title.**

• Oldham received an official complaint from Blackpool in 2003 after their mascot, Chaddy the Owl, attacked the Seasiders' Bloomfield Bear and threw his boots into the crowd.

• **The first World Cup mascot, a Union Jack-draped lion called World Cup Willie, was designed for the 1966 tournament in England. The mascot for the 2014 tournament in Brazil was an armadillo called Fuleco.**

JUAN MATA

Born: Burgos, Spain, 28th April 1988
Position: Midfielder
Club career:
2006-07 Real Madrid B 34 (10)
2007-11 Valencia 130 (33)
2011-14 Chelsea 82 (18)
2014- Manchester United 15 (6)
International record:
2009- Spain 34 (10)

Along with his Spain and former Chelsea team-mate Fernando Torres, Juan Mata is the first player in football history to hold the World Cup, the European Championships, the Champions League and the Europa League simultaneously (if only briefly).

• **After starting out with the Real Madrid B team, Mata made his name with Valencia, with whom he won the Copa del Rey in 2008. He moved to Chelsea in August 2011 for £23.5 million, scoring on his Blues debut as a sub against Norwich at Stamford Bridge. In January 2014 he moved on to Manchester United for £37 million – at the time a record fee for the Old Trafford outfit.**

£37 million man, Juan Mata

• A skilful midfielder with an eye for the killer pass, Mata enjoyed huge success in west London, winning the Champions League and FA Cup in 2012 and the Europa League the following year, after his corner set up Branislav Ivanovic for the winner in the final against Benfica. Mata's consistent performances saw him voted Chelsea Player of the Year in both 2012 and 2013 – only the fourth player to win the award in consecutive seasons – and he was also nominated for the PFA Player of the Year award.

• **Mata made his debut for Spain in a 1-0 win over Turkey in 2009. The following year he was in the Spain squad that won the World Cup and in 2012 he scored in his country's 4-0 thrashing of Italy in the European Championships final in Kiev.**

MATCH-FIXING

The first recorded incidence of match-fixing occurred in 1900 when Jack Hillman, goalkeeper with relegation-threatened Burnley, was alleged to have offered a bribe to the Nottingham Forest captain. Hillman was found guilty of the charges by a joint Football Association and Football League commission and banned for one year.

• **Nine players received bans after Manchester United beat Liverpool at Old Trafford in April 1915. A Liverpool player later admitted the result had been fixed in a Manchester pub before the match. For his part in the scandal, United's Enoch West was banned for life – although the punishment was later waived... when West was 62!**

• In the mid-1960s English football was rocked by a match-fixing scandal when former Everton player Jimmy Gauld revealed in a newspaper interview that a number of games had been rigged as part of a betting coup. Gauld implicated three Sheffield Wednesday players in the scam, including England internationals Tony Kay and Peter Swan. The trio were later sentenced to four months in prison and banned for life from football. Ringleader Gauld fared even worse, receiving a four-year prison term.

• **In December 2013 the Hong Kong FA launched an investigation into match-fixing after a player from Tuen Mun FC scored a last-minute winner for the opposition with a bullet-like header into his own net. As a result of the probe, Tuen Mun and another club, Happy Valley, were suspended from the league.**

• Brazilan referee Edilson Pereira de Carvalho was banned for life from the game in 2005 after being found to have taken bribes to fix a number of games in Brazil's top league. For years afterwards fans would shout 'Edilson!' at referees who they believed had made a bad decision against their club.

• **In 2013 Lebanese referee Ali Sabbagh, who had officiated at a number of World Cup qualifiers, was jailed for six months after offering to fix matches in exchange for sexual favours.**

SIR STANLEY MATTHEWS

Born: Stoke, 1st February 1915
Died: 23rd February 2000
Position: Winger
Club career:
1932-47 Stoke City 259 (51)
1947-61 Blackpool 379 (17)
1961-65 Stoke City 59 (3)
International record:
1934-57 England 54 (11)

Nicknamed 'the Wizard of the Dribble' for his magnificent skills on the ball, Stanley Matthews was one of the greatest footballers of all time. His club career spanned a record 33 years and, incredibly, he played his last game in the First Division for Stoke City five days after his 50th birthday. He remains the oldest player to appear in the top flight.

• **Matthews' England career was almost as lengthy, his 54 appearances for his country spanning 23 years between 1934 and 1957. He made his last appearance for the Three Lions at the age of 42, setting another record.**

• A brilliant winger who possessed superb close control, Matthews inspired Blackpool to victory in the 1953 FA Cup final after the Seasiders came back from 3-1 down to beat Bolton 4-3. Despite a hat-trick by his team-mate Stan Mortensen, the match is remembered as 'the Matthews final'. He had never won an FA Cup winners' medal before and the whole country (outside of Bolton) was willing Matthews to succeed.

• **The first player to be voted Footballer of the Year (in 1948)**

and European Footballer of the Year (in 1956), Matthews was knighted in 1965 – the only footballer to be so honoured while still playing. When he died in 2000 more than 100,000 people lined the streets of Stoke to pay tribute to one of the true legends of world football.

LIONEL MESSI

Born: Rosario, Argentina, 24th June 1987
Position: Striker/winger
Club career:
2004- Barcelona 277 (242)
International record:
2005- Argentina 83 (42)

Rated by many as the best player in the world, Lionel Messi is Barcelona's all-time leading scorer with 354 goals in all competitions. No fewer than 70 of those came in the 2011/12 season and with the little Argentinian also hitting the target twice for his country, his total of 72 goals set a new world record for a player in a single campaign.

Lionel Messi, officially the best player at the 2014 World Cup

MESSI

In recent years, Middlesbrough have moved sideways rather than upwards...

• Life, though, could have been very different for Messi, who suffered from a growth hormone deficiency as a child in Argentina. However, his outrageous talent was such that Barcelona were prepared to move him and his family to Europe when he was aged just 13 and pay for his medical treatment.

• Putting these problems behind him, he has flourished to the extent that in 2009 he was named both World Player of the Year and European Player of the Year, and in 2010 he was the inaugural winner of the FIFA Ballon d'Or – an

IS THAT A FACT?

When Lionel Messi hit four goals for Barcelona in a 5-1 defeat of Osasuna on 27th January 2013 he became, at age 25, the youngest ever player to score 200 goals in La Liga.

award he retained in the following two years, making a remarkable hat-trick. A brilliant dribbler who can bamboozle the most experienced of defenders with his mesmeric ball skills, Messi helped Barcelona win La Liga and the Champions League in both 2009 and 2011. The next year he became the first player to be top scorer in four consecutive Champions League campaigns (2009-12) and he also set another record for the competition when he hit five goals in a single game against Bayer Leverkusen.

• **Messi scored a world record 91 goals in the calendar year of 2012 for club and country, and the following year became the first player to score against every other La Liga club in consecutive matches.**

• Messi made his international debut in 2005 but it was a forgettable occasion – he was sent off after just 40 seconds for elbowing a Hungarian defender who was pulling his shirt. Happier times followed in 2007 when he was voted Player of the Tournament at the Copa America and in 2008 when he won a gold medal with the Argentine football team at the

Beijing Olympics. At the 2014 World Cup he won the Golden Ball as the tournament's outstanding player, but had to be satisfied with a runners-up medal after Argentina's defeat by Germany in the final.

MIDDLESBROUGH

Year founded: 1876
Ground: Riverside Stadium (34,742)
Nickname: Boro
Biggest win: 11-0 v Scarborough (1890)
Heaviest defeat: 0-9 v Blackburn Rovers (1954)

Founded by members of the Middlesbrough Cricket Club at the Albert Park Hotel in 1876, the club turned professional in 1889 before reverting to amateur status three years later. Winners of the FA Amateur Cup in both 1895 and

1898, the club turned pro for a second time in 1899 and was elected to the Football League in the same year.

• In 1905 Middlesbrough became the first club to sign a player for a four-figure transfer fee when they forked out £1,000 for Sunderland and England striker Alf Common. On his Boro debut Common paid back some of the fee by scoring the winner at Sheffield United... the Teesiders' first away win for two years!

• The club had to wait over a century before winning a major trophy, but finally broke their duck in 2004 with a 2-1 victory over Bolton in the League Cup final at the Millennium Stadium, Cardiff.

• Two years later Middlesbrough reached the UEFA Cup final, after twice overturning three-goal deficits earlier in the competition. There was no happy ending, though, as Boro were thrashed 4-0 by Sevilla in the final in Eindhoven.

• In 1997 the club were deducted three points by the FA for calling off a Premier League fixture at Blackburn at short notice after illness and injury ravaged their squad. The penalty resulted in Boro being relegated from the Premier League at the end of the season. To add to their supporters' disappointment the club was also beaten in the finals of the League Cup and FA Cup in the same campaign.

• Former goalkeeper Mark Schwarzer is Boro's highest capped international, playing 51 times for Australia while at the Riverside between 1997 and 2008.

• In 1926/27 striker George Camsell hit an astonishing 59 league goals, including a record nine hat-tricks, for Boro as the club won the Second Division championship. His tally set a new Football League record and, although it was beaten by Everton's Dixie Dean the following season, Camsell still holds the divisional record. An ex-miner, Camsell went on to score a club record 325 league goals for Boro – a tally only surpassed by Dean's 349 goals for Everton.

• In 1997 Middlesbrough became the first club in the world to launch their own TV channel – Boro TV.

MILLWALL

Year founded: 1885
Ground: The New Den (20,146)
Previous name: Millwall Rovers
Nickname: The Lions
Biggest win: 9-1 v Torquay (1927) and v Coventry (1927)
Heaviest defeat: 1-9 v Aston Villa (1946)

The club was founded as Millwall Rovers in 1885 by workers at local jam and marmalade factory, Morton and Co. In 1920 they joined the Third Division, gaining a reputation as a club with some of the most fiercely partisan fans in the country.

• In 1988 Millwall won the Second Division title to gain promotion to the top flight for the first time in their history. The Lions enjoyed a few brief weeks at the top of the league pyramid in the autumn of 1988 but were relegated two years later.

• The club's greatest moment, though, came in 2004 when they reached their first FA Cup final. Despite losing 3-0 to Manchester United, the Lions made history by becoming the first club from outside the top flight to contest the final in the Premier League era, while substitute Curtis Weston set a new record for the youngest player to appear in the final (17 years and 119 days).

• Neil Harris is the club's all-time leading scorer with 125 goals in two spells at the Den between 1998 and 2011. Hardman defender Barry Kitchener has made more appearances for Millwall than any other player, turning out in 602 games in all competitions between 1967 and 1982.

• On their way to winning the Division Three (South) championship in 1928 Millwall scored 87 goals at home, an all-time Football League record.

• In 1974 Millwall hosted the first league match to be played on a Sunday. To get around the law at the time, admission for the Lions' game with Fulham was by 'programme only' – the cost of the programme being the same as a match ticket.

• Millwall splashed out a club record £800,000 on Derby striker Paul Goddard in 1989 – a bit of a waste of money as he only managed one goal in 20 games.

The Lions received a record £2.8 million in 2011 when striker Steve Morison moved to Norwich.

MILTON KEYNES DONS

Year founded: 2004
Ground: stadium:mk (30,500)
Nickname: The Dons
Biggest win: 6-0 v Nantwich Town (2011)
Heaviest defeat: 0-5 v Hartlepool (2005), v Huddersfield (2006), v Tottenham (2006) and v Rochdale (2007)

The club was effectively formed in 2004 when Wimbledon FC were controversially allowed to re-locate to Milton Keynes on the ruling of a three-man FA commission despite the opposition of the club's supporters, the Football League and the FA.

• Despite pledging to Wimbledon fans that they would not change their name, badge or colours, within a few seasons all three of these things had happened, reinforcing the impression amongst many in the game that the MK Dons are English football's first 'franchise'.

• The MK Dons have since handed back to Merton Council all the honours and trophies won by Wimbledon FC and claimed by AFC Wimbledon, the club started up by angry Wimbledon supporters which was promoted to the Football League in 2011 despite the claim by the FA Commission that the creation of such a team would "not be in the wider interests of football".

• The MK Dons won their first trophy in 2008 when they beat Grimsby Town 2-0 in the Football League Trophy final.

• MK Dons captain Dean Lewington has made a record 428 appearances for the club since 2004.

LUKA MODRIC

Born: Zagreb, Croatia, 9th September 1985
Position: Midfielder
Club career:
2003-08 Dinamo Zagreb 112 (31)
2003 Zrinjski Mostar (loan) 22 (8)
2004 Inter Zapresic (loan) 18 (4)
2008-12 Tottenham Hotspur 127 (13)
2012- Real Madrid 67 (4)
International record:
2006- Croatia 78 (8)

Diminutive midfielder Luka Modric enjoyed a sensational second season with Real Madrid in 2013/14, helping the Spanish giants win both the Copa del Rey and the Champions League.

• Modric started out with Croatian side Dinamo Zagreb, winning three league titles and the national Player of the Year award with his hometown club before joining Tottenham in 2008. He recovered from a broken leg to help Spurs qualify for the Champions League for the first time in 2010, but the following summer he agitated for a move to Chelsea until being forced to honour his contract by Tottenham chairman Daniel Levy. He finally left White Hart Lane in 2012, joining Real for around £33 million.

• A gifted playmaker who is known as 'the Croatian Cruyff' in his home country, Modric made his international debut in 2006 and two years later starred at Euro 2008, where he was voted into the Team of the Tournament after some magnificent displays — only the second Croatian player ever to achieve this honour.

• Modric was one of Croatia's best players at the World Cup in 2014, but couldn't prevent his country going out of the tournament at the group stage after defeats to Brazil and Mexico.

Yes, it's still Luka Modric — just without the hairband

MONACO

Year founded: 1924
Ground: Stade Louis II (18,523)
Nickname: Les rouge et blanc (The red and whites)
League titles: 7
Domestic cups: 5

AS Monaco were founded in 1924, following the merger of a number of small clubs in the principality and the surrounding region. In 2011 the club was bought by an investment group led by Russian billionaire Dmitry Rybolovlev and they have since splashed the cash on some high-profile players including Colombian striker Radamel Falcao and Portuguese midfielder Joao Moutinho.

• The club enjoyed a golden period in the early 1960s, winning two league titles under iconic manager Lucien Leduc. More recently, they were managed by a young Arsène Wenger between 1987 and 1994, a team including former Tottenham midfielder Glenn Hoddle claiming the French title in thrilling style in 1988.

• Monaco have never won a European trophy, but they came close in 2004 when they reached the Champions League final, only to lose 3-0 to Jose Mourinho's Porto. The red and whites also reached the Cup Winners' Cup final in 1992, but went down 2-0 to German outfit Werder Bremen.

• Monaco's compact Stade Louis II ground was used as the venue for the UEFA Super Cup between 1998 and 2012. In 2013 UEFA decided to play the prestigious fixture at a different venue every year, ending a 14-year tradition.

HONOURS
French League champions 1961, 1963, 1978, 1982, 1988, 1997, 2000
French Cup 1960, 1963, 1980, 1985, 1991

MONEY

The Premier League is easily the richest league in world football. In the 2013/14 season the league's revenues topped £3 billion for the first time, with domestic and worldwide TV rights accounting for more than half of that money.

• Real Madrid and Portugal star Cristiano Ronaldo is the world's richest footballer. With an estimated wealth of around £130 million, taking into account all streams of revenue, including club wages, image rights, and income from endorsements and advertising. He is followed in the rich list by Lionel Messi, Samuel Eto'o and Wayne Rooney.

• According to Forbes, Real Madrid are the richest club in the world with a total worth of $3.44 billion.

WORLD'S RICHEST CLUBS

1.	Real Madrid	$3.44 billion
2.	Barcelona	$3.20 billion
3.	Manchester United	$2.81 billion
4.	Bayern Munich	$1.85 billion
5.	Arsenal	$1.33 billion
6.	Chelsea	$0.87 billion
7.	Manchester City	$0.86 billion
8.	AC Milan	£0.85 billion
	Juventus	$0.85 billion
10.	Liverpool	$0.69 billion

Source: www.forbes.com

And, despite experiencing their worst ever Premier League season in 2013/14 and missing out on qualification for the lucrative Champions League, Manchester United remain the richest club in Britain with an estimated worth of $2.81 billion.

• **Despite retiring in 2013, former Manchester United boss Sir Alex Ferguson is still the world's richest football manager with a personal fortune of £34 million.** Meanwhile, Bayern Munich's Pep Guardiola is the highest paid manager, pocketing a staggering £14.8 million every year – £6 million more than the Premier League's best-paid boss, Chelsea's Jose Mourinho.

BOBBY MOORE

Born: Barking, 12th April 1941
Died: 24th February 1993
Position: Defender
Club career:
1958-74 West Ham United 544 (22)
1974-77 Fulham 124 (1)
1976 San Antonio Thunder 24 (1)
1978 Seattle Sounders 7 (0)
International record:
1962-73 England 108 (2)

The first and only Englishman to lift the World Cup, Bobby Moore captained England on 90 occasions – a record shared with Billy Wright. When he skippered the team for the first time against Czechoslovakia in 1963 he was aged just 22 and 47 days, making him England's youngest ever captain.

• **Moore's total of 108 caps was a record until it was surpassed by Peter Shilton in 1989, but he was England's most capped outfield player until David** Beckham passed him in 2009.

• At club level, Moore won the FA Cup with West Ham in 1964 and the European Cup Winners' Cup the following year. Then, in 1966, he made it a Wembley treble when England beat West Germany in the World Cup final. England boss Sir Alf Ramsey later paid tribute to his skipper and most reliable defender, saying, "He was the supreme professional. Without him England would never have won the World Cup."

• **In the same year Moore was voted the BBC Sports Personality of the Year – the first footballer to win the honour.**

• The world of football mourned Moore's death when he died of cancer in 1993, but he has not been forgotten. A decade later he was selected by the FA as England's 'Golden Player' of the previous 50 years and, in 2007, a huge bronze statue of England's greatest captain was unveiled outside the new Wembley.

MORECAMBE

Year founded: 1920
Ground: Globe Arena (6,476)
Nickname: The Shrimps
Biggest win: 8-0 v Fleetwood Town (1993)
Heaviest defeat: 0-7 v Leek Town (1998)

Founded in 1920 after a meeting at the local West View Hotel, Morecambe joined the Lancashire Combination League that same year and subsequently spent the next 87 years in non-league football.

• **The greatest moment in the club's history came in 2007 when The Shrimps beat Exeter 2-1 in the Conference play-off final at Wembley to win promotion to the Football League.**

• Veteran midfielder Stewart Drummond has made a club record 265 appearances for the Shrimps since signing from Shrewsbury in 2008. In a previous spell with the club in their non-league days he made another 188 appearances.

• **In 2010 Morecambe reached the League Two play-offs, but a 6-0 hammering by Dagenham and Redbridge – the biggest ever play-off defeat – in the first leg of the semi-final ended their promotion hopes.**

MOTHERWELL

Year founded: 1886
Ground: Fir Park (13,677)
Nickname: The Well
Biggest win: 12-1 v Dundee United (1954)
Heaviest defeat: 0-8 v Aberdeen (1979)

Motherwell were founded in 1886 following the merger of two local factory-based sides, Alpha and Glencairn. The club turned pro in 1893 and, in the same year, joined the newly formed Scottish Second Division.

• **The club enjoyed its heyday in the 1930s, winning the league title for the first and only time in 1932 and finishing as runners-up in the Scottish Cup three times in the same decade.**

• Striker Willie McFadyen scored a remarkable 52 league goals for The Well when they won the title in 1931/32, a Scottish top-flight record that still stands today. His team-mate Bob Ferrier played in a Scottish record 626 league games between 1917 and 1937.

• **Motherwell had to wait until 1952 before they won the Scottish Cup for the first time, and they did it in some style by thrashing Dundee 4-0 in the final. Another success followed in 1991, The Well beating Dundee United 4-3 in an exciting final.**

• Striker Michael Higdon topped the SPL scoring charts in 2012/13 with 26 goals – the first non-Old Firm player to do so since the SPL was founded in 1998. Higdon's goals helped Motherwell to their best ever SPL finish, second behind champions Celtic – a feat The Well repeated in 2014 after accumulating a club record 70 points.

• **In May 2010 Motherwell were involved in the highest scoring game ever in the SPL, coming from 6-2 down to draw 6-6 with Hibs.**

HONOURS
Division 1 champions 1932
First Division champions 1982, 1985
Division 2 champions 1954, 1969
Scottish Cup 1952, 1991
League Cup 1951

MOURINHO

JOSE MOURINHO

Born: Setubal, Portugal,
26th January 1963
Managerial career:
2000 Benfica
2001-02 Uniao Leiria
2002-04 Porto
2004-07 Chelsea
2008-10 Inter Milan
2010-13 Real Madrid
2013- Chelsea

Chelsea manager Jose Mourinho is one of just four coaches to have won the domestic title in four different countries and the only one to have claimed the championship in England, Italy and Spain.

• **Mourinho started out as Bobby Robson's assistant at Sporting Lisbon, Porto and Barcelona before briefly managing Benfica in 2000. Two years later he returned to Porto, where he won two Portuguese league titles and the UEFA Cup before becoming Europe's most sought-after young manager when his well-drilled side claimed the Champions League trophy in 2004.**

• Shortly after this triumph, Mourinho replaced Claudio Ranieri as Chelsea manager, styling himself as a "Special One" in his first press conference. He certainly lived up to his billing, as his expensively assembled Blues team won back-to-back Premier League titles in 2005 and 2006, the FA Cup in 2007 and the League Cup in both 2005 and 2007.

• **Often embroiled in controversy, Mourinho was fined a record £200,000 (later reduced to £75,000 on appeal) in 2005 for breaking Premier League rules by secretly meeting Arsenal defender Ashley Cole to talk about a possible move to Chelsea. Two years later he**

"This football lark is easy when you're a genius like me..."

sensationally left the club after falling out with Blues owner Roman Abramovich.

• A year after quitting Chelsea, Mourinho took charge of Italian giants Inter Milan and led them to the Serie A title in 2009. The following year he did even better, guiding Inter to a treble which included the Champions League, before leaving the San Siro to take over the reins at Real Madrid. He had to be satisfied with

the Spanish Cup in his first season at the Bernabeu, but in 2012 his Real team raced to the title in some style, racking up a record 100 points tally while also scoring a record number of goals, 121. After a disappointing final season in the Spanish capital, he left Real in the summer of 2013 and soon afterwards rejoined Chelsea.

DAVID MOYES

Born: Glasgow, 25th April 1963
Managerial career:
1998-2002 Preston North End
2002-13 Everton
2013-14 Manchester United

Manchester United manager for just 11 months during the 2013/14 season, David Moyes enjoyed the shortest tenure of any United boss in the post-war period. At the time of his dismissal in April 2014 the Red Devils were seventh in the table – their lowest ever placing in the Premier League at such a late stage of the campaign.

• **Moyes' first managerial job was at Preston, who he led to the Division Two (now League One) title in 2000. The following year North End almost made it into the Premiership, but lost out to Bolton in the play-off final.**

• He moved on to Everton in 2002 and in his first season in charge at Goodison Park was voted the League Managers' Association Manager of the Year after guiding the Toffees to a creditable seventh place in the Premier League. Two years later he won the award again after Everton finished fourth, one place ahead of deadly rivals Liverpool, and qualified for the preliminary stage of the Champions League. In 2009 he picked up the award for a third time after taking Everton to the FA Cup final, which they lost 2-1 to Chelsea.

• **A journeyman centre-half in his playing days, Moyes won a championship medal with Celtic in 1982 and later played for a number of clubs, including Bristol City, Dunfermline and Preston.**

Hands up if you've never won the World Cup!!!!

THE NETHERLANDS

First international: Belgium 1 Netherlands 4, 1905
Most capped player: Edwin van der Sar, 130 caps (1995-2008)
Leading goalscorer: Robin van Persie, 47 goals (2005-)
First World Cup appearance: Netherlands 2 Switzerland 1, 1934
Biggest win: Netherlands 11 San Marino 0, 2011
Heaviest defeat: England amateurs 9 Netherlands 1, 1909

Long associated with an entertaining style of attacking football, the Netherlands have only won one major tournament, the European Championships in 1988. In the final that year the Dutch beat Russia with goals from their two biggest stars of the time, Ruud Gullit and Marco van Basten.

• The Netherlands are the only country to have lost all three World Cup finals they have played in. On the first two of these occasions they had the misfortune to meet the hosts in the final, losing to West Germany in 1974 and Argentina in 1978. Then, in the 2010 final, they went down 1-0 in extra-time to Spain in Johannesburg following a negative, at times brutal, Dutch performance which was totally at odds with the country's best footballing traditions.

• A professional league wasn't formed in the Netherlands until 1956, and it took some years after that before the country was taken seriously as a football power. Their lowest ebb was reached in 1963 when they were humiliatingly eliminated from the European Championships by minnows Luxembourg.

• The following decade, though, saw a renaissance in Dutch football. With exciting players like Johan Cruyff, Johan Neeskens and Ruud Krol in their side, the Netherlands were considered the best team in Europe. Pivotal to their success was the revolutionary 'Total Football' system devised by manager Rinus Michels which allowed the outfield players constantly to switch positions during the game.

• At the 2014 World Cup in Brazil the Netherlands used all 23 players in their squad, the first time this had happened at the tournament. Manager Louis van Gaal's 'mix and match' approach worked well, as his team finished in third place.

HONOURS
European Championships *1988*
World Cup record
1930 Did not enter
1934 Round 1
1938 Round 1
1950 Did not enter
1954 Did not enter
1958 Did not qualify
1962 Did not qualify
1966 Did not qualify
1970 Did not qualify
1974 Runners-up
1978 Runners-up
1982 Did not qualify
1986 Did not qualify
1990 Round 2
1994 Quarter-finals
1998 Fourth place
2002 Did not qualify
2006 Round 2
2010 Runners-up
2014 Third place

IS THAT A FACT?
Lacking Robin van Persie through suspension, the Netherlands lined up for the first time since 1996 without a player with 'van' in his name when they faced Chile in a group game at the 2014 World Cup.

MANUEL NEUER

Born: Gelsenkirchen, Germany, 27th
March 1986
Position: Goalkeeper
Club career:
2004-08 Schalke II 26
2006-11 Schalke 156
2007- Bayern Munich 95
International record:
2009- Germany 52

Bayern Munich's Manuel Neuer became
the second most expensive goalkeeper
in the world when he joined the
Bundesliga giants from Schalke for
£19 million in 2011.

• A magnificent shot-stopper with
excellent reflexes and a good
distributor of the ball, Neuer was
voted World Goalkeeper of the
Year in 2013. In the same year he
helped Bayern claim the Treble,
collecting a first winner's medal
in the Champions League when
the Bavarians defeated fellow
Germans Borussia Dortmund 2-1
in the final at Wembley.

• The previous year Neuer's penalty
saves from Cristiano Ronaldo and
Kaka in the semi-final shoot-out
against Real Madrid enabled Bayern
to reach the Champions League
final, where they faced Chelsea at
their home ground, the Allianz
Arena. In the subsequent
shoot-out that settled the
match, Neuer became the
first ever goalkeeper to score
in a Champions League final,
although he still finished on
the losing side.

• Neuer impressed at the
2010 World Cup, helping
Germany come third in South
Africa. Four years later he was
instrumental in Germany's
success in Brazil, keeping
four clean sheets and
collecting the Golden
Glove award.

*Manuel Neuer,
the world's best
goalkeeper
(and not a
bad defender
either!)*

GARY NEVILLE

Born: Bury, 18th February 1975
Position: Defender
Club career:
1992-2011 Manchester United 400
(5)
International record:
1995-2007 England 85 (0)

England's highest capped right-back,
Gary Neville is one of the most
decorated players in the modern game,
winning eight Premier League titles,
three FA Cups, two League Cups and
the Champions League in an illustrious
career with his one and only club,
Manchester United.

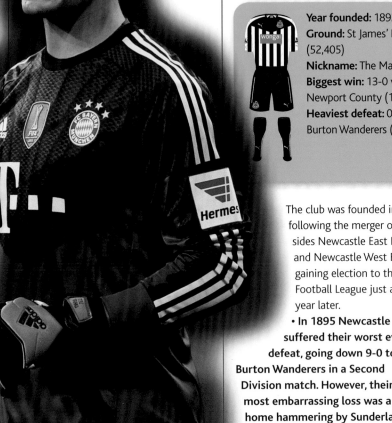

• A fixture in his country's defence
for over a decade, Neville played
in more games in the finals of the
European Championships, 11, than
any other England player. Along with
his younger brother Phil, Neville also
holds the record for the most England
games played by a pair of brothers,
144 – three more than the Charltons
of 1966 World Cup fame managed in
total. In addition, the Nevilles played
in 31 England games together, to set
another record.

• After retiring from the game during the
2010/11 season, Neville became a pundit
for *Sky Sports*, earning rave reviews for
his thought-provoking insights into the
game and surprising those who feared
he would be biased towards Manchester
United with his impartial viewpoint in his
new role.

• In 2012 Neville joined Roy Hodgson's
backroom staff on a four-year
contract, and was part of the coaching
team that assisted the Three Lions
boss at the European Championships
in Poland and the Ukraine, and then at
the 2014 World Cup in Brazil.

NEWCASTLE UNITED

Year founded: 1892
Ground: St James' Park
(52,405)
Nickname: The Magpies
Biggest win: 13-0 v
Newport County (1946)
Heaviest defeat: 0-9 v
Burton Wanderers (1895)

The club was founded in 1892
following the merger of local
sides Newcastle East End
and Newcastle West End,
gaining election to the
Football League just a
year later.

• In 1895 Newcastle
suffered their worst ever
defeat, going down 9-0 to
Burton Wanderers in a Second
Division match. However, their
most embarrassing loss was a 9-1
home hammering by Sunderland
in December 1908. The Toon
recovered, though, to win the title
that season, making that defeat
by their local rivals the heaviest

Remy Cabella is shocked to discover a non-French player has been selected to play in the Newcastle team

record, finding the net 206 times in all competitions after his then world record £15 million move from Blackburn Rovers in 1996. Another famous Newcastle centre-forward, Hughie Gallacher, scored a record 36 goals in the 1926/27 season to help the Magpies win the last of their four league titles.

• The club's leading appearance maker is goalkeeper Jimmy Lawrence, who featured in 432 league games between 1904 and 1921. Another goalkeeper, Shay Given, is easily Newcastle's most honoured international with 83 caps for the Republic of Ireland between 1997 and 2009.

• Newcastle supporters have not had much to cheer about in recent years, their team having failed to win a major trophy since 1969. That was the Fairs Cup, the Magpies beating Hungarian side Ujpest Dozsa 6-2 on aggregate in a two-legged final.

• The mid-1990s, though, promised much. A swashbuckling side managed by Toon legend Kevin Keegan swept to the new First Division title in 1993 before emerging as Premiership title contenders in the 1995/96 season. At one stage during that campaign Newcastle held a 12-point lead over eventual winners Manchester United, but they were unable to hold their advantage and ultimately finished in second place.

• In January 2011 Newcastle sold striker Andy Carroll to Liverpool for a staggering £35 million, the highest fee ever for a British player. Michael Owen is Newcastle's most expensive player, joining the club from Real Madrid for £16 million in 2005.

• Toon legend Alan Shearer scored the fastest ever goal for Newcastle, after just 10.4 seconds against Manchester City in 2003. Shearer's quickfire effort was the second fastest Premier League goal ever, behind Tottenham's Ledley King who scored after just 9.9 seconds against Bradford City three years earlier.

ever suffered by the eventual league champions. The Magpies recorded their best ever win in 1946, thrashing Newport County 13-0 to equal Stockport County's record for the biggest ever victory in a Football League match. Star of the show at St James' Park was Len Shackleton, who scored six of the goals on his Newcastle debut to set a club record.

• Newcastle have a proud tradition in the FA Cup, having won the competition on six occasions. In 1908 the Magpies reached the final after smashing Fulham 6-0, the biggest ever win in the semi-final. Then, in 1924, 41-year-old defender Billy Hampson became the oldest player ever to appear in the cup final, when he turned out for the Toon in

their 2-0 defeat of Aston Villa at Wembley.

• The club's best cup era was in the 1950s when they won the trophy three times, boss Stan Seymour becoming the first man to lift the cup as a player and a manager. Legendary centre-forward Jackie Milburn was instrumental to Newcastle's success, scoring in every round in 1951 and then notching after just 45 seconds in the 1955 final against Manchester City... the fastest Wembley cup final goal ever until Roberto di Matteo scored for Chelsea after 43 seconds in 1997.

• Milburn is the club's leading goalscorer in league matches with 178 strikes between 1946 and 1957. However, Alan Shearer holds the overall club goalscoring

IS THAT A FACT?

In 2002 Newcastle became the first, and so far only, club to make it through the Champions League group stage after losing their first three games.

HONOURS

Division 1 champions 1905, 1907, 1909, 1927
Division 2 champions 1965
First Division champions 1993
Championship champions 2010
FA Cup 1910, 1924, 1932, 1951, 1952, 1955
Fairs Cup 1969

NEWPORT COUNTY

Year founded: 1912
Ground: Rodney Parade (7,850)
Nickname: The Ironsides
Biggest win: 10-0 v Merthyr Town (1930)
Heaviest defeat: 0-13 v Newcastle United (1946)

Founded in 1912, Newport County joined the Football League eight years later. After finishing bottom of the old Fourth Division in 1988 the club dropped into the Conference, only to be expelled in February 1989 for failing to fulfil their fixtures. The club reformed later that year in the Hellenic League, four divisions below the Football League.

• **The road back for Newport was a long one, but they eventually returned to the Football League after beating Wrexham 2-0 in the Conference play-off final in 2013, in the first ever final at Wembley between two Welsh clubs.**

• The club's greatest days came in the early 1980s when, after winning the Welsh Cup for the only time, County reached the quarter-finals of the European Cup Winners' Cup in 1981 before falling 3-2 on aggregate to eventual finalists Carl Zeiss Jena of East Germany.

• **A decade earlier Newport set an unwanted record when they failed to win any of their first 25 league games (losing 21) in the Fourth Division.**

• Goalkeeper Len Weare made a record 526 appearances for Newport between 1955 and 1970.

HONOURS
Division 3 (S) champions 1939
Welsh Cup 1980

NEYMAR

Neymar plays with the weight of Brazil on his shoulders, no wonder he goes bendy at the knees!

South American Footballer of the Year in 2011 and 2012, Brazilian superstar Neymar became the most expensive ever export from South America in the summer of 2013 when he joined Barcelona from Santos for £48.6 million.

• **A superbly talented player who is stronger than his slight frame suggests, Neymar shot to fame soon after making his Santos debut in 2009 when he scored five goals in a cup match against Guarani. He has gone on to become the pin-up boy of Brazilian football, cementing his place in the nation's heart with some outstanding performances at the 2013 Confederations Cup which earned him the Player of the Tournament award. Then, at the following year's World Cup he was Brazil's top scorer with four goals, despite missing his country's last** two matches through injury.

• In April 2011 Neymar was sent off in bizarre circumstances in a Copa Libertadores match against Chilean side Colo Colo. After scoring a magnificent individual goal he celebrated by donning a mask of himself thrown onto the pitch by a Santos supporter. Unfortunately for Neymar, the referee was unimpressed by his antics and showed him a second yellow card.

• Later that year he helped Santos win the Copa Libertadores for the first time since 1963, earning the Man of the Match award for his performance against Penarol in the final. He also won the much-coveted FIFA Puskas Award for the best goal scored in world football in 2011, collecting the honour for a stunning individual effort against Flamengo.

NORTHAMPTON TOWN

Year founded: 1897
Ground: Sixfields Stadium (7,653)
Nickname: The Cobblers
Biggest win: 11-1 v Southend United (1909)
Heaviest defeat: 0-11 v Southampton (1901)

The club was founded at a meeting of local schoolteachers at the Princess Royal Inn in Northampton in 1897. After turning professional in 1901 Northampton were founder members of the Third Division in 1920.

• **The club's first full-time manager was Herbert Chapman (1907-12), who later became the first manager to win the league title with two different clubs, Huddersfield and Arsenal.**

• Despite being injured fighting in France during the Second World War, winger Tommy Fowler went on to make a record 552 appearances for the Cobblers between 1946 and 1961. His team-mate Jack English is the club's record scorer with a total of 143 goals.

• **The Cobblers enjoyed a rollercoaster decade in 1960s, rising from the old Fourth Division to the First in just six seasons. In the process they became the first club to rise through the three lower divisions to the top flight, before plummeting back to the basement by 1969.**

NORTHERN IRELAND

First international: Northern Ireland 2 England 1, 1923
Most capped player: Pat Jennings, 119 caps (1964-86)
Leading goalscorer: David Healy, 36 goals (2000-13)
First World Cup appearance: Northern Ireland 1 Czechoslovakia 0 (1958)
Biggest win: Northern Ireland 7 Wales 0, 1930
Heaviest defeat: England 9 Northern Ireland 2, 1949

Until Trinidad and Tobago appeared at the 2006 tournament, Northern Ireland were the smallest country to qualify for a World Cup finals tournament. They have made it on three occasions, reaching the quarter-finals in 1958 and beating the hosts Spain in 1982 on their way to the second round.

• **Northern Ireland's Norman Whiteside is the youngest player ever to appear at the World Cup. He was aged just 17 years and 42 days when he played at the 1982 tournament in Spain, beating the previous record set by Pelé in 1958.**

• When Northern Ireland thrashed Wales 7-0 on 1st February 1930 to record their biggest ever win, striker Joe Bambrick scored six of the goals – a record for a Home International match.

• **Goalkeeper Pat Jennings won the last of his record 119 caps for Northern Ireland in a 3-0 defeat to Brazil at the 1982 World Cup. Aged 41, he was the oldest ever player at the time to appear at the tournament.**

• During the Euro 2008 campaign Northern Ireland's highest ever scorer David Healy scored 13 goals to set a new record for the competition.

WORLD CUP RECORD
1930 Did not enter
1934 Did not enter
1938 Did not enter
1950 Did not qualify
1954 Did not qualify
1958 Quarter-finalists
1962 Did not qualify
1966 Did not qualify
1970 Did not qualify
1974 Did not qualify
1978 Did not qualify
1982 Round 2
1986 Round 1
1990 Did not qualify
1994 Did not qualify
1998 Did not qualify
2002 Did not qualify
2006 Did not qualify
2010 Did not qualify
2014 Did not qualify

It's tough for Northern Ireland, but they are no pushovers…

NORWICH CITY

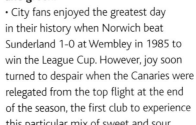

Year founded: 1902
Ground: Carrow Road (27,224)
Nickname: The Canaries
Biggest win: 10-2 v Coventry City (1930)
Heaviest defeat: 2-10 v Swindon Town (1908)

Founded in 1902 by two schoolteachers, Norwich City soon found themselves in hot water with the FA and were expelled from the FA Amateur Cup in 1904 for being 'professional'. The club joined the Football League as founder members of the Third Division in 1920.

• Norwich were originally known as the Citizens, but adopted the nickname Canaries in 1907 as a nod

On the Ball City!

to the longstanding popularity of canary-keeping in the city – a result of 15th-century trade links with Flemish weavers who had brought the birds over to Europe from Dutch colonies in the Caribbean. Soon afterwards, the club changed their colours from blue and white to yellow and green.

• City fans enjoyed the greatest day in their history when Norwich beat Sunderland 1-0 at Wembley in 1985 to win the League Cup. However, joy soon turned to despair when the Canaries were relegated from the top flight at the end of the season, the first club to experience this particular mix of sweet and sour.

• **Ron Ashman is the club's leading appearance maker, turning out in 592 league matches between 1947 and 1964. The Canaries' leading scorer is Ashman's team-mate John Gavin, who notched 122 league goals between 1948 and 1958.**

• Norwich's most capped player is Mark Bowen, who played 35 times for Wales during his Carrow Road career.

• **In 2013 the Canaries splashed out a club record £8.5 million to bring Dutch striker Ricky van Wolfswinkel to Carrow Road from Sporting Lisbon. The following year Norwich received a club record £9 million when they sold midfielder Leroy Fer to QPR.**

• Now under the ownership of cook and recipe book author Delia Smith, Norwich came a best ever third in the inaugural Premiership season in 1992/93 – albeit with a goal difference of -4, the worst ever by a team finishing in the top three in the top flight. The club enjoyed a spirited run in the UEFA Cup in the following campaign, defeating Vitesse Arnhem and German giants Bayern Munich before going out to Inter Milan.

• **Norwich City's anthem, *On the Ball City*, is a music hall song that has been associated with the club throughout their history and is believed to be the oldest fans' song anywhere in the world that is still regularly heard at matches.**

HONOURS
Division 2 champions 1972, 1986
First Division champions 2004
Division 3 (S) champions 1934
League One champions 2010
League Cup 1985

NOTTINGHAM FOREST

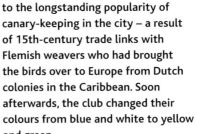

Year founded: 1865
Ground: The City Ground (30,602)
Nickname: The Reds
Biggest win: 14-0 v Clapton (1891)
Heaviest defeat: 1-9 v Blackburn Rovers (1937)

One of the oldest clubs in the world, Nottingham Forest were founded in 1865 at a meeting at the Clinton Arms in Nottingham by a group of former players of 'shinty' (a form of hockey), who decided to switch sports to football.

• **Over the following years the club was at the forefront of important innovations in the game. For instance, shinguards were invented by Forest player Sam Widdowson in 1874, while four years later a referee's whistle was first used in a match between Forest and Sheffield Norfolk. In 1890, a match between Forest and Bolton Wanderers was the first to feature goal nets.**

• Forest adopted their famous red tops in tribute to the Italian patriot Giuseppe Garibaldi, whose followers were known as the 'redshirts'. Legend also has it that the club donated a spare kit to newly formed Arsenal in 1886 and the Londoners have worn red ever since.

• **Forest enjoyed a golden era under legendary manager Brian Clough, who sat in the City Ground hotseat from 1975 until his retirement in 1993. After winning promotion to the top flight in 1977, the club won the league championship the following season – a feat that no promoted team has achieved since. Forest also won the League Cup to become the first side to win this particular double. Even more incredibly, the Reds went on to win the European Cup in 1979 with a 1-0 victory over Malmo in the final. The next year Forest retained the trophy, beating Hamburg 1-0 in the final in Madrid, to become the first and only team to win the European Cup more times than their domestic league.**

• Hardman defender Stuart 'Psycho' Pearce is Forest's most capped international, playing 76 times for England while at the City Ground between 1987 and 1997.

• **In 1959, in the days before subs,**

Forest won the FA Cup despite being reduced to 10 men when Roy Dwight, an uncle of pop star Elton John, was carried off with a broken leg after 33 minutes of the final against Luton Town. It was the first time that a club had won the cup with fewer than 11 players.

• Defender Bobby McKinlay, a member of that 1959 team, is Forest's longest serving player, turning out in 614 league games in 19 seasons at the club. The Reds' record scorer is Grenville Morris, who fell just one short of a double century of league goals for the club in the years before the First World War.

• **Nottingham Forest's City Ground is just 330 yards from Notts County's Meadow Lane, making the two clubs the nearest neighbours in the Football League.**

HONOURS
Division 1 champions 1978
Division 2 champions 1907, 1922
First Division champions 1998
Division 3 (S) champions 1951
FA Cup 1898, 1959
League Cup 1978, 1979, 1989, 1990
European Cup 1979, 1980
European Super Cup 1979

NOTTS COUNTY

Year founded: 1862
Ground: Meadow Lane (20,229)
Nickname: The Magpies
Biggest win: 15-0 v Rotherham (1885)
Heaviest defeat: 1-9 v Aston Villa (1888), v Blackburn (1889) and v Portsmouth (1927)

Notts County are the oldest professional football club in the world. Founded in 1862, the club were founder members of the Football League in 1888 and have since played a record 4,756 matches in the competition (losing a record 1,828 games).

• **In their long history County have swapped divisions more often than any other league club, winning 13 promotions and suffering the agony of relegation 15 times.**

• The club's greatest ever day was way back in 1894 when, as a Second Division outfit, they won the FA Cup – the first time a team from outside the top flight had won the trophy. In the final at Goodison Park, County beat Bolton 4-1,

with Jimmy Logan scoring the first ever hat-trick in the FA Cup final.

• **Striker Henry Cursham scored a record 48 goals for Notts County in the FA Cup between 1880 and 1887, playing alongside his two brothers in the same County team.**

• Giant goalkeeper Albert Iremonger played in a club record 564 games for County between 1905 and 1926, the last occasion when he was 42, making him the club's oldest ever player. A temperamental character, Iremonger was known for running out of his goal to argue with the ref.

• **In their long and distinguished history Notts County have had 58 different managers, a record for an English club.**

HONOURS
Division 2 champions 1897, 1914, 1923
Division 3 (S) champions 1931, 1950
Division 4 champions 1971
Third Division champions 1998
League Two champions 2010
FA Cup 1894

NUMBERS

Shirt numbers were first used in a First Division match by Arsenal against Sheffield Wednesday at Hillsborough on 25th August 1928. On the same day Chelsea also wore numbers for their Second Division fixture against Swansea at Stamford Bridge.

• **In 1933 teams wore numbers in the FA Cup final for the first time. Everton's players were numbered 1-11 while Manchester City's wore 12-22. Six years later, in 1939, the Football League made the use of shirt numbers obligatory for all teams.**

• England and Scotland first wore numbered shirts on 17th April 1937 for the countries' Home International fixture at Hampden Park. Scotland won 3-1. The following year numbers were introduced for the World Cup tournament in France.

• **Celtic were the last club in Scotland to wear numbers, only sporting them for the first time in 1960.**

• Squad numbers were adopted by Premier League clubs at the start of the 1993/94 season. The highest number worn to date by a Premier League player is 62 by Manchester City's Abdul Razak when he came on as a sub against West Brom in 2011. However, Arsenal

Are Forest heading for the Premier League?

OLDHAM ATHLETIC

IS THAT A FACT?

Among the outfield players to have worn the number '1' on their shirts are Charlton's Stuart Balmer in the 1990s, Besiktas' Daniel Pancu in 2005/06 and Barnet player/manager Edgar Davids in 2013/14.

defender Nico Yennaris went two higher in October 2011, when he wore the number 64 shirt in a League Cup tie against Bolton.

• Among the clubs to 'retire' a shirt following the death of a player are West Ham (38, Dylan Tombides), Wycombe Wanderers (14, Mark Philo) and Manchester City (23, Marc-Vivien Foe)

• In 2005 Sao Paulo goalkeeper Rogerio Ceni wore the highest ever shirt number in football history, 618, to commemorate his record-breaking 618th appearance for the Brazilian club.

• In 2010 Australia's Thomas Oar set a world record for a high shirt number in an international match when he sported '121' on his back for an Asian Cup qualifier against Indonesia.

OLDHAM ATHLETIC

Year founded: 1895
Ground: Boundary Park (10,638)
Previous name: Pine Villa
Nickname: The Latics
Biggest win: 11-0 v Southport (1962)
Heaviest defeat: 4-13 v Tranmere Rovers (1935)

Originally known as Pine Villa, the club was founded by the landlord of the Featherstone and Junction Hotel in 1895. Four years later the club changed to its present name and in 1907 Oldham joined the Second Division, winning promotion to the top flight after three seasons.

• The Latics enjoyed a golden era in the early 1990s under manager Joe Royle, reaching the League Cup final (in 1990), two FA Cup semi-finals (1990 and 1994) and earning promotion to the top flight (1991). The club were founder members of the Premier League in 1992 but were relegated two years later. In 1997 Oldham dropped into the third tier, and they are now the longest serving members of League One.

• In 1915 Oldham looked almost certain to win the First Division championship, but they blew the opportunity by losing their last two games, at home to Burnley and Liverpool. Everton took full advantage of Oldham's loss of nerve by claiming the title by a single point.

• In 1989 Oldham striker Frankie Bunn scored six of his side's goals in a 7-0 hammering of Scarborough in the third round of the League Cup. He remains the only player to have notched a double hat-trick in the competition.

• When Oldham manager Lee Johnson met his father's team, Yeovil Town, in April 2013, it was the first father-son clash of this type since Fulham (managed by Bill Dodgin jnr) played Bristol Rovers (managed by Bill Dodgin snr) in 1971.

HONOURS
Division 2 champions 1991
Division 3 (N) champions 1953
Division 3 champions 1974

MARTIN O'NEILL

Born: Kilrea, 1st March 1952
Managerial career:
1990-95 Wycombe Wanderers
1995 Norwich City
1995-2000 Leicester City
2000-05 Celtic
2006-10 Aston Villa
2011-13 Sunderland
2013- Republic of Ireland

Appointed manager of the Republic of Ireland in November 2013 following the departure of Giovanni Trapattoni, Martin O'Neill enjoyed a good start in his new role, leading the Irish to a 3-0 friendly win over Latvia in his first match in charge.

• One of the most articulate managers in the game, O'Neill started out at Wycombe Wanderers in 1990, taking the Chairboys out of the Conference and into the Football League before spending a short period at Norwich. He left Carrow Road in 1995 to move to Leicester, who he guided into the Premier League the following year. He then led the Foxes to the League Cup in 1997, and won the competition again three years later.

• In 2000 O'Neill joined Celtic, with whom he won the Treble in his first season. Dubbed 'Martin the Magnificent' by the fans, O'Neill led the Glasgow giants to two more league titles, four more cups and to the final of the UEFA Cup in 2003 before leaving the club to look after his sick wife in 2005. He returned to management the following year with Aston Villa, making the Villans a regular top six side during his four-year tenure. In December 2011 he

Republic of Ireland manager Martin O'Neill has still got it, you know

OLDHAM ATHLETIC

128

was appointed manager of Sunderland, the club he had supported as a boy, but a poor run of results saw him sacked after just 16 months.

• A one-time law student at Queen's University in Belfast, O'Neill spent most of his playing career with Nottingham Forest, with whom he won the league championship and two European Cups. A hard-working midfielder, O'Neill also played for Norwich, Manchester City and Notts County, and captained Northern Ireland at the 1982 World Cup in Spain.

MICHAEL O'NEILL

Born: Portadown, 5th July 1969
Managerial career:
2006-08 Brechin City
2009-11 Shamrock Rovers
2011- Northern Ireland

A surprise choice as his country's manager in December 2011, Michael O'Neill has endured the worst start of any Northern Ireland boss, winning just one of his first 18 matches in charge – a dismal run which included shock World Cup qualifying defeats to minnows Azerbaijan and Luxembourg.

• After a spell in charge of Brechin City, O'Neill rose to prominence as manager of Shamrock Rovers, who he led to the League of Ireland title in 2010 and the Setanta Sports Cup the following year. In 2011 he became the first manager to lead a League of

BRAZILIANS IN THE PREMIER LEAGUE
1. Oscar (Chelsea, 2012-)
2. Lucas Leiva (Liverpool, 2007-)
3. Philippe Coutinho (Liverpool, 2013-)
4. Paulinho (Tottenham, 2013-)
5. Ramires (Chelsea, 2010-)
6. David Luiz (Chelsea, 2011-14)
7. Sandro (Tottenham & QPR, 2010-)
8. Rafael (Manchester United, 2008-)
9. Willian (Chelsea, 2013-)
10. Fernandinho (Manchester City, 2013-)

Source: www.ftbpro.com

Ireland side into the group stage of a European competition when Rovers beat Partizan Belgrade in the final qualifying round of the Europa League.

• In his playing days O'Neill turned out for a number of clubs, including Dundee United, Hibs and Newcastle, for whom he was the club's leading scorer in the old First Division in 1987/88.

OSCAR

Born: Sao Paulo, Brazil, 9th September 1991
Position: Midfielder
Club career:
2008-10 Sao Paulo 11 (0)
2010-12 Internacional 36 (11)
2012- Chelsea 66 (11)
International record:
2011- Brazil 38 (11)

When Brazilian midfielder Oscar moved from Internacional to Chelsea in the summer of 2012, the £19.35 million transfer fee was the highest ever paid by a Premier League club to a South American one.

• Oscar, whose full name is Oscar dos Santos Emboaba Junior, enjoyed an excellent first season at Stamford Bridge, scoring twice on his Champions League debut against Juventus and then helping the Blues win the Europa League with a 2-1 defeat of Benfica in the final in Amsterdam.

• An intelligent player who possesses sublime ball control, Oscar started out with Sao Paulo but only played 11 games for the club before a contract dispute hastened his departure to Internacional in 2010.

• The following year he scored a brilliant hat-trick for Brazil in the FIFA U-20 World Cup final against Portugal – the first time a player had scored three in a World Cup final of any description since Geoff Hurst in 1966. Since then Oscar has established himself in his country's first team, and he played in all of Brazil's games at the 2014 World Cup, scoring against Croatia and Germany.

MICHAEL OWEN

Born: Chester, 14th December 1979
Position: Striker
Club career:
1997-2004 Liverpool 216 (118)
2004-05 Real Madrid 35 (13)
2005-09 Newcastle United 71 (26)
2009-12 Manchester United 31 (5)
2012-13 Stoke City 8 (1)
International record:
1998-2008 England 89 (40)

Former Liverpool, Newcastle and Manchester United striker Michael Owen is England's joint-fourth highest scorer of all time. He once seemed certain to become his country's record scorer, but his international career came to a juddering halt when he was 28.

• Frighteningly quick in his heyday with Liverpool, Owen enjoyed a golden year in 2001 when he won the FA Cup, League Cup and UEFA Cup in the same season with the Merseysiders, scoring both the Reds' goals in their 2-1 FA Cup final defeat of Arsenal at the Millennium Stadium. In the same year he was voted European Footballer of the Year, the last English player to achieve that distinction.

Was he fouled or is this a case of 'an Oscar for Oscar'?

• Owen joined Real Madrid for £8 million in 2004, but the following year moved back to England when he signed for Newcastle for £16 million. His unveiling at St James' Park was attended by 20,000 excited Toon fans, but after failing to set Tyneside alight he made a surprise move to Manchester United in 2009. In his first season at Old Trafford he helped United win the Carling Cup, scoring in the final against Aston Villa before limping off injured, and in 2011 he picked up his first Premier League winners' medal with the Red Devils. He moved on to Stoke in 2012, before announcing his retirement a year later.

• **Owen is the only England player to have scored at four international tournaments, notching at two World Cups and two European Championships. His strike against Argentina at the 1998 World Cup, when he sped past two defenders before slamming the ball high into the net, is one of the most famous England goals of all time. In the same year he was voted BBC Sports Personality of the Year, becoming only the third footballer to win the award.**

• Of Owen's 40 goals for England, 26 of them came in competitive matches – a figure only bettered by Wayne Rooney. He is also the only England player to have scored for his country at both the old and new Wembleys.

OWN GOALS

The first ever own goal in the Football League was scored on the opening day of the inaugural 1888/89 season, the unfortunate George Cox of Aston Villa putting through his own net in his team's 1-1 draw with Wolves.

IS THAT A FACT?

At the 2014 tournament in Brazil, Honduras goalkeeper Noel Valladares scored the first World Cup goal awarded with the use of goal-line technology in his team's match against France. Unfortunately for Valladares, it was an own goal after he fumbled a Karim Benzema shot which had rebounded off a post.

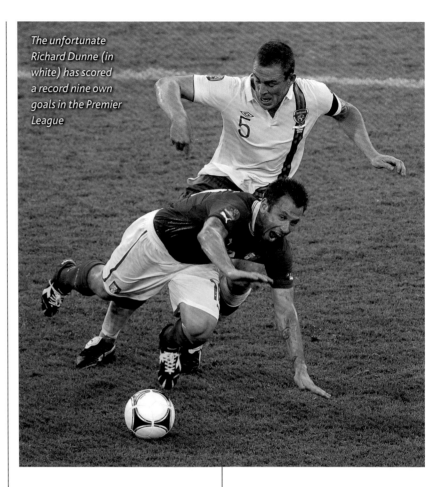

The unfortunate Richard Dunne (in white) has scored a record nine own goals in the Premier League

• **The record number of own goals in a single match is, incredibly, 149. In 2002 Madagascan team Stade Olympique l'Emyrne staged a predetermined protest against alleged refereeing bias by constantly whacking the ball into their own net, their match against AS Adema finishing in a 149-0 win for their opponents. The Madagascan FA took a dim view of the incident and promptly handed out long suspensions to four SOE players.**

• Over the years England have benefitted from 46 own goals, making OGs the Three Lions' third highest scorer after Bobby Charlton (49 goals) and Gary Lineker (48 goals).

• **During the 1934/35 season Middlesbrough's Bobby Stuart scored five own goals – a record for a single campaign.**

• A record 47 own goals were scored in the 2012/13 Premier League season. The unfortunate Richard Dunne of QPR holds the individual Premier League own goal record, with an amazing nine strikes at the wrong end.

• **On 3rd January 1977 Torquay United defender Pat Kruse scored the fastest ever own goal in English football history, netting** at the wrong end against Cambridge United after just six seconds!

• Indonesia defender Mursyid Effendi was banned from international football for life after scoring an intentional own goal in the last minute of a Tiger Cup group match against Thailand in 1998, an encounter neither side wanted to win as defeat would have paired them in the semi-finals with underdogs Singapore rather than hosts and hot favourites Vietnam.

OXFORD UNITED

Year founded: 1893
Ground: Kassam Stadium (12,500)
Previous name: Headington, Headington United
Nickname: The U's
Biggest win: 9-1 v Dorchester Town, 1995
Heaviest defeat: 0-7 v Sunderland, 1998

The club was founded by a local vicar and doctor in 1893 as Headington, primarily as a way of allowing the cricketers of Headington CC to keep fit during the winter months. The name Oxford United was adopted in 1960, six years before Oxford were elected to the Football League.

• **In 1964 Oxford became the first Fourth Division side to reach the quarter-finals of the FA Cup. However, despite being backed by a record crowd of 22,750 at their old Manor Ground, the U's went down 2-1 to eventual finalists Preston.**

• The club enjoyed a golden era under controversial owner Robert Maxwell in the 1980s, although the decade began badly when the newspaper proprietor proposed that Oxford and Reading should merge as the 'Thames Valley Royals'. The fans' well-organised campaign against the idea was successful, and their loyalty was rewarded when Oxford became the first club to win consecutive third- and second-tier titles to reach the top flight in 1985.

• **The greatest day in the club's history, though, came in 1986 when Oxford defeated QPR 3-0 at Wembley to win the League Cup. The following two decades saw a period of decline, however, and by 2006 Oxford had become the first major trophy winners to sink down into the Conference.**

• Oxford splashed out a club record £470,000 on Aberdeen striker Dean Windass in 1998. The previous year the U's received a record £1.6 million when they sold burly defender Matt Elliott to Leicester City.

> HONOURS
> *Division 2 champions* 1985
> *Division 3 champions* 1968, 1984
> *League Cup* 1986

ALEX OXLADE-CHAMBERLAIN

> **Born:** Portsmouth, 15th August 1993
> **Position:** Winger
> **Club career:**
> 20010-11 Southampton 36 (9)
> 2011- Arsenal 41 (3)
> **International record:**
> 2012- England 13 (3)

One of the most exciting attacking talents to emerge in the Premier League for many years, Alex Oxlade-Chamberlain became the youngest English scorer in the Champions League when he netted for Arsenal against Olympiacos at the start of the 2011/12 campaign.

• 'The Ox', as he has been dubbed by fans for his powerful, direct style of play, began his career at Southampton where he became the club's second youngest player (behind Theo Walcott) when he made his debut as a substitute against Huddersfield on 2nd March 2010, aged 16.

• The following season he helped the Saints gain promotion to the Championship, his thrilling displays earning him a place in the League One Team of the Year. A transfer target for numerous Premier League clubs, he moved to Arsenal for an initial fee of £12 million in August 2011. Three years later he was denied a first medal with the Gunners when injury ruled him out of the FA Cup final.

• **After a number of outstanding performances for the Under-21s, Oxlade-Chamberlain made his first appearance for the full England side as a sub against Norway in May 2012. New England boss Roy Hodgson clearly liked what he saw, taking the youngster to the Euros and giving him a first competitive start in the 0-0 draw with France, where he became his country's second youngest player (behind Wayne Rooney in 2004) at the tournament. Later that year he scored his first England goal in a 5-0 thrashing of San Marino.**

• Oxlade-Chamberlain is one of just four England players to have a father who also represented the Three Lions, his dad Mark earning eight caps on the wing during the early 1980s.

Mesut Ozil, Arsenal's record signing

MESUT OZIL

> **Born:** Gelsenkirchen, Germany, 15th October 1988
> **Position:** Midfielder
> **Club career:**
> 2006-08 Schalke 30 (0)
> 2008-10 Werder Bremen 71 (13)
> 2010-13 Real Madrid 102 (19)
> 2013- Arsenal 26 (5)
> **International record:**
> 2009- Germany 62 (18)

An attacking midfielder with skill and creativity in abundance, Mesut Ozil became Arsenal's record signing when he joined the Gunners for £42.4 million from Real Madrid in September 2013. His first season at the Emirates was rather mixed, but he did help the Gunners win a first trophy for nine years when they beat Hull in the FA Cup final.

• Ozil originally captured Real's attention after some impressive performances at the 2010 World Cup for Germany, starring in his side's four-goal thrashings of England and Argentina in the knock-out rounds before a semi-final defeat by eventual winners Spain. Immediately after the tournament Ozil moved to Spain from Werder Bremen, for whom he had scored the winning goal in the 2009 German Cup final and helped reach the UEFA Cup final in the same year.

• In the summer of 2009 Ozil was named as Man of the Match after the German Under-21 side smashed their English counterparts 4-0 in the European Championships final, prompting the manager of the team to hail him as 'the German Messi'.

• Ozil was Germany's top scorer with eight goals during qualification for the 2014 World Cup and he played a full part in his country's success in Brazil, notably scoring the decisive second goal in a last 16 victory over Algeria.

PARIS ST GERMAIN

Year founded: 1970
Ground: Parc des Princes (48,712)
Nickname: PSG
League titles: 4
Domestic cups: 8
European cups: 1

Founded as recently as 1970 following a merger between Paris FC and Stade Saint-Germain, Paris St Germain are now one of the richest clubs in the world after being bought by the Qatar Investment Authority in 2011.

• Since then PSG have splashed out millions on star players like Zlatan Ibrahimovic, Edinson Cavani and David Luiz, and the club's free-spending policy was rewarded when they won the French league in 2013. The club from the French capital repeated the feat in 2014 to claim their first back-to-back titles.

• In 1996 PSG became only the second French club to win a European trophy when they beat Rapid Vienna 1-0 in the final of the Cup Winners' Cup. The Paris outfit had a good chance to become

the only club to retain the trophy the following year, but lost in the final to Barcelona.

• A host of famous names have played for PSG in the past, including ex-Spurs winger David Ginola, one-time World Player of the Year George Weah and, briefly in 2013, former England captain David Beckham.

HONOURS
French league champions 1986, 1994, 2013, 2014
French Cup 1982, 1983, 1993, 1995, 1998, 2004, 2006, 2010
European Cup Winners' Cup 1996

PARTICK THISTLE

Year founded: 1876
Ground: Firhill (10,102)
Nickname: The Jags
Biggest win: 16-0 v Royal Albert (1931)
Heaviest defeat: 1-10 v Dunfermline (1959)

Founded in 1876, the club adopted the name Partick Thistle to distinguish themselves from local rivals Partick FC.

• The club emerged from the shadows of giant Glasgow neighbours Celtic and Rangers to win the Scottish Cup in 1921, and in 1972 Partick enjoyed the greatest day in their history when they thrashed Celtic 4-1 in the League Cup final at Hampden Park.

• The club's longest serving player is goalkeeper Alan Rough, who made 410 league appearances between 1969 and 1982. Rough is also the club's most decorated international, winning 51 caps.

• Partick fans like to point out that their team has always been managed by a Scotsman – a proud record only matched by Ross County among current SPL clubs.

HONOURS
Division 2 champions 1897, 1900, 1971
First Division champions 1976, 2002, 2013
Second Division champions 2001
Scottish Cup 1921
League Cup 1972

PELÉ

Born: Tres Coracoes, Brazil, 23rd October 1940
Position: Striker
Club career:
1956-74 Santos 412 (470)
1975-77 New York Cosmos 56 (31)
International record:
1957-71 Brazil 92 (77)

Born Edson Arantes do Nascimento, but known throughout the world by his nickname, Pelé is generally recognised as the greatest footballer ever to play the game.

• In 1957, aged just 16 years and nine months, he scored on his debut for Brazil against Argentina to become the youngest international goalscorer ever. The following year he made headlines around the globe when he scored twice in Brazil's 5-2 World Cup final defeat of hosts Sweden, in the process making history as the youngest ever World Cup winner.

• Four years later he missed most of Brazil's successful defence of their trophy through injury but was later awarded a winners' medal by FIFA. After being kicked out of the 1966 World Cup, he was back to his best at the 1970 tournament in Mexico, opening the scoring in the final against Italy and inspiring a magnificent Brazilian side to a comprehensive 4-1 victory. He remains the only player in the world with three World Cup winners' medals.

• Fast, strong, tremendously skilful and powerful in the air, Pelé was the complete footballer. He was also a phenomenal goalscorer who remains Brazil's top scorer of all time with an incredible 77 goals (in just 92 games), a record only surpassed in international football by four players. Twelve of

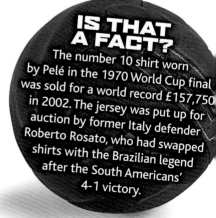

IS THAT A FACT? The number 10 shirt worn by Pelé in the 1970 World Cup final was sold for a world record £157,750 in 2002. The jersey was put up for auction by former Italy defender Roberto Rosato, who had swapped shirts with the Brazilian legend after the South Americans' 4-1 victory.

those goals came at the World Cup, making him the fifth highest scorer in the history of the tournament.

• Pelé's career total of 1,281 goals in 1,365 top-class matches is officially recognised by FIFA as a world record, although many of his goals came in friendlies for his club Santos. The Brazilian ace's most prolific patch saw him score in 14 consecutive games, to set another world record.

MANUEL PELLEGRINI

Born: Santiago, Chile, 16th September 1953
Managerial career:
1987-90 Universidad Chile
1990 Palestino
1991-92 Palestino
1992-93 O'Higgins
1993-95 Universidad Catolica
1998 Palestino
1998-2001 Universitaria Quito
2001-02 San Lorenzo
2002-03 River Plate
2004-09 Villarreal
2009-10 Real Madrid
2010-13 Malaga
2013- Manchester City

Manuel Pellegrini is the first non-European manager to win the Premier League, the Chilean having guided Manchester City to the title in 2014, just a year after replacing Roberto Mancini in the Etihad hotseat. He achieved the feat in fine style, too, as his City side banged in 102 league goals – just one short of Chelsea's Premier League record.

• **After a lengthy apprenticeship in Chile, Ecuador and Argentina, Pellegrini moved to Europe to take over the reins at Villarreal in 2004. During five years with the Spanish club he led them to the semi-finals of the Champions League in 2006, and a best ever second place in La Liga in 2008.**

• The following year Pellegrini took charge at Real Madrid, overseeing the signing of £200 million worth of talent in Cristiano Ronaldo, Kaka, Karim Benzema and Xabi Alonso. His expensively assembled 'galacticos' proceeded to rack up a then club record 96 points, but they were still pipped to the title by arch-rivals Barcelona, and Pellegrini was unceremoniously dismissed.

• Pellegrini moved on to Malaga, guiding 'Los Boquerones' to a creditable fourth place in 2012 and the quarter-finals of the Champions League a year later despite the club suffering a financial crisis which saw it banned from European competition in 2013/14.

PENALTIES

Penalty kicks were first proposed by goalkeeper William McCrum of the Irish FA in 1890 and adopted the following year. Wolves' John Heath was the first player to take and score a penalty in a Football League match, against Accrington at Molineux on 14th September 1891.

• **Francis Lee holds the British record for the most penalties in a league season, scoring 15 for Manchester City in Division One in 1971/72. He earned many of the penalties himself, leading fans to dub him 'Lee Won Pen'. In the Premier League era, Andy Johnson scored a record 11 penalties for Crystal Palace in 2004/05, but to no avail as the Eagles were still relegated.**

• The first penalty awarded in a World Cup final was scored by Holland's Johan Neeskens after just one minute of the 1974 final against West Germany. Only one player has missed a spot-kick in a World Cup final in normal play, Italy's Antonio Cabrini in 1982.

PENALTY SHOOT-OUTS

1. Italy 5 France 3, 2006 World Cup final
2. West Germany 5 France 4, 1982 World Cup semi-final
3. Liverpool 3 AC Milan 2, 2005 Champions League final
4. France 4 Brazil 3, 1986 World Cup quarter-final
5. Brazil 3 Italy 2, 1994 World Cup final
6. West Germany 4 England 3, 1990 World Cup semi-final
7. Germany 6 England 5, 1996 European Championship semi-final
8. Liverpool 4 Roma 2, 1984 European Cup final
9. Manchester United 6 Chelsea 5, 2008 Champions League final
10. South Korea 5 Spain 3, 2002 World Cup quarter-final

Source: www.bleacherreport.com

• Alan Shearer is the most prolific penalty-taker in the Premier League era, scoring 58 times from the spot.

• The most penalties ever awarded in a British match is five in the game between Crystal Palace and Brighton at Selhurst Park in 1989. Palace were awarded four penalties (one scored, three missed) while Brighton's consolation goal in a 2-1 defeat also came from the spot.

• **Argentina's Martin Palermo missed a record three penalties in a Copa America match against Colombia in 1999. His first effort struck the crossbar, his second penalty sailed over, but remarkably Palermo still insisted on taking his side's third spot-kick of the match. Perhaps he shouldn't have bothered, as his shot was palmed away by the goalkeeper.**

• Three players – Craig Burley (Derby), Darren Bent (Sunderland) and Steven Gerrard (Liverpool) – have all taken a record three penalties in a Premier League match. None of the trio, however, managed to score a hat-trick from the spot.

• **The first goalkeeper to save a penalty in the FA Cup final at Wembley was Wimbledon's Dave Beasant, who beat away John Aldridge's spot-kick in 1988 to help the Dons record a shock 1-0 win over hot favourites Liverpool.**

PENALTY SHOOT-OUTS

Penalty shoot-outs were first used in England as a way to settle drawn matches in the Watney Cup in 1970. In the first ever shoot-out Manchester United beat Hull City in the semi-final of the competition, United legend George Best being the first player to take a penalty while his team-mate Denis Law was the first to miss.

• The third/fourth place play-off between Birmingham and Stoke at St Andrew's was the first FA Cup match to be decided by penalties, Birmingham winning 4-3 after a 0-0 draw. However, spot-kicks weren't used to settle normal FA Cup ties until the 1991/92 season, Rotherham United becoming the first team to progress by this method when they beat Scunthorpe United 7-6 in the shoot-out after their first-round replay finished 3-3. In 2005 Arsenal became the first team to win the final on penalties, defeating Manchester United 5-4 after a 0-0 draw.

Losing a penalty shoot-out is not much fun – as the Netherlands discovered at the 2014 World Cup

• The first World Cup match to be settled by penalties was the 1982 semi-final between France and West Germany. The Germans won 5-4 in the shoot-out after an exciting 3-3 draw with France's Jean-Luc Ettori becoming the first goalkeeper to save a spot-kick in the new-style decider. In 1994 the final was settled by penalties for the first time, Brazil defeating Italy 3-2 on spot-kicks after a dull 0-0 draw. The 2006 final also went to penalties, Italy beating France 5-3.

• The first country to win a major international tournament on penalties, though, was Czechoslovakia, who beat West Germany 5-3 in the shoot-out of the 1976 European Championships final. The winning penalty was scored by Antonin Panenka with a delicate chip into the middle of the net.

• Among major nations who have taken part in more than two shoot-outs, Germany have the best record with five wins out of six. England, on the other hand, have the poorest record, with just one win in seven attempts. When the Three Lions lost to Portugal in the 2006 World Cup quater-final, Portuguese goalkeeper Ricardo saved three penalties – a record for a shoot-out at the tournament.

• The longest ever penalty shoot-out was between KK Palace and Civics in the first round of the 2005 Namibian Cup. After an incredible total of 48 kicks, KK Palace emerged victorious 17-16. At junior level, Under-10 sides **Mickleover Lightning Blue Sox and Chellaston required an extraordinary 66 penalties to settle their Derby County Cup match in 1998, before Blue Sox narrowly won 2-1.**

• When Bradford City beat Arsenal in the 2012/13 League Cup quarter-final, they did so in their ninth straight penalty shoot-out win – a record for English football.

PETERBOROUGH UNITED

Year founded: 1934
Ground: London Road (10,102)
Nickname: The Posh
Biggest win: 9-1 v Barnet (1998)
Heaviest defeat: 1-8 v Northampton Town (1946)

Peterborough were founded in 1934 at a meeting at the Angel Hotel to fill the void left by the collapse of local club Peterborough and Fletton United two years earlier.

• The club's unusual nickname, The Posh, stemmed from Peterborough and Fletton manager Pat Tirrel's remark in 1921 that the club wanted "Posh players for a Posh team". When the new club played its first game against Gainsborough Trinity in 1934 there were shouts of "Up the Posh!" and the nickname stuck.

• Peterborough were finally elected to the Football League in 1960... at the 21st attempt. The fans' long wait was rewarded when Peterborough stormed to the Fourth Division title in their first season, scoring a league record 134 goals. Striker Terry Bly notched an amazing 52 of the goals to set a hard-to-beat club record.

• In 1968 the club became the first since the Second World War to be relegated for non-football reasons, dropping from the Third to the Fourth Division after making illegal payments to players and collecting a 19-point deduction as a punishment.

• Striker Billy Assombalonga is the most expensive player to both arrive at and leave London Road, joining the Posh for £1.25 million from Watford in July 2013, before moving on to Nottingham Forest for £5.5 million the following summer.

HONOURS
Division 4 champions 1961, 1974
Football League Trophy 2014

Strange markings left by alien visitors? Or a bunch of football pitches seen from above? You decide...

PITCHES

According to FIFA rules, a football pitch must measure between 100 and 130 yards in length and 50 and 100 yards in breadth. It's no surprise, then, that different pitches vary hugely in size.

• Of Premier League clubs, **Manchester City have the largest pitch, their surface at the Etihad Stadium measuring 115 yards by 74 yards to give a total playing area of 8,710 square yards.**

• At the opposite end of the scale, Stoke City have the smallest pitch in the top flight. The playing surface at the Britannia Stadium is just 7,630 square yards (109 x 70yds).

• **The first portable natural grass pitch was used for the 1993 America Cup clash between America and England at the Detroit Silverdome. The grass was grown in hexagonal segments in the stadium car park and then reassembled in the covered stadium.**

• At the start of the 1981/82 season QPR became the first English club to install an artificial pitch, with Oldham, Luton Town and Preston soon following suit. By 1994, however, Preston were the last club still playing on 'plastic' and at the start of the 1994/95 season the Football League banned all artificial surfaces on the grounds that they gave home clubs an unfair advantage.

• **At 168 metres above sea level, West Brom's pitch at their Hawthorns stadium is the highest among the 92 clubs in the English professional game.**

MICHEL PLATINI

Born: Joeuf, France, 21st June 1955
Position: Midfielder
Club career:
1972-79 Nancy 181 (98)
1979-82 St Etienne 104 (58)
1982-87 Juventus 147 (68)
International record:
1976-87 France 72 (41)

The only man to be voted European Footballer of the Year in three consecutive years (1983, 1984 and 1985), Platini is a legendary figure in world football.

• **An elegant attacking midfielder with a striker's scoring instinct, Platini starred in the French team that reached the World Cup semi-final in 1982 and 1986, only to lose on both occasions to West Germany.**

• In between those disappointments, however, Platini captained France to their first ever trophy when, as the host nation, they won the 1984 European Championships. Again, Platini was the main inspiration, scoring a record nine goals in the tournament, including one from a free kick in his side's 2-0 defeat of Spain in the final.

• **After playing for Nancy and St Etienne, Platini joined Juventus for £1.2 million in 1982. Three-times top scorer in Serie A, he hit the winning goal for the Italian giants in the 1985 European Cup final against Liverpool, although Juventus' victory was completely overshadowed by**

the deaths of 39 fans in the Heysel tragedy.

• After managing France for four years between 1988 and 1992, Platini was elected President of UEFA in 2007. In this role he has opposed the use of goal-line technology in the Champions League but has been a firm advocate of 'Financial Fair Play', preventing clubs with mega-rich owners from spending more than they earn.

PLAY-OFFS

The play-off system was introduced by the Football League in the 1986/87 season. Initially, one club from the higher division competed with three from the lower division at the semi-final stage but this was changed to four teams from the same division in the 1988/89 season. The following season a one-off final at Wembley replaced the original two-legged final.

• **Crystal Palace and Blackpool have been promoted from the play-offs a record four times each, while the Seasiders are the only club to have gone up from three different divisions via the play-offs.**

• Preston have appeared in the play-offs on a record nine occasions, but have never ended up being promoted after losing six semi-finals – most recently against Rotherham in 2014 – and three finals.

• **The Championship play-off final is the most financially rewarding sporting event in the world, its worth to the winners in prize money, TV and advertising revenue, and increased gate receipts, being estimated at around £120 million.**

• Nottingham Forest and MK Dons have the worst record among play-off semi-finalists, appearing in four semis each without once making it through to the final at Wembley.

IS THAT A FACT? The biggest ever crowd at a play-off match (87,347) saw QPR beat Derby County 1-0 in the Championship play-off final at Wembley in 2014.

PLYMOUTH ARGYLE

Year founded: 1886
Ground: Home Park (16,388)
Previous name: Argyle FC
Nickname: The Pilgrims
Biggest win: 8-1 v Millwall (1932) and v Hartlepool (1994)
Heaviest defeat: 0-9 v Stoke City (1960)

The club was founded as Argyle FC in 1886 in a Plymouth coffee house, the name deriving from the Argyll and Sutherland Highlanders who were stationed in the city at the time. The current name was adopted in 1903, when the club became fully professional and entered the Southern League.

• After joining the Football League in 1920, Plymouth just missed out on promotion from the Third Division (South) between 1922 and 1927, finishing in second place in six consecutive seasons... a record of misfortune no other club can match.

• Sammy Black, a prolific marksman during the 1920s and 1930s, is the club's leading goalscorer with 185 league goals. The Pilgrims' longest serving player is Kevin Hodges, with 530 appearances between 1978 and 1992.

• Rory Fallon is the only Pilgrim to appear at the World Cup, featuring in all three of New Zealand's games at the 2010 tournament in South Africa.

• In one of the most bizarre incidents ever in the history of football, Plymouth conceded a goal scored by the referee in a Division Three fixture against Barrow in 1968. A shot from a Barrow player was heading wide until it deflected off the boot of referee Ivan Robinson and into the Pilgrims' net for the only goal of the match.

• The largest city in England never to have hosted top-flight football, Plymouth have won the third tier of English football a record four times, most recently topping the Second Division in 2004.

HONOURS
Division 3 (S) champions 1930, 1952
Division 3 champions 1959
Second Division champions 2004
Third Division champions 2002

MAURICIO POCHETTINO

Born: Murphy, Argentina, 2nd March 1972
Managerial career:
2009-12 Espanyol
2013-14 Southampton
2014- Tottenham Hotspur

Appointed boss of Tottenham in May 2014, Mauricio Pochettino is only the second Argentinian to manage in the Premier League – after Ossie Ardiles, who also enjoyed a spell in the White Hart Lane hotseat in the 1990s.

• Pochettino began his managerial career with Spanish side Espanyol in 2009, but was sacked three years later when the Barcelona-based club slipped to the bottom of La Liga.

• Later that season, however, he was a surprise choice to replace Nigel Adkins at Southampton. Despite never speaking to the press in English, Pochettino soon won over the Saints fans by introducing a vibrant attacking style which made the most of up-and-coming talents like Adam Lallana, Luke Shaw and Jay Rodriguez. In his only full season at St Mary's in 2013/14, Pochettino led Southampton to a best ever eighth place finish in the Premier League.

• A central defender in his playing days, Pochettino twice won the Copa del Rey with Espanyol. He also represented Argentina at the 2002 World Cup, famously fouling Michael Owen in the penalty area to allow England captain David Beckham to score the only goal of the group game between the sides from the spot.

PORT VALE

Year founded: 1876
Ground: Vale Park (19,052)
Previous name: Burslem Port Vale
Nickname: The Valiants
Biggest win: 9-1 v Chesterfield (1932)
Heaviest defeat: 0-10 v Sheffield United (1892) and v Notts County (1895)

Can Mauricio Pochettino get Spurs into the top four?

Port Vale's name derives from the house where the club was founded in 1876. Initially, the club was known as Burslem Port Vale – Burslem being the Stoke-on-Trent town where the Valiants are based – but the prefix was dropped in 1911.

• After a 12-year gap Port Vale returned to the Football League in October 1919, replacing the disbanded Leeds City. Bizarrely, the Valiants inherited the Yorkshiremen's playing record (won four, lost two, drawn two) and went on to finish in a respectable 13th position.

• In their first season as a league club, in 1892/93, Port Vale suffered the worst ever home defeat in Football League history when Sheffield United hammered them 10-0. However, Vale's defence was in much better nick in 1953/54 when they kept a league record 30 clean sheets on their way to the Third Division (North) championship.

• Loyal defender Roy Sproson is Port Vale's longest serving player, appearing in a phenomenal 761 league games between 1950 and 1972. Only two other players in the history of league football have made more appearances for the same club. With 154 league goals in two spells at the club between 1923 and 1933 Wilf Kirkham is the Valiants' record goalscorer.

• Singer Robbie Williams is Port Vale's most famous fan. When he recorded 'It's Only Us', the original theme song for computer game *FIFA 2000*, he did so on the condition that the Valiants would be included in the game.

HONOURS
Division 3 (N) champions *1930, 1954*
Division 4 champions *1959*
Football League Trophy *1993, 2001*

FC PORTO

Year founded: 1893
Ground: Estadio do Dragao (52,399)
Nickname: The Dragons
League titles: 27
Domestic cups: 19
European cups: 5
International cups: 2

Easily the most successful Portuguese side of recent years, Porto were founded in 1893 by a local wine salesman who

had been introduced to football on his regular business trips to England.

• **Seven league title wins in the last nine seasons have taken Porto's total of domestic championships to 27, six behind arch-rivals Benfica. In the three seasons between 2011 and 2013 Porto lost just one league game (to Gil Vicente)... the best run of form of any team in Europe during that period.**

• Porto have the best record in Europe of any Portuguese side, with two victories in the European Cup/Champions League (in 1987 and 2004) and two in the UEFA Cup (in 2003 and 2011), the latter of these triumphs coming under Andre Villas-Boas – at 33, the youngest coach ever to win a European competition.

• **Porto are the only Portuguese club to have been crowned world champions, claiming the Intercontinental Cup in both 1987 and 2004.**

HONOURS
Portuguese League champions *1935, 1939, 1940, 1956, 1959, 1978, 1979, 1985, 1986, 1988, 1990, 1992, 1993, 1995, 1996, 1997, 1998, 1999, 2003, 2004, 2006, 2007, 2008, 2009, 2011, 2012, 2013*
Portuguese Cup *1922, 1925, 1932, 1937, 1956, 1958, 1968, 1977, 1984, 1988, 1991, 1994, 1998, 2000, 2001, 2003, 2006, 2009, 2011*
European Cup/Champions League *1987, 2004*
UEFA Cup/Europa League *2003, 2011*
European Super Cup *1987*
Intercontinental Cup *1987, 2004*

PORTSMOUTH

Year founded: 1898
Ground: Fratton Park (20,668)
Nickname: Pompey
Biggest win: 9-1 v Notts County (1927)
Heaviest defeat: 0-10 v Leicester City (1928)

Portsmouth were founded in 1898 by a group of sportsmen and businessmen at a meeting in the city's High Street. After starting out in the Southern League the club joined the Third Division in 1920.

• **In 1949 the club became the first team to rise from the third tier to claim the league championship, and the following year became the first of just five clubs to retain the title since the end of the Second World War.**

• The most influential player in that team was half-back Jimmy Dickinson, who went on to play a record 764 times for Pompey, the second highest number of Football League appearances with any single club. Dickinson is also Portsmouth's most decorated international, winning 48 caps for England.

• **Another legendary figure from that period, right-winger Peter Harris is the club's leading marksman, with 193 goals between 1946 and 1960.**

• The club won the FA Cup for the first time in 1939, when Pompey thrashed favourites Wolves 4-1 in the final at Wembley. In 2008 they lifted the cup for a second time when a single goal from Nigerian striker Kanu was enough to beat Cardiff City in only the second final at the new Wembley.

• **In the same year Portsmouth splashed out a record £11 million on lanky Liverpool striker Peter Crouch. Midfielder Lassana Diarra is Pompey's record sale, joining Real Madrid for £18 million in 2008.**

• Since those heady days Portsmouth's financial problems have seen the club slide all the way down to League Two, but there was some good news for their long-suffering followers in April 2013 when Pompey were bought by the Portsmouth Supporters' Trust to become the largest fan-owned club in England.

HONOURS
Division 1 champions *1949, 1950*
First Division champions *2003*
Division 3 (South) champions *1924*
Division 3 champions *1962, 1983*
FA Cup *1939, 2008*

IS THAT A FACT?
With a capacity of 20,688, Portsmouth's Fratton Park is the biggest stadium in League Two.

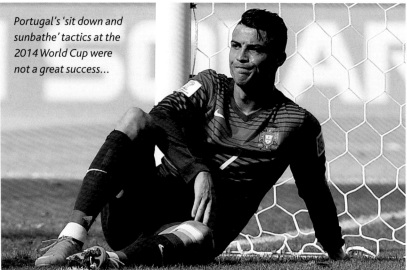

Portugal's 'sit down and sunbathe' tactics at the 2014 World Cup were not a great success...

PORTUGAL

First international:
Spain 3 Portugal 1, 1921
Most capped player:
Luis Figo, 127 caps
(1991-2006)
Leading goalscorer:
Cristiano Ronaldo, 50
goals (2003-)
**First World Cup
appearance:** Portugal 3
Hungary 1, 1966
Biggest win: Portugal 8
Liechtenstein 0, 1994 and 1999
Heaviest defeat: Portugal 0
England 10, 1947

Portugal have never won a major trophy, although they reached the final of the European Championships in 2004. Playing on home soil they were hot favourites to beat Greece, but went down to a surprise 1-0 defeat. Eight years later they missed out on a chance to appear in another final when they lost a Euro 2012 semi-final shoot-out to Spain.

• **Portugal's best showing at the World Cup was in 1966 when they finished third after going out to hosts England in the semi-finals. Much of their success was down to legendary striker Eusebio, who topped the goalscoring charts with nine goals.**

• The southern Europeans also reached the semi-finals of the World Cup in 2006, after beating Holland in 'The Battle of Nuremburg' in the last 16 and England on penalties in the quarter-finals. A 1-0 defeat to France, though, ended their hopes of appearing in the final.

• **Portugal were the first country to beat West Germany at home in a**

competitive match, winning 1-0 a World Cup qualifier in 1985. That victory booked Portugal's passage to the 1986 World Cup in Mexico where they went out in the first round despite recording a shock 1-0 victory over England in their first match.

WORLD CUP RECORD
1930-38 Did not enter
1950-62 Did not qualify
1966 Third place
1970-82 Did not qualify
1986 Round 1
1990-98 Did not qualify
2002 Round 1
2006 Fourth place
2010 Round 2
2014 Round 1

PREMIER LEAGUE

The Premier League was founded in 1992 and is now the most watched and most lucrative sporting league in the world, with revenues of over £3 billion in the 2013/14 season.

• **Initially composed of 22 clubs, the Premier League was reduced to 20 teams in 1995. A total of 46 clubs have played in the league but just five – Manchester United, Blackburn Rovers, Arsenal, Chelsea and Manchester City – have won the title. Of this group, United are easily the most successful, having won the league 13 times.**

• Manchester United recorded the biggest win in Premier League history in 1995 when they hammered Ipswich Town 9-0. In the same match Andy Cole hit a record five goals, a feat since matched by Alan Shearer (Newcastle United), Jermain Defoe (Tottenham) and Dimitar Berbatov (Manchester United).

• Only seven clubs have appeared in the league in every season since its inception: Arsenal, Aston Villa, Chelsea, Everton, Liverpool, Manchester United and Tottenham Hotspur. United lead the all-time table with 1,816 points (including a record 547 wins in 848 games), while Tottenham have lost more games (293) than any other club.

• Alan Shearer is the leading scorer in the history of the Premier League with a total of 260 goals for Blackburn Rovers and Newcastle between 1992 and 2006.

• Ryan Giggs holds the Premier League appearance record, turning out in 632 games for Manchester United between 1992 and 2014.

PRESTON NORTH END

Year founded: 1879
Ground: Deepdale (23,404)
Nickname: The Lilywhites
Biggest win: 26-0 v Hyde
(1887)
Heaviest defeat: 0-7 v
Blackpool (1948)

Preston were founded in 1879 as a branch of the North End Cricket and Rugby Club, playing football exclusively from 1881.

• Founder members of the Football League in 1888, Preston won the inaugural league title the following year, going through the entire 22-game season undefeated and conceding just 15 goals (a league record). For good measure the club also won the FA Cup, beating Wolves 3-0 in the final, to become the first club to win the Double. During their cup run, Preston demolished Hyde 26-0 to record the biggest ever win in any English competition, striker Jimmy Ross scoring seven of the goals to set a club record that has never been matched. Ross went on to score a record 20 goals in the cup that season.

• Of the 12 founder members of the league, Preston are the only club still playing at the same ground, making Deepdale the oldest league football stadium anywhere in the world.

• The legendary Tom Finney is Preston's most capped international, turning out for England in 76 games. The flying winger is also the club's highest scorer, with 187 strikes between 1946 and

1960. North End's leading appearance maker is Alan Kelly, who played in goal for the club in 447 league games between 1958 and 1973.

• Along with Wolves and Burnley, Preston are one of just three clubs to have won all four divisions of English football, achieving this feat in 1996 when they topped the Third Division (now League Two).

• In their proud history Preston have accumulated an impressive 5,442 points – a total only bettered by Premier League giants Manchester United, Liverpool and Arsenal.

> **HONOURS**
> *Division 1 champions 1889, 1890*
> *Division 2 champions 1904, 1913, 1951*
> *Division 3 champions 1971*
> *Second Division champions 2000*
> *Third Division champions 1996*
> *FA Cup 1889, 1938*
> *Double 1889*

PROMOTION

Automatic promotion from the Second to First Division was introduced in the 1898/99 season, replacing the 'test match' play-off-style system. The first two clubs to go up automatically were Glossop North End and Manchester City.

• Birmingham City, Leicester City and Notts County have gained a record 13 promotions, while the Foxes have gone up to the top flight on a record 12 occasions – most recently in 2014, after winning the Championship.

• Not all clubs who have been promoted have done so through playing merit. The most notorious case involved Arsenal in 1919 who were elected to the First Division at the expense of local rivals Tottenham, allegedly thanks to the underhand tactics employed by the Gunners' then chairman, Sir Henry Norris.

QUEEN'S PARK

Year founded: 1867
Ground: Hampden Park (52,025)
Nickname: The Spiders
Biggest win: 16-0 v St Peters (1885)
Heaviest defeat: 0-9 v Motherwell (1930)

Founded in 1867 at a meeting at a house in south Glasgow, Queen's Park are Scotland's oldest club and a genuine sporting institution..

• **The dominant force in the game north of the border in the 19th century, Queen's Park won the first ever Scottish Cup in 1874 and held the trophy for the next two years as well. In all, they have won the competition 10 times... a cup record only bettered by Old Firm giants Celtic and Rangers.**

• Queen's Park's star player of the Victorian era was Charles Campbell, who won a record eight Scottish Cup winners' medals.

• **Queen's Park are the only Scottish side to have played in the final of the FA Cup, losing to Blackburn Rovers in both 1884 and 1885 before the Scottish FA banned its clubs from entering the competition two years later.**

• Despite being the only amateur club in senior football anywhere in Britain, Queen's Park play their games at the home of Scottish football, Hampden Park, but rarely attract more than a few hundred spectators to the 52,000-capacity stadium.

> **HONOURS**
> *Division 2 champions 1923, 1956*
> *Second Division champions 1981*
> *Third Division champions 2000*
> *Scottish Cup 1874, 1875, 1876, 1880, 1881, 1882, 1884, 1886, 1890, 1893*

QUEENS PARK RANGERS

Year founded: 1882
Ground: Loftus Road (18,489)
Nickname: The R's
Biggest win: 9-2 v Tranmere Rovers (1960)
Heaviest defeat: 1-8 v Mansfield Town (1965) and v Manchester United (1969)

Founded in 1882 following the merger of St Jude's and Christchurch Rangers, the club was called Queens Park Rangers because most of the players came from the Queens Park area of north London.

• A nomadic outfit in their early days, QPR have staged home matches at

no fewer than 19 different venues, a record for a Football League club.

• The club enjoyed its finest moment in 1967 when Rangers came from two goals down to defeat West Bromwich Albion 3-2 in the first ever League Cup final to be played at Wembley. In the same season the R's won the Third Division title to pull off a unique double.

• Loftus Road favourite Rodney Marsh hit a club record 44 goals that season, 11 of them coming in the League Cup. George Goddard, though, holds the club record for league goals with 37 in 1929/30. Goddard is also the club's leading scorer, notching 174 league goals between 1926 and 1934.

• In 1976 QPR finished second in the old First Division, being pipped to the league championship by Liverpool. Six years later Rangers reached the FA Cup final for the only time in their history but went down 1-0 to Tottenham in a replay after the original match finished 1-1.

• **No other player has pulled on Rangers' famous hoops more often than Tony Ingham, who made 519 league appearances over 13 years after signing from Leeds in 1950.**

• In January 2013 QPR splashed out a club record £12.5 million when they signed defender Christopher Samba from Russian side Anzhi Makhachkala. It didn't do them much good, however, as they were relegated at the end of a season in which they had the worst ever start to a Premier League campaign – 16 games without a win. However, Rangers bounced back the following season after beating Derby County in the Championship play-off final.

• **The Hoops' most capped international is defender Alan McDonald, who played 52 times for Northern Ireland between 1986 and 1996.**

• Rugby Union side London Wasps shared Loftus Road with QPR between 1996 and 2002, when neighbours Fulham moved in for two years while Craven Cottage was being redeveloped.

• **Famous fans of QPR include actor Martin Clunes, comedian Bill Bailey and bad-boy musician Pete Doherty.**

> **HONOURS**
> *Division 2 champions 1983*
> *Championship champions 2011*
> *Division 3 (S) champions 1948*
> *Division Three champions 1967*
> *League Cup 1967*

Sergio Ramos celebrates his goal in the 2014 Champions League final

SERGIO RAMOS

Born: Camas, Spain, 30th March 1986
Position: Defender
Club career:
2003-04 Sevilla B 26 (2)
2004-05 Sevilla 39 (2)
2005- Real Madrid 287 (36)
International record:
2005- Spain 120 (9)

Real Madrid defender Sergio Ramos is the youngest European player ever to win 100 caps for his country, reaching three figures a week before his 27th birthday when Spain played Finland in a World Cup 2014 qualifier in March 2013. Ramos marked the occasion in style, scoring his side's goal in a 1-1 draw.

• **A strong tackler who can play either in central defence or at right-back, Ramos started out at Sevilla before joining Real for around £20 million in 2005 – aged 19 at the time, he was the most expensive teenager in Spanish football history.**

• Ramos has gone on to win three La Liga titles and the Champions League with Real. The defender played a vital role in his club's triumph in Lisbon against city rivals Atletico Madrid in 2014, heading a last-minute equaliser which enabled Real to go on and win the game in extra-time. Less impressively, Ramos has been sent off a club record 19 times for the Spanish giants.

• Ramos has enjoyed huge success at international level, winning two European Championships (2008 and 2012) and the World Cup in South Africa in 2010.

AARON RAMSEY

Born: Caerphilly, 13th December 1990
Position: Midfielder
Club career:
2007-08 Cardiff City 16 (1)
2008- Arsenal 127 (17)
2010-11 Nottingham Forest (loan) 5 (0)
2011 Cardiff City (loan) 6 (1)
International record:
2008- Wales 30 (8)

Box-to-box midfielder Aaron Ramsey is the youngest player ever to captain Wales, skippering his country for the first time in a Euro 2012 qualifier against England on 26th March 2011 when he was aged just 20 and 90 days.

• **Ramsey is a product of the Cardiff City youth system, and became the club's youngest ever player when he made his debut as a sub against Hull City on the last day of the 2006/07 campaign aged 16 and 124 days. The following season he cemented his place in the Bluebirds' team and played in the 2008 FA Cup final against Portsmouth – aged 17, he was the second youngest player ever to appear in the final after Millwall's Curtis Weston in 2004.**

• In June 2008 Ramsey signed for Arsenal for £4.8 million. When he notched his first goal for the Gunners against Fenerbahce in October 2008, he became only the second player born in the 1990s to score in the Champions League.

• **Ramsey's career stalled after he suffered a double fracture of his right leg in February 2010, but he recovered to enjoy his best season yet for the Gunners in 2013/14. The Welshman's stunning displays saw him nominated for the PFA Young Player of the Year award, and he finished the season in glorious fashion by scoring the winner in the Gunners' 3-2 victory over Hull City in the FA Cup final.**

RANGERS

Year founded: 1873
Ground: Ibrox Stadium (51,082)
Nickname: The Gers
Biggest win: 14-2 v Blairgowrie (1934)
Heaviest defeat: 2-10 v Airdrieonians (1886)

The most decorated club in the history of world football, Rangers were founded by a group of rowing enthusiasts in 1873. The club were founder members of the Scottish League in 1890, sharing the inaugural title with Dumbarton.

Aaron Ramsey is really proud to be Welsh

More goals like this and Rangers will soon be back in the Scottish Premiership

• Rangers have won the league title 54 times, a record of domestic success which is unmatched by any club on the planet. Between 1989 and 1997 the Gers topped the league in nine consecutive seasons, initially under Graeme Souness then under Walter Smith, to equal a record previously set by arch-rivals Celtic.

• In 2000 Rangers became the first club in the world to win 100 major trophies. The Glasgow giants have since extended their tally to 115, most recently adding the League Cup and SPL title in 2011. The club's tally of seven domestic trebles is also unequalled anywhere in the world.

• **Way back in 1898/99 Rangers enjoyed their best ever league season, winning all 18 of their matches to establish yet another world record.**

• The club's record goalscorer is Rangers manager Ally McCoist. In a 15-year Ibrox career between 1983 and 1998 McCoist banged in an incredible 251 goals (355 in all competitions), including a record 28 hat-tricks. McCoist is also the club's most capped international, winning 59 of his 61 Scotland caps while with the Gers.

• **Rangers also hold two important records in the Scottish League Cup, with more wins (27) and more appearances in the final (33) than any other club. The Gers' first win in the competition came in its**

inaugural year when they thrashed Aberdeen 4-0 in the final in 1947.

• The club's record in the Scottish Cup is not quite as impressive, the Gers' 33 triumphs in the competition being bettered by Celtic's 36. However, it was in the Scottish Cup that Rangers recorded their biggest ever victory, thrashing Blairgowrie 14-2 in 1934. Striker Jimmy Fleming scored nine of the goals on the day to set a club record.

• **Despite all their domestic success, Rangers have only won a single European trophy. That was the Cup Winners' Cup, which they claimed in 1972 after beating Dynamo Moscow 3-2 in the final in Barcelona. The club, though, did reach the final of the same competition in both 1961 and 1967 and were also runners-up in the UEFA Cup in 2008, when an estimated 150,000 (mostly ticketless) Rangers fans followed their team to the final in Manchester.**

• No player has turned out in the royal blue shirt of Rangers more often than former captain John Greig, who made 755 appearances in all competitions between 1961 and 1978. The league record, though, is held by Sandy Archibald (513 games between 1917 and 1934).

• **A Scottish League record crowd of 118,567 saw Rangers play Celtic at Ibrox on 2nd January 1939. The home fans went home happy after the Gers beat their city rivals 2-1.**

• In 2000 Rangers splashed out a club record £12 million when they signed lanky Norwegian striker Tore Andre Flo from Chelsea. Eight years later, in 2008, the Ibrox coffers were boosted by a record £9 million when full-back Alan Hutton moved south of the border to join Spurs.

• In 2012 Rangers' massive debts, estimated to be over £130 million, forced the club into administration and then liquidation, prompting the other SPL clubs to vote them out of the league. Starting from scratch in the Scottish Third division, Rangers climbed back to the Championship two years later after going through the entire League One 2013/14 season unbeaten.

HONOURS
Division 1 champions *1891 (shared), 1899, 1900, 1901, 1902, 1911, 1912, 1913, 1918, 1920, 1921, 1923, 1924, 1925, 1927, 1928, 1929, 1930, 1931, 1933, 1934, 1935, 1937, 1939, 1947, 1949, 1950, 1953, 1956, 1957, 1959, 1961, 1963, 1964, 1975*
Premier League champions *1976, 1978, 1987, 1989, 1990, 1991, 1992, 1993, 1994, 1995, 1996, 1997*
SPL champions *1999, 2000, 2003, 2005, 2009, 2010, 2011*
League One champions *2014*
Third Division champions *2013*
Scottish Cup *1894, 1897, 1898, 1903, 1928, 1930, 1932, 1934, 1935, 1936, 1948, 1949, 1950, 1953, 1960, 1962, 1963, 1964, 1966, 1973, 1976, 1978, 1979, 1981, 1992, 1993, 1996, 1999, 2000, 2002, 2003, 2008, 2009*
Scottish League Cup *1947, 1949, 1961, 1962, 1964, 1965, 1971, 1976, 1978, 1979, 1982, 1984, 1985, 1987, 1988, 1989, 1991, 1993, 1994, 1997, 1999, 2002, 2003, 2005, 2008, 2010, 2011*
European Cup Winners' Cup *1972*

READING

Year founded: 1871
Ground: Madejski Stadium (24,161)
Nickname: The Royals
Biggest win: 10-2 v Crystal Palace (1946)
Heaviest defeat: 0-18 v Preston (1894)

Reading were founded in 1871, making them the oldest Football League club south of Nottingham. After amalgamating with local clubs Reading Hornets (in 1877) and Earley FC (in 1889), the club was eventually elected to the new Third Division in 1920.

• The oldest club still competing in the FA Cup never to have won the trophy, Reading experienced their worst ever defeat in the competition when they were hammered 18-0 by Preston in 1894.

• In the 1985/86 season Reading set a Football League record by winning their opening 13 matches, an outstanding start which provided the launch pad for the Royals to go on to top the old Third Division at the end of the campaign.

• Reading's greatest moment, though, came in 2006 when, under manager Steve Coppell, they won promotion to the top flight for the first time in their history. They went up in fine style, too, claiming the Championship title with a Football League record 106 points and going 33 matches unbeaten (a record for the second tier) between 9th August 2005 and 17th February 2006.

• Prolific marksman Ronnie Blackman holds two scoring records for the club, with a total of 158 goals between 1947 and 1954 and a seasonal best of 39 goals in the 1951/52 campaign.

• During the 1978/79 season Reading goalkeeper Steve Death went 1,074 minutes without conceding a goal – a Football League record until 2009, when Manchester United's Edwin van der Sar beat it.

• With 26 caps for the Republic of Ireland between 2006 and 2009, striker Kevin Doyle is Reading's highest capped player.

• In 2007 Reading were involved in the Premier League's highest scoring match, losing 7-4 away to Portsmouth. Five years later they were on the losing side again in the highest scoring League Cup match, going down 7-5 at home to Arsenal.

HONOURS
Championship champions 2006, 2012
Division 3 (S) champions 1926
Division 3 champions 1986
Second Division champions 1994
Division 4 champions 1979

REAL MADRID

Year founded: 1902
Ground: Estadio Bernabeu (81,044)
Previous name: Madrid
Nickname: Los Meringues
League titles: 32
Domestic cups: 18
European cups: 13
International cups: 3

Founded by students as Madrid FC in 1902, the title 'Real' (meaning 'Royal') was bestowed on the club by King Alfonso XIII in 1920.

• One of the most famous names in world football, Real Madrid won the first ever European Cup in 1956 and went on to a claim a record five consecutive victories in the competition with a side featuring

TOP 10

EUROPEAN CUP/ CHAMPIONS LEAGUE FINAL APPEARANCES

1. Real Madrid	13	(10 wins)
2. AC Milan	11	(7 wins)
3. Bayern Munich	10	(5 wins)
4. Liverpool	17	(5 wins)
5. Barcelona	7	(4 wins)
6. Benfica	7	(2 wins)
Juventus	7	(2 wins)
8. Ajax	6	(4 wins)
9. Inter Milan	5	(3 wins)
Manchester United	5	(3 wins)

greats such as Alfredo di Stefano, Ferenc Puskas and Francisco Gento. Real's total of 10 victories in the European Cup/Champions League – their last success coming in 2014 after they beat city rivals Atletico Madrid in the final in Lisbon – is also a record.

• The club have dominated Spanish football over the years, winning a record 32 league titles (10 more than nearest rivals Barcelona) including a record five on the trot on two occasions (1961-65 and 1986-90).

• Real Madrid have broken the world transfer record on the last five occasions, splashing out eye-watering sums on Portuguese star Luis Figo (£37 million from Barcelona in 2000), French midfielder Zinedine Zidane (£46 million from Juventus in 2001),

Some Real Madrid fans complain that their team's players are a bit on the small side

Brazilian playmaker Kaka (£56 million from AC Milan in 2009), Cristiano Ronaldo (£80 million from Manchester United in 2009) and Gareth Bale (£86 million from Tottenham in 2013).

HONOURS
Spanish League 1932, 1933, 1954, 1955, 1957, 1958, 1961, 1962, 1963, 1964, 1965, 1967, 1968, 1969, 1972, 1975, 1976, 1978, 1979, 1980, 1986, 1987, 1988, 1989, 1990, 1995, 1997, 2001, 2003, 2007, 2008, 2012
Spanish Cup 1905, 1906, 1907, 1908, 1917, 1934, 1936, 1946, 1947, 1962, 1970, 1974, 1975, 1980, 1982, 1989, 1993, 2011
European Cup/Champions League 1956, 1957, 1958, 1959, 1960, 1966, 1998, 2000, 2002, 2014
UEFA Cup 1985, 1986
European Super Cup 2002
Intercontinental Cup 1960, 1998, 2002

REFEREES

In the 19th century Colonel Francis Marinden was the referee at a record nine FA Cup finals, including eight on the trot between 1883 and 1990. His record will never be beaten as the FA now appoints a different referee for the FA Cup final every year.

• **The first referee to send off a player in the FA Cup final was Peter Willis, who dismissed Manchester United defender Kevin Moran in the 1985 final for a foul on Everton's Peter Reid. Video replays showed that it was a harsh decision.**

• Michael Oliver became the youngest Premier League referee ever when he took charge of the Birmingham City-Blackburn Rovers fixture on 21st August 2010, aged 25 and 182 days.

• **On 9th February 2010 Amy Fearn became the first woman to referee a Football League match when she took charge of the last 20 minutes of Coventry's home game with Nottingham Forest after the original ref, Tony Bates, limped off with a calf injury.**

• Uzbekistan referee Ravshan Irmatov has taken charge of a record nine matches at the World Cup at the 2010 and 2014 tournaments.

• **In a Premier League career spanning 14 years between 1993 and 2007 Graham Poll issued a record 1,099 yellow cards.**

RELEGATION

Birmingham City boast the unwanted record of having been relegated from the top flight more often than any other club, having taken the drop 12 times – most recently in 2010/11. However, the Blues have not experienced that sinking feeling as often as Notts County, who have suffered 15 relegations in total.

• **In the Premier League era Crystal Palace have been the most unfortunate club, dropping out of the top flight on no fewer than four occasions. In 1993 they were desperately unlucky to go down with a record 49 points, a tally matched by Norwich in 1985 in the old First Division. Southend in 1988/89 and Peterborough in 2012/13 were even more unfortunate, being relegated from the old Third Division and the Championship respectively despite amassing 54 points.**

• Nathan Blake and Hermann Hreidarsson share the unwanted record of having each been relegated from the Premier League an incredible five times during their careers.

• **When Derby County went down from the Premier League in 2008, they did so with the lowest points total of any club in the history of the English league football. The Rams accumulated only 11 points in a miserable campaign, during which they managed to win just one match out of 38.**

• Among the famous clubs never to have been relegated are Ajax, Barcelona, Benfica, Inter Milan and Real Madrid. Arsenal are the least relegated club in English football, having suffered the drop just once in 1912/13.

REPLAYS

In the days before penalty shoot-outs, the FA Cup fourth qualifying round tie between Alvechurch and Oxford City went to a record five replays before Alvechurch reached the first round proper with a 1-0 win in the sixth match between the two clubs.

• **The first FA Cup final to go to a replay was the 1875 match between Royal Engineers and Old Etonians, Engineers winning 2-0 in the second match. The last FA Cup final to require a replay was the 1993 match between Arsenal and Sheffield Wednesday, the Gunners triumphing 2-1 in the second game. In 1999 the FA scrapped final replays, ruling that any drawn match would be settled on the day by penalties.**

• In 1912 Barnsley required a record six replays in total before getting their hands on the FA Cup. Fulham also played six replays in their run to the FA Cup final in 1975, but the extra games appeared to have taken their toll as they lost limply 2-0 to West Ham at Wembley.

• **The World Cup final has never been replayed, but the 1968 European Championships final in Rome went to a second match after Italy and Yugoslavia drew the original game 1-1. Italy won the replay 2-0.**

REPUBLIC OF IRELAND

First international: Republic of Ireland 1 Bulgaria 0, 1924
Most capped player: Robbie Keane, 133 caps (1998-)
Leading goalscorer: Robbie Keane, 62 goals (1998-)
First World Cup appearance: Republic of Ireland 1 England 1, 1990
Biggest win: 8-0 v Malta (1983)
Heaviest defeat: 0-7 v Brazil (1982)

The Republic of Ireland enjoyed their most successful period under English manager Jack Charlton in the late 1980s and early 1990s. 'Big Jack' became a legend on the Emerald Isle after guiding the Republic to their first ever World Cup in 1990, taking the team to the quarter-finals of the tournament – despite not winning a single match – before they were eliminated by hosts Italy.

• **Under Charlton, Ireland were undefeated in four matches against arch-rivals England, pulling off a famous 1-0 win in the 1988 European Championships and drawing three other competitive matches 1-1.**

This record prompted the gleeful chant whenever the teams met of "You'll never beat the Irish!".

• The Republic were the first country from outside the United Kingdom to beat England on home soil, winning 2-0 at Goodison Park in 1949.

• In 2009, in a World Cup play-off against France, the Republic were on the wrong end of one of the worst refereeing decisions of all time when Thierry Henry's blatant handball went unpunished before he crossed for William Gallas to score the goal that ended Ireland's hopes of reaching the 2010 finals in South Africa.

• Republic of Ireland striker Robbie Keane has won more caps (133) and scored more international goals (62) than any other player from the British Isles.

WORLD CUP RECORD
1930 Did not enter
1934 Did not qualify
1938 Did not qualify
1950 Did not enter
1954-86 Did not qualify
1990 Quarter-finals
1994 Round 2
1998 Did not qualify
2002 Round 2
2006 Did not qualify
2010 Did not qualify
2014 Did not qualify

FRANCK RIBERY

Born: Boulogne-sur-Mer, France,
7th April 1983
Position: Winger
Club career:
2000-02 Boulogne 46 (6)
2002-03 Alès 19 (1)
2003-04 Stade Brestois 35 (3)
2004-05 Metz 20 (1)
2005 Galatasaray 14 (0)
2005-07 Marseille 60 (11)
2007- Bayern Munich 176 (63)
International record:
2006- France 80 (16)

Tricky Bayern Munich winger Franck Ribery is the only player to have been voted French Player of the Year and German Footballer of the Year in the same season, winning both awards in 2008.

• After playing for a number of lesser French clubs and Galatasaray, with whom he won the Turkish cup in 2005, Ribery rose to prominence with Marseille. After a fine season in 2006/07, when he was voted French Player of the Year for the first time, he moved on to Bayern in a £20 million deal.

• Ribery, whose scarred face is the result of a serious car accident when he was just two years old, enjoyed his best season with the German giants in 2012/13 when he helped Bayern win the domestic double and the Champions League, following a 2-1 defeat of Borussia Dortmund in the final at Wembley.

• Once described by the legendary Zinedine Zidane as "the jewel of French football", Ribery made his debut for France just before the 2006 World Cup. He played exceptionally well at the tournament, helping Les Bleus reach the final where they lost on penalties to Italy. However, he fared less well at the 2010 World Cup, being one of five players suspended by the French FA after boycotting a training session in support of expelled team-mate Nicolas Anelka, and he missed the 2014 tournament through injury.

ARJEN ROBBEN

Born: Bedum, Netherlands, 23rd
June 1984
Position: Winger
Club career:
2000-02 Groningen 50 (8)
2002-04 PSV 56 (17)
2004-07 Chelsea 67 (15)
2007-09 Real Madrid 50 (11)
2009- Bayern Munich 106 (56)
International record:
2003- Netherlands 82 (26)

Not even Arjen Robben's team-mates can catch him!

Flying winger Arjen Robben is one of a handful of players to have won the domestic league title with four clubs in four different countries, having finished top of the pile with PSV (2003), Chelsea (2005 and 2006), Real Madrid (2008) and Bayern Munich (2010, 2013 and 2014).

• After starting out with Groningen, Robben made his name with PSV, with whom he was named Dutch Young Player of the Year in 2003. The following year he joined Chelsea where, despite suffering a number of injuries and a testicular cancer scare during his three years in London, he enjoyed huge success, collecting five winners' medals before departing for Real Madrid in 2007 for £24 million.

• After two years he was on the move again, to Bayern Munich, where he won the domestic double in his first season and was also voted Player of the Year in Germany – the first Dutchman to receive the honour. Robben, though, was denied a treble when Bayern were beaten in the final of the Champions League by Inter Milan. Two years later, in 2012, he suffered more heartbreak in the same tournament when Bayern were beaten by Chelsea in the final in Munich, but the following year he finally got his hands on the trophy when he scored a last-minute winner against Borussia Dortmund in the final at Wembley.

• The pacy wideman has also experienced much disappointment at international level, being part of the Netherlands team that lost in the 2010 World Cup final to Spain. Four years later he starred in his country's 5-1 hammering of world champions Spain at the World Cup in Brazil, but he was denied another chance to win the trophy when Argentina beat the Netherlands in the semi-final.

ROCHDALE

Year founded: 1907
Ground: Spotland Stadium (10,249)
Nickname: The Dale
Biggest win: 8-1 v Chesterfield (1926)
Heaviest defeat: 1-9 v Tranmere Rovers (1931)

Founded at a meeting at the town's Central Council Office in 1907, Rochdale were elected to the Third Division (North) as founder members in 1921.

• In their long history, Rochdale have gained promotion just three times, most recently to League One in 2014. Long years spent in the bottom tier mean that the Dale have the lowest average position, 76th, of any club since the expansion of the Football League to four divisions in 1921.

• The proudest day in the club's history came in 1962 when they reached the League Cup final. Rochdale lost 4-0 on aggregate to Norwich City, then in the Second Division, but took pride in becoming the first team from the bottom tier to reach a major cup final. The Dale's manager at the time was Tony Collins, the first ever black boss of a league club.

• Rochdale failed to win a single game in the FA Cup for 18 years from 1927 – the longest period of time any club has gone without victory in the competition. The appalling run finally came to an end in 1945 when the Dale beat Stockport 2-1 in a first-round replay.

• Along with Hartlepool, Rochdale have spent more seasons than any other club in the bottom two divisions of English football (86), without ever reaching the top two tiers.

BRENDAN RODGERS

Born: Carnlough, 26th January 1973
Managerial career:
2008-09 Watford
2009 Reading
2010-12 Swansea City
2012- Liverpool

Appointed manager of Liverpool in June 2012 after just one season in the Premier League with Swansea City, Brendan Rodgers enjoyed a superb campaign with the Reds in 2013/14, leading them to second place in the league and qualification for the Champions League for the first time in five years. His achievements saw him awarded the LMA Manager of the Year award, the first Liverpool boss to win this honour.

• After injury forced him to retire aged just 20, Rodgers began his coaching career at Reading, where he was youth team manager. He moved to Chelsea to take a similar role at Stamford Bridge in 2006, where he worked under Jose Mourinho.

• He became Watford manager in 2008 but left after a season to return to Reading. However, after a disappointing run of results, he was sacked by chairman John Madejski in December 2009.

• Rodgers' fortunes turned around at Swansea, who he joined in 2010 and led into the Premier League the following year after a play-off final victory against Reading.

If it doesn't work out as a football manager, Brendan Rodgers would make a great air steward...

Colombia's James Rodriguez, winner of the 2014 World Cup Golden Boot

JAMES RODRIGUEZ

Born: Cucuta, Colombia, 12th July 1991
Position: Midfielder
Club career:
2007-08 Envigado 30 (9)
2008-10 Banfield 42 (5)
2010-13 Porto 63 (25)
2013-14 Monaco 34 (9)
2014- Real Madrid
International record:
2011- Colombia 27 (11)

A talented playmaker who is also a prolific goalscorer, James Rodriguez became the fourth most expensive footballer in the world when he moved from Monaco to Real Madrid for £63 million in July 2014.

• Rodriguez was rated one of the hottest properties in the global game after he enjoyed a sensational 2014 World Cup in Brazil. Not only did he win the Golden Boot with six goals for Colombia, but he also picked up three FIFA Man of the Match awards and was voted into the tournament Dream Team by members of FIFA.com. In addition, his briliant left-footed volley against Uruguay in the first knock-out round was voted the goal of the tournament.

• After starting his career with Envigado in Colombia, Rodriguez soon moved on to Banfield where he became the youngest ever overseas player to score in the Argentinian league. His huge potential attracted the attention of Porto, who signed him in 2010. In just three years with the Portuguese giants Rodriguez won three league titles, the Europa League and the Portuguese Cup. In the last of these competitions, Rodriguez became the first player for 30 years to score a hat-trick in the final when he notched a treble in Porto's 6-2 hammering of Vitoria Guimaraes in 2011. The following year he was voted Portuguese Player of the Season.

• In 2013 Rodriguez moved on to Monaco for around £37 million, making him the second most expensive player ever (behind former Porto team-mate Hulk) in Portuguese football. In his one season in France Rodriguez topped the assists list and was voted into the Ligue 1 XI.

• Rodriguez is married to the sister of David Ospina, the Arsenal and Colombia goalkeeper.

CRISTIANO RONALDO

Born: Madeira, Portugal, 5th February 1985
Position: Winger/Striker
Club career:
2001-03 Sporting Lisbon 25 (3)
2003-09 Manchester United 196 (84)
2009- Real Madrid 165 (177)
International record:
2003- Portugal 114 (50)

In 2013/14 Cristiano Ronaldo set a new record for the Champions League, scoring an incredible 17 goals in the competition, including one in the final as his club Real Madrid won a record tenth title with victory over Atletico Madrid in Lisbon. In the same season, Ronaldo took his total number of Champions League goals to 67, just four behind Raul's all-time record.

• Born on the Portuguese island of Madeira, Ronaldo began his career with Sporting Lisbon before joining Manchester United in a £12.25 million deal in 2003. The following year he won his first trophy with the Red Devils, opening the scoring as United beat Millwall 3-0 in the FA Cup final. He later helped United win a host of major honours, including three Premiership

TOP 10

2013 FIFA BALLON D'OR PLAYERS

1.	Cristiano Ronaldo	27.99%
2.	Lionel Messi	24.72%
3.	Franck Ribery	23.36%
4.	Zlatan Ibrahimovic	5.29%
5.	Neymar	3.17%
6.	Andres Iniesta	2.08%
7.	Robin van Persie	1.79%
8.	Arjen Robben	1.77%
9.	Gareth Bale	1.32%
10.	Andrea Pirlo	1.11%

If Cristiano Ronaldo was just a bit more green, he might pass for The Incredible Hulk!

• After starring for England at Euro 2004 Rooney signed for Manchester United later that summer for £25.6 million, to become the world's most expensive teenage footballer. He started his Old Trafford career in sensational style with a hat-trick against Fenerbahce and has since played a pivotal part in the Red Devils' recent success, winning five Premier League titles, two League Cups and the Champions League. His total of 216 goals for the club in all competitions is only bettered by legendary duo Bobby Charlton and Denis Law.

• **When Rooney made his England debut against Australia on 12th February 2003 he was his country's youngest ever player, but he has since lost this particular record to Arsenal's Theo Walcott.**

England and Manchester United captain, Wayne Rooney

titles and the Champions League in 2008 before signing for Real for a then world record £80 million in 2009.

• In 2007 Ronaldo was voted PFA Player of the Year and Young Player of the Year, the first man to achieve this double since Andy Gray in 1977. The following season he scored a remarkable 42 goals for United in all competitions, and won the European Golden Boot. Three years later, in his second season with Real, he became the first player ever to win the award in two different countries.

• **Ronaldo made his international debut for Portugal against Kazakhstan in 2003 and the following year played for his country in their surprise Euro 2004 final defeat by Greece. Captain of Portugal since 2008, Ronaldo is his country's all-time top scorer with 50 goals and the only Portuguese player ever to score at three World Cups.**

• Arguably the most exciting talent in world football today, Ronaldo is the only player from the Premier League to have been voted World Footballer of the Year, having collected this most prestigious of awards in 2008. After playing second fiddle for some years to his great rival Lionel Messi, he was delighted to win the award for a second time in 2013.

WAYNE ROONEY

Born: Liverpool, 24th October 1985
Position: Striker
Club career:
2002-04 Everton 67 (15)
2004- Manchester United 307 (158)
International record:
2003- England 95 (40)

When Wayne Rooney scored his first goal for England, against Macedonia in a Euro 2004 qualifier on 6th September 2003, he was aged just 17 years and 317 days... the youngest player ever to find the net for the Three Lions.

• **Rooney burst onto the scene with Everton in 2002, scoring his first league goal for the Toffees with a magnificent 20-yarder against reigning champions Arsenal at Goodison Park just five days before his 17th birthday. At the time he was the youngest ever Premiership scorer, but his record has since been surpassed by both James Milner and James Vaughan.**

IS THAT A FACT?

With 33 Champions League goals to his name Wayne Rooney is Manchester United's all-time leading scorer in European football.

• Despite failing to live up to his stellar reputation at international tournaments since Euro 2004, Rooney has scored a record 29 competitive goals for England. In August 2014, following the retirement of Three Lions skipper Steven Gerrard, Rooney was appointed England captain by manager Roy Hodgson.

ROSS COUNTY

Year founded: 1929
Ground: Global Energy Stadium (6,541)
Nickname: The Staggies
Biggest win: 11-0 v St Cuthbert Wanderers (1993)
Heaviest defeat: 1-6 v Alloa (1968) and v Meadowbank (1991)

Founded in 1929, Ross County played in the Highland league until 1994 when they were elected to the Scottish Third Division along with Inverness Caledonian Thistle.

• Ross County enjoyed the greatest day in their history in 2010 when they sensationally beat Celtic in the Scottish Cup semi-final. However, there was to be no fairytale ending for the Staggies as they went down 3-0 to Dundee United in the final at Hampden Park.

• Two years later the club won promotion to the SPL for the first time in their history after a glorious campaign which ended with them a record 24 points clear at the top of the Scottish First Division. The Staggies also put together an incredible 34-match unbeaten run, matching a record for the Scottish second tier set by Aidrieonians way back in 1955.

• With a capacity of just 6,541, Ross County's tiny Global Energy Stadium is the second smallest in the SPL.

ROTHERHAM UNITED

Year founded: 1925
Ground: New York Stadium (12,021)
Nickname: The Millers
Biggest win: 8-0 v Oldham Athletic (1947)
Heaviest defeat: 1-11 v Bradford City (1928)

The club had its origins in Thornhill FC (founded in 1878, later becoming Rotherham County) and Rotherham Town, who merged with County to form Rotherham United in 1925.

• The club's greatest moment came in 1961 when they reached the first ever League Cup final, losing 3-2 on aggregate to Aston Villa. Six years earlier Rotherham had missed out on goal average on promotion to the First Division for the first time in the club's history… the closest they've ever been to playing top-flight football.

• In 1991 Rotherham made history by becoming the first side to win a penalty shoot-out in the FA Cup, defeating Scunthorpe United 7-6 on spot-kicks after a first-round replay.

• Less happily, in 1925 Rotherham failed to keep a clean sheet in 45 consecutive league matches. The run was a record at the time, but Bristol City extended it to 49 games seven years later.

• At the start of the 2012/13 season the club moved from the Don Valley Stadium in Sheffield to a brand-new ground in Rotherham, the 12,000-capacity New York Stadium. The move proved successful, as the Millers gained promotion from League Two at the end of the campaign and another promotion followed immediately as the Millers beat Leyton Orient on penalties in the 2014 League One play-off final.

• With 26 caps for Bermuda between 1989 and 1996, former cult hero Shaun Goater has played more games at international level than any other Rotherham player.

IAN RUSH

Born: St Asaph, 20th October 1961
Position: Striker
Club career:
1979-80 Chester City 34 (18)
1980-87 Liverpool 224 (139)
1987-88 Juventus 29 (8)
1988-96 Liverpool 245 (90)
1996-97 Leeds United 36 (3)
1997-98 Newcastle United 10 (2)
1998 Sheffield United (loan) 4 (0)
1998-99 Wrexham 18 (0)
1999 Sydney Olympic 2 (0)
International record:
1980-96 Wales 73 (28)

One of the most prolific strikers ever, Ian Rush is Liverpool's leading scorer of all time with a total of 346 goals for the club in two spells at Anfield in the 1980s and 1990s.

• Rush has scored more goals in the FA Cup final than any other player, with a total of five for Liverpool in the 1986, 1989 and 1992 finals. His strikes helped the Reds win all three games, two of them against local rivals Everton. With 44 goals in the competition as a whole, Rush is the second highest scorer in the history of the tournament and the leading FA Cup marksman of the 20th century.

• 'Rushie', as he was known to fans, is also the joint leading scorer in the League Cup with Geoff Hurst, the pair both ending their careers on 49 goals. He enjoyed huge success in the tournament, winning the trophy in 1981, 1982, 1983, 1984 and 1995 to become the first player to collect five League Cup winners' medals.

• Rush tops the scoring charts for his native Wales, with 28 goals in 73 appearances. However, he never played in the finals of either the World Cup or the European Championships.

• Rush is the all-time leading scorer in the Merseyside derby with 25 goals against Everton, including a post-war record four goals in a 5-0 thrashing of the Toffees at Goodison Park on 6th November 1982.

• In 1988 Rush returned to Liverpool from Juventus for a then British record £2.7 million.

SACKINGS

A record 10 managers were sacked during the 2013/14 Premier League season, including big names like David Moyes (Manchester United), Andre Villas-Boas (Tottenham) and Michael Laudrup (Swansea City). Fulham showed both Martin Jol and Rene Meulensteen the door, but the Cottagers were still relegated under their third manager of the season, Felix Magath.

• In 1959 Bill Lambton got the boot from Scunthorpe United after just three days in the managerial hotseat, an English league record. His reign at the Old Showground took in just one match – a 3-0 defeat at Liverpool in a Second Division fixture. The shortest Premier League reign, meanwhile, was Les Reed's seven-game stint at Charlton in 2006.

• In May 2007 Leroy Rosenior was sacked as manager of Conference side Torquay United after just 10 minutes in charge! No sooner had the former West Ham and QPR striker been unveiled as the Gulls' new boss when he was told that the club had been bought by a business consortium and his services were no longer required.

• Crystal Palace have sacked more managers since the Second World War than any other league club. The Eagles have made 45 different managerial appointments since 1945, although Steve Coppell and Steve Kember have filled the role on four occasions each.

• Tsanko Tsvetanov was sacked a record three times in one season by the same club, Bulgarian outfit Etar Veliko Tarnovo, in 2012/13. On the first two occasions he got the boot Tsvetanov was reinstated following fan protests, but there was no return after his third dismissal.

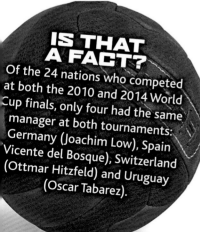

IS THAT A FACT?

Of the 24 nations who competed at both the 2010 and 2014 World Cup finals, only four had the same manager at both tournaments: Germany (Joachim Low), Spain (Vicente del Bosque), Switzerland (Ottmar Hitzfeld) and Uruguay (Oscar Tabarez).

ST JOHNSTONE

Year founded: 1884
Ground: McDiarmid Park (10,696)
Nickname: The Saints
Biggest win: 13-0 v Tulloch (1887)
Heaviest defeat: 0-12 v Cowdenbeath (1928)

St Johnstone were founded in 1884 by a group of local cricketers in Perth who wanted to keep fit in winter.

• The Saints enjoyed their best ever day in 2014, when they beat Dundee United 2-0 in the Scottish Cup final at Celtic Park. Previously, the club had appeared in two League Cup finals, but lost in 1969 to Celtic and again in 1998 to Rangers.

• The Saints' record scorer is John Brogan, who hit 114 league goals for the club between 1976 and 1984. Stalwart goalkeeper Alan Main played in a record 361 games for St Johnstone in two spells at McDiarmid Park between 1995 and 2010.

• Along with Falkirk, St Johnstone have won the Scottish second tier a record seven times, most recently claiming the First Division title in 2009.

• Midfielder Nick Dasovic is the club's most-capped player, turning out 26 times for Canada between 1996 and 2002.

> HONOURS
> **Division 2 champions** 1924, 1960, 1963
> **First Division champions** 1983, 1990, 1997, 2009
> **Scottish Cup** 2014

ST MIRREN

Year founded: 1877
Ground: St Mirren Park (8,023)
Nickname: The Buddies
Biggest win: 15-0 v Glasgow University (1960)
Heaviest defeat: 0-9 v Rangers (1897)

Named after the patron saint of Paisley, St Mirren were founded in 1877 by a group of local cricketers and rugby players. The club were founder members of the Scottish League in 1890, but have never finished higher than third in the top flight.

• The Buddies, though, have won the Scottish Cup on three occasions, most recently in 1987 when they beat Dundee United 1-0 in the final after extra-time – the last time that the winners have fielded an all-Scottish line-up.

• Midfielder Hugh Murray played in a club record 424 games for the Buddies between 1996 and 2012. The club's top scorer is David McCrae, who banged in 222 goals between 1923 and 1934.

• Defender Andy Millen is the oldest player to appear in the SPL, turning out for St Mirren against Hearts for the final time on 15th March 2008 when he was aged 42 and 279 days.

• In 1986 St Mirren's Alex Miller became the first player to receive three red cards in the same match when he was sent off for fighting a Motherwell opponent, and was then shown a further two red cards for dissent.

> HONOURS
> **Division 2 champions** 1968
> **First Division champions** 1977, 2000, 2006
> **Scottish Cup** 1926, 1959, 1987
> **League Cup** 2013

ALEXIS SANCHEZ

> **Born:** Tocopilla, Chile, 19th December 1988
> **Position:** Winger/striker
> **Club career:**
> 2005-06 Cobreloa 47 (12)
> 2006-07 Colo-Colo 32 (5)
> 2007-08 River Plate 23 (4)
> 2008-11 Udinese 95 (20)
> 2011-14 Barcelona 88 (39)
> 2014- Arsenal
> **International record:**
> 2006- Chile 71 (24)

Dynamic Chilean forward Alexis Sanchez became Arsenal's second highest ever signing when the Gunners splashed out £35 million to prise him away from Barcelona in the summer of 2014.

• Sanchez made his name with Italian side Udinese, becoming the first Chilean ever to score four goals in a

Serie A match when he filled his boots in a 7-0 thrashing of Palermo on 27th February 2011.

• Later that year Sanchez moved on to Barcelona, with whom he won the Copa del Rey in 2012 and La Liga in 2013. His most prolific season with the Catalans, though, was in 2013/14 when he scored a career-best 21 goals in all competitions.

• Sanchez made his debut for Chile against New Zealand in 2006. Perhaps his best match for his nation was in a friendly against England in November 2013 when he scored both goals in a 2-0 win. Sanchez also impressed at the 2014 World Cup, netting his country's first goal of the tournament against Australia and then scoring the equaliser against hosts Brazil in a last 16 tie which Chile eventually lost on penalties.

BASTIAN SCHWEINSTEIGER

Bayern Munich vice-captain Bastian Schweinsteiger has enjoyed a magnificent career at the German giants, winning seven Bundesliga titles, seven German cups and the Champions League in 2013.

• A powerful player who can perform capably in either central midfield or on the wing, Schweinsteiger has had mixed fortunes in the Champions

League. He was a runner-up in the competition with Bayern in 2010, but two years later it was his decisive penalty in the shoot-out against Real Madrid that took the Germans through to another final. Unfortunately, Schweinsteiger missed his spot-kick in the shoot-out against Chelsea and allowed Didier Drogba to clinch the trophy for the Londoners. The following year, though, he helped Bayern win the trophy after a 2-1 victory over fellow German outfit Borussia Dortmund in the final at Wembley.

• A talented all-round sportsman who could easily have become a professional ski racer if he had not chosen to concentrate on football, Schweinsteiger made his debut for Germany in 2004 and is now the joint-fifth highest appearance maker for his country with 108 caps.

• Schweinsteiger starred for Germany at the 2014 World Cup in Brazil, his committed performances helping his country to win the trophy for a fourth time. He was handed the captain's armband after Phillip Lahm retired following the World Cup victory.

SCOTLAND

First international: Scotland 0 England 0, 1872

Most capped player: Kenny Dalglish, 102 caps (1971-86)

Leading goalscorer: Denis Law (1958-74) and Kenny Dalglish (1971-86), 30 goals

First World Cup appearance: Scotland 0 Austria 1, 1954

Biggest win: Scotland 11 Ireland 0, 1901

Heaviest defeat: Scotland 0 Uruguay 7, 1954

Along with England, Scotland are the oldest international team in the world. The two countries played the first official international way back in 1872, the match at Hamilton Crescent, Partick, finishing 0-0. Since then, honours have been more or less even between the 'Auld Enemies', with England winning 46 matches, Scotland winning 41 and 20 ending in a draw.

• It took the Scots a while to make an impression on the world scene.

Bastian Schweinsteiger must have one heck of a trophy cabinet!

Bamboozled by Scotland's away kit, the Nigerian keeper missed the cross completely

After withdrawing from the 1950 World Cup, Scotland competed in the finals for the first time in 1954 but were eliminated in the first round after suffering their worst ever defeat, 7-0 to reigning champions Uruguay.

• Scotland have taken part in the World Cup finals on eight occasions but have never got beyond the group stage – a record for the tournament. They have been unlucky, though, going out in 1974, 1978 and 1982 only on goal difference.

• Scotland have a pretty poor record in the European Championships, only qualifying for the finals on two occasions, in 1992 and 1996. Again, they failed to reach the knockout stage both times, although they were unfortunate to lose out on the 'goals scored' rule to Holland at Euro '96. More recently, the Scots made a brave attempt to qualify for Euro 2008 but were narrowly pipped by Italy and France despite beating the French home and away.

• Scotland had a good record in the Home Championships until the tournament was scrapped in 1984, winning the competition 24 times and sharing the title another 17 times. Only England (34 outright wins and 20 shared) have a better overall record.

• **Former Aberdeen and Manchester United goalkeeper Jim Leighton kept a record 40 clean sheets for Scotland, while winning 91 caps between 1982 and 1998.**

• Incredibly, no Scotland player has scored a hat-trick since Colin Stein banged in four goals in an 8-0 hammering of Cyprus at Hampden Park in 1969.

IS THAT A FACT?

Alex McLeish was Scotland's most successful ever manager, winning seven of the 10 matches for which he was in charge. His greatest triumph was a 1-0 win away to France in a Euro 2008 qualifier, shortly before he quit the post to become boss of Birmingham City.

WORLD CUP RECORD	
1930-38	Did not enter
1950	Withdrew
1954	Round 1
1958	Round 1
1962-70	Did not qualify
1974	Round 1
1978	Round 1
1982	Round 1
1986	Round 1
1990	Round 1
1994	Did not qualify
1998	Round 1
2002	Did not qualify
2006	Did not qualify
2010	Did not qualify
2014	Did not qualify

SCOTTISH CUP

The Scottish Cup was first played for in 1873/74, shortly after the formation of the Scottish FA. Queen's Park, who the previous year had competed in the English FA Cup, were the first winners, beating Clydesdale 2-0 in the final in front of a crowd of 3,000 at the original Hampden Park.

• **Queen's Park were the dominant force in the early years of the competition, winning 10 of the first 20 finals, including one in 1884 when their opponents, Vale of Leven, failed to turn up! Since then, Celtic (36 wins) and Rangers (33 wins) have ruled the roost, although Queen's Park (10 wins) remain third in the list of all-time winners ahead of Hearts (eight wins).**

• In 1990 the final was decided on penalties for the first time, Aberdeen beating Celtic 9-8 after a 0-0 draw.

• **Incredibly, the biggest ever victories in the history of British football took place in the Scottish Cup on the same day, 12th September 1885. Dundee Harp beat Aberdeen Rovers 35-0 and were confident that they had set a new record. Yet, no doubt to their utter amazement, they soon discovered that Arbroath had thrashed Bon Accord, a cricket club who had been invited to take part in the competition by mistake, 36-0!**

• A record crowd of 146,433 watched the 1937 Scottish Cup final between Celtic and Aberdeen at Hampden Park.

SCUNTHORPE UNITED

Year founded: 1899
Ground: Glanford Park (9,088)
Previous name: Scunthorpe & Lindsey United
Nickname: The Iron
Biggest win: 9-0 v Boston United (1953)
Heaviest defeat: 0-8 v Carlisle United (1952)

The club was founded in 1899 when Brumby Hall linked up with some other local teams. Between 1910 and 1958 they were known as Scunthorpe and Lindsey United after amalgamating with the latter team.

• Elected to the Third Division (North) when the league expanded in 1950, Scunthorpe won the division eight years later. Their only other honour came in 2007 when the Iron were crowned League One champions under former physio Nigel Adkins. Scunny fans celebrated that triumph by singing, "Who needs Mourinho, we've got our physio!"

• Among the famous names to play for Scunthorpe are England and Liverpool legends Kevin Keegan and Ray Clemence and, somewhat bizarrely, former England cricket captain Ian Botham, who made 11 appearances as a striker for Scunthorpe in the early 1980s.

• In two spells at Scunthorpe between 1979 and 1987, Steve Cammack scored a club record 110 goals for the Iron.

• The club's record signing is defender Rob Jones, who joined Scunthorpe from Hibs for £700,000 in 2009. A year later the Iron sold striker Gary Hooper to Celtic for a club record £2.4 million.

• In 1988 Scunthorpe became the first club in the modern era to move to a new purpose-built stadium when they left their former ground, the Old Showground, for Glanford Park.

HONOURS
Division 3 (North) champions 1958
League One champions 2007

LUKE SHAW

Born: Kingston upon Thames, 12th July 1995
Position: Defender
Club career:
2012-14 Southampton 60 (0)
2014- Manchester United
International record:
2014- England 3 (0)

Attacking left-back Luke Shaw became the world's most expensive teenager when he moved from Southampton to Manchester United for £30 million in the summer of 2014.

Will Luke prove a 'Shaw thing' for England?

• Shaw joined the Southampton Academy aged eight, and came through the ranks to make his debut as a sub in an FA Cup fourth-round tie against Millwall in January 2012. Later that year he became the youngest ever Southampton player to start a Premier League game when he played in a 1-1 draw against Swansea City at St Mary's, when he was aged just 17 and four months.

• After a superb season in 2013/14, during which he was frequently compared to former Saints player Gareth Bale, Shaw was nominated for the PFA Young Player of the Year award and selected for the PFA Premier League Team of the Year.

• Shaw played for the England Under-16, Under-17 and Under-21 teams before making his debut for the senior team as a sub against Denmark in March 2014. Later that year he was chosen by Roy Hodgson for the England World Cup squad, ahead of the ultra-experienced Ashley Cole.

ALAN SHEARER

Born: Newcastle, 13th August 1970
Position: Striker
Club career:
1988-92 Southampton 118 (23)
1992-96 Blackburn Rovers 138 (112)
1996-2006 Newcastle United 303 (148)
International record:
1992-2000 England 63 (30)

Alan Shearer's incredible total of 260 Premiership goals (including a record 11 hat-tricks) for Blackburn and Newcastle is easily a record for the league, none of his rivals having passed the double-century mark. No fewer than 20 of his goals came against Leeds United, a Premier League record for one player against the same opponents.

• Shearer began his career with Southampton, marking his full debut for the Saints in 1988 by scoring three goals in a 4-2 victory over Arsenal. Aged just 17 years and 240 days, he was the youngest ever player to score a top-flight hat-trick.

• In 1992 Shearer moved to Blackburn for a then British record £3.3 million. He helped Rovers win the Premiership title in 1994/95, his impressive tally of 34 goals that campaign earning him one of his three Golden Boots.

• A then world record £15 million move to Newcastle followed in 1996, to the delight of the Geordie faithful. An instant hit at St James' Park, Shearer eventually became the club's all-time record goalscorer, his total of 206 goals in all competitions for the Magpies eclipsing the 49-year-old record of another Toon legend, Jackie Milburn.

• Strong, good in the air and possessing a powerful shot with both feet, Shearer proved a real handful for international defences, too. His five goals at Euro '96 powered England to the semi-finals of the tournament and won him the competition's Golden Boot. By the time he quit international football after Euro 2000 he had scored 30 goals for his country, a figure only surpassed by five other England players.

• Shearer became a pundit for the BBC after hanging up his boots in 2006, but three years later he sensationally returned to his beloved St James' Park as Newcastle caretaker manager. However, in his eight matches in charge he was unable to prevent the Geordies from dropping out of the Premier League for the first time.

SHEFFIELD UNITED

Year founded: 1889
Ground: Bramall Lane (32,702)
Nickname: The Blades
Biggest win: 10-0 v Port Vale (1892) and v Burnley (1929)
Heaviest defeat: 0-13 v Bolton (1890)

The club was founded at a meeting at the city's Adelphi Hotel in 1899 by the members of the Sheffield United Cricket Club, partly to make greater use of the facilities at Bramall Lane.

• **The Blades enjoyed their heyday in the late Victorian era, winning the title in 1898, and lifting the FA Cup in both 1899 and 1902. The club won the FA Cup again in 1915, in what was to be the last final to be played before the**

First World War brought a halt to the sporting calendar. They chalked up another victory in 1925.

• The club's leading scorer is Harry Johnson, who bagged 201 league goals between 1919 and 1930. His successor at centre-forward, Jimmy Dunne, scored a record 41 goals in the 1930/31 season, helped by a purple patch when he found the net in 12 consecutive matches (another club record).

• **The Blades' home, Bramall Lane, is one of the oldest sporting arenas in the world. It first hosted cricket in 1855, before football was introduced to the ground in 1862. Sixteen years later, in 1878, the world's first ever floodlit match was played at the stadium between two sides picked from the Sheffield Football Association, the lights being provided by two generators.**

• During an 18-year career with the club between 1948 and 1966, Joe Shaw made a record 631 appearances for the Blades.

• **Sheffield United hold the record for the most number of points, 90 in 2011/12, for a team failing to win promotion from the third tier.**

• To the dismay of their fans, United have appeared in four play-off finals and lost them all – a miserable record unmatched by any other club. The Blades had another disappointing day at Wembley in 2014 when they lost 5-3 to Hull City in the FA Cup semi-final – only the third time that a semi-final has produced eight goals.

SHEFFIELD WEDNESDAY

Year founded: 1867
Ground: Hillsborough (39,732)
Previous name: The Wednesday
Nickname: The Owls
Biggest win: 12-0 v Halliwell (1891)
Heaviest defeat: 0-10 v Aston Villa (1912)

The club was formed as The Wednesday in 1867 at the Adelphi Hotel in Sheffield by members of the Wednesday Cricket Club, who originally met on that particular day of the week. In 1929 the club added 'Sheffield' to their name, but are still often referred to simply as 'Wednesday'.

• **In 1904 the Owls became the first club in the 20th century to win consecutive league championships. They did so again in 1929/30, but have not won the league since.**

• In 1935 Wednesday won the FA Cup for the third and last time, striker Ellis Rimmer scoring in every round of the competition.

• **The Owls splashed out a club record £5.7 million on Celtic striker Paolo di Canio in 1997. They must have wondered whether they hadn't made a terrible mistake when the volatile Italian pushed over referee Paul Alcock during a match against Arsenal the following year – an action which earned him an 11-match ban.**

• Andrew Wilson holds two significant records for the club. Between 1900 and 1920 he played in 501 league matches, scoring 199 goals. No Wednesday player, before or since, can match these figures.

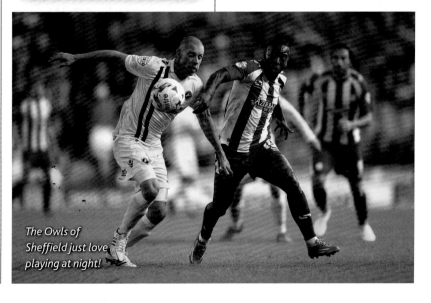

The Owls of Sheffield just love playing at night!

• In 1991, while residing in the old Second Division, the Owls won the League Cup for the first and only time in their history, beating Manchester United 1-0 at Wembley. It was the last time that a club from outside the top flight has lifted a major domestic cup.

• On the opening day of the 2000/01 season Wednesday goalkeeper Kevin Pressman was sent off after just 13 seconds at Molineux for handling a Wolves shot outside the penalty area... the fastest dismissal ever in British football.

HONOURS
Division 1 champions 1903, 1904, 1929, 1930
Division 2 champions 1900, 1926, 1952, 1956, 1959
FA Cup 1896, 1907, 1935
League Cup 1991

PETER SHILTON

Born: Leicester, 18th September 1949
Position: Goalkeeper
Club career:
1966-75 Leicester City 286 (1)
1975-78 Stoke City 110
1978-82 Nottingham Forest 202
1982-87 Southampton 188
1987-92 Derby County 175
1995-96 Bolton Wanderers 1
1997 Leyton Orient 9
International record:
1970-90 England 125

Peter Shilton is the only player in the history of English football to have played 1,000 league games. He reached the landmark, aged 47, while keeping a clean sheet for Leyton Orient in their 2-0 win over Brighton on 22nd December 1996.

• Shilton is England's highest capped player with 125 appearances to his name. In his 20-year international career he played at three World Cups, where he kept 10 clean sheets – a goalkeeping record shared with France's Fabien Barthez.

• A losing FA Cup finalist with Leicester City in 1969 at the age of 19, Shilton had to wait almost 10 years before he collected his first honour, the league championship with Nottingham Forest in 1978. He went on to win two European Cups with Forest before moving on to Southampton in 1982.

• Shilton is the last goalkeeper to be voted PFA Player of the Year,

TOP 10

HIGHEST CAPPED ENGLAND PLAYERS

1.	Peter Shilton (1970-90)	125
2.	David Beckham (1996-2009)	115
3.	Steven Gerrard (2000-14)	114
4.	Bobby Moore (1962-73)	108
5.	Ashley Cole (2001-14)	107
6.	Bobby Charlton (1958-70)	106
	Frank Lampard (1999-2014)	106
8.	Billy Wright (1946-59)	105
9.	Wayne Rooney (2003-)	95
10.	Bryan Robson (1980-91)	90

collecting the award in 1978. The only other keeper to be so honoured was Tottenham's Pat Jennings, two years earlier.

SHREWSBURY TOWN

Year founded: 1886
Ground: New Meadow (9,875)
Nickname: The Shrews
Biggest win: 11-2 v Marine (1995)
Heaviest defeat: 1-8 v Norwich City (1952) and v Coventry City (1963)

Founded at the Lion Hotel in Shrewsbury in 1886, the club played in regional football for many years until being elected to the Football League in 1950.

• **Prolific striker Arthur Rowley is the club's record scorer, hitting 152 goals between 1958 and 1965 to complete his all-time league record of 434 goals (he also turned out for West Bromwich Albion, Fulham and Leicester City). His best season for the Shrews was in 1958/59 when he banged in a club best 38 goals.**

• 'Sir' Mickey Brown is the club's leading appearance maker, playing in 418 league games in three spells at the club between 1986 and 2001. He was 'knighted' by the fans after scoring the winning goal against Exeter on the last day of the 1999/2000 season, thus preserving the club's league status and sending down local rivals Chester City instead.

• **After beating mighty Everton in the quarter-finals of the League Cup in 1961, Shrewsbury came close to**

reaching the final of the competition but were beaten 4-3 on aggregate by Rotherham in the last four. The Shrews have never made it to a semi-final since.

• Shrewsbury have won the Welsh Cup six times – a record for an English club.

HONOURS
Division 3 champions 1979
Third Division champions 1994
Welsh Cup 1891, 1938, 1977, 1979, 1984, 1985

DAVID SILVA

Born: Las Palmas, Spain, 8th January 1986
Position: Winger
Club career:
2003-04 Valencia B 14 (1)
2004-10 Valencia 119 (21)
2004-05 Eibar (loan) 35 (5)
2005-06 Celta (loan) 34 (4)
2010- Manchester City 127 (21)
International record:
2006- Spain 83 (20)

David Silva is blue to his boots

A tricky winger who can wriggle out of the tightest of situations, David Silva is the only Spanish player to have won the Premier League twice after helping his club Manchester City top the table in both 2012 and 2014.

• Prior to moving to the Etihad stadium, Silva was a key player in the Valencia side that regularly managed to upset Real Madrid and Barcelona. His best moment with the Spanish side came in 2008, when Valencia won the Copa del Rey after beating Getafe 3-1 in the final.

• In 2010 Silva joined City for £24 million and in his first season in Manchester helped the Sky Blues win their first trophy for 35 years when they beat Stoke City 1-0 in the FA Cup final at Wembley.

• First capped by his country in 2006, Silva was an integral figure in the Spain side that won Euro 2008, but was restricted to just two appearances as the Spanish became world champions in South Africa two years later. However, he returned to the starting line-up at Euro 2012, heading the first goal in Spain's 4-0 thrashing of Italy in the final.

THIAGO SILVA

Born: Rio de Janeiro, Brazil, 22nd September 1984
Position: Defender
Club career:
2004 Juventude 27 (3)
2004-05 Porto B 14 (5)
2005-06 Dynamo Moscow 0 (0)
2006-08 Fluminense 81 (6)
2009-12 AC Milan 93 (5)
2012- Paris St Germain 50 (3)
International record:
2008- Brazil 52 (3)

Brazil captain Thiago Silva became the world's most expensive defender when he moved from AC Milan to Paris St Germain for around £35 million in 2012, although he has since been knocked down to number two in the list by his club and international team-mate David Luiz, who cost £50 million when he joined PSG from Chelsea in June 2014.

• Silva was something of a late developer, the early part of his career hampered by a bout of tuberculosis while he was with Dynamo Moscow. However, he began to flourish when he returned to Brazil with Fluminense, with whom he was a runner-up in the Copa Libertadores in 2008.

• A brilliant reader of the game who is also extremely composed in possession, Silva has won the Italian league with AC Milan (2011) and the French league with PSG (2013 and 2014)

• First capped by his country in 2008, Silva led Brazil to victory in the Confederations Cup on home soil in 2013. He skippered the South Americans at the 2014 World Cup, but missed out on the semi-final against Germany through suspension and could only watch from the sidelines in horror as his team-mates were thrashed 7-1.

SIZE

The heaviest player in the history of the professional game was Willie 'Fatty' Foulke, who played in goal for Sheffield United, Chelsea and Bradford City. By the end of his career, the tubby custodian weighed in at an incredible 24 stone.

• At just five feet tall, Fred Le May is the shortest player ever to have appeared in the Football League. He played for Thames, Clapton Orient and Watford between 1930 and 1933. The shortest England international ever was Frederick 'Fanny' Walden, a five feet two inch winger with Tottenham who won the first of two caps in 1914.

• No prizes for guessing who the tallest ever England international is. It is, of course, giraffe-like striker Peter Crouch,

Now we know who really did eat all the pies!

who stands six feet seven inches in his socks. Crouch, though, is half an inch shorter than ex-Wolves striker Stefan Maierhofer and Birmingham's Serbian striker Nikola Zigic, who jointly claim the record as the tallest ever Premier League players.

• Yang Changpeng, a striker with Chinese second-tier side Meizhou Kejia, is the tallest player in the world at six foot, eight and a half inches.

MARTIN SKRTEL

Born: Handlova, Slovakia, 15th December 1984
Position: Defender
Club career:
2001-04 Trencin 44 (8)
2004-08 Zenit St Petersburg 74 (3)
2008- Liverpool 187 (14)
International record:
2004- Slovakia 66 (5)

Heavily tattooed Liverpool stopper Martin Skrtel was the most prolific defender in the Premier League in the 2013/14 season, banging in an impressive seven goals as the Reds challenged for the league title right to the last day.

• An aggressive and combative centre-back who is especially strong in the air, Skrtel started out with FC Trencin in Slovakia before moving to Zenit St Petersburg in 2004. He won the Russian league with Zenit in 2007, a year before he joined Liverpool for £6.5 million.

• Skrtel won the League Cup with Liverpool in 2012, scoring in the final against Cardiff at Wembley in normal time before the match was eventually settled on penalties. The following season was a poor one for Skrtel, but he bounced back to become a mainstay of the Liverpool team which finished second in the Premier League in 2014. Unfortunately for the rugged defender, he scored four own goals during the campaign – against Hull, West Ham, Swansea and Newcastle – to set a new record for a single Premier League season.

• Four-times Slovakian Footballer of the Year, Skrtel was part of the Slovakia team which qualified for a first-ever World Cup in 2010 and surprised many by reaching the last 16.

SOUTHAMPTON

Year founded: 1885
Ground: St Mary's (32,589)
Previous name: Southampton St Mary's
Nickname: The Saints
Biggest win: 14-0 v Newbury (1894)
Heaviest defeat: 0-8 v Tottenham (1936) and v Everton (1971)

Founded as Southampton St Mary's by members of St Mary's Church Young Men's Association in 1885, the club joined the Southern League in 1894 and became simply 'Southampton' the following year.

• **The Saints won the Southern League six times in the decade up to 1904 and also appeared in two FA Cup finals during that period, losing to Bury in 1900 and to Sheffield United two years later.**

• The club finally won the cup in 1976. Manchester United were hot favourites to beat the Saints, then in the Second Division, but the south coast side claimed the trophy thanks to Bobby Stokes' late strike. As scorer of the first (and only) goal in the final, Stokes was rewarded with a free car... unfortunately, he still hadn't passed the driving test!

• **Mick Channon, a member of that cup-winning team and now a successful racehorse trainer, is the Saints' leading scorer with a total of 185 goals in two spells at The Dell, the club's old ground. Derek Reeves holds the record for most goals in a season, notching 39 when the Saints won the Division Three title in 1959/60.**

• Legendary winger Terry Paine, a member of England's 1966 World Cup-winning squad, is Southampton's longest serving player. Between 1956 and 1974 he wore the club's colours in no fewer than 713 league games before moving to Hereford United. Paine's amazing total of 824 league games puts him third in the all-time list, behind Peter Shilton and Tony Ford.

• **England goalkeeper Shilton is the club's most capped player, winning 50 of his record 125 caps while at The Dell.**

• In August 2013 the Saints forked out a record £15 million to buy Italian striker Daniel Osvaldo from Roma. The following year they received a club record £30 million when left-back Luke Shaw left the south coast to join Manchester United.

• **Southampton legend Matt Le Tissier was the first midfielder in the history of the Premiership to score a century of goals. His total of 101 strikes included 24 penalties, a figure only exceeded by Alan Shearer and Frank Lampard in the Premier League era.**

• Helped by a superb run of 21 consecutive home league wins in 2011 – equalling the post-war record set by Liverpool in 1971/72 – Southampton returned to the Premier League after a seven-year absence in 2012.

HONOURS
Division 3 (South) champions 1922
Division 3 champions 1960
FA Cup 1976
Football League Trophy 2010

SOUTHEND UNITED

Year founded: 1906
Ground: Roots Hall (12,392)
Nickname: The Shrimpers
Biggest win: 10-1 v Golders Green (1934), v Brentwood (1968) and v Aldershot (1990)
Heaviest defeat: 1-9 v Brighton and Hove Albion (1965)

Southend United were founded in 1906 at the Blue Boar pub, just 50 yards away from the club's home, Roots Hall.

• **After joining the Football League in 1920 the Shrimpers remained in the third tier for a record 46 years, before dropping into the Fourth Division in 1966.**

• The club's top appearance maker is Sandy Anderson, who turned out in 452 league games between 1950 and 1962. His team-mate Roger Hollis is Southend's leading marksman, rifling in 120 league goals in just six years at the club between 1954 and 1960.

• **Southend were relegated from the third tier in 1988/89 despite amassing a record points total for a demoted team, 54.**

• Southend were the only Football League club managed by England World Cup-winning captain Bobby Moore, who was in charge at Roots Hall between 1984 and 1986 and also served on the club's board until his untimely death in 1993.

• **A record six goals were disallowed for offside in Southend's 2-1 defeat at Swindon in 1948.**

HONOURS
League One champions 2006
Division 4 champions 1981

SPAIN

First international: Spain 1 Denmark 0, 1920
Most capped player: Iker Casillas, 156 caps (2000-)
Leading goalscorer: David Villa, 59 goals (2005-14)
First World Cup appearance: Spain 3 Brazil 1, 1934
Biggest win: Spain 13 Bulgaria 0, 1933
Heaviest defeat: Italy 7 Spain 1, 1928 and England 7 Spain 1, 1931

Spain are the first country in football history to win three major international titles on the trot following their successes at Euro 2008, the 2010 World Cup in South Africa and Euro 2012 in Poland and Ukraine.

• **Spain secured their first ever World Cup triumph with a 1-0 victory over Holland at Soccer City Stadium in Johannesburg, midfielder Andres Iniesta drilling home the all-important**

HIGHEST CAPPED SPAIN PLAYERS

1.	Iker Casillas (2000-)	156
2.	Xavi (2000-14)	133
3.	Andono Zubizaretta (1985-98)	126
4.	Sergio Ramos (2005-)	119
5.	Xabi Alonso (2003-14)	114
6.	Fernando Torres (2003-)	110
7.	Raul (1996-2006)	102
8.	Carles Puyol (2000-13)	100
	Andres Iniesta (2006-)	100
10.	David Villa (2005-14)	97

"Now, remind me, how does this 'tiki-taka' work again?"

goal four minutes from the end of extra-time. Despite their entertaining close passing style of play, Spain only managed to score eight goals in the tournament – the lowest total ever by the winning nation at a World Cup.

• Along with Germany, Spain are the only country to have won the European Championships three times. Their first success came in 1964 when they had the advantage of playing the semi-final and final, against holders the Soviet Union, on home soil at Real Madrid's Bernabeu Stadium. Then, in 2008, a single Fernando Torres goal was enough to see off Germany in the final in Vienna. Finally, in 2012, Spain made it a hat-trick of victories after annihilating Italy 4-0 in the final in Kiev.

• Between 2007 and 2009 Spain went 35 matches without defeat (winning 32 and drawing just three) to equal the world record set by Brazil in the 1990s. The run came to an end when Spain lost 2-0 to USA at the 2009 Confederations Cup, but the Spanish were soon back on form, going into the 2010 World Cup on the back of 18 consecutive victories before they surprisingly lost their opening match at the finals against Switzerland. That setback, though, was soon forgotten as Vicente del Bosque's men went on to lift the trophy, sparking jubilant scenes

across Spain from Santander to Seville.
• The cheers turned to tears, however, at the 2014 World Cup in Brazil as Spain were eliminated at the group stage, with their 5-1 drubbing by the Netherlands being the worst ever defeat suffered by the reigning champions at the finals.

HONOURS
World Cup *2010*
European Championships *1964, 2008, 2012*
World Cup record
1930 Did not enter
1934 Quarter-finals
1938 Did not enter
1950 Fourth place
1954 Did not qualify
1958 Did not qualify
1962 Round 1
1966 Round 1
1970 Did not qualify
1974 Did not qualify
1978 Round 1
1982 Round 2
1986 Quarter-finals
1990 Round 2
1994 Quarter-finals
1998 Round 1
2002 Quarter-finals
2006 Round 2
2010 Winners
2014 Round 1

SPONSORSHIP

Manchester United's £45 million-a-year shirt sponsorship deal with US car manufacturers Chevrolet, which started in 2014, is a record for the Premier League.

• **On 24th January 1976 Kettering Town became the first senior football club in the UK to feature a sponsor's logo on their shirts, Kettering Tyres, for their Southern League Premier Division match against Bath City. The Football Association ordered the removal of the logo, but finally accepted shirt sponsorship in June 1977. Two years later Liverpool became the first top-flight club to sport a sponsor's logo after signing a deal with Hitachi.**

• The biggest sponsorship deal in world football was agreed between Manchester City and Etihad Airways in August 2011. The 10-year partnership, which includes stadium naming rights and shirt sponsorship, will boost City's coffers by a staggering £400 million.

• **A kit mix-up in the Tottenham dressing room meant that half the Spurs team wore plain, unsponsored shirts for the 1987 FA Cup final against Coventry City. Needless to say, the Londoners' shirt sponsors, lager manufacturers Holsten, were distinctly unamused.**

• The League Cup was the first major English competition to be sponsored, being renamed the Milk Cup after receiving backing from the Milk Marketing Board in 1982. It has since been rebranded as the Littlewoods Cup, the Rumbelows Cup, the Coca-Cola Cup, the Worthington Cup, the Carling Cup and the Capital One Cup. Since 1994 the FA Cup has been sponsored by Littlewoods, AXA, E.ON and Budweiser, but the competition is still known by its original name. Meanwhile, the Premier League has been sponsored by Carling, Barclaycard and, currently, Barclays.

• **The first competition in England to be sponsored was the Watney Cup in 1971, a pre-season tournament between the highest scoring teams in the different divisions of the Football League.**

RAHEEM STERLING

Born: Kingston, Jamaica, 8th December 1994
Position: Winger
Club career:
2012- Liverpool 57 (11)
International record:
2012- England 7 (0)

Speedy Liverpool winger Raheem Sterling became the third-youngest player ever to make his debut for the Reds when he came on as a sub in a 2-1 home defeat against Wigan Athletic on 24th March 2012. Seven months later he became the club's second-youngest goalscorer (behind Michael Owen) when he notched his first goal for the Merseysiders in a 1-0 win against Reading.

• **Jamaican-born Sterling started his career with QPR, before switching to Liverpool for a bargain £600,000 in 2010. The fee, though, could rise to as much as £5 million, depending on appearances.**

• A star of Liverpool's magnificent 2013/14 Premier League campaign, Sterling was shortlisted for the PFA Young Player of the Year award but missed out on the prize to Chelsea's Eden Hazard.

• **Sterling rose through the England youth ranks to make his senior debut**

Raheem Sterling finds playing for Liverpool a hair-raising experience

in a 4-2 friendly defeat away to Sweden in November 2012. In only his fourth game for the Three Lions he was sent off in a pre-2014 World Cup friendly against Ecuador to become the youngest ever England player to see red.

STEVENAGE

Year founded: 1976
Ground: Broadhall Way (6,722)
Previous name: Stevenage Borough
Nickname: The Boro
Biggest win: 7-0 v Merthyr (2006)
Heaviest defeat: 1-6 v Farnborough (2002)

The club was founded in 1976 as Stevenage Borough, following the bankruptcy of the town's former club, Stevenage Athletic. In 2010 the club decided to become simply 'Stevenage'.

• **Stevenage rose through the football pyramid to gain promotion to the Conference in 1994. Two years later they won the title but were denied promotion to the Football League as their tiny Broadhall Way Stadium did not meet the league's standards.**

• Stevenage finally made it into the league in 2010 after topping the Conference table with an impressive 99 points. If the club's two victories against Chester City, who were expelled from the league during the season, had not been expunged then Stevenage would have set a new Conference record of 105 points. The following season Stevenage were promoted again, after beating Torquay United 1-0 in the League Two play-off final at Old Trafford, but their three-year stay in League One ended in 2014 when they finished bottom of the pile.

• **In 2007 Stevenage became the first club to lift a trophy at the new Wembley, beating Kidderminster Harriers 3-2 in the final of the FA Trophy watched by a competition record crowd of 53,262.**

• In 2012 Stevenage reached the fifth round of the FA Cup for the first time in their history, but were beaten 3-1 in a replay by big boys Tottenham.

STOKE CITY

Year founded: 1863
Ground: Britannia Stadium (27,740)
Previous name: Stoke Ramblers, Stoke
Nickname: The Potters
Biggest win: 11-0 v Stourbridge (1914)
Heaviest defeat: 0-10 v Preston (1889)

Founded in 1863 by employees of the North Staffordshire Railway Company, Stoke are the second oldest league club in the country. Between 1868 and 1870 the club was known as Stoke Ramblers, before simply becoming Stoke and then adding the suffix 'City' in 1925.

• Stoke were founder members of the Football League in 1888 but finished bottom of the table at the end of the season. After another wooden spoon in 1890 the club dropped out of the league, but returned to the big time after just one season.

• The club's greatest moment came in 1972 when they won the League Cup, beating favourites Chelsea 2-1 in the final at Wembley, thanks to a late winner by George Eastham. Aged 35 and 161 days at the time, Eastham is the oldest player ever to win the League Cup. The Potters had a great chance to add to their meagre haul of silverware in 2011 when they reached the FA Cup final for the first time, but they lost 1-0 to Manchester City. At least their fans enjoyed the semi-final, when Stoke thrashed Bolton 5-0 in the joint-biggest win yet by a club side at the new Wembley.

• While playing in his second spell at Stoke, the great Stanley Matthews became the oldest player ever to appear in the top flight. On 6th February 1965 Matthews played his last game for the club against Fulham just five days after celebrating his 50th birthday.

• The legendary Gordon Banks is Stoke's most capped player. The brilliant goalkeeper, a World Cup winner in 1966, won 37 of his 73 England caps while with the Staffordshire outfit.

• **Freddie Steele is Stoke's leading scorer with 140 league goals between 1934 and 1949, including a club record 33 in the 1936/37 season.** Stalwart defender Eric Skeels played in a record 507 league games for the Potters between 1960 and 1976.

• On 23rd February 1957 Stoke thrashed Lincoln City 8-0 in a Second Division match. Incredibly, Neville Coleman bagged seven of the goals to set a club record which has never been matched since.

• **In August 2011 Stoke splashed out a club record £12 million to bring lanky Tottenham striker Peter Crouch to the Britannia Stadium.** Earlier that year the Potters made their record sale when Turkish international Tuncay moved to German club Wolfsburg in a £4.5 million deal.

• On 27th January 1974 Stoke became the first top-flight club to host Sunday football when they played Chelsea at their former home, the Victoria Ground. Ignoring the complaints of religious groups, a crowd of nearly 32,000 turned up to see Stoke win 1-0.

• **For the first time in their history Stoke were the highest-placed Midlands club in the country in the 2013/14 season.** The Potters' ninth-place finish was their best ever Premier League showing and a club best since coming fifth in the old First Division in 1975.

GORDON STRACHAN

Born: Edinburgh, 9th February 1957
Managerial career:
1996-2001 Coventry City
2001-04 Southampton
2005-09 Celtic
2009-10 Middlesbrough
2013- Scotland

Appointed as Scotland manager in January 2013, Gordon Strachan saw his team become the first to be officially eliminated from the UEFA 2014 World Cup section, even ahead of real minnows like Andorra and San Marino. However, he then rallied his troops to impressive home and away victories over Croatia to enable Scotland to finish fourth in their qualifying group.

• Strachan's managerial career began at Coventry in 1996 when he was still playing. The following year he became the first outfield player to appear in the Premier League aged 40. He was sacked by the Sky Blues after taking them down in 2001, but soon moved to Southampton, guiding them to their first FA Cup final in 27 years in 2003.

• In 2005, Strachan was appointed boss of Celtic. Despite losing his first match, a Champions League qualifier against Artmedia Bratislava, 5-0, the little Scot went on to enjoy huge success in Glasgow. Between 2006 and 2008 he won three successive SPL titles, a feat previously only matched by two other Celtic managers. He resigned his position after Celtic were pipped to the SPL title by arch-rivals Rangers on the last day of the 2008/09 season, and then spent an unsuccessful year as Middlesbrough boss before quitting in October 2010.

• Strachan won a host of honours in his playing days as a tireless midfielder, including the European Cup Winners' Cup with Aberdeen, the FA Cup with Manchester United in 1983 and 1985 and the league title with Leeds in 1992. He also won 50 caps with Scotland.

DANIEL STURRIDGE

Born: Birmingham, 1st September 1989
Position: Striker
Club career:
2006-09 Manchester City 21 (5)
2009-13 Chelsea 63 (13)
2011 Bolton Wanderers (loan) 12 (8)
2013- Liverpool 43 (31)
International record:
2011- England 14 (5)

A £12 million signing from Chelsea in January 2013, Daniel Sturridge enjoyed a tremendous season with Liverpool in 2013/14, finishing second in the Premier League goalscoring charts behind his team-mate Luis Suarez with 21 goals and earning a place in the PFA Team of the Year. He also became only the second player (after Manchester United's

Ruud van Nistelrooy) to score in eight consecutive Premier League games.

• A fleet-footed striker who never turns down the chance to shoot, Sturridge started out on the books of Aston Villa and Coventry before making his first-team debut as a 17-year-old with Manchester City. During the 2007/08 season he became the first player ever to score in the FA Youth Cup, the FA Cup and the Premier League in the same season.

• Sturridge joined Chelsea for an initial fee of £3.5 million in 2009, and the following year helped the Blues win the league and cup Double. He spent the second half of the 2010/11 season on loan at Bolton, where he became only the sixth player to score on his first four appearances for a Premier League club. He returned to Chelsea for the start of the 2011/12 campaign, but found his opportunities limited after Roberto di Matteo replaced Andre Villas-Boas in the Stamford Bridge hotseat.

• **Sturridge has played and scored for England at every level from Under-16 upwards. He made his full international debut as a sub against Sweden in November 2011, and in March 2013 notched his first goal for the Three Lions in an 8-0 hammering of San Marino. At the 2014 World Cup he scored England's first goal at the tournament in a 2-1 defeat to Italy.**

LUIS SUAREZ

Born: Salto, Uruguay, 24th January 1987
Position: Striker
Club career:
2005-06 Nacional 27 (10)
2006-07 Groningen 29 (10)
2007-11 Ajax 110 (81)
2011-14 Liverpool 110 (69)
2014- Barcelona
International record:
2007- Uruguay 78 (40)

A quick-witted striker who is famed for his ability to score from the tightest of angles, Luis Suarez became the third most expensive player in football history when he joined Barcelona from Liverpool in July 2014 for £75 million.

• **Suarez enjoyed a rollercoaster three years with Liverpool after signing for the Merseysiders from Ajax for £22.8 million in January 2011.** In his first

Not for the first time, Luis Suarez has bitten off more than he can chew

full season with the Reds he helped them win the Carling Cup but, less impressively, was given an eight-match ban by the FA and fined £40,000 for racially abusing Manchester United defender Patrice Evra. When the two teams met later in the season Suarez hit the headlines again by refusing to shake Evra's hand before kick-off.

TOP 10

MOST EXPENSIVE FOOTBALLERS

1. Gareth Bale (Tottenham to Real Madrid, 2013)   £86 million
2. Cristiano Ronaldo (Manchester United to Real Madrid, 2009)   £80 million
3. Luis Suarez (Liverpool to Barcelona, 2014)   £75 million
4. James Rodriguez (Monaco to Real Madrid, 2014)   £63 million
5. Angel Di Maria (Real Madrid to Manchester United, 2014)   £59.7 million
6. Zlatan Ibrahimovic (Inter Milan to Barcelona, 2009)   £59 million
7. Kaka (AC Milan to Real Madrid, 2009)   £56 million
8. Edinson Cavani (Napoli to Paris St Germain, 2013)   £55 million
9. Radamel Falcao (Atletico Madrid to Monaco, 2013)   £51 million
10. David Luiz (Chelsea to Paris St Germain, 2014)   £50 million
    Fernando Torres (Liverpool to Chelsea, 2011)   £50 million

• The following season Suarez was in hot water again after he bit Chelsea defender Branislav Ivanovic on the arm in an unprovoked attack. The striker, who had been banned for seven games after a similar incident while playing for his previous club Ajax, was hit with a 10-game ban – the fifth longest in Premier League history.

• **However, the Uruguayan appeared to turn over a new leaf in 2013/14 when he topped the Premier League scoring charts with 31 goals, won both Player of the Year awards and became the first player ever to score 10 Premier League goals in a month in December 2013.**

• Sadly for his many admirers, the temperamental Suarez was involved in another shocking incident at the 2014 World Cup when he bit Italy defender Giorgio Chiellini. Despite pleading innocence, the maverick striker was immediately thrown out of the tournament and given a four-month ban from all football activities in the stiffest ever sanction handed out by FIFA at the World Cup for on-field misconduct. In happier days with Uruguay, Suarez was named Player of the Tournament when his country won the 2011 Copa America and two years later he became the South Americans' all-time leading scorer.

SUBSTITUTES

Substitutes were first allowed in the Football League in the 1965/66 season. The first player to come off the bench was Charlton's Keith Peacock, who replaced injured goalkeeper Mike Rose after 11 minutes of the Addicks' match away to Bolton on 21st August 1965. On the same afternoon Barrow's Bobby Knox became the first substitute to score a goal when he notched against Wrexham.

• The fastest ever goal scored by a substitute was by Arsenal's Nicklas Bendtner, who headed in a corner against Tottenham at the Emirates on 22nd December 2007, just 1.8 seconds after replacing Emmanuel Eboue.

• The most goals ever scored in a Premier League game by a substitute is four by Ole Gunnar Solskjaer in Manchester United's 8-1 win at Nottingham Forest in 1999. Incredibly, the Norwegian striker was only on the pitch for 19 minutes. During his United career Solskjaer scored a record 28 goals off the bench.

• Substitutes were first allowed at the World Cup in 1970. The most goals scored by a sub at the tournament in a single match is three by Hungary's Lazlo Kiss against El Salvador in 1982. Brazilian winger Denilson made a record 11 appearances as a substitute at the finals in 1998 and 2002.

• Sunderland goalkeeper Thomas Sorensen is the most substituted goalkeeper in Premier League history, leaving the pitch before full-time on no fewer than 13 occasions.

• Former Newcastle forward Shola Ameobi has made a record 137 appearances as a sub in the Premier League, while Ryan Giggs was substituted a record 134 times in his long Manchester United career.

SUNDERLAND

Year founded: 1879
Ground: Stadium of Light (48,707)
Previous name: Sunderland and District Teachers' AFC
Nickname: The Black Cats
Biggest win: 11-1 v Fairfield (1895)
Heaviest defeat: 0-8 v Sheffield Wednesday (1911), v West Ham (1968) and v Watford (1982)

The club was founded as the Sunderland and District Teachers' AFC in 1879 but soon opened its ranks to other professions and became simply 'Sunderland' the following year.

You can't keep Sunderland quiet these days...

• Sunderland were the first 'new' club to join the Football League, replacing Stoke in 1890. Just two years later they won their first league championship and they retained the title the following year, in the process becoming the first club to score 100 goals in a league season. In 1895 Sunderland became the first club ever to win three championships, and their status was further enhanced when they beat Scottish champions Hearts 5-3 in a one-off 'world championship' match.

• In 1958 Sunderland were relegated after a then record 57 consecutive seasons in the top flight. Arsenal passed this particular landmark in 1983/84 and can now boast an impressive run of 88 successive seasons at the top level.

• Sunderland were the first Second Division team in the post Second World War era to win the FA Cup, beating Leeds 1-0 at Wembley in 1973 in one of the biggest upsets of all time thanks to a goal by the late Ian Porterfield. Incredibly, their line-up featured not one international player.

• Goalkeeper Jim Montgomery, a hero of that cup-winning side, is the Black Cats' record appearance maker, turning out in 537 league games between 1960 and 1977.

• Sunderland's record victory was an 11-1 thrashing of Fairfield in the FA Cup in 1895. However, the club's best ever league win, a 9-1 demolition of eventual champions and arch-rivals Newcastle at St James' Park in 1908, probably gave their fans more pleasure. To this day, it remains the biggest ever victory by an away side in the top flight.

• Sunderland last won the league championship in 1935/36, the last time, incidentally, that a team wearing stripes has topped the pile. The Wearsiders' success, though, certainly wasn't based on a solid defence... the 74 goals they conceded that season is more than any other top-flight champions before or since.

• In 1990 Sunderland became the only team to lose a play-off final yet still gain promotion, the Wearsiders going up to the old First Division in place of Swindon after the Robins were punished for financial irregularities.

SUPERSTITIONS

• Inside forward Charlie Buchan is Sunderland's record scorer with 209 league goals between 1911 and 1925. Dave Halliday holds the record for a single season, hitting the target 43 times in 1928/29.

• Famed for their spending power in the late 1940s and early 1950s, when they were dubbed 'The Bank of England' club, Sunderland coughed up a record £14 million in August 2012 when they signed striker Steven Fletcher from Wolves. The year before the Black Cats sold their previous most expensive signing, Darren Bent, to Aston Villa for a club record £18 million.

• Sunderland have reached the League Cup final twice, losing 1-0 to Norwich City in 1985 and 3-1 to Manchester City in 2014.

> HONOURS
>
> *Division 1 champions 1892, 1983, 1895, 1902, 1913, 1936*
> *Division 2 champions 1976*
> *Championship champions 2005, 2007*
> *Division 3 champions 1988*
> *FA Cup 1937, 1973*

SUPERSTITIONS

Many footballers, including some of the great names of the game, are highly superstitious and believe that performing the same personal routines before every game will bring them good luck. Spain goalkeeper Iker Casillas, for instance, always touches the crossbar when his team scores a goal.

• Cristiano Ronaldo believes it brings him good luck if he has a haircut before a big match and he also insists on being the first player in his team to enter the field of play.

• Kolo Toure's superstition almost cost his then club Arsenal dear in their 2009 Champions League clash with Roma. Believing that it would be bad luck to leave the dressing room before team-mate William Gallas, who was receiving treatment, Toure failed to appear for the start of the second half, leaving the Gunners to restart the match with just nine players!

• France developed a number of superstitions around Fabien Barthez at the 1998 World Cup, one of which demanded that skipper Laurent Blanc had to kiss the goalkeeper's bald head just before kick-off. It may all have been mumbo-jumbo, but the routine

On the first day of the 2014/15 season Swansea recorded their first ever league victory against Manchester United at Old Trafford

worked for the French who won the competition for the first time in their history.

• Some superstitions are not entirely irrational. For example, Arsenal always make sure that a new goalkeeper's jersey is washed before it is used for the first time. The policy stems from the 1927 FA Cup final, which the Gunners lost when goalkeeper Dan Lewis let in a soft goal against Cardiff. He later blamed his mistake on the ball slipping from his grasp and over the line as it brushed against the shiny surface of his new jumper.

• In October 2008 the coach of Zimbabwean side Midlands Portland Cement sent his 17-member squad into the crocodile-infested Zambezi river in a ritual cleansing ceremony ahead of an important match. Unfortunately, only 16 players emerged from the water a few minutes later and, unsurprisingly given the bad omens, the team went on to lose their next game.

• In July 2014 Leeds United owner Massimo Cellini insisted that goalkeeper Paddy Kenny should be excluded from

his team's squad on the grounds that the Irishman was born on 17th May – as Cellini was convinced that the number 17 was extremely unlucky. The wacky Italian also demanded that seat numbers 17 at Elland Road should be changed to 16B.

SWANSEA CITY

Year founded: 1912
Ground: Liberty Stadium (20,750)
Previous name: Swansea Town
Nickname: The Swans
Biggest win: 12-0 v Sliema Wanderers (1982)
Heaviest defeat: 0-8 v Liverpool (1990) and v Monaco (1991)

The club was founded as Swansea Town in 1912 and entered the Football League eight years later. The present name was adopted in 1970.

• Under former Liverpool striker John Toshack the Swans climbed from the

- In 1961 the club became the first from Wales to compete in Europe, but were knocked out of the Cup Winners' Cup in the first round by East German side Carl Zeiss Jena. In the same competition the Swans recorded their biggest ever win over Maltese minnows Sliema Wanderers 12-0 in 1982.

- Some of the club's most famous victories have come in the FA Cup. In 1926 Swansea knocked out Arsenal before losing in the semi-finals to Bolton and in 1964 the Swans again reached the last four after sensationally beating Liverpool at Anfield. Then, in 1999, the Welshmen became the first club from the bottom tier to knock out a Premier League club when they beat West Ham 1-0 in a third-round replay.

- **The Swans made their record signing in July 2013 when Ivory Coast striker Wilfried Bony moved from Vitesse for £12 million. In August 2012 the Welsh outfit sold midfielder Joe Allen to Liverpool for a club record £15 million.**

- In 1936 Swansea set a Football League record for the longest distance travelled for consecutive matches when they visited Newcastle on Easter Sunday just a day after going to Plymouth.

HONOURS
Division 3 (South) champions 1925, 1949
League One champions 2008
Third Division champions 2000
League Cup 2013
Football League Trophy 1994, 2006
Welsh Cup 1913, 1932, 1950, 1961, 1966, 1981, 1982, 1983, 1989, 1991

SWINDON TOWN

Year founded: 1879
Ground: The County Ground (14,700)
Previous name: Swindon Spartans
Nickname: The Robins
Biggest win: 10-1 v Farnham United Breweries (1925)
Heaviest defeat: 1-10 v Manchester City (1930)

The club was founded by the Reverend William Pitt in 1879, becoming Swindon Spartans two years later before adopting the name Swindon Town in 1883. In 1920 Swindon were founder members of the Third Division, kicking off their league career with a 9-1 thrashing of Luton.

- **The Robins' finest moment came in 1969 when, as a Third Division club, they beat mighty Arsenal 3-1 in the League Cup final on a mud-clogged Wembley pitch. Legendary winger Don Rogers was the star of the show, scoring two of Swindon's goals.**

- In 1993, three years after being denied promotion to the top flight for the first time because of a financial scandal, Swindon earned promotion to the Premiership via the play-offs. The following campaign, though, proved to be a miserable one as the Robins finished bottom of the pile and conceded 100 goals... a record for the Premier League.

- **Swindon won the Fourth Division title in 1985/86 with a then Football League best 102 points, a total which remains a record for the bottom tier.**

- John Trollope is Swindon's longest serving player, appearing in 770 league games for the club between 1960 and 1980 – a record for a single club. Harry Morris scored a record 229 goals for the club between 1926 and 1933, including a seasonal best of 47 in the league in his first year with the Robins.

- **On 22nd January 2008 Swindon set an unwanted record when they became the first club to miss all four of their penalties in a shoot-out against Barnet.**

- Inside forward Harold Fleming is Swindon's most-capped international, playing in 11 games for England between 1909 and 1914. He did pretty well, too, scoring a total of nine goals fo his country.

HONOURS
Second Division champions 1996
Division 4 champions 1986
League Two champions 2012
League Cup 1969

old Fourth Division to the top flight in just four seasons between 1978 and 1981, the fastest ever ascent through the Football League. The glory days soon faded, though, and by 1986 Swansea were back in the basement division.

- In 2011, though, Swansea beat Reading 4-2 in the Championship play-off final at Wembley to become the first Welsh club to reach the Premier League. Again, their rise was a rapid one as they had been in the basement tier just six years earlier.

- **The club's greatest day came in 2013 when they won their first major trophy, the League Cup. The Swans triumphed in fine style, too, demolishing League Two outfit Bradford City 5-0 at Wembley in the biggest ever victory in the final.**

- Ivor Allchurch is the Swans' leading scorer, banging in 166 goals in two spells at the club between 1949 and 1968. Allchurch is also the club's most decorated international, winning 42 caps for Wales while with Swansea. One-club man Wilfred Milne is the Swans' leading appearance maker, turning out in 586 league games between 1920 and 1937.

IS THAT A FACT?
The first set of twins to score for the same team in the same Football League match were Swindon's Bill and Alf Stephens in a 2-0 win against Exeter in 1946.

John Terry, Chelsea's most successful ever captain

JOHN TERRY

Born: Barking, 7th December 1980
Position: Defender
Club career:
1998- Chelsea 421 (34)
2000 Nottingham Forest (loan) 6 (0)
International record:
2003-12 England 78 (6)

Chelsea captain since 2004, Terry is the most successful skipper in the club's history, winning three Premier League titles, five FA Cups and two League Cups. In 2012, despite being suspended for the final against Bayern Munich, he added the Champions League to that list, making up for his disappointment four years earlier when he slipped and put his penalty wide in the shoot-out against Manchester United in the final in Moscow.

• A superb tackler who reads the game well, Terry was voted PFA Player of the Year in 2005 after leading the Blues to the first of their back-to-back Premiership titles. With a total of 57 goals for the club in all competitions, he is the highest scoring defender in Chelsea history.

• After making his England debut against Serbia & Montenegro in 2003, Terry went on to represent his country at Euro 2004 and Euro 2012, the 2006 World Cup – where he was the only England player to be selected for the all-star FIFA squad at the end of the tournament – and the 2010 World Cup.

• He was first appointed England captain by Steve McClaren in 2006 and retained the role under Fabio Capello. However, in February 2010 Terry was sensationally stripped of the armband following newspaper revelations about his private life. The following year, though, he reclaimed the captaincy only for the FA to take it off him again in February 2012 after he was charged by police for racially abusing QPR defender Anton Ferdinand earlier in the season. Terry was acquitted at his trial, but when the FA charged him with the same offence he decided to retire from international football.

THROW-INS

Thomas Gronnemark from Denmark holds the world record for the longest ever throw. Employing a forward hand spring technique he hurled the ball an incredible 51.33 metres on 18th June 2010.

• Famous long throw specialists include Ian Hutchinson (Chelsea striker of the 1970s), former England international Malcolm McDonald and, in the Premier League era, ex-Stoke midfielder Rory Delap.

• The most bizarre goal from a throw-in came in a derby between Birmingham City and Aston Villa in 2002. Villa defender Olof Mellberg threw the ball back to goalkeeper Peter Enckelman and it dribbled under his foot and into the net. Despite Villa's protests, referee David Elleray ruled that the goal should stand because Enckelman had made contact with the ball.

• Throw-ins were replaced by kick-ins from the touchline in the Diadora League (now the Ryman League) during the 1994/95 season, but the experiment was abandoned at the end of the campaign.

FERNANDO TORRES

Born: Madrid, 20th March 1984
Position: Striker
Club career:
2001-07 Atletico Madrid 214 (82)
2007-11 Liverpool 102 (65)
2011- Chelsea 110 (20)
2014- AC Milan (loan)
International record:
2003- Spain 110 (38)

When Fernando Torres moved from Liverpool to Chelsea for £50 million in January 2011 he became the most expensive player in British football history at the time. The following year he helped the Blues win the FA Cup and Champions League, despite spending much of the campaign on the bench and struggling to find his best form when he did get on the pitch. He fared better in 2012/13, scoring against Benfica in the final of the Europa League as the Blues won the trophy for the first time.

• Torres began his career with local club Atletico Madrid, where his goalscoring feats earned him the nickname 'El Niño' (The Kid) and the skipper's armband. Aged just 19 at the time, he was the youngest captain in Atletico's history.

• In 2007 Torres signed for Liverpool for a club record £20 million (plus Luis Garcia, who moved in the opposite

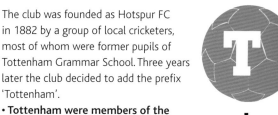

direction). He was an instant hit at Anfield, becoming the first Liverpool player since 1948 to hit hat-tricks in consecutive home matches when he notched trebles against Middlesbrough and West Ham and, later in the season, scoring in eight successive home games to equal a record set by Reds legend Roger Hunt way back in 1962. His total of 24 league goals also set a new record for a foreign player in a debut season in English football.

• Torres carried on his goalscoring form into Euro 2008, hitting the winning goal in the final in Vienna as Spain beat Germany to claim their first trophy for 44 years. To cap a truly memorable year he was named third in the World Footballer of the Year poll behind Cristiano Ronaldo and Lionel Messi.

• Despite playing well below par and failing to score a single goal, Torres ended the 2010 World Cup in South

It's all smiles at White Hart Lane

Africa by picking up a winners' medal. He was back on form at Euro 2012, claiming the Golden Boot after scoring three goals, including one in the final against Italy to help Spain win an unprecedented three consecutive trophies. The following year he won the Golden Boot at the Confederations Cup, although he finished on the losing side in the final as Spain went down 3-0 to hosts Brazil.

TOTTENHAM HOTSPUR

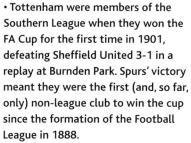

Year founded: 1882
Ground: White Hart Lane (36,284)
Previous name: Hotspur FC
Nickname: Spurs
Biggest win: 13-2 v Crewe (1960)
Heaviest defeat: 0-8 v Cologne (1995)

The club was founded as Hotspur FC in 1882 by a group of local cricketers, most of whom were former pupils of Tottenham Grammar School. Three years later the club decided to add the prefix 'Tottenham'.

• **Tottenham were members of the Southern League when they won the FA Cup for the first time in 1901, defeating Sheffield United 3-1 in a replay at Burnden Park. Spurs' victory meant they were the first (and, so far, only) non-league club to win the cup since the formation of the Football League in 1888.**

• In 1961 Tottenham created history when they became the first club in the 20th century to win the fabled league and cup Double. Their title success was based on a storming start to the season, Bill Nicholson's side winning their first 11 games to set a top-flight record which has not been matched since. By the end of the campaign, the north Londoners had won 31 of their 42 league matches to create another record for the top tier.

• As Arsenal fans like to point out, Tottenham have failed to win the league since those 'Glory, Glory' days of skipper Danny Blanchflower, Dave Mackay and Cliff Jones. Spurs, though, have continued to enjoy cup success, and their total of eight victories in the FA Cup is only surpassed by the Gunners and Manchester United. Remarkably, five of those triumphs came in years ending in a '1', giving rise to the legend that these seasons were particularly lucky for Spurs.

• Tottenham have also enjoyed much success in the League Cup, winning the competition four times – a record which puts them joint third on the all-time honours list behind Liverpool and Aston Villa. The last of these triumphs, in 2008 following a 2-1 defeat of holders Chelsea in the final, saw Tottenham become the first club to win the League Cup at the new Wembley.

• Spurs have a decent record in Europe, too. In 1963 they thrashed Atletico Madrid 5-1 in the final of the European Cup Winners' Cup, the legendary Jimmy Greaves grabbing a brace, to become the first British club to win a European trophy. Then, in 1972, Tottenham defeated Wolves 3-2 on aggregate in the first ever UEFA Cup final and the first European final to feature two English clubs. A third European triumph followed in 1984 when Tottenham beat Anderlecht in the first UEFA Cup final to be settled by penalties.

• Ace marksman Jimmy Greaves holds two goalscoring records for Tottenham. His total of 220 league goals between 1961 and 1970 is a club best, as is his impressive tally of 37 league goals in 1962/63. Clive Allen, though, struck an incredible total of 49 goals in all competitions in 1986/87, including a record 12 in the League Cup.

• Stalwart defender Steve Perryman is the club's longest serving player,

pulling on the famous white shirt in 655 league games between 1969 and 1986, including 613 in the old First Division – a top-flight record for a player at a single club.

• In August 2013 Spurs received a world record transfer fee of £86 million from Real Madrid for Welsh winger Gareth Bale. The club's record buy is midfielder Erik Lamela, who cost £30 million from Roma in the same month.

• Tottenham's first title success was in 1950/51 when Arthur Rowe's stylish 'Push and Run' team topped the table just one year after winning the Second Division championship. In the years since, only Ipswich Town (in 1961 and 1962) have managed to claim the top two titles in consecutive seasons.

• Spurs played just 40 games in the 2005/06 season – a record low for the Premier League era – after being eliminated from both the League Cup and the FA Cup at the first time of asking.

• Spurs' incredible 9-1 trouncing of Wigan on 22nd November 2009 was only the second time a club had scored nine goals in a Premier League game. Jermain Defoe's five-goal haul in the same match also equalled the league's individual scoring record.

• Among the many famous faces who follow Spurs are 'Harry Potter' star Rupert Grint, singing duo Chas and Dave and Lord Sugar of TV show *The Apprentice*.

> **HONOURS**
> *Division 1 champions 1951, 1961*
> *Division 2 champions 1920, 1950*
> *FA Cup 1901, 1921, 1961, 1962, 1967, 1981, 1982, 1991*
> *League Cup 1971, 1973, 1999, 2008*
> *Double 1961*
> *European Cup Winners' Cup 1963*
> *UEFA Cup 1972, 1984*

YAYA TOURE

> **Born:** Bouake, Ivory Coast, 13th May 1983
> **Position:** Midfielder
> **Club career:**
> 2001-03 Beveren 70 (3)
> 2003-05 Matalurh Donetsk 33 (3)
> 2005-06 Olympiacos 26 (3)
> 2006-07 Monaco 27 (5)
> 2007-10 Barcelona 74 (4)
> 2010- Manchester City 134 (38)
> **International record:**
> 2004- Ivory Coast 83 (16)

A nice pic for the Toure family album

Yaya Toure wrote himself into Manchester City folklore when he scored the winning goals in both the FA Cup semi-final and final in 2011, ending the club's 35-year quest for a major trophy. The following season he was a key part of the City side which won the Premier League for the first time, his dynamic displays earning him a place in the PFA Team of the Year. He repeated that feat in 2014 as City won the title again, becoming only the second midfielder ever (after Frank Lampard) to score 20 Premier League goals in a season.

• A powerful midfielder who likes to switch from a defensive to an attacking role during games, Toure began his professional career in Belgium with Beveren. He later had spells in the Ukraine, Greece (where he won the double with Olympiacos in 2006) and France, before moving to Barcelona in 2007.

• Toure was part of the Barcelona team which won an incredible six trophies in 2009, showing his versatility to good effect when he played at centre-back in the Champions League final against Manchester United. The following year he moved to Manchester City for £24 million, teaming up with his older brother, Kolo Toure.

• A member of the Ivory Coast team that competed at the 2006, 2010 and 2014 World Cups, Toure was voted African Footballer of the Year in 2011, 2012 and 2013 – only the second player (after Samuel Eto'o) to achieve this hat-trick.

IS THAT A FACT?
Tottenham became the first club to concede 1,000 Premier League goals when Steven Fletcher scored for Wolves in a 1-1 draw at White Hart Lane on 14th January 2012.

TRANMERE ROVERS

Year founded: 1884
Ground: Prenton Park (16,567)
Previous name: Belmont FC
Nickname: Rovers
Biggest win: 13-0 v Oswestry United (1914)
Heaviest defeat: 1-9 v Tottenham (1953)

The club was founded as Belmont FC in 1884 by members of two local cricket clubs, changing its name to Tranmere Rovers the following year. In 1921 Rovers joined the Football League for the first time as members of the newly created Third Division (North).

• **The club enjoyed their greatest ever moment in 2000 when they played Leicester City in the League Cup final at Wembley. Despite performing well on the day, Rovers lost 2-1.**

• Rovers' best ever league victory, 13-4 against Oldham on Boxing Day 1935, set a record for the highest scoring Football League match which remains to this day. Robert 'Bunny' Bell scored nine goals in the match, a record for the old Third Division (North).

• **Between 1946 and 1955 Tranmere's Harold Bell appeared in 375 consecutive league games, a run unmatched by any other Football**

League player. Bell went on to make a club record 595 appearances before hanging up his boots in 1964.

• In 1964 Tranmere conceded the fastest ever goal in Football League history, Bradford Park Avenue's Jim Fryatt netting against them after just four seconds. Understandably perhaps, Rovers never recovered from that early shock, going down to a 4-2 defeat.

HONOURS
Division 3 (North) champions 1938
Football League Trophy 1990
Welsh Cup 1935

TRANSFERS

The world's most expensive player is Welsh winger Gareth Bale, who moved from Tottenham to Real Madrid in August 2013 for a staggering transfer fee of £86 million. This beat the £80 million which Real paid Manchester United for Portuguese star Cristiano Ronaldo in the summer of 2009.

• **The biggest transfer deal in the British game took place in August 2014 when Manchester United paid Real Madrid £59.7 million for Argentinian winger Angel Di Maria.**

• The first player to be transferred for a four-figure fee in England was Alf Common, who moved from Sunderland to Middlesbrough in 1905. In 1966 World Cup winner Alan Ball became the first six-figure footballer when he joined Everton

from Blackpool, while Trevor Francis broke the £1 million barrier when he moved to Nottingham Forest from Birmingham City for £1,150,000 in 1979.

• **In May 2012 Fleetwood Town striker James Vardy became the first non-league player to fetch a £1 million transfer fee when he joined Leicester City.**

• In 1921 Ernie Blenkinsop, a future England captain, moved from Cudworth to Hull City for £200 and 80 pints of ale. Other strange transfers involving England players include: John Barnes (Sudbury Court to Watford in 1981 for playing kit), Ian Wright (Greenwich Borough to Crystal Palace in 1985 for a set of weights) and Zat Knight (Rushall Olympic to Fulham in 1999 for 30 tracksuits).

TV AND RADIO

The first ever live radio broadcast of a football match was on 22nd January 1927 when the BBC covered the First Division encounter between Arsenal and Sheffield United at Highbury. The *Radio Times* printed a pitch marked into numbered squares, which the commentators used to describe where the ball was at any given moment (which some suggest gave rise to the phrase 'back to square one').

• **The 1937 FA Cup final between Sunderland and Preston was the first to be televised, although only parts of the match were shown by the BBC.**

Arjen Robben has never been one to shy away from the cameras

The following year's final between Preston and Huddersfield was the first to be screened live and in full, although the audience was only around 10,000 as so few people had TV sets at the time.

• The biggest British TV audience ever for a football match (and, indeed, the biggest ever for any TV broadcast in this country) was 32.3 million for the 1966 World Cup final between England and West Germany. The viewing figures for the match, which was shown live by both BBC and ITV, were all the more remarkable as only 15 million households in the UK had TV sets. The biggest TV audience for an FA Cup final was in 1970 when 28.49 million people watched Chelsea beat Leeds 2-1 in a midweek replay at Old Trafford.

• **A record 909.6 million people worldwide watched the 2010 World Cup final between Spain and the Netherlands.**

• The current TV deal between Sky, BT and the Premier League which started in the 2013/14 season is the biggest in the history of the game. Under the terms of the deal the two companies will pay £3 billion over three years to show 154 live games per season – a 71 per cent increase on the previous three-year agreement.

TWITTER

Cristiano Ronaldo has more followers on Twitter than any other footballer in the world, with around 28.2 million at the last count. His onetime Real Madrid team-mate Kaka is second on the footballers' Twitter leaderboard, the Brazilian's popularity being boosted by his well-known devotion to Christianity. Neither player, though, can compete with the world's most popular Twitter celebrity, the singer Katy Perry, who has over 54 million followers.

• **The 2014 World Cup semi-final between hosts Brazil and Germany generated an incredible 35.6 million tweets – a record for a sporting event.**

• A record 672 million tweets were sent during the 2014 World Cup, making the tournament as a whole the most tweeted about event in social media history.

• **Chelsea defender Ashley Cole was fined a record £90,000 for a tweet in October 2012, when he posted abusive comments about the FA after the governing body had questioned the truth of his statements in the John Terry race abuse inquiry.**

MOST FOLLOWED FOOTBALLERS ON TWITTER

1. Cristiano Ronaldo
   28.2 million followers
2. Kaka
   20.3 million followers
3. Neymar
   13 million followers
4. Ronaldinho
   10.2 million followers
5. Wayne Rooney
   9.5 million followers
6. Andres Iniesta
   9.1 million followers
7. Gerard Pique
   9 million followers
8. Xabi Alonso
   7.7 million followers
9. Mesut Ozil
   7.4 million followers
10. Cesc Fabregas
    7.1 million followers

Source: www.twittercounter.com

• Two months earlier Manchester United defender Rio Ferdinand was fined £45,000 by the FA after retweeting a comment by another Twitter user which disparagingly described Ashley Cole as a 'choc ice'.

UEFA

UEFA, the Union of European Football Associations, was founded in 1954 at a meeting in Basel during the Swiss World Cup. Holding power over all the national FAs in Europe, with 54 members it is the largest and most influential of the six continental confederations of FIFA.

• **UEFA competitions include the Champions League (first won as the European Cup by Real Madrid), the Europa League (formerly the UEFA Cup) and the UEFA Super Cup.**

• UEFA President Michel Platini, a former captain of France, is the sixth man to fill the role. The longest serving UEFA President is Sweden's Lennart Johansson, who did the job for 17 years between 1990 and 2007.

• **Controversial UEFA decisions in the past include the introduction of penalty kicks to decide drawn European ties (from 1970) and the ban on English clubs competing in European competitions for five years from 1985 after the Heysel tragedy.**

Uruguay, seen here celebrating a goal at the 2014 World Cup, are the smallest nation to win the tournament

URUGUAY

First international: Uruguay 2 Argentina 3, 1901

Most capped player: Diego Forlan, 112 caps (2002-)

Leading goalscorer: Luis Suarez, 40 goals (2007-)

First World Cup appearance: Uruguay 1 Peru 0, 1930

Biggest win: Uruguay 9 Bolivia 0, 1927

Heaviest defeat: Uruguay 0 Argentina 6, 1902

In 1930 Uruguay became the first winners of the World Cup, beating arch-rivals Argentina 4-2 in the final on home soil in Montevideo. The match was a repeat of the Olympic final of 1928, which Uruguay had also won. In terms of population, Uruguay is easily the smallest nation ever to win the World Cup.

IS THAT A FACT?
Uruguay set a record at the 1970 World Cup when they started their group game with Italy with no fewer than eight players from the same club, Montevideo outfit Nacional. Despite this advantage, the South Americans could only manage a 0-0 draw.

LOUIS VAN GAAL

Born: Amsterdam, Netherlands, 8th August 1951
Managerial career:
1991-97 Ajax
1997-2000 Barcelona
2000-02 Netherlands
2002-03 Barcelona
2005-09 AZ Alkmaar
2009-11 Bayern Munich
2012-14 Netherlands
2014- Manchester United

Manchester United boss Louis van Gaal is the first non-British or Irish manager to occupy the Old Trafford hotseat. The Dutchman was appointed as successor to the hapless David Moyes in May 2014, shortly before leading the Netherlands at the World Cup in Brazil.
• Formerly a midfielder with Dutch and Belgian clubs, Van Gaal first made his mark in management with Ajax, guiding the Amsterdam giants to three league titles, the UEFA Cup in 1992 and the Champions League

Manchester United's first non-British or Irish manager

• In 1950 Uruguay won the World Cup for a second time, defeating hosts Brazil 2-1 in 'the final' (it was actually the last and decisive match in a four-team final group). The match was watched by a massive crowd of 199,854 in the Maracana Stadium in Rio de Janeiro, the largest ever to attend a football match anywhere in the world.
• At the 2010 World Cup in South Africa Uruguay finished fourth, their best showing since Mexico in 1970. However, the South Americans' campaign will mostly be remembered for a blatant handball on the line by striker Luis Suarez, which denied their opponents Ghana a certain winning goal in the teams' quarter-final clash.
• Uruguay are the most successful team in the history of the Copa America. Winners of the inaugural tournament in 1916, Uruguay have won the competition a total of 15 times, most recently lifting the trophy in 2011 after beating Paraguay 3-0 in the final.

HONOURS
World Cup 1930, 1950
Copa America 1916, 1917, 1920, 1923, 1924, 1926, 1935, 1942, 1956, 1959, 1967, 1983, 1987, 1995, 2011
World Cup record
1930 Winners
1934 Did not enter
1938 Did not enter
1950 Winners
1954 Fourth place
1958 Did not qualify
1962 Round 1
1966 Quarter-finals
1970 Fourth place
1974 Round 1
1978 Did not qualify
1982 Did not qualify
1986 Round 2
1990 Round 2
1994 Did not qualify
1998 Did not qualify
2002 Round 1
2006 Did not qualify
2010 Fourth place
2014 Round 2

three years later following victory over AC Milan in the final.

• Van Gaal then moved on to Barcelona, replacing former England manager Bobby Robson at the Nou Camp. He won two league titles with a Barça side that included stars like Rivaldo, Patrick Kluivert and Luis Figo, but quit the club after facing heavy criticism for his use of an attack-minded 4-3-3 system traditionally employed by Ajax since the 1970s.

• **After failing to lead the Netherlands to the 2002 World Cup finals and a brief spell back at Barcelona, Van Gaal restored his reputation by taking outsiders AZ Alkmaar to only their second Dutch league title in 2009. He then became the first Dutch manager to win the Bundesliga title when he triumphed with Bayern Munich in 2010, but he was pipped to the Champions League in the same season by Jose Mourinho's Inter Milan. Appointed Netherlands manager in 2012, he guided the Dutch to third place at the World Cup two years later.**

ROBIN VAN PERSIE

Born: Rotterdam, Netherlands, 6th August 1983
Position: Striker
Club career:
2001-04 Feyenoord 59 (15)
2004-12 Arsenal 194 (96)
20012- Manchester United 59 (38)
International record:
2005- Netherlands 91 (47)

Manchester United striker Robin van Persie is only the third player – after Alan Shearer and Jimmy Floyd Hasselbaink – to win the Premier League Golden Boot with two different clubs. He first won the award with Arsenal in 2012 and then, following a £24 million move to Old Trafford that same summer, retained the trophy in his first season with the Red Devils after his 26 goals powered his new club to the league title.

• **The son of two artists, Van Persie began his career with his local side, Feyenoord, making his first-team debut aged 17 in 2001 and winning the Dutch league's Best Young Talent award at the end of his first season. A UEFA Cup winner the following year, he moved to north London in 2004 for a £2.75 million fee.**

TOP 10

LEADING NETHERLANDS GOALSCORERS

1.	Robin van Persie (2005-)	47
2.	Patrick Kluivert (1994-2004)	40
3.	Dennis Bergkamp (1990-2000)	37
4.	Faas Wilkes (1946-61)	35
	Ruud van Nistelrooy (1998-2011)	35
	Klaas-Jan Huntelaar (2006-)	35
7.	Abe Lenstra (1940-59)	33
	Johan Cruyff (1966-77)	33
9.	Bep Bakhuys (1928-37)	28
10.	Wesley Sneijder (2003-)	27

• In his first season with the Gunners, Van Persie fired his new club to the FA Cup final with two goals in the semi-final defeat of Blackburn Rovers. A month later he collected his first medal in English football when Arsenal defeated Manchester

United on penalties in the final. His personal best tally of 30 league goals for the Gunners in 2011/12 saw him win both Footballer of the Year awards but, frustrated by the club's lack of success over many years, he jumped at the chance to move north.

• **A clean striker of the ball, especially on his preferred left side, Van Persie made his international debut for the Netherlands in a World Cup qualifier against Romania in 2005 and is now his country's all-time leading goalscorer.**

Robin van Persie, the Netherlands' all-time top scorer

THEO WALCOTT

Born: Stanmore, 16th March 1989
Position: Winger
Club career:
2005-06 Southampton 21 (4)
2006- Arsenal 194 (45)
International record:
2006- England 36 (5)

Arsenal winger Theo Walcott is the youngest player ever to represent England, coming off the bench to make his debut against Hungary at Old Trafford in 2006 when he was aged just 17 years and 75 days.

• He has continued to set records for England, becoming the youngest player to score a hat-trick for the Three Lions when he notched three goals against Croatia in a World Cup qualifier in Zagreb in 2008, and finishing on the winning side in his first 14 internationals – the best ever such run by an England player. Despite his status as a 'lucky mascot', he was a shock omission from Fabio Capello's squad for the World Cup in South Africa, although the Italian later admitted leaving Walcott out was "a mistake". He did, though, play at Euro 2012, scoring a goal against Sweden before setting up Danny Welbeck's winner in England's 3-2 victory. After an injury-hit campaign, Walcott missed out on the 2014 World Cup in Brazil.

• Walcott began his career at Southampton and is the youngest player ever to appear for the Saints, making his debut as a sub against Wolves in 2005 when he was aged 16 years and 143 days.

• After attracting huge media attention for his dynamic performances for the south coast outfit, Walcott moved to Arsenal for an eventual fee of £9.1 million, making him the most expensive 16-year-old in the history of the British game. He scored his first goal for the Gunners a year later in the Carling Cup final against Chelsea to become the second youngest scorer in the final of the competition.

• In August 2010 Walcott scored the first club hat-trick of his career in a 6-0 demolition of newly promoted Blackpool at the Emirates. He scored his second hat-trick for the Gunners in an incredible 7-5 victory over Reading in the League Cup in October 2012 – the highest scoring match in the competition's history.

WALES

First international: Scotland 4 Wales 0, 1876
Most capped player: Neville Southall, 92 caps (1982-98)
Leading goalscorer: Ian Rush, 28 goals (1980-96)
First World Cup appearance: Wales 1 Hungary 1, 1958
Biggest win: Wales 11 Ireland 0, 1888
Heaviest defeat: Scotland 9 Wales 0, 1878

Wales are the least successful of the four British national sides, having qualified for just two major international tournaments in their history.

• Their finest hour came in 1958 when a Welsh side including such great names as John Charles, Ivor Allchurch and Jack Kelsey qualified for the World Cup finals in Sweden after beating Israel in a two-legged play-off. After drawing all three of their group matches, Wales then beat Hungary in a play-off to reach the quarter-finals where they lost 1-0 to eventual winners Brazil.

• In 1976 Wales made their best ever showing in the European Championships, reaching the quarter-finals before going down 3-1 on aggregate to Yugoslavia. Since then Wales supporters have had little to cheer, despite the efforts of the likes of Craig Bellamy, Ryan Giggs and all-time leading scorer Ian Rush.

• **Wales winger Billy Meredith is the oldest international in the history of British football. He was aged 45 years and 229 days when he won the last of his 48 caps against England in 1920, a quarter of a century after making his international debut.**

• Wales have the third best record in the British Home Championships with seven outright wins and five shared victories. Their best decade was the 1930s when they won the championship three times.

WORLD CUP RECORD
1930-38 Did not enter
1950-54 Did not qualify
1958 Quarter-finals
1962-2014 Did not qualify

Gareth Bale, Wales' youngest-ever player

WALSALL

Year founded: 1888
Ground: Banks's Stadium (11,300)
Previous name: Walsall Town Swifts
Nickname: The Saddlers
Biggest win: 10-0 v Darwen (1899)
Heaviest defeat: 0-12 v Small Heath (1892) and v Darwen (1896)

The club was founded in 1888 as Walsall Town Swifts, following an amalgamation of Walsall Swifts and Walsall Town. Founder members of the Second Division in 1892, the club changed to its present name three years later.

• **Walsall have never played in the top flight, but they have a history of producing momentous cup shocks, the most famous coming back in 1933 when they sensationally beat eventual league champions Arsenal 2-0 in the FA Cup. The Saddlers' best run in the League Cup, meanwhile, came in 1984 when they reached the semi-finals before losing 4-2 on aggregate to eventual winners Liverpool.**

• Two players share the distinction of being Walsall's all-time leading scorer: Tony Richards, who notched 184 league goals for the club between 1954 and 1963, and his strike partner Colin Taylor, who banged in exactly the same number in three spells with the Saddlers between 1958 and 1973.

• **Club legend Gilbert Alsop scored a club record 40 league goals in 1933/34 and 1934/35, but on both occasions his efforts weren't enough to help the Saddlers gain promotion from Division Three (North).**

• Striker Alan Buckley, who went on to manage the club, is Walsall's record signing, costing £175,000 when he joined the Saddlers from Midlands neighbours Birmingham City in June 1979. No other Football League club's most expensive purchase goes back as many years – although don't expect Walsall fans to get too excited about breaking this particular record!

Watford fell off their Premier League perch in 2007 and are still waiting to get back on

WATFORD

Year founded: 1881
Ground: Vicarage Road (17,477)
Previous name: Watford Rovers, West Herts
Nickname: The Hornets
Biggest win: 10-1 v Lowestoft Town (1926)
Heaviest defeat: 0-10 v Wolves (1912)

Founded as Watford Rovers in 1881, the club changed its name to West Herts in 1893. Five years later, following a merger with Watford St Mary's, the club became Watford FC.

• **The club's history was fairly nondescript until pop star Elton John became chairman in 1976 and invested a large part of his personal wealth in the team. With future England manager Graham Taylor at the helm, the Hornets rose from the Fourth to the First Division in just five years, reaching the FA Cup final in 1984. In the late 1990s Taylor returned to the club and worked his magic again, guiding the Hornets to two successive promotions and a brief** taste of life in the Premiership.

• After finishing second in the old First Division in 1983, Watford made their one foray into Europe, reaching the third round of the UEFA Cup before losing to Sparta Prague.

• **Luther Blissett, one of the star players of that period, is the club's record appearance maker. In three spells at Vicarage Road the energetic striker notched up 415 league appearances and scored 148 league goals (also a club record).**

• In January 2007 Watford received a club record £9.65 million when they sold dynamic winger Ashley Young to Aston Villa. A few months later the Hornets splashed £3.25 million of this cash on West Brom's Nathan Ellington, their most expensive signing ever.

• **Watford are the only non-Premier League club to have had three Italian managers: Gianluca Vialli (2001-02), Gianfranco Zola (2012-13) and Giuseppe Sannino, who was appointed in December 2013.**

DANNY WELBECK

Born: Manchester, 26th November 1990
Position: Striker
Club career:
2008-14 Manchester United 90 (20)
2009-10 Preston North End (loan) 8 (2)
2010-11 Sunderland (loan) 26 (6)
2014- Arsenal
International record:
2011- England 28 (8)

An energetic and quick-thinking striker, Danny Welbeck became Arsenal's record signing from another Premier League club when he joined the Gunners from Manchester United for £16 million in September 2014.

• **A United youth product, Welbeck came to the fore in the 2008/09 season, scoring on his Premier League debut against Stoke City and helping the Red Devils win the Carling Cup. After loan spells at Preston and Sunderland, he returned to Old Trafford to establish himself as Wayne Rooney's main strike partner during the 2011/12 season.**

• Welbeck's impressive displays saw him shortlisted for the 2012 PFA Young Player of the Year award, but he just missed out to Tottenham's Kyle Walker. The following campaign, though, was less memorable for the young striker, as he played second fiddle to Robin van Persie and managed just a single Premier League goal.

• **The son of Ghanaian parents, Welbeck ironically made his full England debut against Ghana in a 1-1 draw at Wembley in March 2011. The following year he scored his first goal for his country, netting the winner against Belgium in a pre-Euro 2012 friendly with a clever lob.**

WEMBLEY STADIUM

Built at a cost of £798 million, the new Wembley Stadium is the most expensive sporting venue ever. With a capacity of 90,000, it is also the second largest in Europe and the largest in the world to have every seat under cover.

• **The stadium's most spectacular feature is a 315m-wide arch, the world's longest unsupported roof structure. Wembley also boasts a** staggering 2,618 toilets, more than any other venue in the world.

• Originally scheduled to open in 2003, the stadium was not completed until 2007 due to a variety of financial and legal difficulties. The first professional match was played at the new venue on 17th March 2007 when England Under-21s met their Italian counterparts, with the first goal arriving after just 28 seconds when Giampaolo Pazzini struck for the visitors. Half an hour later, David Bentley became the first Englishman to score at the new stadium.

• **Chelsea and Manchester United have played at the new stadium a record**

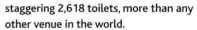

IS THAT A FACT?

Bristol Rovers and Shrewsbury Town were the first Football League teams to play at the new Wembley, appearing in the League Two play-off final on 26th May 2007. Rovers won the game 3-1.

WEMBLEY STADIUM

Wembley pays its respects to the victims of Hillsborough before the 2014 FA Cup semi-final between Hull and Sheffield United

Hillsborough
15 April 1989

NEVER FORGOTTEN 96 25 YEARS

12 times each. Among current Premier League clubs only Newcastle and Leicester have yet to make their debut under Wembley's famous arch.

• The first Wembley Stadium was opened in 1923, having been constructed in just 300 days at a cost of £750,000. The first match played at the venue was the 1923 FA Cup final between Bolton and West Ham, although the kick-off was delayed for nearly an hour when thousands of fans spilled onto the pitch because of overcrowding in the stands.

• **Apart from football, the new stadium has also played host to a number of other sports including rugby league, American football and boxing.**

• Arsenal and England defender Tony Adams played a record 60 games at Wembley between 1987 and 2000, a total boosted by the fact that the Gunners used the stadium for their home games in the Champions League in the 1990s.

ARSÈNE WENGER

Born: Strasbourg, France, 22nd October 1949
Managerial career:
1984-87 Nancy
1987-94 Monaco
1995-96 Nagoya Grampus Eight
1996- Arsenal

Arsenal boss Arsène Wenger is the most successful manager in the Gunners' history, having won the Premier League title three times and the FA Cup on five occasions – most recently lifting the cup in 2014 to end a nine-year trophy drought.

• **After a modest playing career which included a stint with his local club Strasbourg, Wenger cut his managerial teeth with Nancy before moving to Monaco in 1987. He won the league title in his first season there, with a team including English stars Glenn Hoddle and Mark Hateley, and the French Cup in 1991.**

• Following a year in Japan with Nagoya Grampus Eight, Wenger arrived in north London in September 1996. In his first full season at Highbury he became the first non-British manager to win the league and cup Double, and he repeated this accomplishment in 2002.

• His greatest achievement, though, came in 2004 when his Arsenal side won the title after going through the entire Premiership season undefeated. Wenger's 'Invincibles', as they were dubbed, were hailed as the greatest team in English football history, not only for their record 49-game unbeaten run but also for their fluid attacking style of play which made the most of exceptional talents like Thierry Henry, Dennis Bergkamp and Patrick Vieira.

• Wenger is one of just four managers in English football to oversee 1,000 matches with the same club. He reached the landmark when Arsenal played at Chelsea on 22nd March 2014 – but it turned out to be a day to forget as the Gunners crashed to a humbling 6-0 defeat.

WEST BROMWICH ALBION

Year founded: 1878
Ground: The Hawthorns (26,445)
Previous name: West Bromwich Strollers
Nickname: The Baggies
Biggest win: 12-0 v Darwen (1892)
Heaviest defeat: 3-10 v Stoke City (1937)

Founded as West Bromwich Strollers in 1878 by workers at the local Salter's Spring Works, the club adopted the suffix 'Albion' two years later and were founder members of the Football League in 1888.

• **The Baggies were the first club to lose two consecutive FA Cup finals, going down to Blackburn Rovers in 1886 and Aston Villa the following year. In 1888, though, West Brom recorded the first of their five triumphs in the cup, beating favourites Preston 2-1 in the final.**

• In 1931 West Brom became the first and only club to win promotion and the FA Cup in the same season. The Baggies came close to repeating this particular double in 2008, when they topped the Championship but were beaten in the FA Cup semi-finals by eventual winners Portsmouth.

• **West Brom claimed their only league title in 1920, in the first post-First World War season. The 60 points they amassed that season and the 104 goals they scored were both records at the time. The club's manager at the time, Fred Everiss, was in charge at the**

Arsène Wenger, Arsenal's long-serving manager

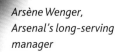

Hawthorns from 1902-48, his 46-year stint being the longest in English football history.

• In 1966 West Brom won the last League Cup final to be played over two legs, overcoming West Ham 5-3 on aggregate. The next year they appeared in the first one-off final at Wembley, but surprisingly lost 3-2 to Third Division QPR after leading 2-0 at half-time.

• The Baggies, though, returned to Wembley the following season and beat Everton 1-0 in the FA Cup final. West Brom's winning goal was scored in extra-time by club legend Jeff Astle, who in the process became one of just 12 players to have scored in every round of the competition. Astle also found the target in his side's 2-1 defeat by Manchester City in the 1970 League Cup final to become the first player to score in both domestic cup finals at Wembley.

• In 1892 West Brom thrashed Darwen 12-0 to record their biggest ever win. The score set a record for the top flight which has never been beaten, although Nottingham Forest equalled it in 1909. The Baggies' worst ever defeat came in 1937 when they suffered a 10-3 thrashing at the hands of Stoke City.

• Cult hero Tony 'Bomber' Brown is West Brom's record scorer with 218 league goals to his name. The attacking midfielder is also the club's longest serving player, turning out in 574 league games between 1963 and 1980.

• Midfielder Chris Brunt has won a club record 36 caps for Northern Ireland since joining the Baggies in 2007.

• The club's record purchase is Nigerian international striker Brown Ideye, who joined the Baggies from Dynamo Kiev for £9 million in July 2014. The club's bank balance was boosted by a record £8.5 million when gangly defender Curtis Davies joined local rivals Aston Villa in 2008.

IS THAT A FACT?
West Brom striker William 'Ginger' Richardson scored four goals in just five minutes in a 5-1 win at West Ham on 7th November 1931 – the quickest four-goal haul in English football history.

• Striker Bob Taylor made a record 78 appearances as a sub for West Brom between 1994 and 2002.

HONOURS
Division 1 champions *1920*
Division 2 champions *1902, 1911*
Championship champions *2008*
FA Cup *1888, 1892, 1931, 1954, 1968*
League Cup *1966*

WEST HAM UNITED

Year founded: 1895
Ground: Upton Park (35,016)
Previous name: Thames Ironworks
Nickname: The Hammers
Biggest win: 10-0 v Bury (1983)
Heaviest defeat: 2-8 v Blackburn (1963)

The club was founded in 1895 as Thames Ironworks by shipyard workers employed by a company of the same name. In 1900 the club was disbanded but immediately reformed under its present name.

• **The biggest and best supported club in east London, West Ham have a proud tradition in the FA Cup. In 1923 they reached the first final to be played at the original Wembley Stadium, losing 2-0 to Bolton Wanderers.**

• The Hammers experienced a more enjoyable Wembley 'first' in 1965 when they became the first English side to win a European trophy on home soil, defeating Munich 1860 2-0 in the final of the Cup Winners' Cup.

• **The following year West Ham were the only club to provide three members – Bobby Moore, Geoff Hurst and Martin Peters – of England's World Cup-winning team. Between them Hurst and Peters scored all four of England's goals in the final against West Germany while Moore, as captain, collected the trophy. The Hammers trio's remarkable contribution to the victory is commemorated by a statue near Upton Park.**

• Striker Vic Watson holds three significant goalscoring records for the club. He is West Ham's leading scorer, with an impressive 298 league goals

between 1920 and 1935, including a record 42 goals in the 1929/30 season. In the same campaign Watson hit a record six goals in a match, a feat later equalled by Geoff Hurst in an 8-0 drubbing of Sunderland at Upton Park in 1968.

• **No West Ham player has turned out more often for the club than former manager Billy Bonds. Between 1967 and 1988 'Bonzo', as he was dubbed by fans and team-mates alike, appeared in 663 league games.**

• In 1980 West Ham became the last club from outside the top flight to win the FA Cup. The Hammers, then residing in the old Second Division, beat favourites Arsenal 1-0 thanks to a rare headed goal by Trevor Brooking. The east Londoners also won the cup in 1975, beating Fulham 2-0 – the last time that the winners have fielded an all-English line-up.

• **The legendary Bobby Moore is the club's most capped international. He played 108 times for England to set a record that has since only been passed by Peter Shilton, David Beckham and Steven Gerrard.**

• In their long and distinguished history West Ham have had just 14 managers, fewer than any other major English club. The longest serving of the lot was Syd King, who held the reins for 31 years from 1901 to 1932.

• **On Boxing Day 2006 Teddy Sheringham became the oldest player ever to score in the Premier League when he netted for West Ham against Portsmouth aged 40 years and 266 days. Four days later he made his last appearance for the Hammers at Manchester City, stretching his own record as the oldest outfield player in the league's history.**

• In March 2011 West Ham's bid to take over the Olympic Stadium in Stratford after the London Games was approved by the Olympic Park Legacy Committee. Two years later the club signed a 99-year lease to play at the stadium and plan to move in for the start of the 2016/17 season.

• **Famous fans of the Hammers include comedian Russell Brand, tough-guy actor Ray Winstone and boxer Lennox Lewis.**

HONOURS
Division 2 champions *1958, 1981*
FA Cup *1964, 1975, 1980*
European Cup Winners' Cup *1965*

WIGAN ATHLETIC

Year founded: 1932
Ground: DW Stadium (25,138)
Nickname: The Latics
Biggest win: 7-1 v Scarborough (1997)
Heaviest defeat: 1-9 v Tottenham Hotspur (2009)

The club was founded at a public meeting at the Queen's Hotel in 1932 as successors to Wigan Borough, who the previous year had become the first ever club to resign from the Football League.

• After 34 failed attempts, including a bizarre application to join the Scottish Second Division in 1972, Wigan were finally elected to the old Fourth Division in 1978 in place of Southport. The Latics' fortunes, though, only really changed for the better in 1995 when local millionaire and owner of JJB Sports Dave Whelan bought the club and announced his intention to bring Premier League football to the rugby-mad town within 10 years. Remarkably, Whelan's dream was fulfilled exactly a decade later.

• In 2006 Wigan played in a major cup final for the first time in their history when they took on Manchester United in the Carling Cup final at the Millennium Stadium in Cardiff. However, the Latics went home empty-handed after losing 4-0.

• In November 2009 Wigan were hammered 9-1 at Tottenham, only the second time in Premier League history that a side had conceded nine goals. The eight goals the Latics let in after the break was a record for a Premiership half.

• The greatest day in the club's history came in 2013 when Wigan won their first major trophy, the FA Cup, after beating hot favourites Manchester City 1-0 in the final at Wembley thanks to a last-minute header by Ben Watson. Sadly for their fans, Wigan's eight-year stay in the Premier League ended just three days after that triumph, meaning that they became the first club ever to win the FA Cup and be relegated in the same season.

• The club's record goalscorer is Andy Liddell, who hit 70 league goals between 1998 and 2003. No player has pulled on Wigan's blue-and-white stripes more often than Kevin Langley, who made 317 league appearances in two spells at the club between 1981 and 1994.

• Wigan made their record signing in 2010 when they bought Mauro Boselli from Estudiantes for £6.5 million. Two years later, after the Argentinian had failed to score a single league goal, he was voted the club's worst ever foreign player by unimpressed Wigan fans.

HONOURS
Second Division champions 2003
Third Division champions 1997
FA Cup 2013
Football League Trophy 1985, 1999

Since the departure of former Chelsea team-mate David Luiz, Willian is officially the frizziest-haired Brazilian in the Premier League

WILLIAN

Born: Ribeirao Pires, Brazil, 9th August 1988
Position: Winger
Club career:
2006-07 Corinthians 16 (2)
2007-13 Shakhtar Donetsk 140 (20)
2013 Anzhi Makhachkala 11 (1)
2013- Chelsea 25 (4)
International record:
2011- Brazil 12 (2)

Frizzy-haired winger Willian became Chelsea's third most expensive signing ever when he joined the Blues from Russian side Anzhi Makhachkala for £32 million in August 2013. He repaid some of that cash by scoring a brilliant goal on his Premier League debut against Norwich, before going on to enjoy an impressive first season at Stamford Bridge

• Willian Borges da Silva, to give him his full name, started out in his native Brazil with Corinthians before moving to Shakhtar Donetsk in 2007 for around £12.5 million. In his first season with his new club he won the Ukrainian league and cup double, and went on to win three more leagues and two more cups over the next five years.

• Willian's greatest triumph with Shakhtar, though, came in 2009 when he helped them become the first ever Ukrainian side to win a European trophy, when they beat German outfit Werder Bremen 2-1 in the last ever UEFA Cup final.

• A skilful player with superb close control who loves to take on and beat defenders, Willian was first capped by Brazil in 2011 in a 2-0 friendly win against Gabon and featured in his country's 2014 World Cup squad.

JACK WILSHERE

Born: Stevenage, 1st January 1992
Position: Midfielder
Club career:
2008- Arsenal 86 (4)
2009-10 Bolton Wanderers (loan)
14 (1)
International record:
2010- England 20 (0)

Tipped as a possible future England captain, Jack Wilshere is one of the emerging stars of the English game. His brilliant performances for Arsenal during the 2010/11 season were rewarded when he was voted PFA Young Player of the Year, an award he was nominated for again two years later.

Jack Wilshere takes time out to ponder life, the future and everything

• The youngest player to appear for Arsenal in the league, Jack Wilshere was aged 16 and 256 days when he made his Premier League debut for the Gunners against Blackburn in September 2008. Two months later he became only the fifth 16 year old in history to play in the Champions League when he came on as a sub against Dynamo Kiev.
• In January 2010 Wilshere went on loan to Bolton, where his dribbling and passing skills impressed both Wanderers fans and neutrals alike. Back in London he won his first trophy with the Gunners in 2014, when he came on as a sub in their FA Cup final defeat of Hull City. In the same year he won the BBC's Goal of the Season award for a deft finish against Norwich following a flowing team move.
• Then England manager Fabio Capello proved to be another admirer of Wilshere's talents, giving the youngster an England debut as a sub against Hungary at Wembley in August 2010. The following year he made his first start for his country, starring in a 3-1 friendly win away to Denmark. He missed Euro 2012 through injury but went to the 2014 World Cup, starting one match against Costa Rica.

WOLVERHAMPTON WANDERERS

Year founded: 1877
Ground: Molineux (30,852)
Previous name: St Luke's
Nickname: Wolves
Biggest win: 14-0 v Cresswell's Brewery
Heaviest defeat: 1-10 v Newton Heath

Founded as St Luke's by pupils at a local school of that name in 1877, the club adopted its present name after merging with Blakenhall Wanderers two years later. Wolves were founder members of the Football League in 1888, finishing the first season in third place behind champions Preston and Aston Villa.
• The Black Country club enjoyed their heyday in the 1950s under manager Stan Cullis, a pioneer of long ball 'kick and rush' tactics. After a number of near misses, Wolves were crowned league champions for the first time in their history in 1954 and won two more titles later in the decade to cement their reputation as the top English club of the era. Incredibly, the Black Country outfit scored a century of league goals in four consecutive seasons between 1958 and 1961 – the only club to achieve this feat.
• When Wolves won a number of high-profile friendlies against foreign opposition in the 1950s in some of the first ever televised matches they were hailed as 'champions of the world' by the national press, a claim which helped inspire the creation of the European Cup. In 1958 Wolves became only the second English team to compete in the competition, following in the footsteps of trailblazers Manchester United.

• The skipper of that great Wolves team, centre-half Billy Wright, is the club's most capped international. Between 1946 and 1959 he won a then record 105 caps for England, captaining his country in 90 of those games.

• Steve Bull is Wolves' record scorer with an incredible haul of 250 league goals between 1986 and 1999. His impressive total of 306 goals in all competitions included a record 18 hat-tricks for the club.

• **Stalwart defender Derek Parkin has pulled on the famous gold shirt more often than any other player, making 501 appearances in the league between 1967 and 1982.**

• In 1972 Wolves reached the final of the UEFA Cup, losing 3-2 on aggregate to Tottenham in the first ever European final between two English clubs. Two years later the club won the League Cup for the first time, beating Manchester City 2-1 in the final, and in 1980 they repeated that success thanks to a single goal by Andy Gray in the final against Nottingham Forest.

• **Wolves were the first team in the country to win all four divisions of the Football League, completing the 'full house' in 1989 when they won the old Third Division title a year after claiming the Fourth Division championship.**

• After suffering consecutive relegations from the top flight for the second time in their history, Wolves bounced back to the Championship in 2014 by claiming the League One title with an all-time third-tier record 103 points.

HONOURS

Division 1 champions 1954, 1958, 1959
Division 2 champions 1932, 1977
Championship champions 2009
Division 3 (North) champions 1924
Division 3 champions 1989
League One champions 2014
Division 4 champions 1988
FA Cup 1893, 1908, 1949, 1960
League Cup 1974, 1980
Football League Trophy 1988

WOMEN'S FOOTBALL

The first recorded women's football match took place between the north and south of England at Crouch End, London in 1895. The north won the game 7-1.

• **The Women's FA was founded in 1969 and the first Women's FA Cup final took place two years later,** Southampton beating Stewart and Thistle 4-1. The Saints went on to win the cup another seven times in the next 10 years, but the most successful side in the competition are Arsenal with 13 victories – most recently beating Everton 2-0 in the 2014 final.

• In a bid to attract more fans to games the top flight was reorganised in 2011 as a semi-professional summer league consisting of eight clubs, the FA Women's Super League. Arsenal won the first two Super League titles before Liverpool claimed the trophy in 2013.

• **The first British international women's match took place in 1972 when England beat Scotland 3-2. In 2005 England recorded their biggest ever win, thrashing Hungary 13-0. Their worst defeat was in 2000 when Norway won 8-0.**

• Winger Rachel Yankey has won a record 129 caps for England, while striker Kelly Smith is the team's top scorer with 46 goals.

• **Since it was first competed for in China in 1991 there have been six Women's World Cup tournaments. The USA were the first winners and also lifted the trophy in 1999, while Germany are the only other country to have won the tournament twice**

England's Lianne Sanderson goes to the same hairdresser as Neymar

It's those pesky Germans again with the World Cup trophy…

(in 2003 and 2007). The holders are Japan who beat the United States on penalties in the 2011 final in Germany.

• The joint top scorers in the World Cup are Birgit Prinz (Germany) and Marta (Brazil) with 14 goals. In 2003 Prinz was offered the chance to join Italian men's side Perugia, but declined the chance to become the first ever woman to play in a professional men's league.

• In May 2014 Portuguese coach Helena Costa was appointed boss of French Ligue 2 outfit Clermont Foot – the first woman to manage at this level in the men's game. However, she quit after just one month, citing 'personal reasons'.

• Caerphilly Castle Ladies suffered the biggest defeat in the history of British women's football when they were trounced 43-0 by Cardiff Metro University in the Women's Welsh Premier League in 2013 and resigned from the league soon afterwards.

WORLD CUP

The most successful country in the history of the World Cup are Brazil, who have won the competition a record five times. Germany and Italy are Europe's leading nation with four wins each, the Germans becoming the first European nation to triumph in South America when they beat Argentina 1-0 in the 2014 final in Brazil. Neighbours Argentina and Uruguay have both won the competition twice, the Uruguayans emerging victorious when the pair met in the first ever World Cup final in Montevideo in 1930. The only other countries to claim the trophy are England, France and Spain, the first two countries taking advantage of their host nation status to win the competition in 1966 and 1998 respectively, while the Spanish triumphed in South Africa in 2010 thanks to a 1-0 win over Holland in the final.

• Including both Japan and South Korea, who were joint hosts for the 2002 edition, the World Cup has been held in 15 different countries. The first nation to stage the tournament twice was Mexico (in 1970 and 1986), while Italy (1934 and 1990), France (1938 and 1998), Germany (1974 and 2006) and Brazil (1950 and 2014). have also welcomed the world to the planet's biggest football festival on two occasions each.

WORLD CUP

• Brazil are the only country to have played at all 20 tournaments and have recorded the most wins (70). Germany, meanwhile, have reached a record eight finals, have played the most games (106) and have scored the most goals (224).

• However, Hungary hold the record for the most goals scored in a single tournament, banging in 27 in just five games at the 1954 finals in Switzerland. Even this incredible tally, though, was not quite sufficient for the 'Magical Magyars' to lift the trophy as they went down to a 3-2 defeat in the final against West Germany, a team they had beaten 8-3 earlier in the tournament.

• Hungary also hold the record for the biggest ever victory at the finals, demolishing El Salvador 10-1 in 1982. That, though, was a desperately close encounter compared to the biggest win in qualifying, Australia's 31-0 annihilation of American Samoa in 2001, a game in which Aussie striker Archie Thompson helped himself to a record 13 goals.

• The legendary Pelé is the only player in World Cup history to have been presented with three winners' medals. The Brazilian superstar enjoyed his first success in 1958 when he scored twice in a 5-2 rout of hosts Sweden in the final, and was a winner again four years later in Chile despite hobbling out of the tournament with a torn leg muscle in the second match. He then made it a hat-trick in 1970, setting a sparkling Brazil side on the road to an emphatic 4-1 victory against Italy in the final with a trademark bullet header.

• The leading overall scorer in the World Cup is Germany's Miroslav Klose with 16 goals between 2002 and 2014. He is followed by Brazil legend Ronaldo, with 15 including two in the 2002 final against Germany.

• England's Geoff Hurst had previously gone one better in 1966, scoring a hat-trick as the hosts beat West Germany 4-2 in the final at Wembley. His second goal, which gave England a decisive 3-2 lead in extra-time, was the most controversial in World Cup history and German fans still argue to this day that his shot bounced on the line after striking the crossbar, rather than over it. Naturally, England fans generally agree with the eagle-eyed Russian linesman, Tofik Bahramov, who awarded the goal.

• Just two players have appeared at a record five World Cups: Germany's midfield playmaker Lothar Matthaus (1982-98) and Mexican goalkeeper Antonio Carbajal (1950-66). Matthaus, though, holds the record for games played, making 25 appearances for his country.

• A record 171 goals were scored at the 1998 finals in France – a total matched at the 2014 tournament in Brazil, when there were a record 121 different scorers. However, the 1954 finals were probably even more exciting with a record average of 5.38 goals per game.

• England are the only country to have been eliminated from the tournament three times without losing a match at the finals, going home with heads held high in 1982, 1990 and 2006.

• The youngest player to appear at the finals is Norman Whiteside, who was just 17 years and 41 days when he made his World Cup debut for Northern Ireland against Yugoslavia at the 1982 tournament in Spain. The competition's oldest player, meanwhile, is veteran Colombia goalkeeper Faryd Mondragon who was aged 43 and three days when he came on as a late sub in his side's 4-1 win over Japan in 2014.

• Brazil suffered the worst ever defeat by a host nation when they were trounced 7-1 by Germany in 2014 – also the biggest ever win in a semi-final.

• A record seven different players scored in Yugoslavia's 9-0 hammering of African no-hopers Zaire in 1974.

• The Dutch East Indies (now Indonesia) are the only country to have played just a single match at the World Cup. In 1938 they travelled all the way to France only to lose 6-0 to Hungary in the first round!

WORLD CUP FINALS

1930 Uruguay 4 Argentina 2 (Uruguay)
1934 Italy 2 Czechoslovakia 1 (Italy)
1938 Italy 4 Hungary 2 (France)
1950 Uruguay 2 Brazil 1 (Brazil)
1954 West Germany 3 Hungary 2 (Switzerland)
1958 Brazil 5 Sweden 2 (Sweden)
1962 Brazil 3 Czechoslovakia 1 (Chile)
1966 England 4 West Germany 2 (England)
1970 Brazil 4 Italy 1 (Mexico)
1974 West Germany 2 Netherlands 1 (West Germany)
1978 Argentina 3 Netherlands 1 (Argentina)
1982 Italy 3 West Germany 1 (Spain)
1986 Argentina 3 West Germany 2 (Mexico)
1990 West Germany 1 Argentina 0 (Italy)
1994 Brazil 0* Italy 0 (USA)
1998 France 3 Brazil 0 (France)
2002 Brazil 2 Germany 0 (Japan/South Korea)
2006 Italy 1* France 1 (Germany)
2010 Spain 1 Netherlands 0 (South Africa)
2014 Germany 1 Argentina 0 (Brazil)
* Won on penalties

WORLD CUP GOLDEN BALL

The Golden Ball is awarded to the best player at the World Cup following a poll of members of the global media. The first winner was Italian striker Paolo Rossi, whose six goals at the 1982 World Cup helped the Azzurri win that year's tournament in Spain.

• Rossi was followed in 1986 by another World Cup winner, Argentina captain Diego Maradona, but since then only one player has claimed the Golden Ball and a winners' medal at the same tournament, Brazilian striker Romario in 1994.

• The only goalkeeper to win the award to date is Germany's Oliver Kahn in 2002. The most controversial winner, meanwhile, was France's mercurial midfielder Zinedine Zidane, who was named as the outstanding performer at the 2006 World Cup before the final – a game which ended in disgrace for Zidane after he was sent off for headbutting Italian defender Marco Materazzi.

TOP 10

GREATEST WORLD CUP PLAYERS

1. Pele (Brazil, World Cups played 1958-70)
2. Diego Maradona (Argentina, 1982-94)
3. Franz Beckenbauer (West Germany, 1966-74)
4. Ronaldo (Brazil, 1994-2006)
5. Zinedine Zidane (France, 1998-2006)
6. Johan Cruyff (Netherlands, 1974)
7. Lothar Matthaus (West Germany/Germany, 1982-98)
8. Gerd Muller (West Germany, 1970-74)
9. Garrincha (Brazil, 1958-66)
10. Michel Platini (France, 1978-86)

Source: www.guardian.co.uk

This stunning volley against Uruguay helped Colombia's James Rodriguez win the 2014 World Cup Golden Boot

• Another much-debated winner of the Golden Ball was Argentina's Lionel Messi, who failed to sparkle in the knock-out rounds at the 2014 finals after a good start to the tournament. Even fellow countryman Diego Maradona described the award as "unfair".

WORLD CUP GOLDEN BALL WINNERS
1982 Paolo Rossi (Italy)
1986 Diego Maradona (Argentina)
1990 Salvatore Schillaci (Italy)
1994 Romario (Brazil)
1998 Ronaldo (Brazil)
2002 Oliver Kahn (Germany)
2006 Zinedine Zidane (France)
2010 Diego Forlan (Uruguay)
2014 Lionel Messi (Argentina)

WORLD CUP GOLDEN BOOT

Now officially known as the 'Adidas Golden Shoe', the Golden Boot is awarded to the player who scores most goals in a World Cup finals tournament. The first winner was Guillermo Stabile, whose eight goals helped Argentina reach the final in 1930.

• French striker Just Fontaine scored a record 13 goals at the 1958 tournament in Sweden. At the other end of the scale, nobody managed more than four goals at the 1962 World Cup in Chile, so the award was shared between six players.

• Surprisingly, it wasn't until 1978 that the Golden Boot was won outright by a player, Argentina's Mario Kempes, whose country also won the tournament. Since then only Italy's Paolo Rossi in 1982

and Brazil's Ronaldo in 2002 have won both the Golden Boot and a World Cup winners' medal in the same year.

• The only English player to win the Golden Boot is Gary Lineker, whose six goals in 1986 helped the Three Lions reach the quarter-finals in Mexico.

• At the 2010 World Cup in South Africa Germany's Thomas Muller was one of four players to top the scoring charts with five goals, but FIFA's new rules gave him the Golden Boot because he had more assists than his three rivals for the award, David Villa, Wesley Sneijder and Diego Forlan.

• The 2014 award went to Colombia's James Rodriguez, who scored six goals, including a brilliant volley against Uruguay which was later voted the best of the tournament by fans on FIFA's website.

WYCOMBE WANDERERS

Year founded: 1887
Ground: Adams Park (10,284)
Nickname: The Chairboys
Biggest win: 15-1 v Witney Town (1955)
Heaviest defeat: 0-8 v Reading (1899)

Wycombe Wanderers were founded in 1887 by a group of young furniture-makers (hence the club's nickname, The Chairboys) but had to wait until 1993 before earning promotion to the Football League.

• Under then manager Martin O'Neill the club went up to the Second Division (now League One) in their first season, beating Preston in the play-off final.

• In 2001 The Chairboys caused a sensation by reaching the semi-finals of the FA Cup where they lost 2-1 to eventual winners Liverpool at Villa Park. Wycombe also reached the semi-finals of the League Cup in 2007, but were beaten 5-1 on aggregate by eventual winners Chelsea.

• On 23rd September 2000 Wycombe's Jamie Bates and Jermaine McSporran set a new Football League record for the shortest time between two goals when they both scored against Peterborough within nine seconds of each other either side of half-time.

• The Chairboys came desperately close to losing their league status in 2014, but survived on goal difference thanks to a last-day win at relegated Torquay United.

HONOURS
Conference champions 1993
FA Amateur Cup 1931

XAVI

Born Barcelona, 25th January 1980
Position: Midfielder
Clubs:
1997-2000 Barcelona B 61 (4)
1998- Barcelona 474 (56)
International record:
2000- Spain 133 (12)

The brilliant Xavi, Barcelona's record appearance maker

The creative heartbeat of Barcelona's hypnotic tiki-taka passing game, Xavi has come through the club's fabled youth system to head the list of the Catalans' appearance makers, having played in 723 games in all competitions (including 147 Champions League matches, a figure only bettered by Ryan Giggs).

IS THAT A FACT?
At the 2012 European championships midfield maestro Xavi completed an astonishing 127 passes – a record for the competition – in Spain's 4-0 defeat of the Republic of Ireland.

• Since making his debut for Barça in 1998, Xavi has won an Aladdin's Cave of silverware, including six La Liga titles and three Champions League winners' medals. His outstanding individual contribution to his team's success was recognised in 2010 when he was voted the third best player in the world, behind club-mates Lionel Messi and Andres Iniesta, for the inaugural FIFA Ballon d'Or award. In the same year he was voted World Player of the Year by the readers of World Soccer magazine.

• Xavi first played for Spain in 2000 and is now the second highest capped player in his country's history. In 2008 he was voted Player of the Tournament when Spain won the European Championships and, two years later, he was a key member of the Spanish side that won the World Cup for the first time after beating Holland in the final in South Africa.

York City celebrate their famous League Cup win over Manchester United in 1995

• To nobody's surprise he was a vastly influential figure at Euro 2012, setting up two goals in the final as Spain ran riot, thrashing Italy 4-0 to win a third successive international trophy. Two years later he retired from international football after Spain's poor showing at the 2014 World Cup.

YEOVIL TOWN

Year founded: 1890
Ground: Huish Park (9,565)
Previous names: Yeovil, Yeovil Casuals
Nickname: The Glovers
Biggest win: 12-1 v Westbury United (1923)
Heaviest defeat: 0-8 v Manchester United (1949)

Founded in 1890, initially as Yeovil and then as Yeovil Casuals (1895-1907), the club had to wait until 2003 before finally entering the Football League when they were promoted as Conference champions by a then record 17 points margin.
• Before they made it into League Two, Yeovil were famed FA Cup giant-killers, knocking out no fewer than 20 league clubs – a record for a non-league outfit. Their most notable

scalp came in 1949 when they beat Sunderland 2-1 in the fourth round on their famously sloping Huish Park pitch.
• Yeovil made it into the second tier of English football for the first time in their history in 2013 when they beat Brentford 2-1 in the League One play-off final at Wembley. Sadly for their fans, the Glovers' stay in the Championship lasted just one season after they finished bottom of the pile.
• Striker Dave Taylor scored a club record 285 goals for Yeovil during their non-league days, including an impressive 59 in 1960/61 – another club record.

> **HONOURS**
> *League Two champions 2005*
> *Conference champions 2003*

YORK CITY

Year founded: 1922
Ground: Bootham Crescent (7,872)
Nickname: The Minstermen
Biggest win: 9-1 v Southport (1957)
Heaviest defeat: 0-12 v Chester City (1936)

Founded in 1922 by former members of an amateur club of the same name, York City joined the Football League in 1929 and rose as high as the old Division Two in the mid-1970s. The Minstermen lost their league status in 2004 but bounced back in 2012 after beating Luton Town 2-1 in the Conference play-off final at Wembley.
• York have a proud tradition in the FA Cup, reaching the semi-final in 1955 before losing to eventual winners Newcastle in a replay. In 1985, a year after becoming the first club to amass 100 points in a season while topping Division Four, the Minstermen performed more FA Cup heroics by beating mighty Arsenal 1-0 in the fourth round. Their cup dream ended, though, with a 7-0 defeat to Liverpool in the next round.
• Perhaps, though, the club's most famous victory came in 1995 when they sensationally beat Manchester United 3-0 at Old Trafford in a League Cup tie – one of the most humiliating defeats suffered by the Red Devils in their long history.
• Full-back Peter Scott made a club record seven appearances at international level for Northern Ireland while with York between 1975 and 1979.

> **HONOURS**
> *Division 4 champions 1984*

The famous 'Zidane step-over' in all its glory

ZINEDINE ZIDANE

Born: Marseille, France, 23rd June 1972
Position: Midfielder
Club career:
1988-92 Cannes 61 (6)
1992-96 Bordeaux 139 (28)
1996-2001 Juventus 151 (24)
2001-06 Real Madrid 155 (37)
International record:
1994-2006 France 108 (31)

Now manager of Real Madrid's B team, Castilla, brilliant French midfielder Zinedine Zidane is one of just two players (with Brazilian striker Ronaldo) to win the old World Player of the Year award three times (in 1998, 2000 and 2003).

• The extravagantly gifted Zidane started out with Cannes and Bordeaux before gaining worldwide attention with Juventus, with whom he won the Serie A title in 1997 and 1998. After five years with the Italian giants he moved to Real Madrid for a then world record fee of £46 million in 2001, and the following year scored a spectacular volleyed winner for his new club in the Champions League final against Bayer Leverkusen.

• Although of Algerian descent, Zidane chose to play for his native France and he became a hero to his fellow countrymen at the 1998 World Cup when he headed two goals in his side's surprisingly comfortable 3-0 defeat of favourites Brazil in the final in Paris. Two years later 'Zizou', as he was known to his team-mates, was voted Player of the Tournament as France beat Italy in the final of the European Championships.

• Zidane came out of international retirement to help a struggling French team qualify for the 2006 World Cup. However, his magnificent career ended on a sour note when he was sent off in the final for headbutting Italian defender Marco Materazzi in the chest after his opponent had made derogatory comments about Zidane's family. Nonetheless, Zidane's sublime performances in the finals ensured that he was awarded the Golden Ball as the outstanding player of the tournament.

DINO ZOFF

Born: Mariano del Fruilli, Italy, 28th February 1942
Position: Goalkeeper
Club career: 1961-63 Udinese 38
1963-67 Mantova 130
1967-72 Napoli 143
1972-83 Juventus 330
International career: 1968-83 Italy 112

Italian goalkeeping legend Dino Zoff holds the world record for international clean sheets, going 1,142 minutes without conceding a goal between September 1972 and June 1974, a run which included 12 consecutive games.

• In 1982, at the age of 40, Zoff became the oldest man ever to win the World Cup when Italy beat West Germany 3-1 in the final at the Santiago Bernabeu in Madrid. As captain of the side, he was only the second goalkeeper to lead his country to World Cup glory (after fellow Italian Giampiero Combi in 1934).